## ALSO BY MORTON HUNT

The Natural History of Love
Her Infinite Variety: The American Woman as Lover, Mate and Rival
Mental Hospital
The Talking Cure (*with Rena Corman and Louis R. Ormont*)
The World of the Formerly Married
The Affair: A Portrait of Extra-Marital Love in Contemporary America
The Mugging
Sexual Behavior in the 1970s
Prime Time: A Guide to the Pleasures and Opportunities of the New Middle Age
  (*with Bernice Hunt*)
The Divorce Experience (*with Bernice Hunt*)

# THE UNIVERSE WITHIN

## A New Science Explores The Human Mind

by Morton Hunt

A TOUCHSTONE BOOK
Published by Simon and Schuster
NEW YORK

Manufactured in the United States of America

10 9 8 7 6 5 4 3 2 1
10 9 8 7 6 5 4 3     Pbk.

Library of Congress Cataloging in Publication Data

Hunt, Morton M., date.
  The universe within.
  Bibliography: p.
  Includes index.
  1. Cognition. 2. Thought and thinking. I. Title.
BF311.H82     153     81-13611
                AACR 2
ISBN 0-671-25258-5
ISBN 0-671-25259-3 Pbk

I am grateful to the following for permission to reproduce brief passages of text from the copyrighted works named:

Academic Press, Inc.: the solution to the DONALD + GERALD cryptarithmetic problem, as given in Peter H. Lindsay and Donald A. Norman, *Human Information Processing: An Introduction to Psychology*, 2nd ed., © 1977.

Addison-Wesley Publishing Company, Inc.: two brief passages (one computer program and one segment of a trace) from Patrick Henry Winston, *Artificial Intelligence*, © 1977.

Cambridge University Press: several brief excerpts from "Modes of Thinking and Ways of Speaking," by Sylvia Scribner, in P. N. Johnson-Laird and P. C. Watson, eds., *Thinking: Readings in Cognitive Science*, © 1977.

Random House, Inc.: two excerpts from E. L. Doctorow, *Ragtime*, © 1974, 1975.

John R. Hayes of Carnegie-Mellon University kindly permitted me to quote at length from a transcript of my own remarks made when performing a writing task in his offices, as part of a study he and Linda Flower are conducting.

Acknowledgment is made to the following for permission to reproduce or adapt copyrighted illustrations from the sources named:

Figure 1: The Salvador Dali Foundation, Inc., St. Petersburg, Fla. 33701.

Figure 2: from "Brain Function and Blood Flow," by Niels A. Lassen, David H. Ingvar, and Erik Skinhøj, *Scientific American*, October 1978; courtesy of W. H. Freeman and Company.

(*Continued on page 401*)

*To the memory of my grandfather,*
*David N. Magill, who made me think*

# CONTENTS

# A WORD ABOUT
# THIS BOOK

The practitioners of a new and all but unknown scientific specialty called "cognitive science"—a hybrid of half a dozen fields of study—have, in a mere handful of years, discovered more about how we human beings think than we had previously learned in all of our time on earth. This book is about those discoveries.

I have written it for two reasons. First, I am greatly intrigued by the explanations that cognitive scientists offer of many ancient mysteries of the mind: how we manage to remember things we have not thought of for years, and why we forget most of what we heard a moment ago; how we reason—and, though usually doing so in nonlogical or illogical ways, generally arrive at sound conclusions; whether we think in words, in images, or in some other fashion altogether; how we are able to solve problems we have never been faced with before, and what it is that experts do when solving a problem that nonexperts do not do; who or what the "I" is that is conscious of its own thinking; how and from where we get original or creative ideas; and many others. I have found all this immensely interesting, and often useful, and suppose that many other people will find it so too.

My second reason for writing this book is that I have long been dissatisfied with, and even actively annoyed by, those several forces in contemporary intellectual life that belittle human thinking and, though we have traditionally thought of it as central to our humanity, relegate it to a position of unimportance. Behaviorists and behavior therapists tell us that thinking is illusory; like lower creatures, they say, we are predictably shaped and reshaped by conditioning, and our every thought is only a kind of conditioned response to a stimulus. The ethologists say that we are naked apes and that our behavior is largely governed by primitive neural structures and the instinctual patterns coded in them, rather than by the thinking processes of the lately developed forebrain. Many participants in the Human Potential Movement look down upon reasoning and intellectual effort, and seek to discover reality through the suspension of thought and the letting-go of feelings. Some animal psychologists claim that human thinking is not unique: they assert that apes and dolphins, among other animals, also think, and that it is only human egotism that makes us suppose we are special. And researchers in artificial intelligence—the programming of computers to perform intelligent tasks—assure us that anything the human mind can do, computers can, or soon will, do far better.

But as a longtime science writer specializing in psychology, I find these several denigrations of human thinking unconvincing and dehumanizing. The evidence of psychology—and of many other disciplines, including history itself—is that there is much more to us than our modern detractors say; we *are* radically different from all other forms of life (and from computers), and it is our thinking that makes us so.

This is not, of course, a new view; indeed, it is at least as old as Western civilization, and probably far older than that. Throughout the ages, we human beings have generally considered ourselves unique and extraordinary—sometimes in an admirable way ("a little lower than the angels," said the Psalmist), sometimes the opposite ("Of all the creatures . . . the most detestable," wrote Mark Twain), and sometimes both ("the glory and the shame of the universe," as Pascal put it). But good, evil, or both, we have always thought ourselves different from the rest of life, and almost always that difference has been linked to the obvious superiority of the human mind. There are rudiments of thought in some other animals, but the human being is the only true thinking animal; the mind is the quintessence of our humanity.

And now this traditional belief, this conviction that we are really different and that all that is wondrous and awesome (and fearful) about us is due to our intellect, is being made credible and respectable again by the new science. But not the ancient belief as such; what cognitive science supports is a wholly modern version of that belief, based not on anthropocentric pride but on a revolutionary understanding of the processes of thought as deduced by a new technology of investigation.

The detailed findings of cognitive science tell us that the human mind is the latest and most superbly adaptive mutation produced by evolution; that as powerful as our minds are, the scientific study of how they function should enable us to use them far more effectively than we normally do; and that the ultimate and most creative miracle of mind is its awareness of itself—a phenomenon not to be found in any other creature and not in any computer. It is nowhere more excitingly exemplified than in the form of cognitive science, the systematic inquiry into our thinking selves.

# EXPLORING THE INTERIOR UNIVERSE

## Everyday Marvels

In the past twenty years—and for the first time in human history—a scientific discipline devoted to exploring how our minds work has emerged. To be sure, ever since the days of the ancient Greeks, philosophers have speculated about what mind is made of, where ideas come from, how logical reasoning is related to reality, and other similarly large issues. But not until the birth of psychology did anyone seek to gather actual experimental evidence as to what goes on, unseen, in the human mind, that interior universe which we take to be a good likeness of the exterior one. Psychology, however, early turned away from these explorations within ourselves and concentrated on observable events—actual stimuli and visible responses. Only within the past generation has there appeared the empirical discipline called cognitive science—a hybrid of psychology, computer science, psycholinguistics, and several other fields—that uses experimental methods to explore those unseeable processes and events that are at once the most commonplace and yet the most marvelous of human accomplishments.

It is just because most of our thought processes are so ordinary that we rarely realize how remarkable, how unlike anything else in the known world, they are. When we watch a bird building a nest, we marvel at the skill and complexity of its performance. Yet we take for granted the vastly more skilled and complex mental acts we ourselves routinely perform every

17

day, and even every waking hour. It is these everyday marvels that cognitive scientists are studying; here is a baker's dozen of them:

1. *Consider this word—the word "word" that you just read. What happened in your mind when you read it?* . . . What happened took place too fast for you to notice it, but the evidence of cognitive science suggests that first you saw the variously shaped letters, then compared those images to your stored memories of printed letters (which you unerringly located someplace in the galactic mass of your brain cells), thereby recognized the ones you had seen, recognized at the same time the word they stood for when assembled, understood its meaning, and fitted that meaning into the context of the sentence. And you did all this in a fraction of a second.

2. *In the place where you lived two residences ago, did your front door open at the left side or the right?* . . . To answer that question, you somehow sent a signal through the unseen branching network of your mind to exactly the right storage place, plucked out a reel of filed imagery, and projected an image upon some inner screen, all in a moment.

3. *What's George Washington's phone number?* . . . Most likely you instantly recognized that the question was absurd. But how did you know it was without even considering the matter? Did you mentally search the phone book of memory in a millisecond? Consult the encyclopedia of history in your head? Look up the dates of Washington and of the telephone and do some logical reasoning based on them? Or none of these? Whatever you did, it was a fine performance.

4. *Tell me, please, how to get from the railroad station nearest your home to your front door.* . . . If you're typical, you visualized a kind of map, translated what you saw into words, and effortlessly assembled them into grammatical sentences, not even bothering to think ahead to see that the sentences would come out right. (They did, anyway.)

5. *What's a seven-letter word ending in y that means "a group of interacting individuals living in the same region and sharing the same culture"?* . . . You probably said "society" before you came to the end of the question—but how did you find that word among the 50,000 to 75,000 in your working vocabulary? Or did you somehow pluck out only seven-letter words—omitting all but those ending in *y?* Or did the definition itself lead you more directly to the place where the word is filed away? In any case, a nice bit of work.

6. *What language other than English do you know? How would you say, in that language, "Excuse me, what's the time?"* . . . It is hard, perhaps impossible, to recapture the impulses that flickered on and off as you linked

the words in English—or, more likely, the meanings behind those words—to the words expressing those meanings in another language. If you are fluent in that second language, you may not even have had any awareness of having done anything like translating; the act was instantaneous.

7. *Here is a joke recorded nearly 2,400 years ago and probably retold ever since:*

> *Talkative barber: How shall I cut your hair, sire?*
> *King Archelaus of Macedonia: In silence.*

. . . If you found this ancient wheeze at least mildly amusing, why did you? No ape or dolphin, as far as we know, can comprehend even so simple a joke, and no computer has yet shown a sense of humor. Even if you made a sour face because you found the joke a poor one, your response was subtle and peculiarly human.

8. *If four days before tomorrow is Thursday, what is three days after yesterday?* . . . To arrive at the answer,* you consciously went through a series of steps of naming, counting, and reasoning. Though the content of the problem is insignificant, the mental processes you used in solving it are highly consequential; they're comparable to the processes we all employ in solving everyday problems in our work and private lives, and even in tackling problems of great moment.

9. *ACORN is to OAK as INFANT is to* ———. . . . Unless your mind was elsewhere, you knew at once that the blank should read *ADULT*. But how did you know? A cognitive-science analysis of this elementary bit of analogical reasoning could fill twenty to fifty pages. But in brief: you compared the attributes of the first two capitalized words, inferred a rule that expressed their relationship, and, applying that rule to the third capitalized word (*INFANT*), extrapolated to get the missing fourth word.

10. *Which word in the following group doesn't belong—rose, lily, hyacinth, potato, tulip?* . . . Yes, I know I've made the example ridiculously easy; still, you did more mental work than you realized. By the time you read the second or third word, you probably were already seeking a higher-level concept or category they could all fit into—perhaps "plant," perhaps "flower"—but knowing that the task was to find a category that included all but one of the terms, you had narrowed it down to "flower" by the time you reached the end of the list.

* ·Tuesday.

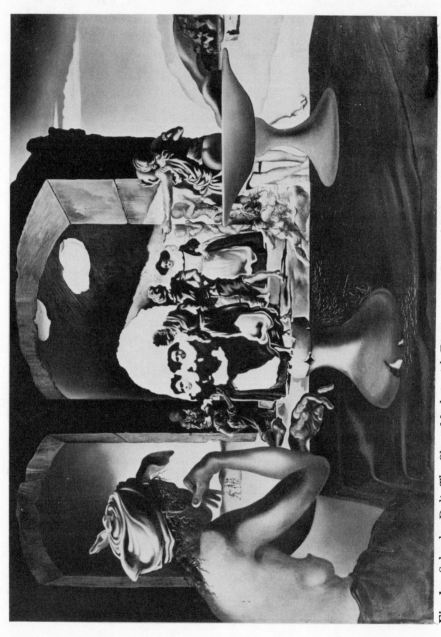

**Fig. 1.** Salvador Dali, *The Slave Market with Disappearing Bust of Voltaire*, 1940, oil on canvas. The Salvador Dali Foundation, Inc., St. Petersburg, Fla. 33701.

11. *What do you see just to the left of the middle of the painting by Salvador Dali in Figure 1?* . . . A bust of Voltaire—but also, when you think about it, two nuns (where Voltaire's eyes and other features seem to be). In fact, once you've seen both images, you can see the painting either way by simply willing to do so. In other words, to some extent you have the capacity to choose how much and what kind of information to supply from your own mind so as to yield one perception or the other; within limits, you can choose what to make of the world outside yourself.

12. *From these two statements—*

> *Fish get oxygen from water.*
> *Clams get oxygen from water.*

*—can you draw this conclusion?*

> *Therefore, clams are fish.*

*If not, why not?* . . . You surely said immediately that the conclusion is *not* valid. Your reason may have been that the first statement doesn't say *only* fish get oxygen from water, or that two objects can have a similar trait without being the same object, or that the syllogism suffers from "undistributed middle." In any case, you saw the invalidity of the conclusion—perhaps, indeed, *visually* saw that fish and clams can both fit within a larger group (creatures that get oxygen from water) without overlapping each other. You're a logician, of sorts; we all are.

13. *"In times past there lived a king and queen who said to each other every day of their lives, 'Would that we had a child!' and yet they had none. But one day when the queen was bathing, a frog jumped out of the water and said, 'Thy wish shall be fulfilled.'"* . . . Whether or not you recognize this as the beginning of *The Sleeping Beauty,* you understand what is happening—and so would a child—not because the words are sufficient, but because you make a dozen inferences, supplying knowledge and meaning from your inner stockpile. Three examples: (1) "In times past"—you recognize that the setting is that of a fable or fairy tale, and you are prepared with all sorts of special expectations; (2) the frog speaks—you know you are in the presence of magical true prophecy; (3) if there were no complications, the birth of the child would be the end of the story; yet you know, somehow, that this will not be so, that there is a tale to be told, and that it will involve problems, perils, and finally some kind of satisfying and sensible ending. You, the listener, do as much in a way as the storyteller.

•

These are but a few of the everyday marvels that we take for granted, and that I will be looking at more closely throughout this book. But there are two others that we are never even aware of, although every thought we think depends on them.

One is the sheer intricacy of the neuronal pathways by which the brain transmits and processes information. Professor Sheldon H. White of Harvard University estimates that the circuitry in the human brain "probably has sixty times the informational complexity of the entire U.S. telephone system."

The second is the mind's huge information-storage capacity—an absolute prerequisite of human thought. How huge? Cognitive scientists struggle to find meaningful ways to express it. Professor Herbert A. Simon of Carnegie-Mellon University calculated some years ago that chess masters know about 50,000 configurations of chess pieces and their manifold implications; he further said that each of us probably knows some 50,000 clusters of information about our own field of expertise. Professor Donald A. Norman, director of the Program in Cognitive Science at the University of California at San Diego, extends this estimate: he believes that each of us knows something like 50,000 facts not just about our own special field but about every topic on which we are reasonably knowledgeable—our own bodies, our personal idiosyncrasies, the arrangement of our homes and environs, the words and grammar of our native language, and so on and on. Plus, of course, that catchall of general information that cognitive scientists call "world knowledge." It comes to a *lot* of information.

How much information is a lot? John Griffith, a mathematician, has calculated that in the course of a lifetime, the average person can accumulate 500 times as much information as is contained in the *Encyclopaedia Britannica*, or 500,000 times as much, if we count redundancies. No doubt about it; that *is* a lot.

### Interesting Questions

In my prefatory remarks, I spoke of thinking as the subject with which cognitive science is concerned, but most cognitive scientists would quarrel with that statement. Many of them have recently come to use "thinking" in a narrow sense, meaning formal, logical reasoning or, perhaps, problem solving; they view all the other higher cognitive processes—perception, memory, learning, inference, concept formation, and so on—as outside thinking proper.

The lay public, however, means all of these things and many others by the term, and unabridged dictionaries usually list nearly a score of mental activities under the heading of "thinking." It is this breadth and variability in the use of the word that bothers cognitive scientists. A few pretend to find the word "thinking" all but meaningless: Professor Gordon H. Bower, who heads the psychology department at Stanford University, said to me rather testily, "I don't work on 'thinking' at all, I work on memory. I don't know what thinking is—I presume it's the study of reasoning." Dr. Elizabeth F. Loftus of the University of Washington, another expert on memory, said more gently that she regarded the term "thinking" as "rather old-fashioned," pointing out that in the last few years textbook and course titles had switched to using "cognition," "information processing," and other words belonging to the jargon of cognitive science. (Every new field of study, like a dog marking its territory, seeks to assert its claim to its area by sticking new labels on the phenomena it is interested in. To be fair, though, the relabeling is sometimes necessary to make finer distinctions than exist in the standard vocabulary, and sometimes to name phenomena not previously recognized or known to exist.)

While a few cognitive scientists avoid the word "thinking" altogether in professional discourse, others still use it but strive—without consensus—to assign it some precise and scientifically workable meaning. Some of them, as I noted a moment ago, equate it with pure reasoning; others, with problem solving or decision making (both of which include reasoning but other processes as well); the coauthors of one popular textbook characterize it more broadly as "the ability to manipulate the environment symbolically"; and certain others, accepting the lay usage but trying to reformulate it in more operational terms, call it "all that goes on [in the mind] between input and output."

None of which need bother you or me. We know what we mean when we say "thinking," for as we grew up we effortlessly learned to use the word correctly in ordinary discourse in any and all of its meanings; the context in which we use it makes the meaning plain. I will therefore continue to use the word in the ways we all do, but I will also use the ingroup terms of cognitive science whenever these are helpful.

It is not surprising that cognitive scientists cannot agree on the meaning of the word "thinking," for coming as they do from a wide variety of academic backgrounds, they agree on very little. One of the few things they are in accord about, however, is that they are concerned with "interesting questions" about the mind. They mean this in a special sense: an "interesting question" is one that does not merely engage the attention, but one that is substantive, important, not yet fully understood, and, above all, difficult to deal with.

Aside from that, cognitive scientists are given to very diverse views of their field. There are two reasons for this. The first is that cognitive science, like all new disciplines that have branched off from a traditional one, has attracted from other areas nonconformists who seek greater freedom in the new territory. The second reason is that, in historical fact, cognitive science came about because of a series of developments in various fields of study that simultaneously cast new light upon the hidden workings of the mind. Twenty years ago, a revolution was brewing within psychology against the dominant school of behaviorism because of its refusal to consider thought processes a fit subject of scientific study (I'll say more about this later). At the same time, a number of other disciplines—computer science, linguistics, formal logic, anthropology, neurology, and child-development studies—were converging from various directions upon the central issue of thinking. This convergence reached a kind of intellectual critical mass by the 1960s, yielding a knowledge explosion and a new field of study.

But explosions are messy, and so is the field this one created. At present, cognitive studies are going on in nearly every major American university, sometimes in one department, sometimes in another—and sometimes in several, either without the people in those departments knowing about one another's work, or knowing but fiercely at odds as to who is doing *real* cognitive science. A handful of universities, however, have created semi-independent institutes of cognitive science within which people of varied intellectual backgrounds work cooperatively. The most notable of these institutes are at the University of California at San Diego, and at Berkeley; Carnegie-Mellon University; Yale University; Stanford University; the University of Texas at Austin; and Massachusetts Institute of Technology. At least a thousand (and perhaps many more) scientists and scholars of various stripes are now full-time cognitive scientists; this estimate was given me by Dr. Kenneth A. Klivington, who is in charge of the Alfred P. Sloan Foundation's eight-year, $20 million program aimed at encouraging the amalgamation of the allied fields of study into a coherent new science. (It would be even less coherent than it is if it included those quasi- and pseudoscientific mental phenomena so congenial to the modern taste for mysticism: altered states of consciousness, precognition and other paranormal abilities, out-of-body experiences, and the like. But none of these is considered, by any cognitive scientist I talked to, to be part of the new discipline.)

So new is cognitive science that almost none of its practitioners are known to the general public as yet. Nobel Laureate Herbert Simon, Noam Chomsky, and the late Jean Piaget are among the few exceptions, but most of the people in this young field are quite young themselves and known only to one another. This suits them fine; at the moment, they expect no one else to understand them. Offsetting this isolation is the heady sense of being in on the beginning of great things and of taking part in a race to find the answers to profoundly interesting questions. As one participant in a seminar sponsored by the Sloan Foundation put it, "We may be at the start of a major intellectual adventure . . . somewhat comparable to the position in which physics stood towards the end of the Renaissance." But more often, I have heard people say that they find the situation more like that of the same science in the early seventeenth century, just before Newton. One cognitive scientist says that many of his colleagues already fancy themselves the field's Newton, although as yet none but each one's own graduate students agree.

And as far as I could see, no one of them is doing work that unifies or synthesizes what all the others are doing. For even to the outsider such as myself, it is plain that, aside from a handful of persons trying to spin broad theories, cognitive scientists are engaged in a variety of very special and dissimilar activities aimed at discovering the answers to a wide range of different interesting questions.

Those questions are serious and significant, but the techniques used to research them often look and sound like games, puzzles, and other mere diversions. The topic under investigation may, for instance, be the very weighty one of problem solving—the processes the mind goes through in seeking solutions to problems as complex as, say, diagnosing a rare disease, designing a space vehicle, or working out a peace treaty—but the most feasible way of studying it may be to offer a group of laboratory volunteers (usually the researcher's own undergraduate students) problems of a far simpler sort, such as this:

> Three missionaries and three cannibals are on one side of a river. They all have to get to the other side via a canoe that can hold only two persons. At no point can there be more cannibals than missionaries on either bank of the river, or the

cannibals will kill the missionaries they outnumber. How do they all get across?*

Or this:

|  |  |
|---|---|
| LETS | Each letter stands for a one-digit number. When |
| +WAVE | decoded, the first line added to the second line |
| LATER | will yield the third line. What are the numbers?† |

Or a problem created and used by none other than Nobelist Simon and a colleague, Dick Hayes (John R. Hayes), having to do with "three five-handed extraterrestrial monsters" of three sizes who are juggling crystal globes of three sizes, and who want to—well, never mind. The point is that experimenters, by having their subjects talk out loud while solving such small-scale artificial problems, can observe the mind doing many of the same things it does when solving large real-life problems.

A quite different approach to studying problem solving is to try to write computer programs that will enable machines to play chess, backgammon, or Go in the same way human beings appear to. Some computer specialists have written game-playing programs that use nonhuman methods—they test many thousands of possibilities per second—but the inquiry into human problem solving involves programs that do what we do instead, namely, narrow down drastically the number of possibilities we look at. Those who are pursuing this line of inquiry develop their own theories as to how we do this, write game-playing computer programs that are based on their theories, and then test them by playing actual games against their own begotten offspring.

From the perspective of the outsider, this looks more like fun than serious research, though it is, of course, the latter. It also has a faintly spooky air at times, since the creators of such programs often refer to their own programs as if they were sentient creatures. "What's he up to, now?" I heard Professor Walter Reitman of the University of Michigan say while playing Go

---

* I'll talk about such problems at greater length in Chapter 7, but if you would like to work this one out now, you'll find the answer on page 365. It calls for eleven trips across the river. You might need ten to twenty minutes to solve the problem if you've never done one like it before.

† Cryptarithmetic problems like this will also be dealt with in Chapter 7. If you want to try this one now, here's a hint: it should be obvious what numeral L must stand for. The solution to the problem is on page 366. You might need an hour or so to work it out if you are a newcomer to cryptarithmetic. Someone familiar with such problems might do it in ten or fifteen minutes.

against his own program, whose moves appeared in the form of a printout issuing from a desk-top terminal. "Ah!" said Reitman in a moment. "Look how he's trying to build up his influence in this sector!" At Carnegie-Mellon University, I sat in a room filled with computer terminals and watched Dr. Hans J. Berliner play chess against his own program; he punched a move on the keyboard, looked at the screen, and when nothing happened immediately, said to me, "Now it's thinking. . . . *There!* . . . It took sixty-three seconds to work out that move, but it did well. It's really very cute and clever! And now it knows there's only one move I can make, and it's ready to mate me without delay. Watch. Here's my move—*there!* It's got me."

Another important question—whether the ability to do formal logical reasoning is innate or is culturally acquired—also involves some curious research. The best way to seek an answer is to go to some place where Aristotelian syllogisms have never been heard of and see what the local people make of them—a method which sometimes yields surprising and improbable dialogues such as this one between psychologist Sylvia Scribner and an illiterate Kpelle farmer in a tiny Liberian village:

> SYLVIA SCRIBNER: All Kpelle men are rice farmers.
> Mr. Smith is not a rice farmer.
> Is he a Kpelle man?
> KPELLE FARMER: I don't know the man. I have not laid eyes on the man himself.
> S.S.: Just think about the statement.
> K.F.: If I know him in person, I can answer that question, but since I do not know him in person I cannot answer that question.
> S.S.: Try and answer from your Kpelle sense.
> K.F.: If you know a person, if a question comes up about him, you are able to answer. But if you do not know the person, if a question comes up about him, it's hard for you to answer it.

While that interchange may have something of the flavor of a discussion between Laurel and Hardy, it (and other such experiences) shows, or at least suggests, that formal logical thought is not a natural or inevitable outcome of human mental development, but a cultural artifact acquired along with literacy. For other Kpelle persons in the same village, who had been to school, could provide the valid conclusion to the syllogism even though they had never laid eyes on the hypothetical Mr. Smith either.

Or consider the equally serious question of how the human mind reaches political decisions—a complex process that involves dealing with factual news by drawing upon stored information and preconceptions to interpret that news, make predictions, decide on a course of action, and resolve conflicts that appear in the process of thinking. A weighty question, indeed, but the research methodology sometimes looks like political spoofing. A handful of AI (artificial intelligence) researchers, for instance, have been writing programs that think right-wing thoughts when confronted with an international situation and come to appropriately right-wing conclusions; an early version of such a program was even called by its designer "the Goldwater machine." (Such programs can be equally well tailored to simulate left-wing thinking.) A politically conservative program, endowed by its creator with a mass of suitable opinions and general information, might be presented with this situation: "The Russians massed troops on the Czech border." The computer is allowed to absorb this information into its electronic brain and integrate the news with its previously stored notions and information. The researcher then asks it, "Why did Russia do this?" to which the answer appears, glowing green on the terminal, "BECAUSE RUSSIA THOUGHT THAT IT COULD TAKE POLITICAL CONTROL OF CZECHOSLOVAKIA BY SENDING TROOPS." "What happens if Czechoslovakia does not give in?" asks the creator, and his Adam replies, "RUSSIA MAY DECIDE TO START THE INVASION." "What should the United States do?" "THE UNITED STATES SHOULD INTERVENE MILITARILY."

A number of substantial questions are involved in the study of how we learn or fail to retain new information; the research methods often seem, on the surface, to be trivial, if not inane, but there is good reason for the triviality or inanity. Any list of words that one tries to memorize, for instance, will yield skewed or contaminated results depending on the particular meanings and associations of the words used; accordingly, psychologists often make up nonsense syllables devoid of any such content. (Try making up such a list; it's not easy.) Here's one such list: BEM, TAQ, MUZ, PEZ, LUF, ROH, VID, JOP, KUG, GAV. Another psychologist studying memory solemnly intoned to his research subjects, "Bah, gah, gah, bah, dah, bah, dah," following this with a somewhat jazzier utterance, "Bah, bee, bah, boo, bah, bee, boo." He, too, had a serious purpose: he was seeking to find out by what handles of sound we hold onto spoken words in memory long enough to make sense of a heard sentence.

With equally serious motives, one psycholinguist asked his subjects to memorize sentences that sound like stuff Lewis Carroll had crossed out. Here are two such sentences; the object was to see which one took longer to memorize:

The yigs wur vumly rixing hum in jegest miv.
yigs rixing wur miv hum vumly the in jegest

The first one, as you may have sensed, is much easier to memorize; although it is just as nonsensical as the second, it has normal syntactical (grammatical) structure and therefore is easily handled by our mental circuitry (which, some linguists believe, is wired that way genetically, grammar being built into it in advance of actual speech).

Finally, a team of psychologists seeking to measure the human capacity to store and recognize visual materials seen only one time showed 2500 slides consecutively to a group of subjects; it took four hours a day, for four days, to get through the lot, which said something about the doggedness of the researchers—but also yielded valuable information about the capacity of human visual memory. (Afterward, subjects were able to recognize correctly 91 percent of the pictures they had seen—that is, on a second viewing, they could nearly always tell whether they had seen any picture before or not.)

Thus, behind the various entertaining (or boring) research procedures of cognitive science there is a solid structure of complex hypothesizing, theorizing, and data analysis, all of it looking for answers to a number of interesting questions.

Among these are: Do we learn what we learn primarily as a result of mere repetition—or of comprehension—or of the linkage of new material to previously known material? How can things as unlike as visual images, heard words, and ideas all be recorded in our brain cells—which, under the microscope, show no trace of such recording? By what methods do we locate, in our memories, whatever we want to remember? Has what is forgotten faded out, or been erased, or is it merely misfiled? Does the human mind spontaneously come to reason along the lines of formal logic or does it, instead, have a quite different natural logic of its own? What do we do that enables us to see, at some point, that certain things can be grouped into a coherent category, or that a general rule can be extracted from a series of experiences? Do we learn to imitate grammatical speech as we grow up, or are grammatical structures genetically prewired in the brain's language area? What are the processes we use consciously and unconsciously when solving problems both great and small, and can the individual's problem-solving ability be improved by training? What do highly creative people do that ordinary people don't do (and can the latter learn to do it)? What kinds of thinking go on unconsciously, as contrasted to those kinds that are conscious? How is our thinking affected or skewed by our sex, age, personality, and background? Will everything about the human mind someday be duplicated and surpassed by artificial intelligences, or are there aspects of the human mind that are unique not only today but likely always to be so?

All these are distinctly interesting questions, yet even they are not the deepest and most challenging matters that concern the new discipline. For throughout the journals, textbooks, and monographs of cognitive science one also finds much philosophic discussion and assorted batches of laboratory evidence dealing with the classical "Mind-Body problem" that has vexed philosophy since the time of Plato, and religion since time immemorial. Is the mind, the thinking self, something incorporeal—something like soul or spirit? If so, how and in what place does it store its ideas and conduct its processes? Why does it need the physical brain to manifest itself; or if it does not, why does damage to the brain cause the mind to operate imperfectly? If, on the other hand, there is no mind separate from the body—if mind is only the sum total of operations of the brain itself—how can it be aware of itself? Who or what steps back and observes the thoughts in the brain, as we seem to do when considering our own ideas? Who or what thing chooses when we make a choice—a neuron or string of neurons? What caused them to choose—some other neuron? But that, clearly, is no answer either. Must we hypothesize a "ghost in the machine," as one anti-ghost philosopher sneered? Or can one dispense with the ghost and still explain how we can be observers of our own mind's workings, and choosers of what thoughts we choose to think? A major issue, this—and of deep interest not just to the cognitive scientist but to everyone, since all of us must, from an early age, learn to live with the fact of mortality either by believing in an afterlife or by accepting death as the end of the individual self.

Equally significant is the ancient "Nature-Nurture problem," which, within cognitive science, is focused upon the extent to which our mental functions are the result of experience and teaching, or, instead, of neural wiring and preprogramming laid down by our genes—or, perhaps, of an unfolding interaction, during childhood, between built-in structures and formative experiences. On this issue, too, there is continual heated argument within the field, plus a great deal of new evidence derived from hundreds of studies of infants and young children. And again, this is a matter of great pertinence to everyone since it has so much to say about how we became the persons we are, about our power—or limits—as parents to influence our own children, about the effectiveness or ineffectiveness of various educational programs, and about the reasons why so many human beings think so differently from ourselves.

Lastly, cognitive scientists have all but preempted from philosophers the profoundly interesting question of how our impressions of the world are related to reality. All we actually know of what exists outside our heads are the perceptions inside them; but of course perceptions can be falsehoods, as is the case with delusions, hallucinations, and dreams. Bishop George Berkeley, in the eighteenth century, carried subjectivist doubt to its furthest possible limit: he speculated, in *A Treatise Concerning the Principles of Human Knowledge*, that nothing outside our minds has any independent existence, but that our experiences of the world are all impressions put into our minds by God. The commonsense answer to this is the one Samuel Johnson gave when Boswell suggested that Berkeley's theory seemed impossible to refute: Johnson, kicking a large stone with great force, exclaimed, "I refute it *thus.*" But that is no refutation: the sensations of the solidity of the stone and the resultant pain in the foot could both have been created in Johnson by the Deity.

Cognitive scientists don't debate this issue: they assume there *is* a world out there, since that is the most parsimonious and therefore scientific explanation of experience. But they do spend a good deal of time trying to spell out the exact steps by which the mind forms its notions of what exists outside. For instance, while they don't trouble themselves about the ultimate meaning of cause and effect, some are spending their lives trying to find out how and why the mind of the growing child spontaneously develops the notion that certain events, preceding others, have "caused" the latter to happen.

Nor do cognitive scientists care much whether the mind's representations of the world outside are accurate or, instead, are a limited and selective view of it, like, say, a fish's notion of geography. What does intrigue them is the machinery by which the mind manipulates its own symbols for objects and occurrences in the outside world (however distorted those symbols might be), comes to some conclusions about them, and then proceeds to deal with the outside world on the basis of its conclusions. None of us, for instance, need ponder the ultimate nature of gravity as Einstein did in order to deal with it in our daily life; we manage the gravity that is involved in walking, eating, and tennis playing on the basis of our perceptions and the uses we make of them in the mind.

In view of the size and scope of these questions, it is little wonder after all that so many cognitive scientists consider themselves Newtons of a sort, and that they are a prideful and contentious lot—and an interesting lot, in the everyday sense of the word.

## The Mind's Machinery

Thus far I have said nothing about psychobiology or "brain research," a specialized area of neurophysiology that might seem the most likely place to seek answers to the questions I have been discussing. If you want to know how the mind works, why not study the mind's actual machinery in operation? Why not look to the brain's design, the special functions of its various parts and several kinds of neurons (nerve cells), and the multitude of electrical and chemical events that take place during mental activity?

But knowledge of this kind, though now increasing rapidly, only occasionally tells us anything at the level that interests cognitive scientists. For psychobiology is usually *too* basic. It deals chiefly with such minute events that it says little or nothing about the *mass effects*—memories, concepts, problem solving, and so on—that are the collective product of millions or billions of neural and molecular microevents. To scramble an egg, you need to know about turning on the range to the right heat, melting butter in a pan, and stirring the egg in the pan until it is done; your technique will not be helped at all by a study of the chemical reaction between burning gas and oxygen, the molecular movements by which the pan transmits heat, or the chemical and physical reorganization of the proteins in the egg as it cooks.

Cognitive scientists themselves often use an analogy closer to their subject. A knowledge of psychobiology, they say, is no more important to the study of cognitive processes than a knowledge of computer design is to computer programming. If you want to write a program that will enable a computer to play chess, translate English to French, or prove algebraic theorems, you need to know first how to talk to the machine in a "language" (a code) it can understand, then how to feed a program of information and procedures into its memory bank, and finally how to issue it a carefully constructed set of commands. But you do not need to know whether its transistors are made of silicon or germanium, what its circuitry looks like, or how it is powered.

Similarly, to investigate how we learn, remember, or go about solving problems, you need to know about such phenomena as association, cued retrieval, and the generating and testing of hypotheses. But you do not need to know about processes such as the flow of sodium and potassium ions into and out of tiny passages in the nerve fibers as each nerve impulse travels along them. As Allen Newell, Herbert Simon, and others in the field have said, useful theories of thinking deal not in neural processes but in *epineural* ones—highly complex events that are several layers of organization above the molecular and cellular events of which, ultimately, they consist.

All the same, psychobiology is beginning to provide at least some kinds of information that bear directly on the understanding of human thinking and its special place in the spectrum of living behaviors.

In recent years, for one thing, brain researchers have been able to map more accurately than before which areas of the brain perform specific functions and which operate more generally. (This, as we will see in a moment, tells us a good deal about the human mind as compared with minds of nonhuman animals.) For some years, neurophysiologists had to gather this kind of information chiefly by studying the behavior of persons with localized brain damage or brain tumors. Recently, however, a new technique has been added: a Danish team has been measuring the blood flow through the brain during different mental activities by injecting harmless radioisotopes into the bloodstream and recording the varying levels of radioactivity throughout the brain.

These studies have shown that much of the rear part of the brain is specialized and is committed to bodily functions—the interpretation of incoming sensations, the control of movement, and so on—as shown in Figure 2. The forebrain, however (chiefly the frontal and temporal lobes), which is very much larger in the human being than in any other animal, is relatively nonspecific; freed from bodily functions, its various areas interact in highly complex ways to produce the processes we call thinking. In the computer-generated diagrams in Figure 3, the darker areas show where there is increased blood flow during higher mental activities. The top two show the activity of the left and right hemispheres during speech; the middle two— the left hemisphere in both cases—show the difference in activity during silent reading (left diagram) and reading aloud (right diagram); and the bottom one shows left hemisphere activity during silent counting.

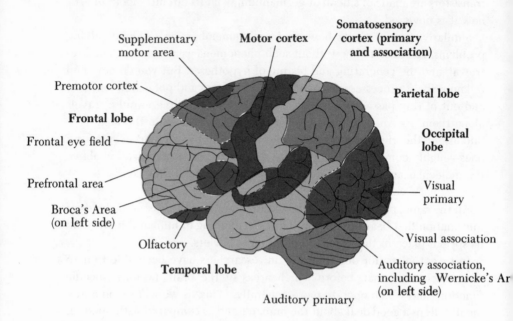

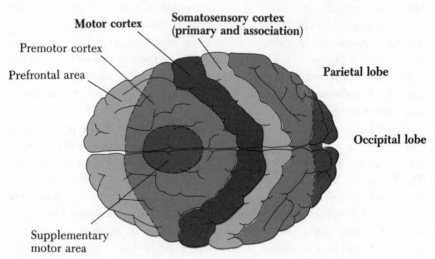

**Fig. 2.**   Functional map of the human brain

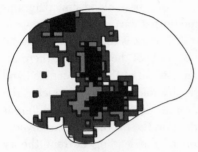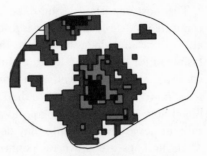

Speaking activates three centers in each hemisphere; left hemisphere
(*left*) is the busier one.

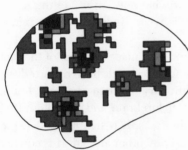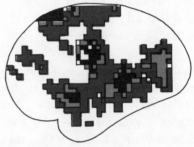

Reading silently (*left*) activates four areas; reading aloud (*right*) involves
two more.

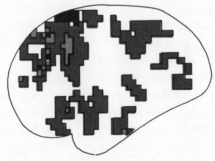

Counting silently—"internal speech"—activates frontal regions but not
the areas normally involved in speech.

**Fig. 3.**   Specific kinds of mental activity cause increased blood flow (gray
tones and black) in various areas of the brain.

The most important lesson to be learned from these blood-flow diagrams is not that one area or another is associated with a particular activity, valuable as that knowledge is. Rather, the crucial point is that complex mental tasks call for the interaction of a number of parts of the brain—in the rearward parietal lobes as well as the forebrain—some of them specialized and some not. "This system," write the Danish physiologists who conducted the blood-flow studies, "is analogous to a computer program in which different subroutines are brought into play depending on the problem to be solved." Their findings are powerful confirmation of the leading current theory about thinking—the theory called "information processing," which we will look at later on—which analyzes each act of thinking as a series of subroutines. The blood-flow data also repudiate the behaviorists' doctrine that nothing can be said, or need be said, about what goes on inside the mind, and that all one need or should consider is what kinds of input produce what kinds of output.

Those ethologists and others who have recently made so much of the fact that we still have ancient animal brains inside our heads have distorted the reality of what is there: a very small evolutionary remnant of animal brain, and a very large evolutionary innovation of forebrain and "uncommitted cortex"—gray matter—unassigned to bodily tasks. It is significant that the human brain is far larger than that of almost any other animal. It is equally significant that we have a far higher ratio of brain to body weight than the others—hundreds of times higher than the rat, five to ten times higher than the apes. But what is crucial is that so much of the brain in us, and so little in other animals, is uncommitted to sensory and motor functions and therefore available for higher mental processes.* Figure 4 is a comparison of the brains of six creatures (drawn as if they were the same size), showing in white what part of each is uncommitted cortex.

Don't be misled by the fact that in this diagram the chimpanzee's brain seems much like the human one; when these two brains are drawn to the same scale, showing their true relative sizes, they look as shown in Figure 5. The difference in the amount of thinking brain between chimpanzee and human is thus not only large in percentage, but very large in absolute quantity. If you've been impressed by the reports of chimps and gorillas who have conversations with their trainers, using American Sign Language or plastic chips as words, remind yourself that the smartest trained ape who has ever lived knows some 400 words, while you yourself know nearly two

---

* A few animals such as the elephant and the blue whale have an even higher brain-to-body ratio than we—but a far smaller proportion of uncommitted cortex.

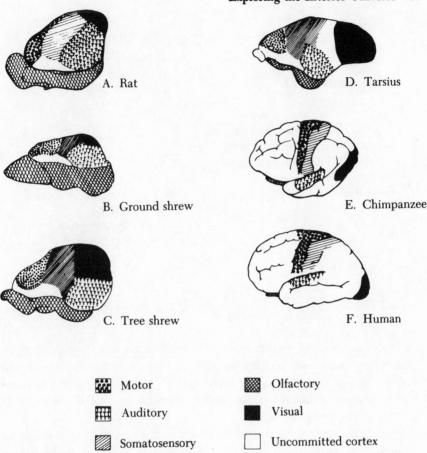

A. Rat

B. Ground shrew

C. Tree shrew

D. Tarsius

E. Chimpanzee

F. Human

Motor

Auditory

Somatosensory

Olfactory

Visual

Uncommitted cortex

**Fig. 4.**   Why humans think: their brains aren't otherwise occupied.

hundred times that many. That suggests the order of magnitude by which human thinking (assuming you're an average person) outdoes ape thinking.

The macroview of the human brain may be impressive, but hardly so much as the microview. It is when we look at the brain's individual functioning units—the neurons—and their connecting circuitry that we get some idea of how complex and highly organized our brains are. Let's start with Figure 6, a diagram (drawn from microphotographs) of the spatial arrangement of a handful of neurons in the six layers of human cerebral cortex. In this highly simplified drawing, each of the sixteen neurons connects to—or, really, comes close to—other neurons at only a few points. But

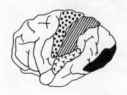

**Fig. 5.**   Chimp and human
brains drawn to the same scale;
it's the total amount of uncommitted cortex (white) that makes
the difference.

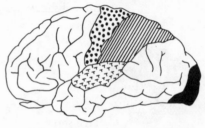

to appreciate how your brain is actually constructed, stretch your imagination to the uttermost: imagine not sixteen but *ten billion* neurons in the
cortex alone (a *hundred billion,* if you include the interior of the brain)—
each of them connected to hundreds of others by anywhere from 1000 to
10,000 synapses or relay points.

One cannot, of course, actually envision such numbers. But perhaps the
following comparison will be useful: if you were in a very large city library
with a million volumes, and every volume were five hundred pages long,
and every page reproduced the neuron diagram, there still wouldn't be as
many neurons pictured as you have in your cortex alone. As for the total
number of interconnections and pathways through your brain, it must be of
the order of trillions. The drawings in Figure 7 may give you some hint of
what that means. They show how minuscule fragments of cerebral cortex
look at different times during the first two years of life, as the network of
neural connections is being woven. The intricate tangle of the two-year-old
segment is far less than a billionth part of the network in your cortex alone.

Such data tell us something significant about human thinking. They tell
us that the human brain has an astronomical number of pathways through
its cells, with the result that any neuron or group of neurons can contact a
vast number of others via innumerable circuits. Nothing made by human

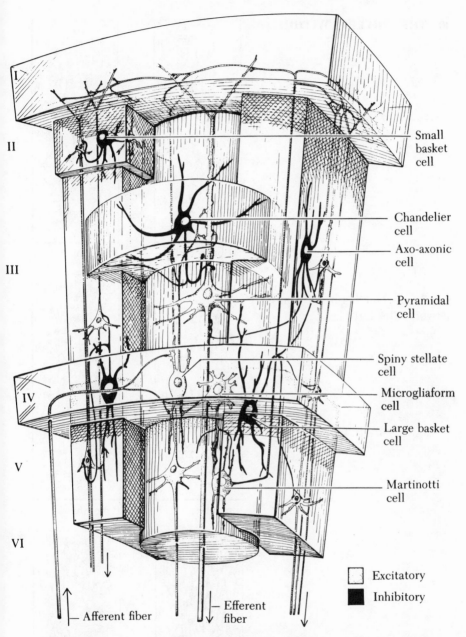

I

II — Small basket cell

Chandelier cell

Axo-axonic cell

III Pyramidal cell

Spiny stellate cell

Microgliaform cell

IV Large basket cell

Martinotti cell

V

VI

☐ Excitatory
■ Inhibitory

Efferent fiber

Afferent fiber

**Fig. 6.** The cerebral cortex is made up of columnar modules of special-ized neurons; this typical column is one-one hundredth of an inch in di-ameter. The boxlike structures are, of course, diagrammatic and do not exist in reality.

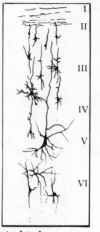

At birth

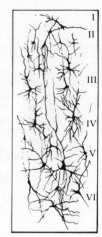

1 month

**Fig. 7.**  Assembling of the neuron
network after birth

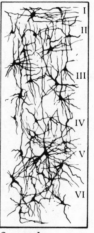

3 months

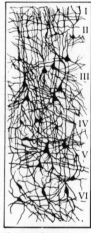

6 months

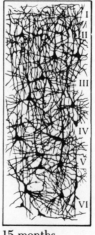

15 months

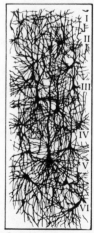

2 years

beings begins to approach this mechanism in complexity. Or in *redundancy:* apparently, many functions are duplicated in several regions of the cortex, and there are a great many alternate pathways by which impulses can get from any one point to any other.

This may explain how we can store so immense a quantity of facts, why we have so many different methods of locating things in memory, and why we can think about problems in such diverse ways—often with such unexpected results. And why most accidents, illnesses, and even the supposed daily loss of 100,000 brain cells due to aging leave us fully capable of normal thinking until old age; it is the redundancy of our brains—their excess of parts and circuits—that keeps them running smoothly. In business terms, it would be a wasteful and unprofitable way to build a machine; in evolutionary terms, it's a triumph of good design.

At least one other area of psychobiological research is of direct concern to cognitive scientists: this is the study of the way nerve impulses cross the synaptic cleft or gap separating one neuron from another. Most neurons have a single large branch, the axon, extending out some distance from the cell body and ending in terminal fibers or smaller branches; its job is to send outgoing messages to other neurons. Each neuron also has a set of many smaller branches, the dendrites, whose job is to receive incoming signals from other neurons. A typical neuron is shown in Figure 8; in this diagram, the axon is folded regularly in order to show its length, although in reality it would be straight or wandering in shape. Between the tip of each of the axon's terminal fibers and the dendrite of another neuron—the junction point known as a synapse—is the tiny synaptic gap or cleft; in Figure 9 we see the knoblike tip of an axon terminal above, and a receptor region of a dendrite below. The message of one neuron crosses the synaptic gap to another neuron by means of a complicated event: an electrical impulse traveling down the axon manufactures and releases into the gap a burst of molecules of norepinephrine, dopamine, or any one of some twenty to thirty other "neurotransmitter" substances. These molecules cross the gap and either excite or dampen activity in the second neuron, which then either "fires" an electrical impulse along its own axon or not, depending on the total impact it receives from hundreds of such incoming messages at the synapses connecting it to other neurons; at each synapse, meanwhile, the neurotransmitter chemicals that carried these messages are either reabsorbed by the other neurons or chemically destroyed hundreds of times per second. When we think, this activity takes place in millions or billions of

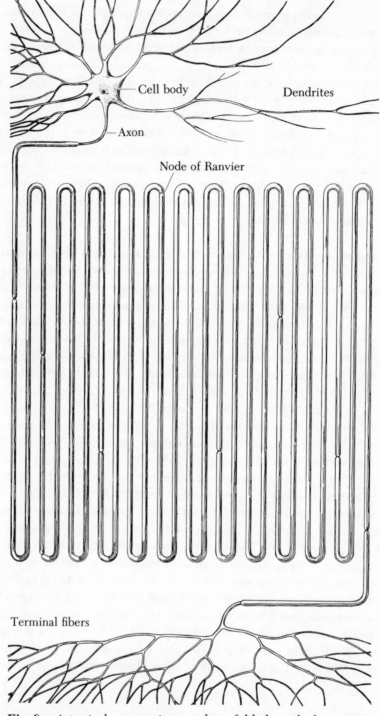

**Fig. 8.** A typical neuron, its axon here folded neatly for artistic convenience

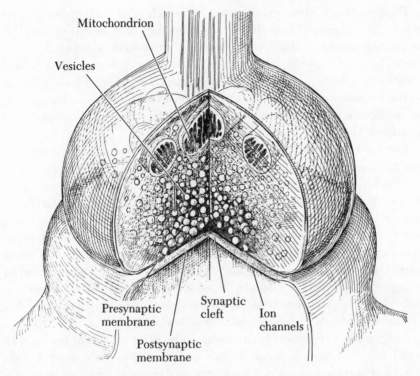

Mitochondrion

Vesicles

Presynaptic
membrane

Synaptic
cleft

Ion
channels

Postsynaptic
membrane

**Fig. 9.**   A typical synapse or junction point between two neurons. The neurons do not touch; bursts of neurotransmitter chemicals carry the message across the synaptic cleft.

active neurons at a rate of several hundreds of cycles per second in each one; even as you register this fact, billions of such events are taking place in your brain to make the thought happen.

While this may seem as remote from the larger issues of thinking as the chemistry of proteins is from egg-cooking technique, it does explain the impact of the psychoactive drugs on thinking. "Uppers," "downers," hallucinogens, and the like do their work right at the synapses: chemically, they either facilitate or interfere with the neurotransmitters, and so affect the speed and the pattern of our thought processes. Some of the effects are temporary, others are long-lasting, and some may even be irreversible. Thus, while many of the psychoactive drugs are medically valuable when administered by expert practitioners, taking such drugs according to folk wisdom for fun or adventure is playing a chemical version of Russian roulette.

Disappointingly, too, psychoactive mood elevators and hallucinogens don't really improve the quality of one's thinking; they merely speed it up or produce a sense of illumination that vanishes when the drug wears off. As we will see in Chapter 8, the evidence is that drugs do not yield heightened creativity; at best, they may sometimes permit a creative process going on in the unconscious to make itself manifest. But hard work—or fatigue and relaxation after hard work—will do as much. The chemical route to art, and to Higher Wisdom, is an illusion.

But it is no illusion that some of the new neurochemical knowledge has practical uses other than the tranquilizing of the disturbed and the mood elevation of the depressed. Some people with insomnia, and some aging persons with failing memories, simply suffer from inadequate production of one or another of the neurotransmitter chemicals. For them, daily extra doses of certain natural food substances may be helpful: L-tryptophan for the person whose mind won't shut down at night, lecithin for the aging person whose memory is weakening. Here, chemotherapy isn't intended to change the nature of the mental processes; it merely is meant to restore the individual's normal capacity for relaxation or for remembering, if either has been diminished by abnormal body chemistry.

Certain other avenues of brain research also yield insights at the level at which cognitive science operates. They include studies of the mental functioning of persons with various kinds of brain damage and persons who have undergone brain surgery, and they yield important information about the storage of memories, the processing of language, and so on. I'll discuss them as we come to the relevant topics.

For now, I want to add one more group of basic findings about the brain, some from neurophysiology and some from fossil discoveries, that tell us highly significant truths about the human mind. These findings make clear that we are not just smarter apes, but that our minds represent a quantum leap of evolution and make us qualitatively different from all other forms of life.

Consider, first, that the brain of the human infant, unlike that of any other animal, triples in size during its first year. This is an extraordinary development, an amazing accommodation between the limits of the birth canal and the prodigious brain size we have achieved through evolution.

Moreover, that increase in brain size appears to have come about explosively. Most major evolutionary developments have taken place over many millions of years, but not this one. About twenty million years ago our prehominid ancestors, Dryopithecus and Ramapithecus, had brains no bigger than monkeys'. Virtually no change occurred for the next seventeen million years or so, but then, rather abruptly, the australopithecine hominids appeared, with larger brains of about 500 cc in volume. Currently, there is considerable disagreement as to whether another line, genus Homo, branched off and the australopithecines died out, or whether the australopithecines evolved into Homo, but in either case, the first human being, Homo habilis, appeared—again, rather abruptly—about two million years ago, with 750 cc of brain. And rather swiftly, in evolutionary terms—only half a million years later—Homo erectus showed up, with 900 to 1300 cc of brain. Then evolution went berserk: a mere 200,000 to 300,000 years ago an early form of Homo sapiens appeared, with a 1400 cc brain, and by 40,000 years ago the modern human being, Homo sapiens sapiens, emerged, with a brain averaging 1500 cc.

What happened? What caused evolution to accelerate in this way, and to produce, as if overnight, modern humankind with its highly special brain? Here we enter an area of speculation—but not guesswork—for recent fossil discoveries give us a toehold on reality.

What, for instance, is the connection between standing up straight and having a large brain? Not what you might suppose—not a better brain first, and upright posture afterward, as a result of doing things with the hands in a human way. Rather, the data now seem to show that our ancestors stood upright three to four million years ago, when their brains were still small. Why did the brain only then increase? Apparently, having hands free to pick up and wield sticks and stones gave a tremendous evolutionary advantage to those whose brains were a little better than their fellows, a little quicker to realize the possibilities of using sticks and stone. We stood up—and this favored those who were smart enough to make the most of it; the brightest—the fittest—survived. So brain growth followed hard upon the upright posture: within half a million years, the larger-brained hominids appeared, and began using simple tools and weapons, and hunting animals.

And with the advent of toolmaking, the brain grew still faster. The connection isn't the obvious one: it wasn't only that better brains improved the tools, but that the use of tools made for better brains. Anthropologist Sherwood L. Washburn of the University of California at Berkeley says the evidence shows that it was *after* early humans started making tools and weapons that the real explosion in brain size took place. He suggests that since stone tools are hard to make but highly effective in the race for survival, there was a feedback effect from tool to brain. Those individuals who could make better tools were the ones with larger and better brains; by virtue of their tools they had a better chance of surviving, and therefore of producing larger-brained offspring. As Washburn puts it, "The anatomy of the human brain reflect[s] a selection for success in manual skills." It was our hands, obeying our forebrains, that made better tools—and better tools that then in turn promoted the rapid growth of the forebrain.

But an upright, toolmaking, large-brained human being is not necessarily a speaking, thinking one. We have no way of knowing whether early humans spoke or not, but it seems unlikely that they were mute—and likely that their verbal communication was of a very low order. In consequence, for hundreds of thousands of years there was little change in their way of life. But perhaps toolmaking helped select ever-larger brains, capable of dealing with communication of a simple sort, until at last the expanding brain somehow—perhaps by a sudden mutation—developed language centers (Broca's Area and Wernicke's Area, in Figure 2) such as neither the apes nor early humans had.

This most recent and most significant evolutionary development made all the difference. Modern humankind appeared only 40,000 years ago—and, says Washburn, "What we see in the last 40,000 years of prehistory may have been triggered by the development of speech as we know it today." In less than 1 percent of the time since our ancestors stood up on two feet, humans learned to make all sorts of new and complex tools and weapons, build shelters, design and construct boats, travel across the sea, domesticate animals, paint and draw and, later, write; and finally, transform the entire nature of society and daily life through technology and science. Language, Washburn suggests, may have been "the critical new factor that provided a biological base for the acceleration of history."

Somewhere along this course of evolutionary development, we acquired one other special trait: self-awareness. Animals are aware of their environment, but not of themselves in the sense that we are. No animal except a chimpanzee or an orangutan, seeing itself in a mirror, knows whose image it is seeing. (I've sometimes watched a male pheasant furiously attacking his own reflection in a sliding glass door, thinking it a rival for his females' favors.) But we not only know who it is that we see in the mirror, we actively think about ourselves and about our own thoughts; there's no evidence at all that the chimpanzee or orangutan, though it knows itself in a mirror, does anything of the kind.

Is self-awareness a by-product of the most recent burst of brain evolution and another function of Broca's Area? Or did self-awareness come earlier, as a happenstance mutation that made its owner more thoughtful than others and therefore more human? Camus said that an intellectual is someone whose mind watches itself, but this is true of all human beings, more or less, and it is surely part of what makes us so different from the rest of life on earth. And it is surely, too, the driving force behind cognitive science, the first rigorous effort of the human mind to explore its own workings.

# THE GREAT BLACK BOX DEBATE

## The Human Being as Dog, Pigeon, Rat, or Sheep

Looking within the human mind has been unfashionable, at least among research psychologists, during much of this century. In the five decades during which behaviorism dominated experimental and theoretical psychology, the study of inner mental processes—sometimes derisively referred to as "mentalism"—was considered old-fashioned and even benighted; rather akin, indeed, to feckless mystical and religious speculations about the soul. All such studies, behaviorists held, were purely conjectural; moreover, they were simply unnecessary. Human behavior could be explained in the same concrete, nonmentalistic terms as those by which we explain the behavior of a dog, a pigeon, a rat, or a sheep—the very animals used in a number of psychological experiments from which analogies to human behavior were drawn, profoundly influencing childrearing, psychotherapy, and many other areas of daily life.

*The human being as dog.* . . . It all began with Pavlov's dog. Early in this century, in what is surely the most famous experiment in psychology, the Russian physiologist-psychologist Ivan Pavlov strapped a dog in a test chamber and connected a tube from one of its salivary glands to a recording device. When Pavlov set a metronome ticking, the dog did not salivate— why should it?—but when he put food in the dish, it did; the stimulus of food produced the reflexive or "unconditioned response" of salivation. But then Pavlov set the metronome ticking each time he put out food; after a while, the dog would salivate as soon as it heard the sound, even before receiving food and, eventually, even when it got no food. Salivation had become a "conditioned response" to the ticking. This exemplified what emerged as the basic law of conditioning: a stimulus can be made to produce a reaction that is not a reflex to it but is a learned or conditioned response.

This and a number of similarly simple and objective principles (I will come to them shortly) seemed to Pavlov's followers sufficient to explain all of animal behavior, including that of the human being. Dogs, for instance, tend to behave in certain ways that are natural to them, but conditioning can produce in them all sorts of other special behavior: they can be trained to relieve themselves only at the curb, to sniff out drugs in luggage, to attack intruders (but not people they know), to prance or mince before dog-show judges, to lead the blind, to locate truffles, to leap through flaming hoops, and so on, all depending on the administration of rewards and punishments at appropriate moments in their training.

As with the dog, so with the human being. The American psychologist John B. Watson, who brought Pavlov's work to the attention of Americans in 1913 and who coined the name "behaviorism" for the new school of psychology, made this famous boast in 1925, when behaviorism was flushed with its early successes in the laboratory:

> Give me a dozen healthy infants, well-formed, and my own specified world to bring them up in, and I'll guarantee to take any one at random and train him to become any type of specialist I might select—a doctor, lawyer, artist, merchant-chief, and, yes, even into a beggar-man and thief, regardless of his talents, penchants, tendencies, abilities, vocations and race of his ancestors.

*The human being as pigeon and as rat.* . . . Watson's most famous disciple, B. F. Skinner, is the dean of today's behaviorists and was for several decades a major force in American psychology. Along with his additions to behaviorist theory, Skinner developed the technique of "operant conditioning" or behavior shaping, an advance on conditioning technique by means of which all sorts of complicated and unlikely behavior can be induced in fairly stupid animals. The principle of operant conditioning is to give an immediate reward or "reinforcer" for any bit of desired behavior or even any tiny movement in the desired direction, but none, or even a mild punishment, for the opposite.

With patience, one can push this process to the point where a mindless creature will do seemingly intelligent tasks. In one celebrated experiment, Skinner taught two pigeons to play a kind of table tennis: with their beaks they shoved a Ping-Pong ball back and forth across a table at each other, each pigeon receiving a bit of food for each push. Another experiment yielded a pigeon who played a toy piano: it would peck a key, run over to a food trough into which a pellet had fallen as a reward, then back to the keyboard, then back to the trough, and so on. Even more seemingly intelligent and purposeful was the performance of one of Skinner's rats: it would pull a chain to get a marble, pick up the marble in its paws, carry it to an upright tube and drop it in, and rush to the food trough to get its reward.

These complex and apparently intelligent behaviors had been fashioned, a bit at a time, out of random and reflexive movements by means of operant conditioning. There was no need to suppose that the animals understood what they were doing or to speculate about their inner mental processes. Or those of human beings. Human behavior, Skinner has repeatedly said in his own characteristically gentle and rational way, is shaped by the environment, not by internal cognitive processes. "We're always controlled and we're always manipulated," he says. "I don't believe that people control people [that is, themselves], I believe that environment controls people." Accordingly, he has long urged the use of operant conditioning to produce the kinds of human behavior we want: "By rearranging the controls over people," he has said, "the world could be improved." Seeking to modify human behavior through mental processes, or to explain it in terms of what goes on in the mind, seems to Skinner to be akin to primitive animism, and to have no place in scientific psychology:

> We do not need to try to discover what personalities, states of mind, feelings, traits of character, plans, purposes, intentions, or other perquisites of autonomous man really are in order to get on with a scientific analysis of behavior. . . . As the interaction between organism and environment has come to be understood . . . effects once assigned to states of mind, feelings, and traits are beginning to be traced to accessible conditions.

The science of behavior, he has said at other times, need deal only with external causes of behavior and the observable results of that behavior; such data will yield "a comprehensive picture of the organism in a behaving system."

*The human being as sheep.* . . . By the 1930s and 1940s, it had occurred to various behaviorists that not only desirable behavior but behavioral malfunctioning might be explicable in terms of conditioning. Howard Liddell, a psychobiologist at Cornell University, was the leading investigator of this subject several decades ago. In a typical experiment, he would attach a wire to a sheep's front leg and, after a warning signal—a ten-second dimming of the lights in the animal's cubicle, for instance—would give it a mildly painful electric shock. After a few shocks, the sheep would respond to the dimming of the lights by running around frantically, its head held high and its heart racing, and would jump convulsively when the shock came. But after many more shocks, it would be a wretched sight: at the signal—or even without it—it would crouch rigidly in a corner, grinding its teeth and twitching, but making no effort to escape. Some sheep even had hallucinations—they jumped time and again without shocks—and still others, put out to pasture with their fellow sheep, stayed as far from the flock as possible in trembling isolation.

The sheep, to come to the point, were displaying physical symptoms and behavior strongly reminiscent of those exhibited by human beings suffering from neuroses or even psychoses. One could not and need not ascribe the sheep's troubles to an unhappy childhood, unloving parents, or sexual repression and other inner conflicts; sheep were only sheep, and their conditioning to shock was a sufficient explanation. The inevitable inference was drawn by clinical psychologists: it was not necessary to explain human neuroses and psychoses in the complicated and speculative terms of psychodynamic psychology when those disorders could be so much more simply explained in terms of the conditioning produced by bad experiences that had been conjoined to normal desires or to ordinarily benign stimuli. Why not abandon all efforts to get one's patients to achieve insight and simply provide them with counterconditioning experiences? As Joseph Wolpe, a leading exponent of behavior therapy, put it several years ago, the Freudian explanations of neuroses were simply unnecessary; a neurosis was "just a habit—a persistent habit of unadaptive behavior" that could be cured by counterconditioning techniques such as "systematic desensitization." Typically, a female patient with a morbid fear of the penis was induced to relax and think pleasant thoughts, and then to envision a nude male statue far off (where the penis was relatively unthreatening). When the association of relaxation and pleasant thoughts with the remote nonliving penis made it tolerable, the patient was then told to envision it closer and closer, and eventually to practice this association with images of a live male. This was reported to have led her to be able to tolerate the real thing.

Other behavior therapists have used "aversive" conditioning techniques to link unwanted behavior to unpleasant experiences and so eliminate that behavior. Some have given electric shocks to male homosexuals as they looked at erotic photos of nude males. Others have sought to combat overeating by training their patients to imagine themselves vomiting in public when they feel like gorging themselves, or giving them pills that produce nausea shortly after eating. Early reports claimed considerable success with these efforts.

Many contemporary marriage therapists, similarly, do not try to get troubled couples to look for insights into the causes of their feelings about, and behavior toward, each other; rather, the therapist asks the couple to talk to each other about some problem, and abruptly orders them to stop whenever they say or do something hurtful and to learn and rehearse substitute forms of talking and behaving that the therapist prescribes. The theory behind this method is that the old behavior produces pain while the new behavior produces satisfaction or even pleasure; therefore, substituting and practicing the new behavior will be enough to make it habitual and self-reinforcing. Understanding isn't necessary.

Thus, from the third decade of the century until about ten years ago, experimental and theoretical psychology in this country were dominated by a school whose central doctrine was that mental processes do not matter and are probably only labels we vain and credulous creatures give to certain of our illusions. (The influence of psychoanalytic psychology, which held very much the opposite, was limited chiefly to the psychotherapies, and even there ceased to be dominant by the 1960s.) A lot may happen in our minds, but according to behaviorism none of it can be examined, and none need be in order to predict what we will do or account for what we have done. We are brother and sister to the dog, the pigeon, the rat, and the sheep; the same principles explain our behavior and theirs, and it is only ignorance and pride that makes us think we are thinking animals, different from them in any important way.

And this simplistic doctrine was the reigning view of the human mind during those same years in which the products of that mind radically transformed Western culture by means of electric lighting, the automobile, the airplane, and television; produced a dozen phases of artistic radicalization; totally changed the nature of warfare, and led to two world wars; discovered the secret of atomic power and the nature of the genetic code; pushed back the age of the universe threefold, and its dimensions by far more than that; increased the human life span, in the developed nations, by more than a generation; and restructured morals, customs, and the law so that divorce, remarriage, and a variety of variant forms of family life could take their place in modern society and fill a number of new social needs.

Wonders all. But the wonder of wonders is that so many intelligent and thoughtful people could have believed that behaviorism was an adequate explanation of human behavior.

## Simple Answers to Difficult Questions

Yet behaviorism had (and still has) an enormous appeal for many people. In part, that's because it is in harmony with democratic and liberal sentiments; it says that the human being is only a collection of conditioned responses that we can remold nearer to the heart's desire.

But perhaps in larger part, its appeal stems from the fact that it seems to answer several of those difficult questions I referred to earlier that have so long plagued philosophers and psychologists. Among them: What is the mind made of—the same kind of stuff as the body, or something else (and if so, what)? How can we ever be sure that the world inside the mind corresponds to the reality outside it? How does the mind come by abstract ideas such as "beauty," "humanity," or "infinity" when we can experience only individual beautiful objects, or people, or a finite number of actual things?

The unsatisfactory answers that most philosophers gave to these questions for well over two thousand years were based not on observation but on the metaphysical view that there are two kinds of substance or being, namely, matter and spirit, and that our minds are made of the second kind.

Religion had long distinguished between body and soul, but it was Plato who turned this into a metaphysical system with psychological consequences. He held that there are two levels of being: a superior one, composed of timeless ideas or abstract forms, and an inferior one, composed of mere appearances or individual physical objects. (Beauty, for instance, is timeless, and therefore more real than any beautiful object or person.) In this way, Plato identified the mind with disembodied thought, and later on Christian theologians identified it further with the soul.

What this implied, psychologically, was that the mind is made of something incorporeal—spirit or pure thought or soul; that it can perceive true reality outside itself by dealing in timeless ideas rather than physical appearances; and that it possesses such ideas innately, as part of its very nature. Such were the beliefs that so long served as answers—thoroughly unsatisfactory ones—to the psychological questions posed by the Platonic metaphysic.

Even when science began to blossom in the seventeenth and eighteenth centuries, the leading European philosophers—Descartes, Leibniz, and Kant among them—followed this tradition. But across the Channel in England, where philosophizing tended to be more commonsensical and practical, an opposite tradition was developing. Its major figures were the philosophers Thomas Hobbes, John Locke, and David Hume; they are known as empiricists because they regarded observation of actual events rather than metaphysical reasoning as the foundation of knowledge.

Locke, in particular, considered the doctrine of innate ideas to be without any proof and contrary to everyday experience. In 1690, he stated his view in its most extreme form: he likened the mind of the infant to a tabula rasa—a clean slate—on which everything that later appeared was written by experience. How does such a mind extract ideas from its sense impressions and so understand reality? By comparing and connecting images in various ways; the details were vague.

Hume went further: although the mind, he said, has no power to perceive any metaphysical reality behind appearances, it makes sense of the world by simply *assuming* that there is some real connection between events that are experienced in sequence; in other words, it *associates* them. He gave this homely example: if a man eats a loaf of bread and is nourished by it, the next time he sees an object that looks just like that loaf of bread, he will expect it to be edible and nourishing—not because his mind sees through to the inner nature of the bread, but because he merely associates with its appearance those qualities that went with such an appearance before. As Hume put it:

> All belief of matter of fact or real existence is derived merely
> from some object, present to the memory or senses, and a cus-
> tomary conjunction between that and some other object.

Which is an eighteenth-century way of saying what Pavlov later observed in his dog: it acted as if it expected the metronome to produce food because there had been a "customary conjunction" between ticking sounds and food in the past. The seed of behaviorism had been sown.

•

But when psychology emerged as a science somewhat over a century after Hume wrote these words, it did not begin as behaviorism; the first psychologists were interested in consciousness and in the exploration of mental processes. Like the English empiricists, they believed that all thoughts are made up of perceptions, combined and recombined in the mind. So to investigate thinking, men like Wilhelm Wundt in Germany and Edward B. Titchener in America asked their subjects to perform certain little mental tasks (such as adding, or completing analogies) and then to report the images their thoughts had been composed of.

Unfortunately, introspectionism, as this method was called, was a failure. The subjects often couldn't say what had happened; they got the answer without any awareness of their own thoughts. When they were aware of them, those thoughts often involved no images. In any case, as critics of the technique asked, how could one trust the subjects' reports when the only tool used to examine their thoughts were their own thoughts? How can one use a lens to examine its own substance?

It was just at this time that behaviorism appeared and seemed to offer a far more solid approach to research. Pavlov was discovering laws of associative learning by purely objective methods, without any assumptions about unseen processes or any effort to look into the mind. In America, Watson, greatly impressed by this method, began to argue that psychology should give up seeking to be a science of mental life; instead, it should become a science of observable behavior. Only objective observations should be acceptable in that science; introspectionism and theorizing about the mind should not. The proper goal of psychology, he wrote, is "to be able, given the stimulus, to predict the response—or, seeing the reaction take place, to state what the stimulus is that has called out the reaction."

Behaviorism thus answers the ancient intractable questions by saying, in effect: We can explain human behavior without talking about mind; therefore the question of what it's made of is irrelevant. The same thing is true of the other questions (how the mind's world corresponds to the outside one, and how the mind comes by its ideas); we simply don't need to know what occurs inside. If, knowing what goes into a black box, we can confidently say what will come out, what is in it doesn't matter; it might as well be empty.

Simple answers to difficult questions. Of course, they're evasions rather than answers, but they swept the field, particularly after Pavlov's work appeared in English in 1927. Aside from a handful of experimental psychologists who still wanted to study the mind's processes, and the Freudians who were probing the inner mental life of their patients, American psychology was dominated by behaviorism for the next four decades. For much of that time it put an end to nearly all efforts to see into the black box.

## The Rat, et al., as Human Being

People who do not admire behaviorism sometimes refer to it as "rat psychology," and with reason. During the decades when behaviorism dominated American psychology, the bulk of basic research in the field consisted of studying rats made to run through mazes, push levers for a food reward, choose between doors of different colors, and so on. Sometimes, the researchers used chicks, pigeons, dogs, and other small animals, but in any case, they weren't interested in the behavior specific to the rat or any of these other species. They were looking for general principles of conditioning that they believed held true of all sentient creatures, much as the principles of valence are true of all elements in chemical compounds. It was exciting to think that one might discover, in these small, simple, controllable subjects, laws of psychology that would apply to all animals, including human beings.

Imagine that we are viewing a few minutes of a documentary film consisting of scenes shot in various laboratories in the twenties, thirties, and forties. We see in short takes—mostly in harshly lit black and white—a tiny sample of the thousands of experiments by which a number of principles were discovered and verified during that period:

—We look down on a maze—a series of alleys wide enough for a rat to run through or turn around in (Fig. 10). A hand belonging to some unseen researcher places a twitchy-nosed laboratory rat in the start box. The rat begins exploring, sniffing, and moving about. It runs a little, turns into the first blind alley, then turns around and runs the other way. After three wrong choices and three right ones at the intersections, it reaches the goal box; the hand removes the rat and, a little later, puts it back at the starting point. Finally, on the seventh run there is a pellet of food at the goal; the rat smells it, then gobbles it down. Then another rat gets the same training, but with no food reward, not even at the last run.

After a week during which the rats receive the same training every day, we see the first rat run swiftly through the maze without a mistake (it had made fewer errors each day, and at last knows the route perfectly). Next, we

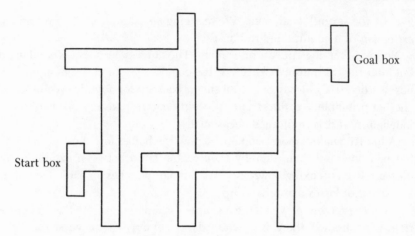

**Fig. 10.**  A maze used in studying how rats learn their way around

see the second rat; it still makes as many mistakes as ever. But now, for the first time, it gets a bit of food at the end of its run and—presto!—on the very next trial it makes almost no mistakes. It has learned as much, in one rewarded trial, as the first rat learned in a week. We are seeing two principles revealed: first, *reward produces learning*—but also, even without reward, *latent learning* takes place and becomes manifest as soon as a reward is given. The second rat had been learning the maze in some sense, but what it had learned was not activated until the right route was associated with a reward.

(Does the principle apply to humans? Ask any teacher. A child practicing handwriting—or any similar skill—may seem to make little progress until the teacher has time to bestow a word of encouragement; then, abruptly, the child shows improvement. A novice at tennis may spend half a summer trying to hit a decent backhand; one day things suddenly fall together and he hits a beautiful one, his partner praises him, and from then on—though with frequent lapses—he's "got it," or at least knows what it is that he wants to do.)

—We see a medium-sized, perky dog strapped in a cage. A metronome begins to tick; the camera pans down to a nearby recording graph, where a pen moves upward, showing that thirteen drops of saliva were produced—as much as if the dog were getting fed. On the second trial, somewhat later, still without food, the pen records only seven drops. The third time, only five. By the seventh trial, none. We're seeing an example of the principle of *extinction* of a conditioned response.

Now another dog appears on-camera. The same experiment is conducted, but after the third unrewarded trial the dog does get food—and on the next unrewarded trials his saliva output shoots back up for a while. We're seeing another principle: *reinforcement.* A conditioned response can be kept intact indefinitely if it is reinforced occasionally.

(A human analog: most people who play the horses lose most of the time, but win now and then, thereby keeping the bond between gambling and pleasure from breaking down. But the gambler who has an extended unbroken string of losses may give it up.)

—On the screen, now, we see a simple T-shaped maze. At the end of the right-hand branch there is a white door, behind which we see a bit of cheese; at the end of the left-hand branch there is a black door behind which there is only a metal grid floor that will give an electric jolt to the rat's feet after it enters.

We see a number of rats put in, one at a time, to run this maze; they learn, after a while, to choose the right-hand branch with the white door. Once they've learned, the situation is reversed: the white door and food are now at the left side, the black door and shock at the right. The rats run to the right, jump when shocked, run again, and soon learn to turn left.

And again the situation is reversed. But now the rats learn at once. They've associated reward and punishment with the colors of the doors, not their direction; the rats are demonstrating the principle of *discrimination,* or the association of one cue, in a two-cue situation, with the rewarding outcome.

(A human parallel: a novice at cocktail-party behavior finds that he feels poor after a jolly evening during which he had a good deal of Scotch. At the next party, on a friend's advice, he tries vodka instead, and suffers no ill effects. But at a third party, where he has a good time and stays a long while, he drinks a lot of vodka, and the next day feels rotten. He now puts two and two together: it wasn't the choice of liquor but the excess of it that made the trouble.)

—A small cage with metal sides and with glass walls at the front and back. Inside, a rat is sniffing, exploring, bustling about. After a while, standing on its hind legs, it happens to lean on a small metal bar set in one wall. At once, a food pellet falls into a little trough below. (This is the famous "Skinner box" invented by B. F. Skinner himself.) The rat notices the food, drops down and eats it, but makes no connection between the lever and the food. Awhile later, it again accidentally pushes the bar down and gets a second pellet. After a number of such episodes, the connection becomes established: the rat stands up, presses the bar, drops down and eats, stands up and presses the bar again, and keeps this up until it is sated. We've just seen *operant conditioning;* unlike classic (Pavlovian) conditioning, this links spontaneous normal behavior, such as the animal uses in operating in the world around it, to a reward, and thereby modifies the behavior.

There is almost no limit to what the experimenter or animal trainer can do with this technique. In quick takes we see a rabbit that picks up a coin with its mouth and drops it into a piggy bank, a pigeon that pecks a sign reading BLUE (out of four signs naming various colors) when a blue light flashes on, and a show-business pig named Priscilla that turns on the TV set, eats breakfast at a table, picks up dirty clothes and puts them in a hamper, and runs a vacuum cleaner over the floor.

(In Skinnerian terms, much of childrearing is operant conditioning: the innumerable disapproving looks and words, when a child is annoying, and the innumerable smiles and words of encouragement when he or she is pleasing, are minuscule punishments and rewards that organize and mold the child's behavior. The same is true at the adult level: the recruit in the service, the freshman on campus, the employee new to the firm, all rapidly shape up—or, more precisely, are shaped up—by the multitude of subtle responses that they sense to their clothing, their demeanor, and their conversation.)

—Another Skinner box, another rat. Suddenly the rat jumps, begins to scurry around, and tries to climb the walls. It is feeling an unpleasant electric current in its feet. After a while, in its random movements it happens to push down on the bar, and the current goes off. Soon the rat has learned to turn off the current whenever it starts; we are seeing *operant escape.*

But operant escape, unlike conditioning to a reward, can become a fixation—a pattern resistant to extinction. We see a larger cage with a dog inside; a buzzer sounds, the dog gets a shock in its feet, and in its discomfort jumps over a hurdle in the middle of the cage. On the other side, there is no current. Soon the dog jumps over the hurdle as soon as it hears the buzzer, avoiding the shock altogether. But what happens if there is no more current being sent into this cage, and no reason to jump? The dog keeps jumping; we see it do so for the hundredth time and the two hundredth time. The response hasn't been extinguished because as far as the dog is concerned, it has avoided the shock each time; it doesn't know there is no longer anything to avoid.

(Much human behavior resembles the dog's operant escape pattern. The child of critical or harsh parents, for instance, may discover that it is possible to avoid their criticism by being inconspicuous; such a person may be self-effacing all through life on the erroneous assumption that were he or she otherwise, other people, too, would be critical and harsh.)

—Another **T** maze. In it, rats are learning to choose the right side. There's no punishment for choosing the left, merely a lack of reward. Some rats, if they choose the right side, find food behind the door every time, but a less lucky group find food there only once in every four times. As we watch, it's clear that the unlucky rats are much slower to learn than the lucky ones; we're seeing that *partial reinforcement* is measurably less effective, in learning, than continual reinforcement.

The situation changes: now there is no reward at all for either group. Curiously, the rats who were rewarded every time lose their conditioning rapidly, while those who were rewarded only intermittently keep choosing the right branch every time for a long while. This is the *partial reinforcement effect*. If rats had expectations, like people, you might say that the less lucky rats, expecting less, were far slower to grasp the reality of the new situation, while the luckier rats, unaccustomed to disappointment, were quick to be disillusioned. But behaviorists don't talk in such terms about rats. Or about the human beings rats substitute for in the laboratory.

No wonder behaviorists have so often sounded like cult leaders or bringers of the Word. Wielding such power to alter small creatures—and seeing in the behavior of those creatures principles that seemed to be universal—they felt certain that their theory could encompass all of psychology. This heady sense of power was coupled to an optimistic liberalism; like Watson and Skinner, many behaviorists felt that since human nature was so malleable, there was no limit to the social improvement that could be brought about by the application of scientific psychology.

Moreover, they were equally sanguine about the prospect that psychology would soon cease to be a "soft" science and would rapidly become as precise and capable of correct prediction as chemistry or physics. That, at any rate, was the hope of one of Watson's disciples named Clark L. Hull, who fostered a behaviorist specialty known as "mathematical learning theory." In Hull's view, the rate at which responses are learned or extinguished can be predicted with mathematical precision. This Hullian equation—

$$_SH_R = M\ (1 - 10^{-iN})$$

—says that the strength of any habit can be computed from the number of reinforced trials, the size of the reward, the individual's learning rate, and so on. This and a number of more complicated equations and formulae offer a mathematically exact explanation of behavior in terms of the various independent variables (the conditions of input) and dependent variables (the measurable variations in response)—but omit altogether the intervening variables, or whatever is inside the black box.

The goals of complete objectivity and of mathematical precision are admirable. But in ignoring or dismissing whatever might take place in the human mind, behaviorists were prone to look upon the human being as no more than a rat of larger stature and with a quicker learning rate. With the best of intentions and the most decent of social values, it was all too easy for scientists holding such views to begin to treat human beings like laboratory animals.

The classic example is that of Watson himself. In 1920, he and an associate, Rosalie Rayner, working at Johns Hopkins, decided to do an experiment in the acquisition and extinction of fear. Their subject was Albert B., a healthy eleven-month-old infant who lived in a home for invalid children, where his mother was a wet nurse. In the experiment, a white rat was presented to Albert, who immediately reached for it. Just as he touched it, a steel bar was struck with a hammer right behind his head. Albert jumped, fell forward, and buried his face in the mattress. The process was repeated; this time Albert jumped, fell forward, and began to whimper. A week later, when the rat was again offered to Albert, he was hesitant and withdrew his hand when the rat nosed it. The next six times that the rat was brought to him, the steel bar was banged; Albert's fear reactions grew stronger and he burst out crying. At last, the instant the rat was shown him—even without the noise—Albert began to cry, turned over, and tried to crawl away as fast as possible. By now, he was just as frightened of a rabbit; he had generalized his fear to other furry things, including a dog, a fur coat, and a Santa Claus mask. Watson and Rayner had meant to countercondition him, if possible, but he and his mother left the home and Albert's fate is unknown.

Skinner never did anything quite like this, but his own well-intentioned experiments in infant care seemed, at least to outsiders, chillingly devoid of human feeling. In 1945, newsreel headlines billed him as "the man who keeps his baby in a box." He had designed a glassed-in, insulated crib with filtered and temperature-controlled air; in this environment, the baby needed no clothing or bedding but only a diaper. Skinner's own daughter, Deborah, spent two and a half years in the "air crib," and grew up to be a normal, successful adult, but to many people the air crib sounded like an experiment in isolation of the infant, and Skinner's efforts to market the device failed.

More to the point, perhaps, Skinner's own notions of behavior shaping, as outlined in his utopian novel, *Walden Two,* have struck many critics as being applicable to evil social ends as well as good ones, and uncomfortably akin to the outlook of those leaders of dictatorial governments who treat their citizens much like domestic animals in which desired behavior is induced by the skillful application of carrot and whip.

But no controlled society and no cult has ever long remained without dissidents, reformers, revisionists, and break-away revolutionaries. The view of the human being as rat is simply too narrow: people do think and, thinking, find reason to reshape their own behavior; they follow their own minds despite all the external pressures of reward and punishment.

For much the same reason, many of the behavior therapies have failed to live up to their first promise. The short-term sex therapies, for instance, originally seemed to cure most of the disabilities they were used to treat, but follow-up studies have shown that there is a high relapse rate; only when treatment includes more searching forms of psychotherapy are most of the gains permanent. Similarly, behavioral marriage therapy seems to have no higher a success record than insight-using therapies (and, according to some studies, has a lower one), although if its theory were sound, it should be far more effective than the more cerebral methods.

The most disappointing results of all have been those of the aversive therapies: the association of homosexuality, overeating, alcoholism, and other behaviors with sharply unpleasant stimuli has shown a high rate of cessation of those behaviors—but the results have been largely ephemeral. For in contrast to laboratory animals, human patients in aversive therapy *know* that the painful stimulus is being given them for a purpose. Unlike the dog jumping over the hurdle, they know that after the conclusion of therapy, if they wish to engage in homosexual behavior, overeat, or drink too much, they can do so without fear of shock or nausea. And that knowledge can, of itself, wipe out the aversive conditioning.

## Dull Blade

William of Ockham, a fourteenth-century Franciscan philosopher, is remembered today chiefly for the maxim known as "Ockham's razor": "Entities are not to be multiplied without necessity," or, in plain words, the simplest explanation is the best one.* In modern science this is called the principle of parsimony: it says that if you can explain a phenomenon without assuming this or that hypothetical entity, there is no reason to assume it.

Behaviorism wielded Ockham's razor with a vengeance: it explained human behavior without making any assumptions about what happens in the mind. But the razor proved to have an exceedingly dull blade; it hacked off what was necessary along with what was not and, in its simplicity, simply could not explain most of human behavior.

In fact, it couldn't even explain much of animal behavior. Watson, ever a confident sort, had said in 1924, "We can take any stimulus calling out a standard reaction and substitute another stimulus for it," but he was wrong: not all stimuli can be replaced by others, not even by the most persistent researchers. Followers of Skinner, using operant conditioning, discovered that while they could easily get a pigeon to peck at a key for food, they could not get it to flap its wings for the same reward. They could easily get a rat to lean on a bar for food, but found it almost impossible to get a cat to do so. They gave rats sour blue water to drink, followed by a sickness-producing drug; afterward, the rats associated sickness with sour water and shunned it but continued to drink blue water—but quail, given the same treatment, thereafter avoided the blue water and drank the sour water. These and hundreds of similar findings show that the behaviorist laws of learning are too general; they do not allow for built-in neural circuitry—instinctual tendencies—that differ greatly from species to species.

Nor did the behaviorist theory of learning allow for any cognitive processes in the animal mind. It viewed the rat as an automaton, driven this way and that in its environment by stimuli, but even in the heyday of behaviorism, Edward C. Tolman—who considered himself a behaviorist—no-

* Actually, this quotation does not appear in his works; he did say something that has the same force, but I am citing the maxim as it is usually stated.

ticed that his rats weren't passive automata. A rat, at a choice point in a maze it had run a few times, did not automatically turn and run one way or the other but paused, looked this way and that, took a few steps, and perhaps turned around, all before making a final choice. To Tolman, this called for a cognitive explanation, not a behaviorist one: the rat was sampling cues and going through a process of "vicarious trial and error"—a simple version of what human beings do when they consider the various possibilities ahead of them before actually trying to solve a problem.

Sometimes, indeed, rats seemed to do all the vicarious trial and error in their heads, without any physical movement. In 1930, Tolman and a colleague built a maze with three routes to the food: a short one, a medium-length one, and a long one (see Fig. 11). Behaviorist theory predicted—

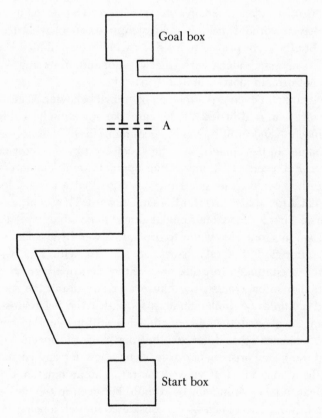

**Fig. 11.** When Tolman closed the barrier at *A*, his rats knew which way to go.

correctly—that the rat would get to the food by each of the routes, and would then learn to take the shortest one because that was the easiest habit to establish. But then Tolman dropped a barrier at point A. According to behaviorist theory, the rat should have tried the medium-length route—the next most easily established habit—but it did not; it took the longest route. Tolman held that this showed it had some kind of mental map of the maze and knew that the barrier blocked all but the longest route. Such assumptions were forbidden in orthodox behaviorism—which therefore failed to predict the rat's choice.

Human beings, of course, can do as well—but why can they? It's certainly not an instinctive ability, because very young children haven't got it. Professor Herbert L. Pick, Jr., of the Center for Learning at the University of Minnesota, is one of a number of researchers who have recently studied the ways in which children deal with space. A few years ago, Pick and several of his graduate students assembled a set of little cubicles in different arrangements. Figure 12 shows a typical one. They led children through the cubicles, each of which contained a different toy animal by way of identification. Rather quickly, young children learned the route; they knew what room came after the one they were in, what one came after that, and so on. But they couldn't invent detours through the closed doors, nor could they say what room was on the other side of the wall from the one they were in unless it was next in the series.

Yet as children get older, they acquire the ability to do both; they are able to correctly imagine routes and spatial relationships they have never directly experienced. Since this behavior is not instinctive, it must be learned—although it is not part of experience. Pick and some of his colleagues believe this is strong evidence that children assemble the acquired information into a kind of map from which, by analogy and inference, they can relate any point to any other point even though they have never experienced a connection between the two. And this is crucial: analogy and inference are thought processes—the very kind of entities that behaviorists consider unnecessary hypotheses.

Just as children develop this capacity to deal with space, so do they develop capacities to deal with a number of other subtle aspects of the world around them. This was the message of the work of the Swiss psychologist Jean Piaget that belatedly reached American psychology in the 1960s. Piaget's work—I pass over it in a sentence or two until later—showed that children spontaneously acquire certain sophisticated ideas about the world

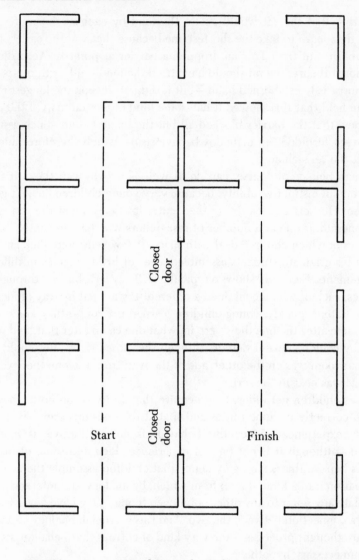

**Fig. 12.** A maze used in studying how young children learn their way around

they live in. "Conservation" of quantity is an example: a preschooler who sees water poured from a short wide glass into a tall thin one thinks the second glass has more water in it—but a few years later, without actual instruction, the same child will realize that the amount of water doesn't change. Such concepts, neither instinctual nor directly experiential, indicate that the developing mind has dealt in some way with the data of experience and gone beyond them.

It is true that we are far less instinct-guided than the other animals. But the view of the infant brain as tabula rasa, based on the infant's incompetence, fails to recognize that the brain, directed by heredity, is destined to develop complex circuits and systems as the child matures. Look back at Figure 7 (p. 40); obviously the wiring has only been begun in the newborn infant. But the latest evidence of brain research is that the multiplying and growing neurons of the child's brain, guided by chemical tags, knit together according to an immensely complex and precise plan. This does not give us instincts, but it does give us innate tendencies to see the world and to deal with experiences in specific, cognitive ways, none of which is admissible in behaviorist theory.

Take the matter of human memory. Behaviorists dealt with it in mathematical terms: the more trials, reinforcements, and so on, the more certain it was that a stimulus would produce a given response. The stimulus might be a question: What comes after 2? The response would be the answer: 3. Or: What is your Social Security number? The answer is a nine-digit series in which each number is the stimulus for the next; that is, a chain of little associative links.

But psychologists before the behaviorist era had found it necessary to hypothesize that there were two distinct kinds of human memory: short-term and long-term. The need to invoke this distinction did not disappear merely because behaviorists ignored it. It was still true, even in the behaviorist era, that you would look up a phone number, remember it long enough to dial it—and usually forget it at once; yet innumerable things you had looked up or seen only once would remain long, or permanently, in your memory— the price you paid for a suit, a joke you found particularly funny (or unfunny), a special look on someone's face. Repetition and reward aren't a good enough explanation; other things happen in the mind that enable it to hold briefly—and then discard—what is only briefly wanted, but to register and keep what is wanted permanently.

Learning theory was based for years on the principles of associationist psychology as derived from laboratory research. It didn't work as well in the classroom as in the laboratory, but Skinner said that that was because, among other things, teachers couldn't immediately reinforce every student's correct responses simultaneously. The training of rats and pigeons by machines, however, was highly effective because every desired movement was instantly rewarded. So a generation ago Skinner campaigned for the use of teaching machines that would require the student to make an overt response (not just think it, but write it down) and would then immediately reinforce the response if it was correct, or fail to do so if it was not.

Skinner expected teaching machines to bring about a revolution in pedagogy. They didn't. It turned out that in human beings, delayed reinforcement is often more effective than immediate reinforcement, and that overt responses may slow down learning while merely thinking one's responses may speed it up. Rat and pigeon learning isn't a good model for human learning, for we use words and other symbols internally as vicarious experience, and this is not part of rat psychology or pigeon psychology. Ignoring our internal machinery produced a wrong prediction—and wrong predictions are the disproof of a theory.

Language was another area in which behaviorism fell on its face. Language acquisition by the child, behaviorists held, took place by means of imitation. The production of language—in speech or writing—they saw as simply a train of associative linkages between words in a series.

But language has a special role in human behavior; it is not merely another group of stimuli like any other. For one thing, it easily overrides and supersedes routine stimulus-response conditioning. A few years ago, a team of researchers used classical methods to condition their human subjects to expect a shock after they saw a red light but not after a green one. After thirty trials, the subjects had sweaty palms when they saw the red light go on, but not when they saw the green. According to behaviorist theory, if the signals were then switched it should take a number of trials to extinguish the fear response to red and to establish it to green. But the subjects were told beforehand that the switch was about to be made—and instantly responded on the first trial with full-scale extinction of the fear response to red and acquisition of it to green. The message: human beings learn by stimulus and response—but even more swiftly and powerfully by the use of a linguistic representation of reality.

So much for that; think now, for a moment, about this sentence you are reading—a sentence I have never written before or heard before in my life. How can associationism explain the phenomenon of my writing a sentence that is new to me? It can't. I may have associative links between any two or three words in that sentence, but the sentence as a whole is a complex thought that I constructed, not a chain of S-R links that was determined from the moment I started with the first words.

Similarly, children, early in their mastery of speech, can be heard to produce all manner of sentences they have never heard uttered. Psycholinguists maintain that this proves the children must have developed a set of rules (or perhaps have such rules genetically encoded in their developing brain networks), and that they use these rules to build any number of grammatical sentences they have never heard.

Language offers innumerable other examples of behavior not explainable by behaviorism, one of the most striking being the shift from active voice to passive voice, a procedure every normal English-speaking adult and teenager can effortlessly do. But how do we do it? Take a simple example:

The boy caught the butterfly.

It becomes:

The butterfly was caught by the boy.

What is the procedure? The behaviorist explanation: we learn a rule; the conditioned stimulus is the wish or need to shift from active to passive, the conditioned response is the use of that rule, to wit: ignoring the word "the," switch the first word and the last word, and stick "was" before the verb and "by" after it.

Splendid. Now let's try the rule on another sentence:

Yesterday Jeffrey bought a raincoat.

It becomes:

A raincoat Jeffrey was bought by yesterday.

Something wrong there. It seems the rule has to be more complicated, specifying not the first word and last word but "agent" and "object of the action," and excluding adverbs of time like the introductory "yesterday."

Now let's try the revised rule in a slightly more involved sentence:

Today the author used the *Encyclopædia Britannica* to answer a question.

It becomes:

> Today the question was used by the *Encyclopædia Britannica*
> to answer the author.

There is no need for more examples; it's clear that invoking the kinds of rules that can be learned by imitation proves to be thoroughly unwieldy, and certainly doesn't seem to be the way we actually turn active into passive. Evidently another explanation is called for. Psycholinguists have one to offer: they say that our minds deal with sentences in terms not of surface structure—schoolbook grammar, word sequence, and such—but in terms of *deep structure:* an intuitive, possibly innate, recognition of the relationships among the things in the sentence, by means of which we easily and correctly shift not just words but related clusters of words, and so reconstruct the sentence. We don't mechanically apply learned rules; we *understand* the deep significance of the sentence, and so can transform it without losing meaning or comprehensibility.

Awhile back, I pointed out that you, the perceiving organism, can to some extent choose what it is that you see, as for instance in the ambiguous painting by Salvador Dali (Fig. 1, p. 20). Figure 13 is another and more familiar example. You can see this drawing as a cube that you are looking down on (that is, if you imagine point $X$ as the corner nearest you, you can see its top). But with very little effort, by imagining point $Y$ as the corner nearest you, you can perceive it as a cube you're looking up at (you can see its bottom). Associationist theory would say that you have learned to associate a

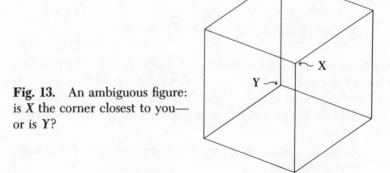

**Fig. 13.**   An ambiguous figure: is $X$ the corner closest to you— or is $Y$?

line drawing such as this with a three-dimensional object, and, in fact, with that object in either of two positions. That sounds reasonable. But what can account for your ability to *choose* which view you want to see, and to deliberately shift from one to the other? Only something we call *will,* or perhaps *selective attention;* you will yourself to attend to the cues in a certain way, then in another way.

Another example may make this even clearer: in Figure 14 you can look at the combined drawing in panel *C,* and then make yourself see in it either panel *A* or panel *B,* with the unwanted material becoming only a kind of background noise.

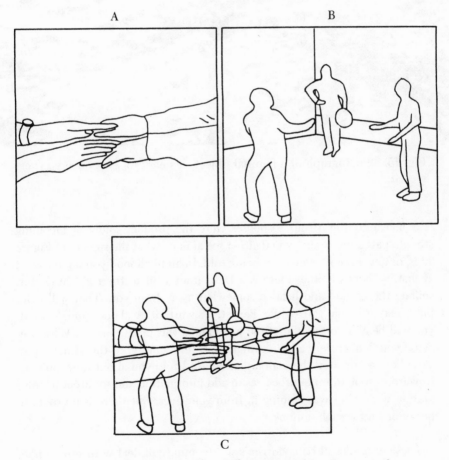

**Fig. 14.** In panel *C,* we can will ourselves to see *A* or *B,* as we choose.

**Fig. 15.** Photograph of a familiar object. It's easy to see—once you've seen it.

A final example: if our responses were the product solely of incoming stimuli, past and present, you'd either see at once what the subject of Figure 15 is, or never see it, even after being told. In all likelihood you do not see it at first. So here's a clue: there is a Dalmatian a bit to the right of center, sniffing the ground and headed somewhat away from you. That will help, but it may still take you awhile. Persist; it's worth it. And once you do see it, you will be able to see it anytime you look at this picture again. Why? Because you deliberately add information, from memory, to the visual input. Whether you created the Dalmatian before I told you about it, or only afterward, it took internal processes to add information and to direct its integration with what was coming in from your eyes. But there is no room in behaviorism for such notions.

These examples of behaviorism's shortcomings all deal with simple phenomena. What is true of them is true all the more of complex ones that we will be looking at in later chapters, such as comprehending allusive speech, where most of what is meant is left unsaid. Or answering a question we have never been asked before. Or solving problems as simple as this:

Form a word from these scrambled letters:

TARIL

Or solving problems as complex as deciding whom to marry, designing a space shuttle, or negotiating a union contract.*

Yet all of the above doesn't mean that behaviorism is wrong in the sense that Ptolemaic (earth-centered) astronomy is wrong. Rather, it means that behaviorism is incomplete. It does describe a kind of primitive learning that takes place in lower animals such as worms and fish, and that also takes place in higher animals but is often dominated and overridden in them by complex mental processes.

To make a higher animal into a behaviorist automaton, you have to get rid of its cognitive mechanisms. Rats that have undergone surgical removal of the hippocampus (an infolded area of forebrain cortex) do act according to pure behaviorist rules; they don't anticipate or perform vicarious trial and error, like Tolman's rats. In human beings, classical conditioning and operant conditioning work according to behaviorist theory in very young children, in the mentally retarded, and in normal people who are asleep. In these cases, consciousness and the internal representation of the world outside are undeveloped or turned off; when that is so, people do behave according to stimulus-response theory.

Thus the principles of behaviorism are not wrong, but describe elementary processes that are only a small part of the psychology of higher vertebrates and only a minuscule part of the psychology of the human being.

What *is* resoundingly wrong about behaviorism is its stand that there is nothing in the black box or, at least, nothing worth speculating about. William of Ockham was quite right—entities are *not* to be multiplied without necessity—but even in the case of the rat, and to a vastly greater extent in the case of the human being, the necessity exists. There is a great deal inside the black box; without hypothesizing what it might be and finding ways to test those hypotheses, we cannot begin to understand ourselves.

* The easy solution to TARIL is TRAIL; most people get it in about 7 seconds. For some reason, a second solution—don't look ahead—takes about 240 seconds. (The second solution: TVIAL.)

## A Mechanism of Elegance and Depth

The evidence piling up, even in the heyday of behaviorism, made it obvious that the mind, far from being empty, is filled with cognitive devices of one sort or another; it is what these devices do to an input that accounts for the output.

But the evidence gave nothing like a picture or plan of the mind's interior. There was only a conglomeration of hypotheses about the different mechanisms that account for memory, language, reasoning, and so on; each seemed to have its own rules and its own kind of action. What was lacking was an overall theory of the human mind—some unifying principle that underlay all of them, some overall function they all subserved, as in an automobile the gears, drive shaft, universal, and differential all subserve the end of power transmission.

About two decades ago such an overview began to emerge—but not, oddly enough, from within psychology. It arose from the confluence of several other disciplines, most notably formal logic, information theory, and computer science.

The digital computer, in its early years, had been viewed as a machine for dealing with numbers. But theoretical work in formal logic and mathematics by several men whose names are unfamiliar to many laymen—Alan Turing, John von Neumann, Claude Shannon, and others—endowed the computer with far broader abilities adding up to general intelligence.

In this view, a number is only one kind of information-conveying symbol, and arithmetical steps are only one genre of symbol manipulation or *information processing*. But in theory any symbol can be translated into another (a common example is any code in which numbers are turned into letters, or letters into numbers), and any form of symbol manipulation can be turned into mathlike computations (the words "is the same as" can be turned into "="; the words "is not the same as" can be rendered "≠"; and so on). And therefore, given a set of rules by which to translate, a computer can become not a mere number-calculator but a general information-processing machine; it can perform operations analogous to human thinking.

By the 1950s, the inevitable happened: psychologists began to turn the analogy around and liken the mind to an intelligent machine—that is, view it as an extremely sophisticated information-processing mechanism, and all the devices inside it as stages in an information-processing sequence.

If, for instance, you read the question, *What is the largest number (other than itself) that will go into one hundred an odd number of times with no remainder?* you first turn the perceived shapes of the letters and words into neuronal impulses (one step in information processing); then, by a series of steps I mentioned in the first chapter, you make sense of the words and the sentence; then you reason about a way to find such a number, and fix upon a method; then you test the method, trying one candidate number after another until you get one that seems to meet the criteria; and finally you check your work.* Each of these steps is part of an information-processing program.

Ever since information-processing theory emerged, cognitive scientists have been drawing flow diagrams made up of arrows and boxes to show how incoming information moves from one process to the next. No two of them draw the diagram quite the same way, but Figure 16, by Gordon Bower, will give you the idea. The diagram isn't self-explanatory, but there's no need for a detailed explanation here; the point is simply that cognitive scientists see information processing as a set of operations that take place between the environmental input and the eventual response or output. Whatever the exact details of the diagram any cognitive scientist draws, it expresses this same general view—a view that encompasses all the mental devices that behaviorism refused to consider, and links them into a single immensely effective information-processing system.

Information-processing theory is an intellectually satisfying, plausible hypothesis, but is it anything more than that? We still cannot see into the black box; even when the skull is open, in brain surgery, we cannot see thought processes. But we can hypothesize how some particular process takes place inside, according to our theory, and then do experiments that will either prove the hypothesis or disconfirm it. An analogy: suppose you had to drive an unfamiliar vehicle—a backhoe or some other earthmover, perhaps—and you found in it something that looked like a gearshift lever but bore no indication of how it should be used. You might hypothesize that in the gearbox there were gears that would make the machine go forward in various speeds or backward. You might further hypothesize that if you pushed the lever hard to the left and away from you, it would make the machine back up. You try it and let out the clutch: if the machine backs up,

* The answer: 0℥.

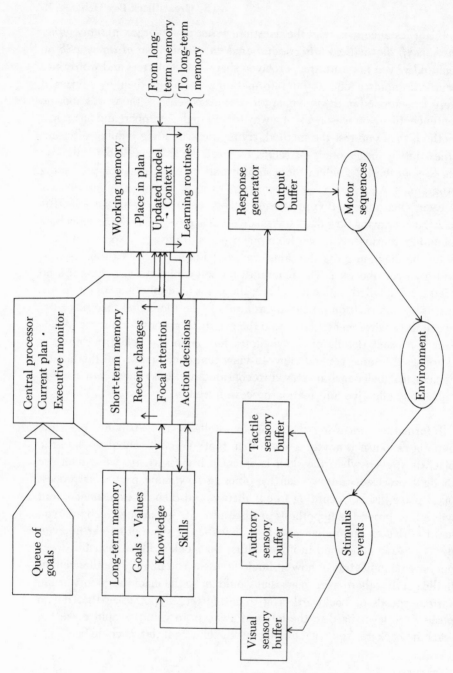

**Fig. 16.** One cognitive scientist's diagrammatic picture of the flow of information into and within the mind

your hypothesis about the inside of the gearbox is confirmed, though you have not looked into it; if it goes forward, your hypothesis is disconfirmed—and you have learned something.

Throughout the rest of this book we will see how cognitive scientists go about putting a wide variety of hypotheses to the test, thereby learning something of what takes place in the black box of the mind even though they can never actually look inside it. For now, here are a few brief examples of the principal methods they use.

Imagine that you are a volunteer in a simple experiment. You sit before a small screen on which pairs of letters are about to be projected; you are to say aloud, as fast as you can, whether the two letters you see have the same name or different names. This is what appears:

AA

and immediately you say "Same." Then this appears:

Aa

and again, immediately you say "Same." But the researcher, measuring your response with a highly accurate timer, finds that it took you a little longer to judge the second pair: if you're average, you replied to AA in something like 549 milliseconds (549 thousandths of a second) and to Aa in 623 milliseconds.

In such a mote of fact, there is a large principle to be discerned. According to information-processing theory, you had only to go as far as visual pattern recognition to know that the letters in AA—which are visually identical—were the same. But Aa required more processing: since the letters are not visually identical, you had to produce the *name* of each letter from memory and see whether the names were the same; this took 74/1000ths of a second more—not much more, but enough to prove the point.

Now imagine yourself taking part in another experiment. On the screen you will see two words appear; you are to decide as quickly as possible whether they belong to the same semantic category or not. On comes this—

LION
HORSE

—and you push a button signifying "Same." Then on comes this—

LION
APPLE

—and you push "Different." In each case, it took you about 750 milliseconds, or three quarters of a second. But now the researcher turns on only one word, and adds the second one nearly a second later. You can feel the difference: you are able to call out "Same" or "Different" in only a little over half a second. Why? Philip Gough and Michael Cosky, of the University of Texas at Austin, devised this experiment to test their hypothesis that before a word is understood, it must be carried from the retina to a part of the brain where it is briefly retained while you locate its meaning in your mental lexicon. If one word is shown you first, they speculated, you should finish looking it up before the second one comes along—and thus the time you need to decide "Same" or "Different" when the second word appears should be shorter than if both words appeared at once. And that's exactly what Gough and Cosky found.

These are examples of *reaction time* studies, which have become a basic tool of cognitive-science research. Professor Robert G. Pachella, who heads the Human Performance Center at the University of Michigan, explained it to me: "If you want to study the mind in its normal mode of functioning and not disturb it by your observation, the major property of mental processes that you can actually observe while they're taking place is the amount of time between input and output. That information enables you to say which one of several explanations is the likeliest."

But it is also possible to study mental events by having subjects say what is going on in their minds while they are performing some task—anything from a missionaries-and-cannibals problem to writing a fugue. Everything said is recorded and later analyzed by the researcher; the procedure is called *protocol analysis.*

Protocol analysis is very different from the introspective technique used unsuccessfully early in the century. For one thing, subjects don't look back and comment on the thoughts that have passed through their minds; instead, they simply turn those thoughts into words as quickly as possible. This brings researchers in touch with—or only one remove from—the actual events or as many of them as the subjects are conscious of; what remains unspoken can often be inferred. By analyzing the content of the protocol, step by step, researchers can see patterns that either confirm or disconfirm a hypothesis they hold about some aspect of thinking, or that lead them to construct one.

Protocol analysis is lengthy and complicated, but a few sample sentences, and the meaning extracted from them by cognitive scientists, will give you some idea of how much more objective this is than the method of the introspectionists, early in the century, whose subjects tried to think about their own thoughts. These examples come from a landmark work by Allen Newell and Herbert Simon called *Human Problem Solving*, published in 1972. One chapter in it analyzes in great detail the complete protocol of one student's solution of this cryptarithmetic problem:*

DONALD
+ GERALD        Given: D = 5
ROBERT

The student, known to history as S3, solved the puzzle in a series of 311 statements or voiced mental events; the protocol runs 15 pages and the analysis of it 66 pages. The theory behind the analysis is complicated and subtle, but here are three simple examples of how S3's words were raw material that fitted into the Newell and Simon theory:

—S3: "If we assume that L, is, say, 1 . . ."

(Newell and Simon: this is "assignment," or one process derived from S3's general view of the task ahead.)

—S3 (after working out a series of steps): "Of course, this is all going on the assumption that R is 7."

(Newell and Simon: this is an example of his making *inferences* based on an assignment.)

—S3 (after trying E as 9): "I seem to be running into trouble the way I am here. Having trouble getting this E. . . . I can't make E a 9."

(Newell and Simon: this is "evaluation" occurring at a "terminal node"—the point where a line of reasoning comes to a dead end, blocked by contradictions—a situation every crossword puzzle fan is familiar with.)†

---

* As with the cryptarithmetic problem presented in Chapter 1, this can take an hour or so to solve unless you are an old hand at it. The solution is on page 367. The problem will be discussed in detail in Chapter 7.
† If you have not yet attempted to solve DONALD + GERALD and decide to do so, don't assume that S3 was right—or that he was wrong—about the value of E. Follow out the implications of your own assumptions, not his.

This, however, is only the beginning of the protocol analysis. The end product is a theory of the methods, both general and specific, by which the human mind works its way through a "problem space," even as an explorer, in unfamiliar territory, must reconnoiter and tentatively probe various routes in order to make his or her way through it.

Protocol analysis is not limited to the study of problem solving; by now it is widely used in studies of memory, reasoning, teaching, writing, creative thinking, and so on. It is even the basis of a kind of intellectual cloning. From protocol analysis, a cognitive scientist may construct a theory as to how the mind of the subject did a particular thing, then translate the theory into computer language (that is, write a computer program), and finally try it in a computer. If the theory is correct, the computer will be able to go through the hypothesized steps in the same sequence that the subject did, and arrive at the same answer. No wonder I heard artificial intelligence people talking about their programs as "he" or even "the guy."

Information-processing theory has been the "guiding metaphor" (as Gordon Bower puts it) of cognitive science for the past ten years, and to many people in the field it offers a deeply satisfying view of the human intellect.

It also meets head-on difficult philosophic questions that behaviorism sought to avoid. Not that it answers them all; it simply makes some of them irrelevant—a phenomenon that Thomas S. Kuhn, the noted philosopher of science, says is typical of revolutionary theories. One such question is: How can we ever know that the world inside the mind is a faithful representation of the one outside? It's irrelevant because it now seems clear that what is inside cannot be identical with what is outside; it is a selection and transformation into neural impulses, a *processed* version, of what is outside. Yet since the mind uses these materials to decide what to do, and since most of its decisions, when carried out, do in fact produce the predicted results, it is clear that there is a reliable correspondence between the symbols in our heads and the realities outside. If I reach out to shake your hand, I will receive new input that something has happened that corresponds to our hands joining and shaking. If, instead, I punch you in the mouth, I can be fairly sure that the ensuing input into my processing system is going to be of another and less agreeable kind.

The mind-body problem, on the other hand, is one that information-processing theory does answer. What has seemed to philosophers to be mind—a different sort of stuff from the brain—is not a separate stuff at all, but a series of processes of immense complexity, the integration of millions or billions of neural events. We call some of these macroevents "ideas," but they are actually *sets of physical microevents*—concatenations of impulses, coded and processed and stored in memory. A computer has no soul but only tangible parts, yet by means of its programs, it can simulate certain aspects of human thought. So, too, with our mind: it is not something apart from the brain, but is the brain's programs, the brain's total set of symbol manipulations.

Those mental processes we call thoughts or, more broadly, mind, are thus *epiphenomena*—secondary or collective effects of the brain's biological processes, much as a flame is the composite effect of trillions of chemical microevents occurring at the molecular level. Those who argue that mind must be something more, that it cannot be "only an epiphenomenon," misuse the word "only" to denigrate the concept. A flame, a flower, a thought can all be theoretically analyzed as nothing more than trillions of events at the molecular level, but it is the clustering, the organization, the coherence of these microevents that we experience and interact with. Yet that overall organization does not confer independent existence on the epiphenomenon; were its constituent parts to dissipate, it would cease to exist. Figure 17 is a simple example of an epiphenomenon (my thanks to Douglas Hofstadter, from whose remarkable book, *Gödel, Escher, Bach*, I borrowed the idea of this illustration).

That, of course, is only an analogy to the relationship of mind and brain. Another analogy is given by William R. Uttal, a psychobiologist, who says, "Mind is to the nervous system as rotation is to the wheel"—rotation being a mass effect of organized movement, and not an independently existing thing. Perhaps an even closer analogy is that mind is to the brain as digestion is to the stomach: the brain is what *is*, the mind is what the brain *does*.

All of these analogies suggest that an epiphenomenon is reality on another and higher level than the phenomena of which it is composed, but that it is not in any way a separate essence or spirit. Who would argue that

**Fig. 17.**   Brain and mind; phenomenon and epiphenomenon

digestion is a spirit that inhabits the stomach? And why then suppose that mind is a spirit or incorporeal stuff that inhabits the brain?*

The third of the most difficult old questions, however, is one that the new theory has not yet answered but only caused to proliferate. It asks whether our abstract ideas are innate, or whether we derive them in some way from our experiences. This question now has spawned a whole litter of offspring: Is logic innate or acquired? Is there a "language organ," as the noted psycholinguist Noam Chomsky puts it, that shapes our language use, no matter what we hear? Do we have some kind of number sense built into our mental circuitry? And so on.

That is what has become of one old question. But many new ones have been created by the new theory (Kuhn says this, too, is typical). Information processing may indeed be the guiding metaphor of cognitive science, the central conception that knits together the many pieces of special theory that had existed, but there are numerous schisms in the new faith, fierce doctrinaire battles, intellectual differences as sharp as any that have ever existed within a science. But after all, it is a brand-new discipline, still in its formative period—and one that deals with the most complex, mystifying, and intriguing subject possible for the mind to study: itself.

In any case, one great question to which it has given a clear and unarguable answer is whether the black box is empty or full. It is full—full of information-processing mechanisms of the most stupendously intricate, yet efficient, sort. Consequently, far from seeing the human being as a large rat, cognitive scientists have rediscovered much of the traditional respect and awe with which humankind has long regarded its mental superiority to the other animals.

One day last spring, two psychologists at the University of Pennsylvania expressed this to me—independently of each other—as well as I have heard it said. Rochel Gelman, who, though still quite young, is a leading investigator of the development of children's mental abilities, said, apropos of her own discoveries, "The human mind, as I see it in my work, is a wonderful, a magnificent structure created by evolution. Nothing resembles it or comes close to it—not the mind of the smartest ape, and not even any AI program."

Later that day I spoke to Lila Gleitman, a professor of psychology who

---

* A few cognitive scientists do, however, cling to the dualist position, among them the distinguished neurophysiologist and Nobel Laureate Sir John C. Eccles, a highly vocal advocate of the view that mind exists apart from, and interacts with, the biochemical events occurring in the brain.

has long specialized in studying how children acquire language. What she sees in her work has given her an almost passionate admiration of the structure of the human mind, even in the least of us. "You take the most primitive man you ever meet in the most backward society you can find," she said, "and there is such elegance and depth to this being's mind that his life is precious. *Every* human life is precious."

# 3

## Q.: WHAT DO YOU DO WITH 100 TRILLION— OR IS IT 280 QUINTILLION—BITS OF INFORMATION? A.: EVERYTHING.

### The Workshop of Thought

Recently, while reminiscing, I happened to think of an actor I used to be friendly with some years ago, and realized that I could recall his jovial face and deep resonant voice but not his last name. Bill . . . I said to myself. Bill . . . what? So I looked in an old address book that I have kept even though it is falling apart and was supplanted several years ago by a new one. I had to thumb nearly all the way through the old book before I found Bill because he turned out to be William Woodson, and in so doing I was dismayed to see how many of the people listed there, but omitted from the newer book, I would not have been able to call to mind unaided—and, worse still, how many of the names in it meant nothing to me.

It's not because I'm middle-aged; young people, too, experience the fading of unused memories. Nearly every recent college graduate has discovered, in the course of some conversation, how little remains of a subject he or she knew thoroughly only a few years earlier, and it is well established that about four fifths of what is learned in classrooms in higher education is forgotten by students by the time they complete their training.

And indeed most of us, when we think about our memory, do so chiefly in a negative context. If memory works well, we take it for granted, as we do breathing; we notice it only when it fails us. But the attitude of most cognitive scientists is very different: they are deeply impressed by, and respectful of, what they have been discovering about both the size and the efficiency of the human memory system.

As to its size, there are various estimates—all of them staggering. John Griffith, the mathematician I cited earlier, plausibly calculates that the lifetime capacity of the average human memory is up to $10^{14}$ (one hundred trillion) bits.* But the late John von Neumann, the distinguished information theorist, just as plausibly put the figure at $2.8 \times 10^{20}$ (280 quintillion—that is, 280,000,000,000,000,000,000) bits. To be sure, von Neumann had assumed that nothing is every truly forgotten, but even if one were to figure, more conservatively, that we keep very little in active memory—only, say, one tenth of 1 percent of whatever we learn in life—it would still mean that our active memories hold several *billion* times more information than a large contemporary research computer.

What impresses cognitive scientists even more than memory capacity is the efficiency with which the human memory system retrieves information. Much of the time we don't have to hunt widely through the huge storehouse of memory for everyday information or think about how to find it; we go directly, unerringly, to the item we need. For instance: *Which of the disciples betrayed Christ?* Without going through any process of search, you immediately answer: *Judas.* But try answering that question by using any printed reference work; it's a slow business, looking for the right index heading, turning to the proper volume and page, and reading through a lot of irrelevant material before finding the answer. In human memory, however, searching is often quite unnecessary; many items of information are linked directly to the question.

Many others are found nearly as quickly because we go straight to the right category, in memory, and so need make only a limited search. An example: *Name three mammals that live in the sea.* Probably you had to do a little scanning before you found such answers as *whale, seal,* and *dolphin* or, perhaps, some other trio, but undoubtedly you searched around only in that area of memory where you have *sea creatures* (or some such category) stored; you wasted no time hunting around in inappropriate groupings such as *fruit trees, woodworking tools,* or *authors.*

But the function of memory is far larger and more important than conve-

---

* A bit, in information theory, is the smallest unit of information—the equivalent of a simple yes or no. An ordinary decimal-system digit or a letter in the English alphabet can be equal to several bits. This is discussed more fully in Chapter 9.

nient and easily accessible storage. As we have already seen, to understand even such a question as *Which of the disciples betrayed Christ?* you had to call upon your memory in order to recognize the letters, the words, and the meaning of the sentence, as, of course, I had to use my memory to recall that same information when I thought of the question and wrote it down. Memory is not an inert resource used now and then by the thinking mind, but an active and ever-present component of all thinking processes. Until recently, psychologists viewed memory as a reference facility, but today's cognitive scientists consider it the sine qua non of intellect, or, as one of them puts it, "the workshop of thought."

Although every act of thinking involves the use of images, sounds, symbols, meanings, and connections between things, all stored in memory, the organization of memory is so efficient that most of the time we are unaware of having to exert any effort to locate and use these materials. Consider the range of kinds of information you keep in, and can easily summon forth, from your own memory: the face of your closest friend . . . the words and melody of the national anthem . . . the spelling of almost every word you can think of . . . the exact place where you keep the pliers . . . the words and tone of voice suitable for greeting an old friend—or, conversely, a neighbor you have had some differences with . . . the name of every object you can see from where you are now sitting . . . the way your room looked when you were eight . . . the set of skills you need to drive a car in heavy traffic . . . and enough more to fill many shelves full of books the size of this one.

These are all examples of *recall*—the active, deliberate retrieval of information from memory, a mental function that, in all likelihood, only human beings perform. But a vastly greater store of information, not subject to recall, serves us by way of *recognition*—a passive and primitive process in which we rely on memory to tell us what we are experiencing. We recognize thousands of faces that we cannot visualize, thousands of melodies that we cannot summon up at will, and so on. We could not begin to make our way through life successfully without this elemental animal ability to recognize innumerable objects, places, and situations that we need not and cannot call to mind.

Since recall is the far more advanced memory function, and is indispensable for all but the simplest thought processes, it has long intrigued psychologists and other cognitive scientists, who see in its workings a variety of special and highly efficient mechanisms—most of which operate without our being aware of them. Herewith a few brief notes on some of these devices:

—It takes most of us only a fraction of a second to answer the question *What is your name?* We find the answer by means of "direct retrieval"— the process used in answering the question about Christ's betrayer. Without direct retrieval of a multitude of materials, almost every conversation would be filled with long pauses while we searched for answers—and even for ordinary words. At the opposite extreme from direct retrieval is "sequential scan"—a system commonly used in computers, involving a rapid systematic search through the entire contents of memory until the wanted information is found; if human beings had no better method than that, a fifty-year-old person would need something like four hundred years to reply to the question, "What is your name?"

—Much of what we can't find by direct retrieval we find almost as quickly by "hierarchical inference." Example: *Does a whooping crane have feathers?* A person who has never seen a whooping crane—and few people have—recognizes that it is a bird, then turns, in memory, to the category of birds, and notes that having feathers is one of its characteristic traits, and thereupon infers that the whooping crane does have feathers. Typical time needed, by laboratory measurement: less than two seconds.

—A computer may search its memory for a requested item and report back that the item is not available; human beings often can tell beforehand that no search is necessary, since either they have never learned the answer or they recognize that the question is absurd. If I ask you, "What is Deng Xiaoping's phone number?" you do not bother to think about it; you say, "How should I know?" If I ask you, "What was Socrates' zip code?" you waste no time searching for it; you sense that no search could produce an answer.

—Much long-forgotten material can be retrieved if one works at it. How many of the people in your high-school graduating class—or any similar group you knew five or ten years ago—can you name? Most people would say "Only a handful," assuming that the rest have been irrevocably forgotten. But in several studies, volunteers have spent many hours, over a period of weeks, reminiscing—and thereby recovering forgotten names—as they envision scenes and experiences that bring the people to mind. Typically, one volunteer was able, in the course of several months, to remember the names of two hundred of her high-school fellow graduates.

—The human memory spontaneously compresses information into what researchers call "chunks." A chunk is any coherent group of items of information that we can remember as if it were a single item: a word is a chunk of letters, remembered as easily as a single letter (but carrying much more information); a well-known date—say, 1776—is remembered as if it were one digit; and even a sentence, if familiar ("A stitch in time saves nine"), is remembered almost as effortlessly as a much smaller unit of information. I referred earlier to Herbert Simon's estimate that a chess master has roughly 50,000 patterns of pieces (board situations) stored in memory; by means of these chunks, he can rapidly recognize what is happening in a game and make his moves without deep analysis, whereas the novice must laboriously work out the outcome of each possible move. In the same way, the person with a good deal of experience in business and social life has chunked all sorts of interpersonal information, and can therefore recognize at a glance what is happening in many a situation and act appropriately; the novice flounders and makes gaffes.

—The ability of actors and opera singers to commit long roles to memory through study and repetition impresses most of us. But equally impressive is what we all do every day with material we see or hear only once: we remember not the precise form but the meaning. Within a handful of seconds (by actual laboratory measurement) we forget the verbatim details of a heard or read sentence, yet remember its content. Chances are that right now you can accurately restate the substance of the first sentence of this paragraph—dealing with actors and opera singers—but are unable to recall its exact wording. We do this all the time, with virtually everything we experience; the system in our heads files away a great deal of meaning without any need for repetition or memorization.

—Dr. Stephen M. Kosslyn, a young psychologist I met at Harvard (he is now at Brandeis), has for several years been exploring the ways we use visual images stored in memory; he has come up with some striking discoveries, one of which he demonstrated to me with great simplicity. "Imagine a tiny bee, off in the distance," he said, and I did so. "Now," he said, "tell me: does the bee have a dark head or a light head?" My eyes went blank as I did what he knew I would do—zoomed in mentally to take a closer look. (The bee, I saw, had a dark head.) Kosslyn had made his point: we use stored images as if they were film or tape that we project in the mind, and then inspect them as if they had become actual pictures. A lot of thinking takes place in this way: we use stored images to answer questions such as how to get from where we are to some other place, whether the trunk of the car will hold all our luggage, and so on. Some psychologists even maintain that much of our most important and creative thinking takes place in images rather than in words.

We rarely notice any of these powers of memory; what we notice are its limitations or defects. We are often aware, for instance, that we cannot recall things we think we know like the back of our own hands—which, in fact, we don't know all that well; try, without looking, to visualize the back of your own hand in detail, and then look and see how much you've missed. Try to draw the telephone dial that you have used a thousand times this past half year; you'll be surprised. Or try to draw a common penny: including the features on both sides, there are eight things to be remembered, but in one recent study most people could recall and correctly locate only three.

There is probably good evolutionary reason for this limitation of memory: survival, as I've said, depends on our ability to recognize innumerable things, and recognition is vastly more economical of storage space than detailed recall. Still, we tend to perceive the restriction as a *failure*.

Here are a few other limitations of memory of which we are often, and uncomfortably, aware:

—Under stress we may forget things that we know well. Junior executives, at a company dinner, may fumble the name of the superior they are introducing to their mate. Performers about to go onstage to make a debut may forget the words or music they have rehearsed so long and thoroughly; desperate efforts to remember are of no avail. Cognitive science has an explanation: the stressful input takes up most of the mind's conscious equipment and so impedes the retrieval of information from long-term memory. But let the performance actually begin, and the unconscious automatically fetches forth the desired material.

—At times we are unable to think of some word or name we know but use only occasionally. We may feel we almost have it—for instance, we feel sure that it starts with *b*, or has three syllables, or has the sound "on" in it (and research shows that such intimations are correct more often than not)—yet the word "bubonic" remains tantalizingly on the tip of the tongue. The suggested explanation: we file words and names in memory in several ways—by their meaning, by their initial sound, and so on—but with infrequently used words or names these cues may not supply enough information to lead us to the word or name; we need still more.

—Slips of the tongue are near-misses in retrieval; usually, the slip is a word close to the target in sound, but off-target in meaning. Such errors embarrass us, particularly when (as Freud thought was always the case) the slip is an inadvertent admission of a hidden feeling. Some slips are surely just that: one woman I know of, after a particularly inedible dinner at a friend's house, met the friend on the street and, intending to say, "I've been meaning to reciprocate," said instead, "I've been meaning to retaliate." Psycholinguists, however, now say that only a minority of slips of the tongue have Freudian significance; most are simply errors in retrieval due to the use of inadequate phonetic information. Thus "cavalry" becomes "Calvary," "relegate" becomes "regulate," or the initial sounds of two words are switched, as in Dr. Spooner's own grand line, "I assure you the insanitary specter has seen all the bathrooms."

—Events we witness do not always, or even usually, remain unchanged in memory; we fill in missing details by inference, or alter them in accordance with questions we are asked or suggestions made to us, and have no way of retrieving the original—and are not even aware that anything has happened to it. Elizabeth Loftus of the University of Washington, who, as noted earlier, specializes in memory research, has shown brief films of auto accidents to students and then asked them loaded questions about what they saw. When she asked, "Did you see the broken headlight?" one out of every seven said yes, although no broken headlight had appeared. She also showed students a videotape of a disruption of a class by eight demonstrators; then she asked half the students, "Was the leader of the four demonstrators who entered the classroom a male?" but, with the other half, replaced the word "four" by the word "twelve." A week later she asked both groups how many demonstrators there had been; the answers of the "four" group averaged 6.4, while those of the "twelve" group averaged nearly 9.

Similarly, as other studies have shown, all of us continually revise our memories of our lives to harmonize with the events that have happened or are happening to us; we are unable to distinguish between what really happened and what we now think happened, since the original memory no longer exists. In one study, a majority of people interviewed in 1964 and again in 1974 recalled, at the second interview, earning a considerably higher income and having far greater work drive in 1964 than had been the case. Seemingly crucial childhood experiences that we clearly remember may never have happened. Jean Piaget himself once wrote that until he was fifteen, he had a vivid memory of a man trying to kidnap him in the Champs

Élysées when he was only two; his nurse fought the man off until a policeman came up and the kidnapper fled. But many years later the nurse, guilt-ridden, wrote his parents a letter returning a watch they had given her as a reward and confessing that she had made the whole thing up. Piaget, however, having heard the story from his parents, had believed he remembered the event—down to the scratches the nurse suffered and the details of the policeman's uniform.

—By far the most severe limitation of memory is the size of short-term memory. This label does not refer to a location in the brain but to whatever new information we are keeping in mind at any moment. Some years ago, the psychologist George A. Miller concluded from various experiments that we can retain only about seven items in short-term memory. Since then, others have put the figure a little higher or a little lower, but the differences are not important; the salient fact remains that we cannot hold onto more than a mere handful of new and unmemorized numbers, letters, or words at any one time.

Test your own short-term memory. Here is a seven-digit number: 3169675. Read it once, twice; now look away and repeat it; then check your memory. If you had it right, read and repeat this one: 1294508. Have you got it? If so, can you still remember the first one without looking back?

Or try this. Look at the following number for a few seconds, then close your eyes and see if you can repeat it: 7340017. . . . That should have been fairly easy. Now try this one: 10009642301001. . . . If you correctly repeated that one after only a few seconds of study, you have an unusual memory—and if you can still repeat it at this moment, a few seconds afterward, you have a *most* unusual memory.

One more: try to solve the puzzle in Figure 18 in your head: making use of the empty space, slide the pieces about until they are in ascending numerical order. It's hard enough to do when you can actually move the pieces about, but it's almost impossible when you have to maintain the positions of fifteen items in short-term memory.

Since long-term memory has an astronomical capacity, it is puzzling and exasperating that short-term memory is so tiny. Yet this, too, may have been an evolutionary advantage, according to George Mandler, director of the Center for Human Information Processing at the University of California at San Diego, who explained it to me as follows: "If I paid attention to all the things my senses are reporting at any moment and took them all into account, I'd have great difficulty acting. It would be very hard for me to de-

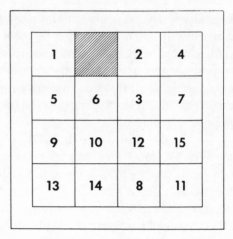

**Fig. 18.** The fifteen-number puzzle—too much for the human memory to handle

cide what to do. But I can attend only to a few things—only to what I can hold in short-term memory—and that's what enables me to focus on what's important and to make decisions quickly. If you go to a restaurant and there are fifty entrées on the menu, you can't deal with it—you first have to narrow it down to, maybe, chicken dishes, or to veal dishes. Why are we like this? It's simple—if our ancestors had paid attention to fifty things at once, they would never have made up their minds what to do in time to escape the saber-toothed tiger bearing down on them. That's why the memory system developed the way it did."

## Why Most of What You've Always Heard About Memory Is Better Forgotten

Two questions have been asked about memory from time immemorial: How does it work—and how can we make it work better?

By way of answer, there have long existed at least three major theories—or, more accurately, three metaphorical likenesses—of memory, each of which purports to explain some things about it. The first views memory as a kind of intellectual muscle; the second likens it to writing (or some other kind of inscription or recording); the third describes it as a reference work—a sort of encyclopedia, dictionary, or even library.

The human memory, of course, is not literally any of these, but since it is invisible and intangible, philosophers have had to think about it in terms of metaphors. For that matter, scientists, too—even in the physical sciences—often couch their theories in metaphorical terms; they cannot say what reality actually *is*, but they can say what it is *like*. They describe light in terms of waves, portray evolution as a sort of tree, and speak of superdense objects in space as black holes, but all these are only metaphors; they are what light, evolution, and superdense objects resemble, not what they are in some ultimate sense. Yet such metaphors enable scientists to organize their information, perceive relationships among phenomena, and make reasonable cause-and-effect predictions.

So it is with metaphors of memory. The reality of the trillions—or quintillions—of neural events that make up memory is incomprehensible, but the overall process of memory itself can be likened to some comprehensible object or action; and to the extent that the comparison clarifies and explains, it is a valid theory, even though a metaphor.

The three metaphors of memory all seemed, at various times, to explain it quite well, but today none of them does so. Then why talk about them? Because news about the mind filters only slowly through society; the old theories of memory are the bases of deeply rooted beliefs that many of us still cling to and seek to apply, with disappointing results. It is therefore worth seeing what memory has been said to resemble, but doesn't, before looking at its present-day likeness.

No one has ever actually called memory a kind of muscle, but a very old and still popular view holds that, like a muscle, it can be developed and strengthened only through hard, regular exercise.

For many centuries, this belief was the basis for the emphasis, in education, on the study of rhetoric, Greek, Latin, and mathematics. These subjects, apart from any intrinsic merit they have, were viewed as a form of mental gymnastics that would increase the powers of the mind, especially memory. Some decades ago, rhetoric and the classic tongues disappeared from the curriculum, but children were still made to memorize masses of material—poems, Shakespearean soliloquies, geometrical proofs, algebraic procedures, dates of wars and treaties—because it was thought that the effort spent in memorizing these materials would make the children better able to remember any and all other kinds of subject matter. Even today many people believe that exercising the memory has value in itself, and our schools rely heavily on multiple-choice testing in which the student need only remember the right answer, not *do* anything with it, a pedagogical technique that embodies the old belief in a new form.

The exercise theory of memory was long taken on faith and not subjected to scientific test until less than a century ago. It was William James,

America's first psychologist, who, using himself as a subject, first tried measuring the power of memory before and after a period of exercise to see if, indeed, there were any change. Over a period of eight days, James memorized 158 lines of *Satyr*, a poem by Victor Hugo, finding that it took him an average of fifty seconds per line. Next, during thirty-eight days he memorized the entire first book (798 lines) of Milton's *Paradise Lost*. This prolonged exertion should have built up the strength of his memory, but when he went back to Hugo's *Satyr* and memorized another 158 lines, he found that it took him seven seconds longer per line than it had the first time. Exercise, he concluded, hadn't increased the power of his memory but diminished it, at least temporarily.

Many experiments by later psychologists have yielded similar results; some have even shown that the more memorizing one does, the poorer one's ability to memorize becomes. Psychologist Benton J. Underwood of Northwestern University performed a classic study in 1957 which showed that typical subjects, twenty-four hours after memorizing a list of nonsense syllables, would remember about 80 percent of it; if they then memorized a second list, their twenty-four-hour recall would be somewhat less than 80 percent; and with each subsequent list they would do worse until, twenty-four hours after memorizing the twentieth list, they would remember only 20 percent of it. Such evidence has disposed of the exercise theory, at least among psychologists if not the general public.

The second metaphor (or, actually, group of metaphors) likens memory to a kind of writing or recording. At various times, memory has been compared to a wax tablet on which experience makes marks with a stylus, a sheet of paper on which it writes with a pen, and a canvas on which it paints with a brush; and in recent decades it has been thought of as a record inscribed in the brain in the form of conductive pathways laid down by experience.

This metaphor, unlike the exercise theory, is concerned not with what makes memory itself strong but with what makes any particular item remain in, or disappear from, memory. A single experience of that item is like a message set down faintly on any of the recipient media, while repetition—writing on top of the message again, or laying down more conductive material on the electrical pathway—makes the message more distinct and long-lasting. And it is true enough that repetition is a basic way to fix something in memory; thousands of experiments have shown, for instance, that a subject who sees a list of letters or syllables four or five times will be able to recall several times as many of them as after seeing the list only once.

But why does any image, whether faint or dark, ever disappear? Why do we tend, as time passes, to forget things unless we reuse them? The metaphor has two answers. First, just as ink or colors on canvas tend to fade with the passage of time, so memories suffer from fading unless renewed; it is in their nature to disintegrate.

The wax-tablet and electrical-pathway versions of the metaphor don't lend themselves to this account of forgetting, but they and the others all provide another one; later messages, written or recorded on top of the first one, blur it or even conceal it altogether; this is known in psychology as the "interference theory" of forgetting. An old joke, popular in psychological circles, tells of the professor of ichthyology who complained that every time he learned the name of a new student, he forgot the name of a fish. But interference can also work the other way, with the oldest message being the most vivid and interfering with later ones, as was the case with Underwood's subjects, who remembered less and less of each subsequent memorized list. Similarly, travelers abroad often find that when they try to say something in a newly crammed language, words and phrases of some other foreign tongue, studied long ago, keep popping into their minds.

Such phenomena, attributable to interference, are very comfortably explained by the writing or recording metaphor; unfortunately, it doesn't handle a number of others nearly as well. It casts no light on why we should be able to keep so few items in short-term memory, or why those items disappear the moment we turn our attention elsewhere. Nor does it explain how we can keep something in short-term memory as long as necessary by means of "rehearsal" (saying it to ourselves over and over, as we do with the phone number we have looked up but not yet dialed), yet have no permanent trace left by that repeated rewriting.

Another flaw in the writing or recording metaphor is that it does not picture what happens when we learn items in a series. A list of items written with steady effort is of even density, and length, but that's not the way we record a series of items in memory; innumerable experiments have shown that when subjects briefly see or hear a list of letters, numbers, or words, they remember the first ones and the last ones considerably better than those in between. In a typical experiment using a thirty-two-word list, nearly half the subjects remembered the first word and nearly three quarters the last word, but only about a fifth remembered the larger part of the

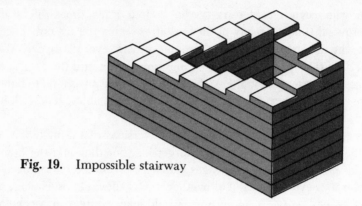

**Fig. 19.**   Impossible stairway

words in between. This is not just a curiosity of memory; it relates to the crucial issues of how we hear and comprehend speech. Apparently, we notice first sounds and last sounds of long words more than we do the middle sounds (perhaps because in order to minimize effort, we attend to those cues that are most useful to memory), but the writing/recording metaphor tells us nothing about this important phenomenon.

Finally, the metaphor deals with memories as traces that are recorded separately or in pure form; this may be true of nonsense syllables in the laboratory, but in real life, we perceive and remember nearly everything in terms of what we already know—we modify the input, and remember not what our senses perceived but what our minds made of it. Many optical illusions exemplify this principle. Consider, for instance, Figure 19. This impossible stairway baffles the mind because, as Douglas Hofstadter says of a similar illusion created by the artist M. C. Escher, it relies upon "the recognition of certain basic forms, which are then put together in nonstandard ways; and by the time the observer sees the paradox on a high level, it is too late—he can't go back and change his mind about how to interpret the lower-level objects." It is extremely difficult to remember this drawing or reproduce it without looking, because one assimilates its details to drawings of real stairways already in memory. I have just tried to draw the impossible stairway without looking at the figure, and made a mess of it; I could produce only a possible one.

What this suggests is that the extent to which we remember a new experience has more to do with how it relates to existing memories than with how many times or how recently we have experienced it, or how much interfering scribble there is. But this is tantamount to saying that the writing or recording metaphor makes true but largely unimportant observations about how we remember and forget.

The third metaphor pictures memory as a kind of reference work or library. Materials stored in it are classified logically by subject, and these subjects are grouped together in progressively more inclusive categories; the overall structure is therefore hierarchical. In such a system, memories are "content addressable"—that is, if you know the subject or content of a memory, you know where to look for it in the reference work or library. If your knowledge is only general, you have to search a large area; if your knowledge is detailed and specific, you can go at once to the precise place where it is located.

This fits in with much of what we have already seen about how memory works. Moreover, certain recent research findings support the image. A few years ago, for instance, Elizabeth Loftus (who did the intriguing studies on how eyewitness memories change) and a colleague presented two groups of subjects with a written command to name a fruit beginning with $P$. The first group saw the letter $P$ first and then, after a brief pause, the word "fruit"; the second group saw the word "fruit" first, and a moment later the letter $P$. Quite consistently, those who saw "fruit" first were able to say "peach," "pear," "plum," and so on a quarter of a second sooner than those who saw $P$ first. This lends credence to the hypothesis that to find the answer to a question, one first has to get to the right category of memory; by the time the second group heard the letter $P$ they were already in the right place— the "fruit" category—while the first group, who heard "fruit" last, still had to get there. ("Words beginning with $P$" isn't a natural or conceptual category—or, one might say, not a fruitful one.) Similarly, Loftus later found that if she asked subjects to name a fruit beginning with $A$ and then asked them to name one beginning with $P$, they answered the second question faster than the first because they were already in the right memory location.

Another kind of evidence that fits the reference-work metaphor is a by-product of efforts to write a computer program that can understand language. Some years ago, psychologist Allan Collins and AI researcher Ross Quillian drew up a plan for such a program in which they assembled nouns in a network of locations or "nodes" and, around each of these, clustered the traits that belong to it (see Fig. 20). This hierarchical structure is quite similar to that of many reference works and libraries. Collins and Quillian then sought to find out whether the scheme, which made a priori sense, did

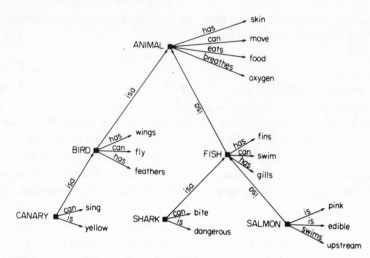

**Fig. 20.**  A piece of the semantic memory network

in fact represent the way the human memory stores materials. They asked people to answer "True" or "False" to statements like "A canary can sing," the answer to which exists at a single node, and other statements like "A canary has skin," the answer to which requires looking up canary in the category "bird," and "bird" in the more general category "animal." And indeed the second kind of question took longer to answer than the first, as it should if memory is arranged in reference-work fashion.

Nevertheless, the reference-work metaphor has fallen somewhat out of favor of late because many other issues involve research data that don't fit it or raise questions it can't answer. One such problem is: In what form is material stored in memory—are words stored as words, images as images, sounds as sounds, and so on? If this is the case, it is hard to see how they can all be classified under the same system. If I ask you to think of a number of yellow objects, or sweet-tasting foods, or cheerful melodies, you almost certainly will do so without working within a hierarchy of nouns. And you will answer many kinds of questions by using images alone (for instance: *At which time is the angle between clock hands larger—4:25 or 9:10?*), or by reviving physical experience (*In the house you lived in last, how many windows were there?*—a question most people answer by mentally walking around in that house and counting). You can recognize a piece of music or a work of art you've never heard or seen before as being by a composer or painter whose other work you know. In these and many similar cases, the mechanisms of classification and of retrieval don't seem to have anything to do with the reference-work model.

On the other hand, there are some cognitive scientists—particularly those in the artificial intelligence camp—who see human memory strictly in computerlike terms; they argue that nothing is stored as it is perceived, but that everything is coded into some other "propositional" form, as information is in a computer. Even the lineaments of a beloved face could be stored as a group of numbers in some arbitrary code—from which the original could be reconstructed whenever we needed it. And why not? A videotape contains imagery and sound converted into electrical impulses and stored magnetically; yet both can be recovered and turned back into a replica of the original. Why not something of the sort with human memory? It would certainly be a neater and more consistent system than one in which there are multiple forms of storage and multiple systems of classification.

Furious debates about this have raged within cognitive science, but most of the people I asked about it seemed weary of the question, which has proven unprofitable in terms of research. The majority opinion seems to be that we store a variety of materials—verbal, semantic, visual, aural, and so on—and that each kind has its own laws, and is classified and retrieved in its own way. That leaves a great many questions unanswered, but it answers one rather clearly: the reference-work metaphor, as good as it is in some ways, isn't good enough. Perhaps it is part of some larger metaphor; in itself, it's too confining.

In any case, there are two other very considerable issues that make the reference-work metaphor seem inadequate.

One is a biological question: Where are memories of various sorts stored? In a reference work or library—or computer memory—there is one right place for each item (plus, of course, some cross-referencing). The brain is nothing like that. Nearly everyone now knows that the two hemispheres of the brain are somewhat specialized, with language and semantic functions being handled chiefly by the left half (at least, in most right-handed people), while music, imagery, and other sensory functions are more under the control of the right half. But this distinction has been greatly exaggerated by neomystics who claim that Reason is in the left hemisphere and Feeling— the Real Self—is locked up in the right half. In actual fact, information of all sorts is passed back and forth from one half of the brain to the other and each half has some capacity to store materials that the other half specializes in. That is why people with brain damage, and even people who have undergone operations to disconnect the two halves in order to control certain disorders, can still remember a great deal that they would not remember if memories were neatly sorted out by hemispheric function.

Even more important: with a few exceptions, no one class of memories is stored in a single area. Language, to be sure, is located largely in Broca's Area and Wernicke's Area, and recognition of faces takes place in a particular part of the underside of both occipital lobes, but most other memories are spread all around the brain. Many years ago, the psychologist Karl Lashley tried to locate what he called the "engram," or neural trace of a particular memory. He taught animals certain tasks and then surgically destroyed different parts of their brains, seeking to identify the part in which that memory had been registered. He never found it; instead it turned out that the memory of a learned task diminished in proportion to the total amount of brain he destroyed. The same thing has been found true of human beings who have suffered brain damage or undergone brain surgery. Apparently, memories are stored redundantly, in the form of a disseminated but interconnected set of patterns in various places—a seemingly untidy and illogical scheme, quite unlike that of any reference work or library, but possessing the great advantage that we can still remember most things even after accidents or the erosion of aging.

The second troublesome matter is a philosophic question known in cognitive-science circles as "the problem of the homunculus." If you look up something in your memory according to reference-work rules, who or what knows the rules and does the looking up? Is there some tiny separate You inside—the homunculus—running around the library stacks? Or if you visualize something in your mind's eye, who or what is in there looking at the picture? Who or what is it that tries to remember something, and then remembers it? In all our talk about memory, we sound as if we are postulating a distinction between the observer and the observed—between the homunculus and the memory. Is there, after all, a ghost in the machine, a bodiless Something that observes and uses the brain?

Cognitive scientists dismiss such a notion for all the good reasons we heard awhile back. And yet whenever we try to remember something, or do remember it, we are aware of the remembering self that makes the effort and experiences the retrieved memory. It's the "I" that we are aware of in all our thinking—the "I" of Descartes' historic assertion *Cogito ergo sum*—I think, therefore I am. Francis Crick, the codiscoverer of the double-helix structure of DNA, whose interest has now shifted to neurobiology, writes that the "fallacy of the homunculus" is to be avoided at all costs—but that "it is easier to state the fallacy than to avoid slipping into it. The reason is that we certainly have an illusion of the homunculus: the self." Some cognitive scientists think that the perceiving self is nothing but the process of interaction between various parts of the mind; others say it is a series of mental events, as a flame is a continuous flow of chemical combinations; and still others suggest that the self is a feedback effect—the reactions of the brain's circuitry to its own processes.

Whatever the answer to these large issues, the questions themselves make it plain that the reference-work metaphor succeeds only up to a point. Our minds are far less tidy and far more complex—and much more capable of surviving disasters—than the information-storage systems they have thus far designed.*

## The IP Memory System

Information-processing (IP) theory has, not surprisingly, produced its own metaphor of memory; that metaphor fits the facts better, answers more of the familiar old questions, and raises fewer new questions, than any of the older models.

Although the information-processing model is adapted from computer science, the computer memory itself is not a good analog or model of human memory; its hardware—and consequently the details of how it operates—differs too much from our own. (Much later in this book, I'll discuss those differences.) What does work as a metaphor is a somewhat computer-like *set of transformations* of information from the moment of perception on; these transformations change the incoming information anywhere from slightly to greatly, and thereby cause it to be retained anywhere from momentarily to permanently. In short, the new likeness of memory is not that of a structure but of a *series or system of processes.*

This abstract language becomes concrete the moment one looks at a diagram of the memory system, with tidy little boxes and arrows that represent the flow of information from process to process. But no two researchers specializing in memory draw it the same way, for a diagram is, like an ex-

---

* A fourth metaphor, of recent provenance, likens memory to a kind of rather chaotic information exchange run by a number of "demons" or "frame keepers"—imaginary operators, each of whom is in charge of a particular directory or batch of information. I do not discuss this provocative metaphor in detail because it is not a major historical model. Those who are interested can find references in the Notes.

planation in words, only an individual's way of putting things, and not reality itself. So I've borrowed from various versions and drawn my own; it represents what is currently the median position in the field.° First, then, the diagram (Fig. 21); afterward, an explanation of what's going on in it.

A disclaimer: the boxes do not represent sharp, distinct stages in the memory process but are merely convenient labels for what is happening along the way. A more accurate picture would show a continuous pipeline of some sort, with gradual and continuous changes throughout, but this would be difficult to portray and confusing to read.

And now a step-by-step tour through the diagram:

THE SENSORY BUFFERS. Everything in memory begins as a sensory input from the environment. Whatever the form in which it impinges on us—light on the retina, sound waves on the auditory nerves, and so on—it is transformed in sensory organs into a pattern of neural excitation; this is the first step of processing. So far, there is nothing that can be called a memory.

Almost instantly, however, the neural excitations travel to the sensory buffers—parts of the brain where they are briefly retained until we can notice them. (If these excitations were retained in the sense organs themselves for more than a tiny fraction of a second, we would perceive everything as a blur.) Much more information arrives in the buffers than we can pay attention to, but it stays there long enough for us to be able to select what we want to notice, even after the event itself has ended. The excitations held in the buffer thus constitute very short-term memories. Just how short has been determined by a number of fascinating experiments. In one of them, for instance, the following pattern was flashed on a tachistoscope screen before subjects for fifty milliseconds (one twentieth of a second):

R    B    L    A

T    Y    Q    N

G    K    R    X

It disappeared from the screen too quickly for the subjects to have seen all of it and yet they could write down, afterward, the letters of any line. (A tone, *after* the flash, told them which line to write down.) That meant they could still "see" all three lines in the visual buffer. Yet while they were writing down any one line of letters, the others would disappear and could

---

° It corresponds to only part of what appears in Figure 16—Gordon Bower's diagram—and differs, even in that part, from his in many ways, but most of the differences are stylistic rather than substantive.

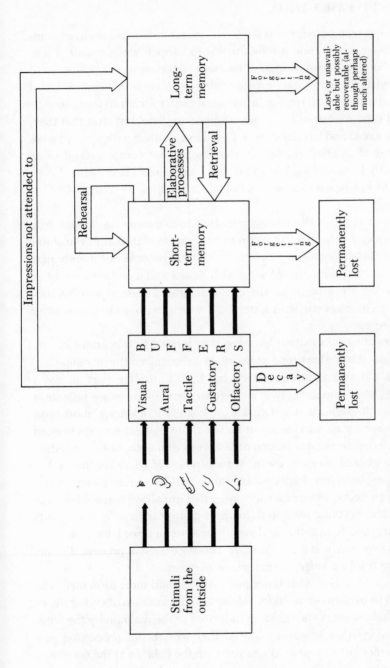

**Fig. 21.** Flow chart of the human memory system

no longer be remembered; the trace in the visual buffer had decayed completely. The length of time it took for this to happen was, at most, a second—the shortest measured span of memory in the system.

In somewhat the same way, experiments have shown that sounds heard but not paid attention to remain in the aural buffer for up to four seconds; during that time we can still turn our attention to them, but after that they, too, have decayed and left the system. I used to go sailing with a friend who, when engrossed in chart reading or steering a close course, would often make no reply to something I had said. But long seconds later, when I concluded he hadn't heard me, he would look around, say, "What?—Oh!"— and reply.

SHORT-TERM MEMORY. By paying attention to a sensory impression in a buffer, we process it further; we begin to make sense of it, that is, transform it into a meaningful symbol. Numbers and letters become not merely perceived shapes but informational signs with names and a certain amount of meaning. A "3," for instance, is "three" and signifies a known quantity; similar transformations occur with letters and words, with sentences read or heard, and so on.

When incoming information has been transformed to this extent but no further, we say it is in short-term memory. We recognized the incoming "3" by comparing it to long-term memory, but the "3" itself as part of, say, a telephone number remains only in short-term memory unless we take steps to remember it permanently. Outside of cognitive science, "short-term memory" is loosely used to mean our recollections of what we experienced earlier in the day, or the day before, or last week or month. But to cognitive scientists, short-term memory means our awareness of whatever things that have been processed just deeply enough to be part of current mental activity—the seven items, give or take a couple, that are all we can hold onto at any moment. Everything we stop thinking of disappears rapidly from short-term memory, and is forgotten and out of the system; if we later seek to retrieve some experience and can do so, it is because we had processed it further, turning it into a longer-term form of memory.

How fast do we forget what is not processed beyond short-term memory? Fast enough to explain our need for rehearsal—the business of saying something to ourselves again and again, as indicated in the diagram by the feedback loop. We either rehearse material that we are not processing into longer-term memory or lose it. When you note the balance at the bottom of the page in your checkbook, you repeat it to yourself as you turn the page and write it at the top of the new one; then you stop rehearsing it, and forget it within a few seconds. Experiments have measured short-term retention time objectively by making rehearsal impossible. For instance, one research team gave their subjects an extremely easy task—remembering a set of three consonants—but as soon as the subjects had seen the letters, they were required to count backward by threes in time with a metronome (this prevented rehearsal). The counting was stopped at different times, with different subjects, to see whether they could still remember the consonants; no one could remember the letters by the time eighteen seconds had passed.

In addition to the arrows showing input to short-term memory from the sensory buffers and rehearsal, I have drawn an incoming arrow marked *Retrieval*, to indicate the return flow of long-term memories to attention (short-term memory)—a process that goes on continually in every kind of thinking. (Some cognitive scientists prefer to show such retrieved material as flowing not to short-term memory but to yet another box called "working memory"—into which the contents of short-term memory also flow.)

ELABORATIVE PROCESSES. Sometimes a sensory input goes directly from the buffer into long-term memory without further processing (note the arrow marked *Impressions not attended to*). We often recognize a face, an object, or a melody that we never were aware of or paid any attention to. But most of what we remember over any period of time does require processing of various sorts to transform it from the immediate images and preliminary meanings of short-term memory to more permanent forms that can be classified and filed in long-term memory. Rehearsal alone doesn't do that because it doesn't make any changes in the information; what does do it are those activities labeled *Elaborative processes* in the diagram.

To transform material by these processes, we need to maintain it in short-term memory long enough to do the work. Anything that disrupts short-term memory therefore prevents our adding new information to long-term memory. An accident or blow on the head, for instance, often causes "retrograde amnesia"—a forgetting of what took place just before it, but not of the more distant past; apparently, events that haven't yet been processed very deeply are lost because processing is interrupted. And certain people have undergone brain damage that destroys short-term memory, causing them to become unable to add anything new to long-term memory. One man, famous in the literature of psychology as "H.M.," suffered such severe epileptic seizures that at age twenty-seven he agreed to an operation removing part of the hippocampus (see Fig. 2, p. 34). The epilepsy was relieved, and H.M.'s IQ remained unimpaired, his speech normal, and his memory intact for events up to a year or so before the operation. But he could learn nothing new. When his family moved, he could never remember the new address; he mowed the lawn regularly but could not learn where the lawn mower was kept; he treated the neighbors as strangers no matter how often he met them; and he could rework the same puzzles every day without any awareness of having done them before.

The elaborative processes that transform short-term memories into long-term ones may, in some cases, consist largely of repetition—not the kind we do in rehearsal, but repetition in which we look for patterns, chunks, clusters of sounds, or associations that enable us to commit to memory a series of items with little meaning. It's what children do when they learn the alphabet by making a singsong jingle of it, using chunking, rhythm, and rhyme ("Ab—cd—ef—g; hi—jk—lmno—p," and so on). Some opera singers learn entire roles in a foreign language they do not understand, and in Nigeria there are some Hausa-speaking people who have committed the entire Koran to memory although they understand not a word of the Arabic in which it is written.

But by far the greatest part of elaborative processing consists of quite a different kind of activity: the extraction of deeper meanings from words, sentences, images, and the like; classification of those meanings; and the linking of this new information to some part of our organized mass of long-term memories. All this can take place with remarkable speed. It's what has happened when, in a matter of seconds, you have forgotten the words of a sentence but registered its content.

One example: Let us suppose you have never seen or heard of a certain animal, and now you are shown one by a friend. You process the information: you classify the animal as a rodent and as a pet called a "gerbil," and you file the data in the appropriate part of your long-term memory reference system. You also file with it the substance of whatever your friend told you about its habits and its temperament. In the future, even if you forget the word "gerbil," you will still know what *kind* of animal it is and a lot about it; you have an encoded and classified set of data about it, located in an identifiable part of your semantic memory network.

LONG-TERM MEMORY. The semantic network, and all the images, sounds, and other sensory data associated with the meanings in it, fill the last box in the diagram. It is not identical with the neuron network of the brain, for that, as I've said, is intricate beyond all possible imagining or reckoning. Rather, the semantic network is only a *symbolic* picture of how remembered information is assembled; it is, once again, a metaphor.

Nonetheless, we can draw a fairly specific picture of it. The bit of hierarchical network shown above in Figure 20 is one such picture, but more recent research indicated that it needed some tinkering; it was too neat and regular. For instance, people take longer to answer "True" or "False" to the statement "An ostrich is a bird" than they do to the statement "A canary is a bird," though they shouldn't, according to the Collins and Quillian diagram. That, and many similar findings, have led memory researchers to envision the network as somewhat irregular and distorted: a *typical* bird, such as a canary, is closer to the node or center of the category *bird* than the atypical ostrich. So Collins and Elizabeth Loftus recently modified and stretched the network to allow for typicality, and made it look as in Figure 22.

New material is added to this network by being plunked down in a hole in the middle of an appropriate region, and then gradually is tied in, by a host of meaningful connections, to the appropriate nodes in the surrounding network. That's why cramming for a test is so impermanent; it doesn't knit

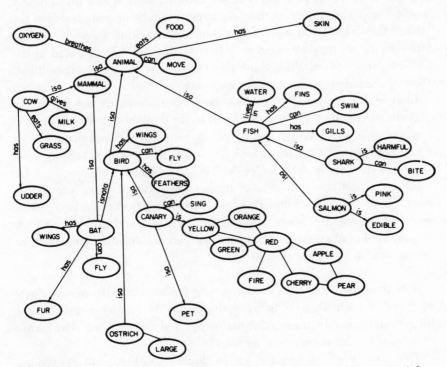

**Fig. 22.** A piece of the semantic memory network—a later view (cf. Fig. 20)

the new material into the long-term web. In contrast, discussing or using the new material in working on a research paper does interweave it until it is a fixed part of long-term memory.

Thus, although remembered information is arranged by categories of subject matter, the arrangement is far less orderly and regular than in reference works or libraries. But also far more redundant: we have many ways of getting to something filed in long-term memory, many cues and routes to the item we are seeking. When no cue or route takes us directly to it, we can guide ourselves to the general area and then mentally run through the items in that area until we come across the one we're looking for.

And this implies that there is more to memory than a semantic network; there seem to be other networks woven in and around it. We have all sorts of nonlogical and even nonmeaningful cues associated with the information we are looking for, and we can often retrieve the wanted material by recalling the irrelevant accompaniment. In a recent study, a group of students in a basement lounge at Texas A & M University were read a list of ninety words. The next day they returned for a recall test. Some were tested in the lounge; they recalled an average of eighteen words. Others were tested in a fifth-floor room; they averaged only twelve. But still others, tested in the fifth-floor room, were told to think about the lounge for a few minutes first; they recalled an average of seventeen words.

In everyday life we often use not the semantic network but the others that are woven in and around it. If you try to think of rhymes for "boat," you don't do it by looking in that part of the semantic network that contains means of transportation. If you look for objects that resemble bulging eyes, you don't do it by looking under "vision" or "organs" or "faces," but by making connections with similar images—hard-boiled eggs, protruding navels, large marbles, onions. Perhaps there are networks interlacing with networks—a semantic one, a visual one, an aural one, and so on—each with its own kind of organization, and each with an unthinkable number of interconnections to the other networks.

If information we process deeply is so well woven into the memory network and is reachable by so many methods, why do we ever forget? Except for material erased by trauma due to illness, accidents, or aging, why is anything ever lost from long-term memory?

This, too, is well accounted for by Figure 21. First, not everything processed beyond short-term memory is thoroughly transformed or strongly woven into the network. You can remember today where you were last Saturday night, but a year from now you probably won't be able to; you can remember a good deal of the content of a book you read a month ago or even a year ago, but very little of one you read five or ten years ago. In contrast, you have not forgotten your name, or how to speak English, or the principles of combustion, or any of millions of pieces of information that are well locked into the network, and available by a multiplicity of routes.

What actually becomes of material that is forgotten? Theorists disagree, and adhere to one or another of two general schools of thought. The first holds that unused long-term memories do decay and eventually disappear, leaving no trace whatever. The second holds that the trace remains as long as we live, but that changes in the organization of the network, due to new experiences, altered habits of thought, and the like, break the bonds or cues that enabled us to retrieve the trace. We lose the memory in the same sense that a book misplaced in a library is lost, even though it still exists and has not left the building.

The issue is hotly disputed, much evidence being offered on each side. Some intriguing evidence for the misplaced-but-not-erased theory comes from hypnosis, under which people often remember names, faces, and other information they cannot otherwise recall. In July 1976, for instance, three masked men kidnapped a busload of children from the California farming town of Chowchilla and forced the children and the bus driver into an abandoned trailer truck buried underground. Eventually the driver and the children dug themselves out and were rescued. The FBI, called into the case, found that the school bus driver could remember nothing specific about a white van used by the kidnappers, but under hypnosis he recalled all but one digit of its license plate number—enough to crack the case.

But such instances are rare. In studies similar to those performed by Elizabeth Loftus, hypnotized subjects have recalled not the correct details of a videotape but the modified or altered memory that results from suggestions, later information, and inferences; the memory that exists is not identical to the original experience, and that original is no longer to be found. What hypnotized people come up with, according to Loftus, is on occasion a new important fact, but is all too often totally false information.

The most frequently cited evidence for the permanence of memories is the work of the eminent brain surgeon Wilder Penfield; in the 1940s, while performing operations on conscious patients, he experimentally touched electrodes carrying a weak current to various parts of the brain, and some of the patients promptly relived long-forgotten experiences. One man heard a piano playing just as he'd heard it long ago. A woman heard a mother calling her little boy; it had happened in her neighborhood many years ago. Penfield concluded that the brain contains a permanent record of every experience, even though much of the record is unavailable and seems to us to be lost.

But although these findings captured the imagination of Americans, and are periodically repeated in articles about memory, the actual evidence is very weak, as Elizabeth Loftus points out. Of some 1100 patients on whom Penfield used electrode stimulation, only 40 had memory responses; of the 40, many had only fragmentary memories—the sound of music, a voice calling—and even some of the fragments, when looked at closely, seem more like dreams than true recall. The woman who heard a mother calling her boy, for instance, was stimulated by the electrode a second time and heard it again, and this time said it was not in her neighborhood but at a lumberyard; she added, however, that she had never been at a lumberyard in her life.

And yet nearly everyone has had an experience suggesting that *some* forgotten memories do remain, in some form, and can on occasion be retrieved. When I was seventeen, I heard Smetana's "The Moldau" for the first time and suddenly remembered being carried on my father's thick muscular shoulder, when I was a year or two old, as he walked back and forth in the upstairs hall of our house and sang to me. Perhaps I had been awakened by a nightmare and he was calming me; the melody he sang was that of "The Moldau," and for a second or two I saw, I heard, I *felt* that moment. Then, as if a camera diaphragm were closing, it disappeared during the next second or two, leaving me possessing—but no longer experiencing—the memory.

But neither such episodes nor the fragmentary surviving evidence of hypnosis and brain stimulation proves that everything remains in memory; they prove only that *some* forgotten things remain. It still may be true that a great majority of our long-term memories do fade away and eventually disappear altogether.

Of the evidence supporting this view, perhaps the most intriguing involves a heroic feat of patience and painstaking record-keeping. Some years ago, a psychologist named Harold E. Burtt read to his very young son passages of Sophocles in the original Greek (alternating with more suitable nursery materials) from the time the boy was fifteen months old until he was three. Then Burtt waited five years, at which time he asked the eight-year-old boy to memorize some of those passages, as well as others that hadn't been read to him, to see if there was any trace left of the sounds the boy had heard earlier. It took the diligent lad 435 repetitions to learn the new passages but only 317 to learn the previously heard ones; evidently, something of the sounds he'd heard before had indeed remained. But the patient Burtt repeated the experiment, using other previously heard passages, when his son was fourteen and again when he was eighteen; by the latter year, there was no difference in the effort the youth had to exert to memorize new passages and those heard fifteen years before. Fading, though slow, had evidently been complete.

In any case, forgetting, while it is often annoying, sometimes costly, and occasionally catastrophic, is probably essential to our mental well-being and our ability to function. Psychologists like to point out how crippled we would be if every familiar object caused our minds to be filled with recollections of every past experience we have had with such an object. In *The Processing of Memories*—a thorough review of recent research on both remembering and forgetting—psychologist Norman E. Spear writes, "Forgetting is more a blessing than a curse. We would be in a sorry state indeed if our awareness were bombarded by all the telephone numbers we had ever learned each time we used the telephone, or by the name of every person we had ever met each time we approached a friend on the street."

This is no idle speculation; just such a problem afflicted a man with the most astonishing memory ever closely observed by psychologists. The man was a Russian, Solomon V. Shereshevskii, who was studied from the 1920s to the 1950s by the great Russian psychologist Aleksandr R. Luria. Shereshevskii, after trying various professions, earned his living during most of his life by putting on public exhibitions of his superhuman ability to remember large sets of numbers, letters, or words after only a very brief look at them. But he was plagued by his inability to forget the materials he had memorized at earlier performances. He even tried writing them down and burning the paper, but they kept reappearing in his mind. In ordinary conversation, the flood of memories produced by various words made his conversation all but incoherent; he would become verbose, digress endlessly, and clutter his speech with details and irrelevancies. Apologizing to Luria, he said that it was these unwanted memories that made it impossible for him to stick to the subject, adding plaintively, "It's not that I'm talkative."

I sometimes regret that I have forgotten so much, and wish I could remember everything I have ever learned. But when I think of Shereshevskii, I marvel that evolution, proceeding by trial and error, produced in us a mind so much better adapted to survival than the one we ourselves might design according to our own wishes.

## Learning How to Remember

Ask a small child what he or she did in nursery school or kindergarten today, and the answer is likely to be "Nothing," although later, unbidden, the child will trot out various memories of the day, one by one. The problem is not, as we may suppose, that young children invariably resent questioning by their parents, but that often they simply don't realize there are ways to remember things. They haven't yet acquired an awareness of their own memory capabilities—a body of self-knowledge that cognitive scientists call "metamemory."

The result is that young children, though they're pretty good at recognition, are very poor at recall. Dr. Marion Perlmutter, a psychologist at the University of Minnesota, has been investigating the development of memory in children by showing them a series of ten or twenty toys, and then concealing the toys and asking the children how many they can name. At age three, she finds, children can typically recall only two items. But after starting school, their recall ability begins to increase, and continues to do so for many years. It is the demands and procedures of the classroom that awaken them to the existence of elementary memory skills such as chunking, the use of simple mnemonic devices like rhythm and rhyme, and self-cuing in such ways as visualizing some past event in order to stir up associations, or starting at the beginning of some activity and thereby recalling what came next, and next after that. Even so common a short-term memory technique as rehearsal is probably learned by example rather than developed spontaneously.

Formal education is also responsible for the set of skills by which we make use of "external memory"—notes, reminders, study outlines, textbooks, reference books, calendars, address books, datebooks, and the like, all of which add immensely to the capability of the human memory system. Anything we learn to write down or to locate in recorded form is a thing we need not commit to memory; we need remember only some economical procedure for finding what exists in that recorded form. The historians of preliterate societies were the bards who memorized their people's epics; it was a labor of many years to learn such a body of material by heart. (Historians now believe, on the basis of recent studies of preliterate peoples, that the *Iliad* and *Odyssey* were passed down by oral tradition until Homer wrote them down.) Yet any historian today, working for a few years on some project, can learn scores and perhaps hundreds of times as much: he holds it in memory in the form of his notes, and of his familiarity with the articles and books in which the details exist. He remembers chiefly a retrieval system, but the great volume of the material exists in external memory where, barring fire or some other catastrophe, it won't fade in his time.

Almost as important as external memory are the various mnemonic techniques we learn to use, the most potent of which is the deliberate creation of associations. How can one remember which way we turn the clock when going from standard time to daylight saving, or back? "Spring ahead, fall back"; the association of other meanings to the words for the seasons fixes the rule in our minds. How can the novice sailor remember which side is starboard and which is port? "Starboard" is longer than "port," and "right" is longer than "left"; problem solved.

One can create mnemonic associations for almost anything—phone numbers, license numbers, the names of new acquaintances—and even seemingly surmount the stringent limitations of short-term memory. In a recent experiment at Carnegie-Mellon University, an undergraduate named Steve Faloon over a period of a year and a half increased his ability to remember lists of numbers from seven, at the outset, to seventy-nine (he could remember and correctly repeat a list of seventy-nine digits read to him just once). Faloon achieved this by building up a complicated system of mnemonic associations (he might, for instance, think of a series of four digits as the running time for a race—3492 became "3 minutes and 49 point 2 seconds, near world-record mile time"; or as dates—1944 was "near the end of World War II"; these chunked associations were, in turn, combined into superchunks, and so on). Though his short-term memory actually remained unchanged—he never could reliably remember more than four unchunked items—he was able, thanks to his mnemonic tricks, to perform on a level with Luria's Shereshevskii.

Mnemonic tricks are, in fact, the secret behind the astonishing performances of the memory experts who appear on television and the stage, and who teach courses in memory improvement. Of the techniques they teach, the most important ones involve the creation of a train of associations that serve as cues to memory. There's nothing new about this basic principle; it was known to Greek and Roman orators in the form of "the method of loci." The orator would first think of some easily recalled series of loci (places)— the rooms, doors, and even furnishings of some familiar house or public building, for instance—and then would turn the major points of his oration into images he could connect in some way to those loci in the sequence that he would find them in that building. Had Shakespeare's Antony been such a Roman orator, he might have memorized the funeral oration by visualizing himself at the entrance to a particular temple, where someone asks him, "Why are you here?" to which he answers, "I come to bury Caesar." Having dealt with that topic, he enters the temple; the statue in the first niche has an *ambiguous* expression on its face—ah, the next topic is Caesar's alleged *ambition*—and so on.

The "peg-word" method taught by many memory experts in recent years relies on the same principle but in a different form. Here's how one peg-word system works. First, you memorize the following set of ten words that rhyme with the numbers one to ten (which makes them easy to learn):

> one—bun
> two—shoe
> three—tree
> four—door
> five—hive
> six—sticks
> seven—heaven
> eight—gate
> nine—line
> ten—hen

You now take another numbered list of any ten words, and hang each one, from one to ten, onto the peg word with the corresponding number by creating an image that links them. Suppose the first word is "light bulb"; you might attach it to "bun" by imagining a bun being warmed over a lighted bulb. Suppose the second word is "desk"; you might visualize a muddy shoe inappropriately resting on a desk. And so on. Spending no more than five to ten seconds per word, you can process a list of ten words in one minute and then recall them flawlessly—even hours or days later.*

* If you'd like to try it, first commit the above peg words to memory. Then, in one minute's time, associate the following words to them:

| | |
|---|---|
| one—bowl | six—cigarette lighter |
| two—log | seven—cup |
| three—painting | eight—spotlight |
| four—lollypop | nine—sock |
| five—chair | ten—television set |

Not only will you be able to reproduce the list without effort afterward, but, in all likelihood, you will still be able to days from now.

Such mnemonic devices are highly effective in memorizing the points to be made in a lecture, the names of business associates, or lists of any kind. But, alas, they do not enable us to deal with the vast wide-ranging body of material we learn and need in daily life. What does help us to remember general knowledge is hierarchical classification—one of the basic principles of the network of long-term memory. In a sense, this is the most valuable mnemonic device of all.

Many an experiment has shown how much better we remember items we see meaningfully organized than those we see in random order. Gordon Bower and a couple of associates showed two groups of subjects cards with words on them; the first group saw twenty-six words arranged hierarchically, like this:

Minerals

| Metals | | | Stones | |
|---|---|---|---|---|
| Rare | Common | Alloys | Precious | Masonry |
| Platinum | Aluminum | Bronze | Sapphire | Limestone |
| Silver | Copper | Steel | Emerald | Granite |
| Gold | Lead | Brass | Diamond | Marble |
| | Iron | | Ruby | Slate |

while the second group saw twenty-six words arranged randomly, like this:

Knee

| String | | | Ruby | |
|---|---|---|---|---|
| Drum | Arm | Lead | Percussion | Head |
| Flower | Slate | Instrument | Hand | Trumpet |
| Tuba | Foot | Maple | Rose | Marble |
| Neck | Piano | Toe | Birch | Aluminum |
| | Oak | | Gold | Violin |

The first group was able to remember several times as many of the words as the second group. Evidently, hierarchical arrangement furnishes the mind with a multitude of associations or retrieval cues.

People who must memorize large and complex bodies of material—a symphony or an opera, for example—often say that they do so in a hierarchical way rather than starting at the beginning and working straight

through. Eugene Kohn, my stepson, an assistant conductor at the Metropol-
itan Opera, told me how he memorizes the score of an opera: "I try to get
an overall view of the entire thing first. I memorize the order of the acts,
and then of the scenes within each act. Only then do I start to learn the
music itself, scene by scene and measure by measure. That way, I know
what's going on at every point."

The mnemonic power of good organization may account for an intriguing
and paradoxical finding that I learned about from Marion Perlmutter, who,
in addition to investigating children's memory, is also studying memory in
aging people. Perlmutter (herself barely thirty) told me about comparisons
she has made between the memories of people in their sixties and those in
their twenties. "People in their sixties and up," she said, "definitely recall
and recognize lists of words less well than people in their twenties—but interestingly, they recall and recognize facts *better*. I interpret this as meaning that while there is some increase of memory failure with age, it's not
serious—and if, in fact, the memory task is not a rote one but a real-life one,
involving a well-stocked mind, older people definitely perform better than
young people."

There are probably two reasons why this is so. First, the more real-life
information we possess, the denser is the network of linkages in long-term
memory; a new fact is caught and held in it like a fly in a spider web. This
doesn't contradict what we've heard about interference; older people do
worse at rote memorization but better at the recall of information that is
*meaningful*—that is, woven into the experiential memory network.

The second reason mature people remember facts better than young
people is that it takes time and experience to arrange and rearrange what
we know until it is in thoroughly hierarchical form. Many of the researchers
I have spoken to, especially those working on problem solving, told me that
nothing seems as productive of good retrieval as the hierarchical arrangement of information. In a memory so ordered, an individual looking for the
answer to a problem does not rummage around among a thousand specific
possibilities but starts at a high level of abstraction and works downward toward a more and more specialized level, arriving finally at the right answer.
(I'll say more about this in Chapter 7.) But this high degree of organization
and retrieval skill is not something most people can achieve all at once.
Time and again I heard, even from young cognitive scientists, that there
seems to be no substitute for experience in one's field—about twenty-five
years of it.

## On Knowing What People Mean

"Mary heard the ice-cream truck coming down the street. She remembered her birthday money, and ran into the house."

David E. Rumelhart, of the University of California at San Diego, read these two unremarkable sentences—the beginning of a children's story—to the crowd jamming a lecture hall at the 1979 meeting of the American Educational Research Association in San Francisco. He asked us what we made of them. "Most readers," he said, "recognize that Mary is a little girl, that she wants ice cream when she hears the truck, and that she goes into the house to get money in order to buy some ice cream." Isn't that obvious? Yes, but where does it say any of those things in the two sentences? Most readers, he explained, add that information (and a lot more) to the fragment when they read it; they fill in the missing material by making a set of inferences that draw upon their personal stockpile of world knowledge. The same sentences, with a change of one noun, would cause those readers to make a wholly different set of inferences and to supply a completely different body of missing material. "Change 'ice-cream truck' to 'bus,' for instance, or 'birthday money' to 'gun,' " said Rumelhart, "and see how different the interpretation is."

Rumelhart, tweedy, bearded, and young (like so many male cognitive scientists), was introducing the audience to "schema theory." This recent development in research on language comprehension seeks to explain how we understand even the most straightforward communications from other people, since, upon inspection, it is evident that communication consists not just of words and their meanings, but of what is left out and mutually understood. Our normal mode of communicating with each other in speech and writing is highly abbreviated and elliptical; listeners and readers supply far more information than is overtly contained in the words of the speaker or writer. But how do we do it, and why can the communicator count on us to do so in the way he or she means us to?

Rumelhart is only one of many cognitive scientists who now believe—and have good experimental evidence to support their view—that the answer lies in the fact that knowledge in the memory network is "packaged": it exists in the form of stereotypical routines, expected patterns of behavior, or clusters of cause-and-effect relationships within various subjects.

Cognitive scientists have a variety of names for these packages (Rumelhart calls them "schemata," Marvin Minsky at MIT speaks of "frames," Roger C. Schank at Yale uses the term "scripts"). They describe the structures in somewhat different terms, but they are all talking about coherent areas within the memory network. What is included within the boundary of any such area is a set of familiar events that we expect will be part of a given situation and that we link in a cause-and-effect relationship. A schema—I'll use that term to refer to all of them—is thus something like a play whose plot we know. It is a hypothesis that leads us to expect or predict a great deal more than the explicit words we are hearing or reading; we supply far more information than the speaker or writer does.

Rumelhart went on to describe his own method of investigating the existence and use of schemata. He reads stories like the one about Mary and the ice-cream truck to his subjects, one sentence at a time, and, after each sentence, asks them what they think is happening; he can thus see how early and how heavily they draw on various schemata to supply meaning to what would otherwise be obscure. For instance, he said, when he read to his subjects this first sentence of a story:

> I was brought into a large white room, and my eyes began to
> blink because the bright light hurt them.

some 80 percent of them immediately assumed they were hearing about either an interrogation scene or a hospital scene, and began to supply a wealth of information to the handful of words they'd heard. Whichever hypothesis they hold, if the next sentence or two furnish clues that conflict with it, they draw back, form a second and probably correct hypothesis, and flesh out the words with a different mass of background and expectations.

All of this is true not only of such stories but of everyday human speech. Cognitive scientists have their own favorite examples of brief spoken interchanges that are instantly comprehensible to any normal person but that it might require a page or more to explicate for an intelligence from another solar system. Here's one mentioned to me by linguist Herbert H. Clark of Stanford University:

> Do you know what time it is?
> It's ten past five.

Clark pointed out that the question doesn't mean "Do you *know* what time it is?" since the simple answer yes or no would be taken to be hostile. But also, to understand the question and the answer the participants must share a knowledge of how we keep track of time, how we express time, the cases in which it is unnecessary to say whether it's A.M. or P.M., and even why we regard it as valuable to know what time it is. As Clark summed up, "We bring to bear an enormous amount of knowledge to even the simplest utterances, in order to comprehend them."

Similarly, on a recent trip, I had this exchange with a waiter:

> I:   I'd like the duck, but I have a plane to catch.
> WAITER:   Better order something else, sir.

It would take pages to spell out the detailed knowledge of flight scheduling, restaurant procedures, and duck preparation that was mutually taken for granted in these two lines.

The principle applies not just to the simple stories used in schema research, and to ordinary conversation, but to all human communication. Indeed, it may be most true of the most sophisticated forms of speech and writing. Public speeches and lectures, newspaper and magazine articles, nonfiction books, novels, plays, and poems all rely on the listener or reader to furnish far more information than the speaker or writer can possibly find time or space for. No life would be long enough and no book big enough, if we had to say everything. And, of course, no one would listen or read; it is a cardinal rule of human communication that we are supposed not to tell what the listener or reader may be presumed to know.

To illustrate this point, I went to our library and, without hunting for an ideal example, pulled a familiar great book from the shelf and opened it to the first page, where the writer could not draw on anything he had already said but had to rely on the reader to make the words comprehensible. Here is the first sentence of Gibbon's *Decline and Fall of the Roman Empire:*

> In the second century of the Christian era, the Empire of
> Rome comprehended the fairest part of the earth, and the
> most civilised portion of mankind.

A reader who finds this sentence perfectly intelligible does so not because Gibbon was a lucid stylist but because he or she knows when the Christian era began, understands the concept of "empire," is familiar enough with history to recognize the huge sociocultural phenomenon known as "Rome," has enough information about world geography so that the phrase "the fairest part of the earth" produces a number of images in the mind, and, finally, can muster a whole congeries of ideas about the kinds of civilization that then existed. What skill, to elicit that profusion of associations with those few well-chosen cues—but what a performance by the reader! One hardly knows which to admire more: Gibbon's craft as a writer, or the performance of one's own memory in using these shards to reconstruct a world.

# THE PRACTICAL COGITATOR

### A Flunking Grade in Logic for the World's Only Logical Animal

For many centuries, philosophers and others who have studied the human mind have believed that reasoning takes place according to the laws governing logic. Or rather, that it should, but regrettably often fails to do so. Ideal reasoning, they have held, is *deductive:* one starts with statements that are self-evidently true or taken to be true and, by means of logical processes, sees what other true statements can be derived from them. When we violate the principles of logic, or when we reason *inductively*—moving from particular examples to a generalization that goes beyond them—we often fall into error or reach invalid conclusions.

Such is the tradition that runs unbroken from Aristotle to Piaget. But the findings of cognitive science run counter to it: logical reasoning is not our usual—or natural—practice, and the technically invalid kinds of reasoning we generally employ work rather well in most of the everyday situations in which one might suppose rigorous deductive thinking was essential.

First, a look at our ability to reason deductively, and at its severe limitations. Let's start with a syllogism concocted by psychologist John L. Horn of the University of Denver (a syllogism is a basic form of logical reasoning in which two statements, known as "premises," lead to a third one, the "conclusion"):

No Gox box when in purple socks.
Jocks is a Gox wearing purple socks.
Therefore Jocks does not now box.

Is the conclusion warranted by the premises? That is, if the first two statements are true, is the third one true or not? Many people find it hard to say—and yet the syllogism is quite simple, structurally speaking; if it had dealt with familiar, sensible subjects rather than silly and confusing ones, the answer would have been immediately obvious even to a fifth- or sixth-grade child. For instance, this syllogism uses the same syntactical structure as the first one:

No cars run when they're out of fuel.
My car is out of fuel.
Therefore my car does not now run.

Clearly, the conclusion is valid—and, therefore, so is the conclusion to the first version of this syllogism. But if we were truly logical thinkers, we would find the first one just as easy to evaluate as the second one.

Syllogistic reasoning, one of the basic forms of deductive inference, is most familiar to us in the configuration that Aristotle called "perfect" because we intuitively recognize the validity of the inference in it; we can *feel* how the statements fit into each other. The following example is the one that has been used more often than any other since Aristotle's day:

All men are mortal.
Socrates is a man
Therefore Socrates is mortal.

We can sense without effort that this conclusion validly follows from the premises. But there are many other kinds of syllogisms with different configurations (different arrangements of the terms in the subjects and predicates), negative statements rather than affirmative ones, and particulars rather than universals. Some of these syllogisms are quite difficult for people untrained in formal logic to evaluate correctly. Professor Philip N. Johnson-Laird, a leading British investigator of deductive reasoning, found that more than half of a group of people whom he asked about the following incomplete syllogism felt that no valid conclusion could be drawn from the premises:

Some of the beekeepers are artists.
None of the chemists are beekeepers.
Therefore —————?

Yet according to formal logic, a valid conclusion does exist; before reading on, you might like to say what you think it is. . . . It is this:

Some of the artists are not chemists.

If that is hard for you to see, here's the same form of syllogism, using nouns that make sensible familiar statements:

Some birds can swim.
No fish are birds.
Therefore some animals that can swim are not fish.

In this form, it's easy to perceive the validity of the conclusion. As Johnson-Laird and his longtime collaborator, Peter C. Wason, have concluded from their research, our ability to judge the validity of a syllogism or to draw a valid conclusion from premises is much heightened or diminished by the subject matter; we're far more likely to be logical when the content is real or familiar, and far less likely to be so when it is unreal or unfamiliar.

If we can be logical when the subject matter is real or familiar, what does it matter that we have trouble reasoning about Jocks and Gox or fictitious beekeepers, chemists, and artists? It *does* matter; it is just when the subject matter is hypothetical or unfamiliar that the need for rational thinking is most important—as in identifying the cause of a mysterious outbreak of illness, deducing the characteristics of a new subatomic particle, or drafting a piece of innovative legislation.

Even if the subject matter is both real and familiar, recent studies show, we are more capable of logical reasoning when the content doesn't matter to us, and less capable of it when the content does matter. We tend to think that conclusions we approve of are valid when they are not, and to judge those we disapprove of not valid when they are. How, for instance, would you rate the conclusion to this syllogism?

Those who believe in democracy believe in free speech.
Fascists do not believe in democracy.
Therefore Fascists do not believe in free speech.

And this one?

Whatever makes for full employment is socially beneficial.
Being in a state of war tends to make for full employment.
Therefore war is socially beneficial.

The conclusion about Fascists is invalid, even though undoubtedly you agree with it. (It may, however, be validly inferred from other premises.) If you do not recognize that it is invalid, here is the same form of syllogism, dealing with another topic:

> Robins have feathers.
> Chickens are not robins.
> Therefore chickens do not have feathers.

A way to visualize the flaw in the reasoning is to draw a set of Euler's circles that show, diagrammatically (Fig. 23), how the classes named in the premises fit together (Leonhard Euler, an eighteenth-century Swiss mathematician, was the first to use this way of checking the validity of a syllogism). Euler's circles show, in graphic form, what cognitive scientists say is the es-

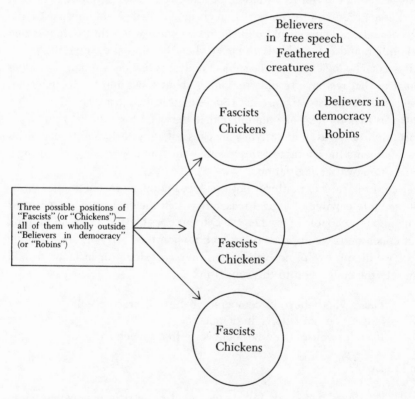

**Fig. 23.**   Euler's circles—a visual way of testing whether a given syllogism is or is not valid

sence of logical thinking: it is fundamentally a kind of spatial mapping—a mental perception of what areas of discourse overlap other areas. The first premise says that believers in democracy are a part of, or fit within the area of, the class of believers in free speech. The second premise maps out the class of Fascists: it lies wholly outside the area of believers in democracy. Yet the diagram shows that this does not necessarily put Fascists outside the area of believers in free speech. Even though in actual fact they are not believers in free speech, this particular syllogism doesn't prove it.

On the other hand, the conclusion that war is socially beneficial is perfectly true, provided the premises are true; it is the valid conclusion of a "perfect" syllogism. What is wrong with it is the false assumption of the first premise, but not the reasoning; yet even a logician might unthinkingly label that wretched conclusion invalid. As Wason and Johnson-Laird put it, "At best, we can all think like logicians; at worst, logicians all think like us."

We are equally likely to make logical errors in another kind of deductive reasoning known as conditional argument or conditional inference. Here is a simple example:

A

If it's raining, the streets are wet.
It is raining.
Therefore the streets are wet.

Is this reasoning valid or invalid? The answer seems obvious, but in certain other versions of the conditional argument it is not so obvious. For instance:

B

If it's raining, the streets are wet.
It isn't raining.
Therefore the streets aren't wet.

C

If it's raining, the streets are wet.
The streets are wet.
Therefore it's raining.

D

If it's raining, the streets are wet.
The streets aren't wet.
Therefore it isn't raining.

Many people find it easy to decide whether versions A and D are valid or not, but curiously difficult to do so about B and C—and they often arrive at the wrong decisions about these two. Yet logically speaking, the answers to all four are equally clear.

Of the four versions, A and D are valid, since if it is raining, the streets are sure to be wet, and if they're dry, it can't possibly be raining. In the terminology of logic, we reach a valid conclusion to a conditional argument if we "affirm the antecedent" or "deny the consequent," as in these two examples.

But if we do the opposite—"deny the antecedent" or "affirm the consequent"—we cannot draw any valid conclusion: in B, even if it isn't raining, the streets might be wet for some other reason (dewfall, a broken water main, a street-washing machine), and in C, even if the streets are wet, that doesn't mean it must be raining, since there are other possible explanations.

As simple as this may seem, the principles involved in the invalid cases aren't obvious or natural to us; or to put it another way, most people do find it natural to make these invalid inferences. John E. Taplin and Herman Staudenmayer of the University of Colorado recently showed subjects who had had no formal training in logic a series of ninety-six simple conditional syllogisms, of which these are examples:

> If there is a Z, then there is an H.
> There is no Z.
> Therefore there is no H.

> If there is a Z, there is an H.
> There is an H.
> Therefore there is a Z.

Nearly two thirds of the subjects thought the first of these examples was valid, and over two thirds thought the second one was, yet neither one is; the first denies the antecedent, and the second affirms the consequent.

A few years ago, Wason devised a fascinating little problem that demonstrates this tendency visually. The problem looks simple enough for a child, yet most adults cannot answer it correctly—and many cannot understand it when it is explained to them. Suppose you are shown four cards that look like those in Figure 24. Each of them, you are told, has a letter on one side and a number on the other. The following rule is supposed to be in effect: *If a card has a vowel on one side, then it has an even number on the other side.* The problem: Which of the cards must you turn over to see whether the rule is true or false?

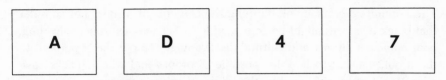

**Fig. 24.**   Peter Wason's four-card problem. Most people get it wrong—
and have trouble understanding the right answer.

Of course, you could turn them all over, but that's not the task; the task is
to say which ones—and only which ones—will prove or disprove the rule.
Let me warn you (if you are about to try to answer the question) that in
Wason's first study using this problem, only 5 of his 128 subjects got the answer right.

Most of those who got it wrong said that they needed to turn over the *A*
and the 4, or only the *A*. But the right answer is the *A* and the 7: it is necessary to see whether the *A* does have an even number on the other side, but it
is also necessary to make sure the 7 does *not* have a vowel on its other side,
since if it did, that would disprove the rule. The *D* needn't be turned over
because the rule says, *If a card has a vowel on one side,* and so on, and since
this card does not have a vowel on one side, it makes no difference what's on
the other. But why did so many people erroneously pick the 4? Because
they misinterpreted the rule to work both ways around, but in fact it does
*not* say that if there's an even number on one side, there will be a vowel on
the other. *If Z, then H,* isn't the same as *If H, then Z;* if the street is wet,
that doesn't mean it must be raining.

Wason and a number of other cognitive scientists conclude that human
beings find it much more natural to look for proof than to look for disproof;
we tend to think only in terms of tests that will confirm a hypothesis we
hold but not tests that might disconfirm it. And while this matters little if
we are turning over numbered and lettered cards, it can matter greatly
when we are thinking about larger issues.

An example. An old, and recently revived, explanation of the fact that
black children get lower scores on IQ tests, on the average, than white children is that blacks, by racial inheritance, have inferior mental equipment.
Stated in logical form:

> If blacks have inferior brains, they will get lower IQ scores
>    than whites.
> They do get lower IQ scores.
> Therefore they have inferior brains.

This commits the fallacy of affirming the consequent; it does not consider that black IQ scores might be depressed for other reasons—poor schooling, poor home conditions, and cultural disadvantage. To put the hypothesis to the proof, one has to look for possible disproof—and where blacks have educational and social equality, that disproof exists in the form of IQ scores close to, or equal to, those of whites. Where there is such disproof—that is, denial of the consequent—the antecedent is denied, and the racial hypothesis is disproved. And that's valid reasoning.

In these and many other ways most human beings earn a failing grade in elementary logic. But we're not just frequently incompetent, we're also willfully and skillfully illogical. When a piece of deductive reasoning leads to a conclusion we don't like, we often rebut it with irrelevancies and sophistries of which, instead of being ashamed, we act proud. Recently, a new mortality study released by the State Mutual Life Assurance Company of America reported that at all ages the death rate among smokers is more than twice as high as that among nonsmokers. That night on a television news program, a reporter was shown asking various smokers what they thought of the findings: one man sarcastically replied, "So nonsmokers don't die, right?"—and looked immensely pleased with himself; a young woman, with equal self-satisfaction, said, "Nobody lives forever, anyway." Such rebuttals are not at all unusual; many psychological studies have shown that smokers tend to reject logical inferences about smoking by means of a variety of distortions and rationalizations. They may assert that the evidence is incomplete or biased, or cite the case of someone they know who smoked heavily and lived to be ninety, or, like the man and woman on television, rebut conclusions other than the one that was actually drawn.

Similarly, most people are little influenced by the reasoning, however cogent, of campaigners, organizers, and other public persuaders. Jeanne B. Herman of the Graduate School of Management at Northwestern University has studied the reactions of people subjected to company and union arguments prior to voting on some issue, and found that few of them change their attitudes as a result of such exposure. By a variety of nonlogical cognitive techniques they "insulate" themselves from the reasoning they are exposed to unless it confirms their preexisting attitudes. To be sure, some part of every voting population changes its views in the course of a campaign, but the causes of shifts are factors such as the personalities of the campaigners, changing economic conditions, threats or promises, and so on; the noble ideal of persuasion by means of the clash of ideas in the marketplace has little to do with it.

Even within the cerebral ranks of foreign-policy decision makers, rationality is the ideal but rarely the reality. The classic theory of high-level decision making views it as a process in which the theoretical rational man weighs costs against benefits and inexorably comes to the optimal decision, but many recent studies find that this is rarely the case. Political scientists Ole R. Holsti of Duke University and Alexander George of Stanford University have analyzed various examples of such decision making and found that only when a problem is trivial do foreign-policy decision makers behave rationally; far more often, such factors as stress, the complexity of the problem, and their own conflicting motives cause them to make decisions by irrational processes.

The failure of human beings to be led by logic is perhaps most noteworthy in the areas of religion and law. Look at the variety of doctrines within Christianity—most of them derived by deductive reasoning from the same original body of evidence, the Scriptures, rather than later revelations. From those premises, some churches conclude that we have free will, but others that we are predestined to behave as we do; some churches infer that we achieve salvation through private repentance, but others through public rebirth, and still others through good works; and so forth.

If we need any final piece of evidence that even fine minds are not so much led by logic as prone to bend logic to their own conclusions, look at the output of the United States Supreme Court. In recent decades, many important cases dealing with constitutional guarantees have resulted in split decisions; the constitutional guarantees are the premises all nine justices start with, and many of their decisions involve deductive reasoning of a high order, yet they arrive at disparate and even diametrically opposite conclusions. How can this be? But the question is a rhetorical one; we all know the answer: the justices *interpret* the language of the Constitution in their own ways, so as to derive from it justification for their own social values. As Chief Justice Charles Evans Hughes said to William O. Douglas, when Douglas was new to the Supreme Court, "You must remember one thing. At the constitutional level where we work, ninety percent of any decision is emotional. The rational part of us supplies the reasons for supporting our predilections."

Thus there is yet another paradox about the human ability to reason deductively: those who are best at logical reasoning often use it—as the rest of us use illogic—to get where they want to go, rather than where reason would naturally lead them.

## Reason and Reality

So we flunk in logic. But like other flunking students, let us dare to ask whether the fault is not in the subject matter. Do we have difficulty thinking logically because our minds are feeble or flawed—or because there is something unnatural about the laws of deductive inference? If logic is the model of normal human reasoning, why is most human reasoning abnormal? It would make more sense, and be more in keeping with an evolutionary view of the human intellect, to suppose that logical reasoning is in large part abnormal, unnatural, and not generally applicable to everyday experience and to the problems of survival. It consists of a set of artificial rules that we can learn and can apply—indeed, *must* apply—in order to solve certain kinds of important intellectual problems, but it is not a means by which our minds can effectively interpret the larger part of the reality around us; our natural way of reasoning, however, is just such a means.

This is the very opposite of what most Western philosophers have long believed. The ancient Greeks were the first to maintain that the way to explore the nature of reality was by means of rigorously deductive thinking of the sort that leads to mathematical discoveries. Plato even maintained that mathematics should be a prerequisite to the practice of philosophy, and Aristotle termed deductive reason "divine" because it deals with timeless and perfect realities such as the truths of mathematics and so enables us to share in God's immortality.

From Aristotle's time on, this was the dominant philosophic tradition. Even when science was beginning to flourish and the empirical and experimental approach was yielding rich returns of new knowledge, many philosophers were intent on trying to decipher the nature of the world by means of pure deductive reasoning. Spinoza, in the seventeenth century, derived his entire *Ethics* in a Euclidean manner, starting with definitions and self-evident axioms, and proving everything else theorem by theorem. Here is a specimen of his psychology, from Part Four of the *Ethics:*

> Prop. XIX—*According to the laws of his own nature each person necessarily desires that which he considers to be good, and avoids that which he considers to be evil.*
>
> *Demonst.*—The knowledge of good and evil (Prop. 8, pt. 4) is the affect itself of joy or sorrow, in so far as we are con-

scious of it, and therefore (Prop. 28, pt. 3), each person necessarily desires that which he considers to be good, and avoids
that which he considers to be evil. But this desire is nothing
but the essence itself or nature of man (Def. of appetite in
Schol. Prop. 9, pt. 3, and Def. 1 of the Affects, pt. 3). Therefore, according to the laws of his nature alone, he necessarily
desires or avoids, &c.—Q.E.D.

Leibniz, similarly, believed that logic could provide the final answers to
both metaphysical and moral questions. All his life he hoped to discover a
new form of mathematical logic that would replace ordinary thinking with
a species of rigorous calculation. If we had such a system, philosophers who
disagreed about the nature of the world or about some moral issue would
not dispute each other but instead, said Leibniz, "take their pencils in their
hands, sit down to their slates, and say to each other (with a friend as witness, if they liked): Let us calculate."

The triumph of the scientific method eventually brought about a reappraisal and devaluation of deductive reasoning. But philosophers and mathematicians themselves were partly responsible for this shift. Kant, in the
eighteenth century, showed that pure reason, when applied to subjects outside of possible experience such as God, soul, and immortality, can be made
to lead to contradictory conclusions; hence, he said, it cannot possibly en-
lighten us about such things. Various nineteenth-century and twentieth-
century mathematicians invented geometries that start from premises different from Euclid's but are as internally consistent and as valid as his. The
same is true in other areas of mathematics. Thus, contrary to what the ancients thought, there is not one single set of mathematical and logical truths
that corresponds to reality; there can be many such systems, each arbitrary
and derived from definitions and rules we create, each having some degree
of correspondence with what we actually experience.

Accordingly, early in this century Alfred North Whitehead, Bertrand
Russell, Rudolf Carnap, and other "logical positivists" took the view that
the laws of logic deal with the relationships among statements we make but
have no direct bearing upon reality other than the reality of thoughts. Logic
and mathematics are extremely valuable ways of *handling* the knowledge
we acquire, but neither one, said Russell, can *produce* new knowledge—except about itself. As he put it, "All the important inferences outside logic
and mathematics are inductive, not deductive; the only exceptions are law
and theology, each of which derives its first principles from an unquestionable text, viz., the statute books or the scriptures." But we have already seen

how different minds, starting from an unquestionable text, can use logical means to come to different conclusions.

A few philosophers, even today, argue that the laws of modern symbolic logic are rooted in reality, and express properties common to the relationships found in all the sciences. But they are a tiny enclave in modern intellectual life; most scientists regard logic and mathematics as tools of thought, not as principles of reality.

None of this means that deductive thinking is valueless. On the contrary, it plays an indispensable, though limited, part in both scientific thinking and everyday life. In almost every scientific investigation, deductive reasoning is used to set up the basic hypothesis to be investigated and to extract the implications of the findings. When we perform analytical and computational acts such as those involved in working out a family budget or filling out an income-tax report, we are using deductive processes. When we play bridge, chess, or even ticktacktoe, we reason deductively. When we are jurors or plaintiffs or defendants, we make deductive use of both the law and the evidence in judging, complaining, or defending. When we talk or plead or argue with each other, or grapple with the everyday problems in our lives, much of our reasoning consists of inferences which, valid or invalid, are deductive—that is, logically inferred from what we already know, or think we know.

And yet formal logic is not a good description of how our minds usually work, or even how they should usually work. Logic tells us how we should reason when we are trying to reason logically, but it does not tell us how to think about reality as we encounter it most of the time.

For one thing, its rules cause it to generate a world of thought that is in many ways alien to our realistic needs and our perceptions. Here is part of the opening statement in a rather upper-brow contemporary textbook of formal logic:

> It *is* the job of pure logic to point out that if it is true to say
>
> > *Tom stole it,*
>
> then it is equally true to say
>
> > *Tom stole it or Dick stole it.*
>
> It is *not* the job of pure logic to point out that someone who makes the second statement, knowing that the first is also true, may be seriously misleading his hearers and slandering Dick.

The second statement is, of course, a valid inference from the first one; it says only that one or the other of the two men stole it—and since it is true that one of them (Tom) did steal it, the second statement is also true—but useless, and even potentially harmful. Yet by various logical steps, an *infinite number* of such true but useless statements can be derived from any true statement. For instance, from *Tom stole it* we can also validly infer this:

> *It isn't true that: Tom didn't steal it, and either Tom stole it or Dick didn't steal it, and Dick didn't steal it.*

Whether this statement is useful or comprehensible or represents anything real that we might experience has nothing to do with the case; it is exactly as true as the original statement, *Tom stole it.*

It is for such reasons that Professor Marvin Minsky of MIT, a senior figure in cognitive science whose work spans artificial intelligence, psychology, psycholinguistics, and epistemology, recently concluded that no cognitive system, whether human or artificial, can operate according to the laws of formal logic. Such programming, he said, would churn out any number of valid but useless inferences from every true statement, and unfortunately "there simply is no direct way to add information to tell such a system about kinds of conclusions that should *not* be drawn." Or, conversely, what kinds *ought* to be deduced under ordinary circumstances. The human mind, in contrast, avoids making irrelevant inferences; it may not be as logical as a computer, but it possesses something the computer does not—common sense.

Not only does the human mind avoid making inferences that do not represent anything real, but in nonlogical ways it makes sense of a great many experiences that logic cannot admit or cannot encompass. The same textbook says that since there are albino crows in the world, it is false to say *All crows are black;* the statement is *nearly* true but "a near truth is a kind of falsehood, and in logic . . . we do not distinguish degrees of truth or falsehood." That, however, is something the human mind often needs to do, and does.

Logic enables us to judge the validity of our own deductive reasoning, but much of the time we need to reason nondeductively—either inductively, or in terms of likelihoods, or of causes and effects, none of which fits within the rules of formal logic. The archetype of everyday realistic reasoning might be something like this: *This object (or situation) reminds me a lot of another that I experienced before, so probably I can expect much to be true of this one that was true of that one.* Such reasoning is natural and utilitarian—but logically invalid.

Another major divergence between formal logic and natural reasoning is that while in logic every statement is either true or false, in normal discourse many statements are neither true nor false—nor even mostly true or false—because the terms simply don't apply to them. Johnson-Laird and Wason give this example: If someone says, "All of John's children are asleep," and in fact John has no children, the assertion is certainly not true—but neither is it false, since logically that would be the same as saying, "Some of John's children are not asleep." Rather, the statement is *void* or *irrelevant*—conditions that the normal mind recognizes but that logic does not.

Nor does formal logic accommodate temporal or causal relationships, yet the human mind cannot make sense of the world without them. Compare these two statements:

> She inherited a fortune and he married her.
> He married her and she inherited a fortune.

In formal logic, say Johnson-Laird and Wason, the two are identical, but there is, to say the least, a great difference between them in real life.

Even so simple and seemingly clear a sentence as "If $X$, then $Y$" has a distinctly different meaning in logic than it does in natural language and thought. We normally mean by it that if $X$ occurs, it will *cause* $Y$ to occur, as in our old friend, *If it's raining, the streets are wet;* in logic, however, a conditional doesn't signify causality, but only that if the first thing is so, then the second is, too. For instance: If the forsythia is in bloom, the robins are reappearing (but one thing isn't the cause of the other).

That's realistic enough, but logic doesn't stop there: it says that even if the first thing is absurd and false, it still "materially implies" the second. Daniel N. Osherson, a psychologist at MIT, who concerns himself with just such knotty philosophic problems as they affect cognitive science, gives this peculiar example:

$$\text{If } 2 + 2 = 5, \text{ then } 2 + 2 = 4$$

In a logical sense, he says, this statement is true. But how can it be? Well, since the first part is false, it can't affect the second part one way or the other, so the overall statement is true. "If pigs had wings, fish could fly" is just as true a statement as "If pigs had wings, fish couldn't fly." In more formal terms, an established theorem of logic says that "a false statement materially implies any statement." This paradox follows from the rules of logic, but it runs counter to our intuition of what "If . . . then" means. More than that, it simply has no meaning or reality outside the world of logic. Our intuition is right after all.

And yet the view persists, chiefly among the followers of Jean Piaget, that formal logic represents the way the normal mature mind works. This is only part of Piagetian psychology—but it is the part that has recently been rejected by most cognitive scientists for all the reasons we have just seen, and others.

Among those others is the evidence of recent experiments testing whether the human mind, confronted by problems in logic, solves them by means of formal logic. In one series of such experiments conducted a few years ago, Osherson presented children and adults with brain twisters like this:

> HINT:   All the red jars and all the large jars have tacks.
> QUESTION:   Can you be sure that every jar that does not have tacks and is not large is not red?

There were twenty-eight problems in all, some more complicated and some less complicated than this one (for the answer, see below\*). The way one solves such a problem logically involves a series of steps testing the implications of each constituent part of the problem; the more negatives, conjunctions, and disjunctions there are, the more steps, and hence the longer the problem should take. But Osherson found that there was no significant relation between how complex a problem was and how long it took his subjects. Evidently they didn't use formal logical processes to solve the problems; whatever they did—and he couldn't ascertain what it was—it was something else.

They might have solved the problems even faster and with fewer errors if they had done what logicians do, which is to get rid of words altogether, rewriting the problem in letters and other symbols that they can manipulate without being distracted by meaning. The red-jar-and-large-jar problem can be expressed in logical notation as follows:

$$(A \vee B \rightarrow C) \rightarrow (- C \And - B \rightarrow - A)$$

The logician is now able to mechanically transform, reverse, cancel out, and otherwise juggle the symbols according to the rules of the "propositional

---

\* Yes; no small tackless jar is red.

calculus" until he or she arrives at the answer to the question. But as tidy and efficient as this process may be, it is not a recognizable likeness of normal human reasoning: we think not in terms of symbols and quasi-algebraic manipulations but in terms of words and meanings, for this is how several million years of evolution shaped us; this is how we naturally represent the real world in our minds and think about it. At a recent conference, one scholar even termed it a "scandal" that logicians have been so little interested in natural language—or, he should have added, in natural reasoning.

Finally, according to Marvin Minsky, formal logic is irrelevant to real life because of its lack of flexibility. He gives this illustration: Suppose the thought we want to implement is, "Don't cross the road if a car is coming." In a cognitive system that operated according to pure logic, it would be necessary to *prove* that no car was coming—an unfeasible if not impossible requirement. What we actually do is look both ways and, if we see no car, cross the road, assuming that it is very unlikely a car will suddenly whiz around the corner at high speed or materialize out of thin air. We trade a limited amount of risk for the benefit of getting the job done—a trade that cannot be made in a purely logical system. Logic requires total consistency, total certainty; we do not require it, and could not manage if we did. If we had to be wholly consistent and certain, we could hardly think at all, for most of our thinking is as imperfect as it is functional—and as functional as it is imperfect.

## Intellectual Messing Around

Our natural reasoning is thus a kind of mental puttering or tinkering with thoughts—the intellectual equivalent of what a child does when it messes around with some new toy or unfamiliar object. After a spell of mental messing around, we may put our reasoning into logical terms, but the explanation comes after the fact; the actual process took place according to some other method.

Even without the evidence of cognitive science, some thinkers have known that this is the case. Three centuries ago, for instance, Pascal grumbled that many mathematicians "make themselves ridiculous" by beginning with definitions and principles, and trying to deduce everything logically from them; the mind, he said, reasons "more naturally and artlessly" than this. The late Richard Courant, a distinguished mathematician, once told me that it is common for mathematicians to ponder long over a problem, eventually have an intuitive insight into the solution, and then carefully construct a proof that makes it sound as if they had reached the conclusion by impeccably logical steps.

The rest of us often find solutions to our problems, by means of mental fumbling, that we cannot or do not bother to justify logically. We simply "know" that the solution is correct; we can *feel* that it is. In Virgil's account of the legend of Dido, he tells how she was granted as much land in Africa as she could enclose with an oxhide, and how she cleverly cut the hide into long thin strips, tied them together, and laid out the site of Carthage in the form of a circle, so as to gain the largest possible area. How did she know a circle was the optimum shape? No doubt this was intuitively obvious to her, as it is to most of us, on the basis of physically similar experiences—tying as many sticks as we can into a bundle with a piece of string of a given length, for instance. But obvious though it may be, almost none of us can prove it mathematically—and, indeed, professional mathematicians were unable to do so until recent times.

Protocol analysis—one of the important tools of cognitive-science research, as we saw earlier—reveals an interesting enigma about such natural reasoning: people often arrive at a correct answer for wrong reasons or, at least, they consciously use only wrong ones. At MIT, Professor Andrea di Sessa, a physicist who has been investigating how high-school students think about physics problems, drew for me on the blackboard in his office the diagram shown in Figure 25 and said, "$M$ is a monkey and $W$ is a weight. They weigh exactly the same. Assume there is no friction, and that the rope and pulley have no mass—that is, no weight. The monkey starts to climb the rope. What happens to the weight?"

Grasping at a straw of thought, I said, "Well, the energy he expends has to go someplace, so I guess the weight rises as high as he climbs."

"That's right, it does," said di Sessa. I felt pleased with myself. "And many students get the right answer," he went on, "but can't explain how they got it—or, like you, get it right for the wrong reasons." I felt less pleased.*

Yet we all do this a good deal of the time; natural reasoning often succeeds even when it violates or ignores the laws of logic. What laws, then, does it obey? The cognitive scientists who are tackling this question have a variety of tentative answers that don't hang together very well yet, but two

* The problem is one of the laws of motion: since the forces acting on the two objects are always equal, their motions must be equal. Viewing the problem as one of the conservation of energy, or one of balance, may lead to the right answer, but ought not.

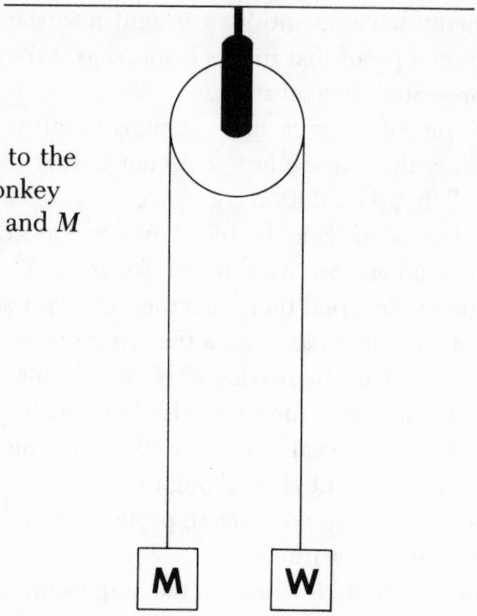

**Fig. 25.** What happens to the weight (*W*) when the monkey (*M*) climbs the rope? (*W* and *M* weigh exactly the same.)

words that occur again and again in their reports and discussions indicate a core of agreement: the words are "plausible" and "probable." For in contrast to logical reasoning, natural reasoning proceeds by steps that are credible but not rigorous, and arrives at conclusions that are likely but not certain.

Plausible reasoning operates by means of analogy and experience rather than the laws of deductive inference: we know enough about enclosing space or climbing ropes to make a skilled guess at an answer when faced with a problem like Dido's or the monkey's, though we can't—and don't try to—get to that answer by formal deductive means. As Carnegie-Mellon's Professor John R. Anderson, a leading theoretician of thinking, said to me, "Naturalistic reasoning doesn't use the rules of general inference but tends to be 'content-specific'—it uses rules that work in a particular area of experience." To put it in William James's terms, we are pragmatists by nature; what *feels* right we take to *be* right. And most of the time it *is* right; were this not so, we would long ago have disappeared from the earth. Our pragmatism, our natural mode of reasoning, is not anti-intellectual but is the kind of effective intellectuality that was forged in the evolutionary furnace.

Plausible reasoning is a "hot topic" in cognitive science today. Until quite recently, research in reasoning consisted chiefly of efforts to see how the mind handles logical problems, and when and why it makes errors in formal reasoning. But lately, interest has shifted to plausible reasoning, which is now seen not as logically defective or incompetent thinking, but as highly competent thinking of a different and natural kind.

One fundamental process involved in plausible reasoning is the recognition of similarities between two or more things, leading to the inference that they are probably alike in ways other than the observed ones. If in the past I have bought goods from street-corner peddlers, and then found them to be junk, I may well infer that the next street-corner peddler I see is selling junk. Put this reasoning into syllogistic form, and it's blatantly invalid:

> The people who sold me junk were street-corner peddlers.
> This fellow is a street-corner peddler.
> Therefore he sells junk.

Such reasoning commits the fallacy of undistributed middle, as is easily seen in a more obvious example:

> All herbivores are mammals.
> A lion is a mammal.
> Therefore a lion is a herbivore.

The "middle" term—the one that appears in both premises—should serve as the bridge between those premises, but in this example neither premise says anything about *all* mammals, and so the bridge doesn't carry us across. Yet in real life undistributed middle is a plausible form of reasoning, since it asserts that things that are similar in a number of significant ways are probably related in an overall way. Shabby, shifty fellows who hawk goods from open suitcases and are ready to flee at the sight of a policeman probably have a lot in common; the similarities I reason from are predictive.

This is how experts in medicine, engineering, and other skilled professions think when solving professional problems, according to psychologist Paul E. Johnson of the University of Minnesota. Johnson has been analyzing the protocols of cardiologists, commodity brokers, and other experts who have talked out loud while solving problems he has set them in their own fields of expertise. "I'm continually struck by the fact," he told me, "that the experts in our studies very seldom engage in formal logical thinking. Most of what they do is plausible-inferential thinking based on the recognition of similarities. That kind of thinking calls for a great deal of experience, or, as we say, a large data base. If anybody's going to be logical in a task, it's the neophyte, who's desperate for some way to generate answers, but the expert finds logical thinking a pain in the neck and far too slow. So the medical specialist, for instance, doesn't do hypothetical-deductive, step-by-step diagnosis, the way he was taught in medical school. Instead, by means of his wealth of experiences he recognizes some symptom or syndrome, he quickly gets an idea, he suspects a possibility, and he starts right in looking for data that will confirm or disconfirm his guess."

This, too, is invalid, since it commits the fallacy of undistributed middle, as one can see by forcing it into the mold of syllogistic inference:

> Disease X is known to produce various symptoms, including A, B, and C.
> This patient has symptoms A, B, and C.
> Therefore (I suspect) this patient has disease X.

That's logically impermissible—but it's a highly plausible way to begin a diagnosis.

One could also cast the doctor's thinking into the conditional mode, as follows:

> If the patient had disease X, I would see symptoms A, B, and C.
> I do see A, B, and C.
> Therefore (I suspect) he has disease X.

This, too, is technically invalid, since it affirms the consequent. But as Johnson-Laird and Wason point out, such reasoning often leads from true premises to a probably true conclusion—which is all right, they say, as long as one is aware that it is only *probably* true. They quote an example given by George Polya, a mathematics professor at Stanford University: "If it's good, then it's expensive. It's expensive. Therefore (probably) it's good." The reasoning is fallacious but, in terms of everyday experience, quite plausible: most often, expensive things *are* good, for they have to be, to compete in the market. That may not be logical, but it's realistic.

Some cognitive scientists prefer to talk about natural reasoning as being largely *analogical.* This seems to say no more than I've already said, since to draw an analogy is to note the likenesses between two objects or events, and to reason by analogy is to make an inference based on these likenesses. But it does go further: it accounts for reasoning that uses no words, analogizing

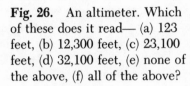

Fig. 26. An altimeter. Which of these does it read— (a) 123 feet, (b) 12,300 feet, (c) 23,100 feet, (d) 32,100 feet, (e) none of the above, (f) all of the above?

from images or other sensory data. We reason by analogy when we merely recognize that two objects look alike or are comparable, and therefore deal with the second one as we do the first. When our familiarity with tying up bundles of sticks leads us to sense that a circle will enclose the largest area within a given length of perimeter, we are doing analogical reasoning. When a child who has learned to turn the water off and on at the sink sees an outdoor faucet and turns it to get water, he or she is reasoning by analogy. If you were to poke your head into the cockpit of a plane and see a common type of altimeter (Fig. 26), you might, if you had never seen one before, be momentarily unsure how to read it. But by analogy to the sweep-second, minute, and hour hands of a clock or watch, you'd quickly infer that the hands of the altimeter, in order of decreasing size, are probably indicating altitude in hundreds, thousands, and tens of thousands of feet.*

And you'd be right; your inference was only probable, but it was based on salient characteristics. If, however, you reason analogically on the basis of unimportant characteristics, or fail to notice a salient one, you can easily reach a wrong conclusion. If you see a graph that looks like Figure 27, you might, by analogy to temperature and stock market graphs, conclude that you're looking at a record of something that is increasing at a steady rate. If so, you failed to notice that the vertical scale is exponential and is constantly changing; the graph actually shows not a steady increase but an explosive growth that gets faster, the faster it gets. If redrawn on a steady-

* The altimeter reads 32,100 feet.

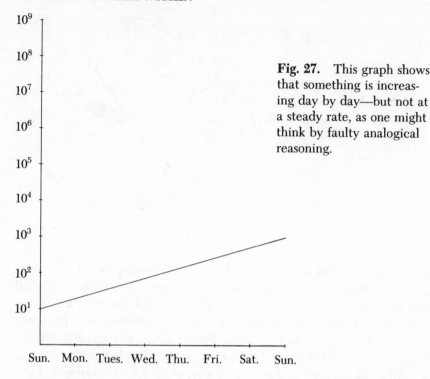

**Fig. 27.** This graph shows that something is increasing day by day—but not at a steady rate, as one might think by faulty analogical reasoning.

scale graph like that of a temperature or stock market record, it would look something like Figure 28.

Thus, analogical thinking, whether it deals with words or images, is plausible and its conclusions are only likelihoods and possibly wrong. But according to some cognitive scientists, it is the most important of our reasoning processes, and is the chief way in which we interpret and deal with the physical world around us.

Analogical reasoning is, in fact, a major component of general intelligence, and analogical problems using geometrical figures rather than words have long been used to measure intelligence without the misleading influence of cultural background. Here is an easy figural analogy: in Figure 29, which of the two figures, $D$ or $E$, will complete the series? That is: $A$ is to $B$ as $C$ is to —? Undoubtedly you saw that to get from $A$ to $B$, you had to take away the little box underneath and put a dot in the middle of what remained; when you did the same to $C$, you got $D$.

But since analogical reasoning is only plausible and probable, it is possible to focus on aspects of the figure that yield the wrong solution, or to

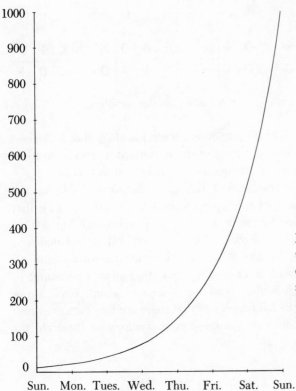

**Fig. 28.**   The data of Figure 27, transferred to a conventional uniform scale, show an explosive rather than a steady-rate increase.

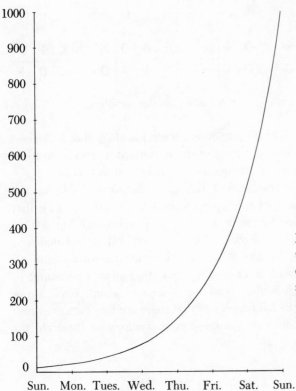

**Fig. 29.**   *A* is to *B* as *C* is to____? An easy problem.

A         B         C         D         E

| X | O | + |
|---|---|---|
| + | O | X |

| O | X | + |
|---|---|---|
| + | X | O |

| O | + | X |
|---|---|---|
| O | X | + |

| + | O | X |
|---|---|---|
| + | X | O |

| X | + | O |
|---|---|---|
| X | O | + |

**Fig. 30.**  *A* is to *B* as *C* is to____? A rather harder problem.

overlook certain salient traits. Figure 30 is a figural analogy that is difficult because one tends to notice only some of the important factors or to focus on irrelevant ones; once again, the question is, *A* is to *B* as *C* is to —?

You may well have had trouble with that one. The answer is *E*, but the reason is not at all obvious: what happens from *A* to *B*, and *C* to *E*, is that the pairs of symbols linked by the broken lines are exchanged (Fig. 31).

Robert J. Sternberg, a psychologist at Yale, has used both verbal analogies and figural analogies like Figures 29 to 31 (which are borrowed from his book, *Intelligence, Information Processing, and Analogical Reasoning*) to discover how the mind goes about making an analogical inference. From the analysis of protocols, he has concluded that there are four (or sometimes five) steps involved. He uses this simple verbal analogy to illustrate his major findings:

*Washington* is to 1 as *Lincoln* is to (a) 10, (b) 5.

In solving this tiny problem, Sternberg says, people first identify various attributes of the first term, *Washington*, among them, *first president, war hero, face on the one-dollar bill*. Second, they infer the rule that relates *Washington* to *1; war hero* drops out but the other two possibilities remain. Third, they "map" *Washington* onto *Lincoln*—that is, they look for a higher rule that relates these two terms: it could be either the number of the presidency or the denomination of the bills each one's portrait is on. Finally, they apply the two possible rules to the possible answers; since Lincoln was

A         B         C         D         E

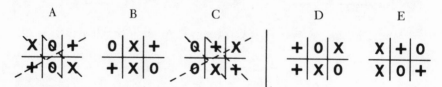

**Fig. 31.**  Solution to the problem in Figure 30

the sixteenth president, not the fifth or tenth, it becomes clear now that the only rule that can complete the analogy has to do with faces of presidents on paper money, and that the correct answer is 5.

These processes, Sternberg believes, underlie the analogical reasoning that pervades daily life. "We reason analogically," he writes, "whenever we make a decision about something new in our experience by drawing a parallel to something old. When we buy a new goldfish because we liked the old one, or when we listen to a friend's advice because it was correct once before, we are reasoning analogically." But daily life doesn't present us with pairs of possible answers from which to pick the right one; we experience only two pieces of the analogy—the familiar item and the new item—and the similarities we notice and the rules we extract are only as good as our perception and judgment make them. The friend's previous advice might have been right by accident or because it dealt with a subject he or she knows a lot about; if we are unaware of this, we may draw the risky conclusion that our friend's advice is worth taking on all kinds of matters.

Everyday analogical reasoning is thus conjectural and probabilistic. And yet it is a natural tendency of the human mind to interpret new experiences in the light of old ones, and to make inferences based on similarities. Despite the uncertainties of such reasoning, it seems to have been fixed in us, over the span of time, by success; the errors we make are small in comparison to our gain in coping with the world. Like language, analogical reasoning is part of the human difference; logicians may look down upon it, but we could not survive without it.

Allan Collins, the psychologist whose diagram of the memory network we saw in the last chapter (pp. 97–98), has been working for seven years on a theory of plausible thinking that may eventually weave the various preceding threads together. Collins, who works for the Cambridge consulting firm of Bolt Beranek and Newman Inc., talked about his work at a colloquium on plausible thinking at the University of Minnesota one afternoon in 1979 when I was visiting there. A small scholarly man in a baggy sweater, Collins spoke in a low-keyed, understated fashion, but what he said was galvanizing: he was developing a theory that would enable him to simulate, on a computer, not logical reasoning but natural human reasoning—"it would make plausible inferences, and know their limitations." That, I thought, would be a genuine triumph: a computer that was not superhuman but humanlike—a machine that would hold up the mirror to humankind.

Collins had asked a group of subjects some sixty different questions, ranging from whether there are black princess phones to when the subject first drank beer. He was seeking to find out how people reason when they do not have direct and certain knowledge. From their protocols he had so far identified hundreds of types of plausible inference, three of which he singled out as particularly important.

One, he said, is what he calls the "lack-of-knowledge inference." He asked his subjects, "Is the Nile longer than the Mekong River?" and one young man, identified as JB, said, "I think so." "Why?" asked Collins. JB replied, "Because in junior high I read a book on rivers and I kept looking for the Hudson River because that was the river I knew about and it never appeared, and the Amazon was in there and the Nile was in there and all these rivers were in there, and they were big, and long, and important. The Mekong wasn't in there."

Collins extracted from this statement no less than seven different inferential steps, the crucial ones of which could be restated as follows:

> I know the Amazon is extremely long.
> I know the Nile is extremely long.
> I would know the Mekong is extremely long if it were.
>
> I don't know the Mekong is extremely long.
>
> Probably the Mekong is not extremely long.

A second major kind of plausible inference, Collins said, is the "functional analogy." A simple analogy stresses superficial resemblances; a functional analogy looks for cause-and-effect relationships behind the resemblances. "Can a goose quack?" he asked subject BF. "No," said BF, but then began to think about it. "A goose—well, it's like a duck, but it's not a duck. It can honk, but to say it can quack . . . No, I think its vocal cords are built differently. They have a beak and everything, but no, it can't quack."

Collins saw a great deal more in this protocol than appears on the surface. "In analogical reasoning," he said, "the protocols often reveal a thrashing around and searching for knowledge, a matching of similarities, and then a plausible inference from that knowledge." BF had said "no" at once, but then thought of similarities ("it's like a duck"—a simple analogy); then, however, BF thought of dissimilarities (the remark about different vocal cords, Collins said, probably was based on a mental image of the different neck lengths); and finally, on the basis of this functional analogy— which shows a mismatch—BF concluded that a goose doesn't quack.

The third example dealt with plausible inferences about spatial relationships—a common kind of inference in which we draw upon memory for images of two objects or events and try to find some degree of overlap or relationship between them. "Is Texas east of Seattle?" Collins asked JB, who replied, "Texas is south and east of Seattle." "How did you get that?" asked Collins. JB: "I essentially looked at a visual image of the U.S. where I remembered that Seattle was in Washington and know that it's up in the left corner and I know that Texas is in the middle on the bottom. Sometimes you get fooled by things like that, like for example Reno being further west than San Diego. This case I think we're O.K."

In each of these statements, the subjects indicate the degree of their certainty about the correctness of their conclusions; this, Collins said, is an essential feature of human plausible reasoning. We are not, after all, unaware of the hazards of plausibility. Yet it is true that we can be misled by what memory furnishes us to think with. Psychologists Daniel Kahneman of the University of British Columbia and Amos Tversky of Stanford University have found that we tend to use what is most easily available in memory rather than what is most appropriate, and make resultant errors in reasoning. For instance, when Kahneman and Tversky asked subjects whether there are more English words that begin with *r*, or more that have *r* as their third letter, most people said the former, although the latter is correct; they did so because it's easier to think of words by their first letters than their third ones. Similarly, Kahneman and Tversky found that people often make mistakes in judgment due to faulty notions of what is typical or representative. The "gambler's fallacy" is a case in point: when tossing coins, most people think that if heads has come up several times in a row, tails must be about to come up, but it is no more likely to do so than at any other time. (Before you start tossing a coin, for instance, the chance that ten heads will come up in a row is 1 in 1024; if you've just tossed nine heads in a row, however, the chance of the tenth flip coming up heads is the same as ever, namely 1 in 2.) The gambler's miscalculation arises from his or her expectation that the fifty-fifty chance on each toss results, usually, in an alternation of heads and tails; in actual fact, it results in an equal number of heads or tails in the long run but does not govern any particular toss, no matter what has gone before it.

But in the main, Collins concluded, when we reason we are usually aware of the degree of uncertainty in our conclusions. A number of conditions that are part of the thinking process make us either more or less sure of the correctness of our inferences. And indeed Collins himself, at the start of his talk, had mockingly referred to his research project as a "very grandiose scheme" that still had some "bugs" in it—his way of saying that his own reasoning is plausible and that his own conclusions are only probably true.

## Who Can Think Logically? Why Can They?

Despite the pervasiveness of plausible reasoning, it is still true that most of us think in logical, deductive fashion from time to time, and some of us—especially those whose work requires it—do so very often. But such logical competence seems to be very unevenly distributed. The question arises, therefore, as to whether it is a special gift—an unusual genetic endowment, perhaps—or the product of special experiences. In a technological society, where much of the research and methodology that keep us going depends in part on deductive reasoning, this is an interesting question, and one to which new and surprising answers are beginning to appear.

And we need new ones, for the old ones have proven untenable—most notably, the deep-rooted traditional belief that logical reasoning is sex-linked. Plato, long ago, asserted that women were inherently inferior to men in all their mental abilities, of which, of course, reasoning was the highest. This view, or something much like it, has been widely held by men—and women—throughout Western history, and firmly buttressed by Saint Paul's low opinion of woman's judgment and his edict that she was not to teach but "to be in silence." For over two thousand years there were almost no female philosophers, mathematicians, or jurists; this is hardly surprising, since women had no chance to learn to use their minds, but men took the lack of female intellectual achievement to be absolute proof of female mental inferiority. Long after girls had begun going to school, and even after they had started going to college, the view persisted; only a few decades ago national opinion polls showed that most men and most women still thought that women were, by nature, less logical than men. In the 1950s, Broadway audiences still roared with laughter when crotchety Professor Higgins, in *My Fair Lady*, demanded to know why a woman can't be more like a man, accusing women, among other things, of never thinking logically, and of always straightening up their hair but never "the mess that's inside."

And, true enough, school records and intelligence tests had long shown boys to be superior to girls at mathematical reasoning and deductive problem solving. But there was something odd about the data: girls were as good as boys at such reasoning during grade school, and fell behind only after puberty. A generation ago, social scientists and eductors began to think that the explanation had to be cultural rather than biological. At puberty, they said, girls became sharply aware of their classic social roles, and realized that they were expected to be emotional and intuitive rather than rational and that mathematical and logical reasoning was considered masculine. Accordingly—so the new view held—they became inferior at mathematics and deductive reasoning either because they expected to be so, or because they feared that being good in these subjects would mark them as unfeminine.

Recent social trends seem to bear this out. Between the late 1960s and the late 1970s, as the women's movement counteracted women's traditional fears about their own mental abilities (and opened job possibilities to them), the number of women majoring in mathematics or science in college doubled. Unlike earlier studies which showed sharp differences in logical and mathematical reasoning ability appearing after adolescence, a number of more recent studies showed only minor differences developing. Public opinion began to swing toward an egalitarian view: a 1976 Gallup Poll found that a majority of American men thought women were just as logical as men.

And yet social conditioning does not account for all of the differences between male and female thinking observed in the past, or those remaining today. A number of recent studies by neurophysiologists and others have found that there is at least a modicum of structural difference between the male brain and the female brain. Based on observations of brain-damaged people, and on a variety of laboratory experiments involving such activities as listening to words with one ear or the other by means of earphones, researchers are coming to believe that there is somewhat more difference between the right and left hemispheres in the male brain than in the female brain. This might well account for two sex differences in mental function that have no apparent social cause: from infancy on, males have greater visual-spatial ability while females have greater verbal ability. And these differences might explain the greater tendency of males, even as infants, to be attracted to objects they can manipulate—actually or mentally—and of females to respond to social stimuli such as facial expressions and tones of voice.

Do men and women, then, think differently? Many people would like a flat yes or no, but there is no good simple answer. It is undeniable that men and women think somewhat differently, some of the time, and that these differences are largely taught to them; both history and the study of other societies show that what is thought of as typical male and typical female thinking can vary greatly. And yet some part of the traditional difference is built in—not much, but some of it. Male and female brains are organized very much alike, but not altogether; consequently, the average of male performance in logical and spatial thinking remains a little higher than the average of female performance, and probably would do so even in an ideally egalitarian milieu.

Still, the important thing is that this is only an average difference, and a minor one at that. By far the largest part of the male population and of the female population overlap in logical thinking ability. It is something like height: men tend to be a little taller than women, on the average, but nearly all men and women in this country are between five and six feet tall. And many a woman is taller—as many a woman is more logical—than most men.

Even those who still maintain that logic is the model of normal human thinking do not say it is inherited; rather, they picture logical thinking as the product of our first dozen to fifteen years of life, during which we slowly and with considerable effort evolve for ourselves a pattern of logical reasoning in order to make sense of our experiences.

That, in simplest terms, is what Jean Piaget told us. His theory of the mental development of the child, which we will hear more of in Chapter 6, pictures a stage-by-stage progression in the child's ability to organize his or her perceptions of the world and to adapt to that world. The developing brain, interacting with the environment, builds cognitive "structures" such as number, causality, time, constancy, and change in order to deal effectively with the world and to organize its experiences coherently. At each stage the child reconstructs his or her modes of thinking, remaking simple structures into more complex ones. The summit of this developmental process, reached between the ages of eleven and fourteen or fifteen, is what Piaget calls "formal operations"—that is, mature logical thinking. In Piaget's own words:

> The principal novelty of this period is the capacity to reason in terms of verbally stated hypotheses and no longer merely in terms of concrete objects and their manipulation. This is a decisive turning point because to reason hypothetically and to deduce the consequences that the hypotheses necessarily imply (independent of the intrinsic truth or falseness of the premises) is a formal reasoning process.

From then on, Piaget believed, the child thinks in terms directly comparable to those of symbolic logic—implication (if-then), disjunction (either-or), affirmation or denial, and so on, with all the inferences that these syntactical operations permit. We are not born with the patterns of logic innate in our brains, but our developmental history—the interaction between our brains and the environment—inevitably leads to logical thinking as the culmination of mental development.

The evidence for this theory comes from protocols: over many years, Piaget and his colleagues presented children with problems of various kinds, and recorded what they said as they solved them and replied to the examiner's questions. The more complicated problems involved such tasks as determining what factors affect a pendulum's frequency of oscillation (length, weight, height, or force of the push), what factors affect the bending of rods under weight (length, shape, or the material), and so on.

Children under seven make random efforts to solve such problems: such a child, given materials with which to solve the pendulum problem, might first try a long string with a light weight, then a short one with a heavy weight, and so on. From the inconclusive results, the child would reason incorrectly; for instance, because a short heavy pendulum swings faster than a long light one, the child might incorrectly conclude that weight is the important factor. Adolescent children, in contrast, plan and design their experiments properly, and draw logical conclusions from them: for instance, they try different weights with the same length string, then different lengths of string with the same weight, and make legitimate inferences from what they see.

In another problem, children are shown four vials of colorless liquid plus a dropper bottle of reagent. Two of the liquids are chemicals that, when mixed, turn yellow if a drop of reagent is added; a third is pure water; the fourth is a chemical that can prevent the yellow reaction in the first two. The child, not knowing which liquid is which, is asked to find out how to produce the yellow color by using or mixing any of the four liquids. Faced with this complicated problem, one seven-year-old boy typically tried the liquids one at a time, then two at a time, but not systematically; he was unable to reach any conclusion. A thirteen-year-old boy, in contrast, not only went through the various combinations systematically, but speculated correctly that one liquid might cancel the yellow and another have no effect at all. This was a typical speculation: "If this liquid 4 is water, when you put it in with 1 plus 3 it wouldn't completely prevent the yellow from forming. It isn't water [because it does prevent the yellow from forming]; it's some-thing harmful." This "if-then" reasoning, where the consequence turns out to be contradicted by the experiment, is a type of advanced hypothetical reasoning foreign to younger children but the logical implications of which lead to the solution of the problem. And it is only one of a series of logical operations that Piaget says adolescent children use, which, taken together, constitute formal logical reasoning.

Yet all the evidence we have seen in this chapter indicates that most of the time, we do not reason logically about most things. How can one ac-count for this contradiction? There are several possibilities—all of which may be true. For one thing, many people have repeated Piaget's experi-ments but gotten the same results only some of the time; in England and Australia, only half the teenage children tested performed as Piaget's theory says they should. This may mean that Piaget's findings do not have universal validity. Perhaps the children Piaget worked with were a special, privileged group; perhaps the way Piaget and his co-workers asked questions of the children elicited reasoning the children might not have done spontaneously; or perhaps Piaget, who by training was strongly predisposed to favor logic, overinterpreted the children's answers.

A second major possibility is that the children used nonlogical procedures to arrive at answers, but then, questioned by Piaget or a colleague, cast their answers in logical-sounding form. Daniel Osherson, among others, has performed experiments which—like the red-jar-large-jar problem—seem to indicate that this is a common occurrence.

A third possibility, suggested by psychologist Daniel Keating of the Uni-versity of Maryland, is that other cognitive skills may account in large part for the adolescent's ability to solve problems. The adolescent has learned to use memory effectively, to apply rules adeptly, and in general has become an efficient manipulator of information; this, rather than logical reasoning per se, may account for much of the increased ability to deal with reasoning problems.

But there is a fourth argument that is even more persuasive. It acknowl-edges that, through everyday experience and schooling, we gradually ac-quire the rudiments of logical thinking and become capable of abstract de-ductive reasoning, though most of us master it only in part and easily fall into various errors. But the fact that we have more or less learned how to reason logically doesn't mean that this is how we normally reason. We rea-son logically when we are asked to, or when the task before us requires it; the rest of the time, we reason plausibly. Piaget presented his adolescents with problems that require logical reasoning, and, since they solved those problems, concluded that their overall thinking had become logical—that formal thought had become their "generalized orientation" toward the world around them. But that is like saying that because I see you swimming, swimming is your normal way of getting around. Piaget, in effect, threw his adolescents into the water; no wonder he saw them swimming. Had he watched them under ordinary conditions, he might have seen that usually they walk. A good many people doing research in child development told me that there is mounting evidence that this aspect of Piagetian psychology is simply wrong. We may learn to be logical when we need to be, but it is a special set of skills rather than the basic shape of adult reasoning; it is a way we reason when we must, but not the way we naturally reason most of the time.

One other body of recent evidence supports the view that logical reasoning uses skills acquired through schooling and is not, as Piagetians believe, a universal outgrowth of everyday life experience. The evidence comes from cross-cultural studies that reveal how people in preliterate cultures reason.

For ideological reasons, the nature of preliterate peoples' reasoning has long been a hotly debated issue. In 1910 the anthropologist Lucien Lévy-Bruhl asserted that "natives" (preliterate peoples) think in a "prelogical" fashion—in emotional, magical, and wholly personal terms, very much like small children. But others angrily rushed to the defense of the preliterates; Franz Boas regarded Lévy-Bruhl's view as culturally biased, and argued that despite superficial differences, all human beings think in the same fashion.

Boas' ideologically liberal stance marked the start of "cultural relativism"—the view that no culture is superior to any other, only different. This may have been a necessary corrective to the self-satisfied smugness of Victorian anthropology, but in some ways it is simply wrong—and where thinking is concerned, it is more wrong than right. Later fieldwork among primitive peoples repeatedly showed that while we human beings all think alike in some respects, we do not all think in terms of formal logic—not even when we are asked to do so.

Specifically, people in preliterate cultures are strongly disinclined to follow the rules of formal reasoning; they can't see the point of making deductions from premises that aren't part of their own experience, and firmly stick to their own commonsense ways of reasoning despite the best efforts of anthropologists and psychologists to get them to do otherwise. I mentioned earlier that when Sylvia Scribner put to a typical illiterate Liberian farmer a simple syllogism involving a fictional "Mr. Smith," he politely replied, "I don't know the man. . . . I can't answer the question." But forty years earlier, Aleksandr Luria had had the same experience in Uzbekistan, Central Asia. He had said to illiterate Moslem women in that region, "In the far north all bears are white; Novaya Zemlya is in the far north; what color are the bears there?" and got answers such as, "You should ask the people who have been there and seen them," or "We always speak only of what we see; we don't talk about what we haven't seen." And as far away as the Yucatán, psychologist Michael Cole and a colleague got almost identical answers a few years ago from Mayan villagers. Even when such people do answer the question, they may simply refuse to accept a premise they know or believe to be contrary to fact. When Scribner said to one illiterate Vai, "All women who live in Monrovia are married; Kemu is not married; does she live in Monrovia?" her subject, rejecting the first premise, said, "Yes. Monrovia is not for any one kind of people, so Kemu came to live there."

This is only one of the reasons why preliterate peoples, in all the cultures studied, do only slightly better than chance in their answers as to whether conclusions to simple syllogisms are true or false. The word "preliterate" may be misleading; it is not literacy per se, but formal education in general, that makes the difference. In Liberia and in the Yucatán, some of the people had been to, or were in, school—and as little as two years of schooling produces a sharp rise in the ability to give correct answers to syllogisms. The more schooling people have, the better they are at it; those who have gone as far as high school in each culture answer correctly in the majority of cases.

What schooling does is discipline people to accept the ground rules of logic, in particular the rule that says: Base your answer on the terms defined by the questioner. Nonschooled people, not having been trained to think in this special and artificial way, reason in a commonsense, empirical way, relying on personal knowledge (which they insist on adding to the premises given them), or rejecting premises they find unreasonable, or finding rationales to allow them to reach a conclusion they consider sensible. Scribner put this syllogism to Vai villagers:

> All people who own houses pay a house tax.
> Boima does not pay a house tax.
> Does Boima own a house?

Those Vai who had been to school gave purely logical answers such as, "If you say Boima does not pay a house tax, he cannot own a house." But nonliterate villagers were more apt to suppose that Boima did own a house and to look for ways to maintain this stance. "Boima does not have the money to pay a house tax," one said, while another made up a justification: "Boima has a house, but the government appointed Boima to collect the house tax so they exempted him from paying house tax."

Such answers do not indicate stupidity, nor do they mean that preliterate people think in childlike ways. They think in nonschooled ways; that is, they have not learned to accept artificial premises as true and to manipulate them without adding conjectures, personal information, or general knowledge. Perhaps that is why Piagetian studies show that people with little schooling do not possess formal logical ability. But Scribner, Cole, and their colleagues believe that their data show preliterates to be capable of deductive reasoning—on their own terms, which are not those of formal logic. Most of the time they do plausible reasoning, but they can also make logical inferences, provided the premises contain personal knowledge or general commonsense information. Scribner cites this example of a conversation with a Kpelle farmer, which on the surface sounds like logical error:

EXPERIMENTER:  If Sumo or Saki drinks palm wine, the Town Chief gets vexed. Saki is drinking palm wine. Is the Town Chief vexed?

FARMER:  The Town Chief was not vexed on that day.

E:  The Town Chief was not vexed? What is the reason?

F:  The reason is that he doesn't love Sumo.

E:  He doesn't love Sumo? Go on with the reason.

F:  The reason is that Sumo's drinking is a hard time. That is why when he drinks palm wine, the Town Chief gets vexed. But sometimes when Saki drinks palm wine he will not give a hard time to people. He goes to lie down to sleep. At that rate people do not get vexed with him. But people who drink and go about fighting—the Town Chief cannot love them in the town.

The farmer's answer is logically wrong because he ignores the fact that the first premise says that if *either* man drinks palm wine, the Town Chief gets vexed. But taking the farmer's own fantasies about the two men as his premises, one can see, says Scribner, that he did some perfectly valid deductive reasoning. She recasts his statements to show his reasoning:

> Sumo's drinking gives people a hard time.
> Saki's drinking does not give people a hard time.
> People do not get vexed when they are not given a hard time.
> The Town Chief is a person.
> Therefore, the Town Chief is not vexed at Saki.

Thus, it seems that the human mind, by virtue of its neural capabilities and the experiences that each culture feeds into it, can to some extent reason logically. Without education, that reasoning is limited to inferences based on personal experience and common knowledge. With education, we become capable of thinking in more abstract and general terms—concerning ourselves with the inferential relationships, and not the subject matter.

Perhaps the value of formal reasoning, as opposed to plausible reasoning, is just this, that it enables us to escape from the confines of personal knowledge and belief. As Michael Cole puts it, "It's very hard to get traditional [nonliterate] people to see the point of reasoning about things they don't know personally." That's why they do poorly at logical problems, and yet think cogently about things they know; but it is this that limits them and that makes preliterate societies static. Of itself, logic may not generate new knowledge about the world, but it allows us to think in terms of "what if," and so to find out where to go in search of it.

## LET THERE BE ORDER

### Hubris Justified

*So God created man in his own image, in the image of God created he him; male and female created he them.*

How presumptuous, how prideful, of those barely civilized herdsmen-warriors, the nomadic Hebrew tribesmen of long ago, to see themselves as little replicas of the Almighty! And yet in a way that they surely did not realize, their view had some merit: their God had made order out of chaos, and like Him, every human being fashions a world out of the formless tumult, and sets each thing in its proper place. Not, of course, in actuality, but in the model of actuality within the mind, where the inane welter of incoming sense impressions is sorted out, shaped, and assembled into a coherent representation of the outer world.

This genesis, taking place within every human head, is the result of inductive thinking. Deductive thinking, as we have just seen, is an information-rearranging process; we start with statements taken to be true and see what other, more special statements can be logically produced from them. But inductive thinking is an information-extending process; we start with a set of special observations and, by extrapolation or analogy, make a generalization based on them. Deductive thinking extracts the implications of what is already known; inductive thinking expands from the known to the unknown.

Take the matter of human mortality. Deduction, in the form of that well-known perfect syllogism, says that all men are mortal, Socrates is a man, and therefore he is mortal. Induction works just the other way; from individual cases, we construct the overall rule. When my son was four and a half, his pet hamster and his grandfather both died in the same week, and he started thinking about life and death. "Dad," he asked me in a small, tremulous voice, "will Mommy ever die?" I said that she would, but not for a very long while—probably not until he himself was a middle-aged man. Not at all comforted, he next asked, "Will you die?" I said much the same thing. At that point he was able to make the inductive leap: "Then everybody dies?" he asked, knowing the answer. When I confirmed his inductive conclusion, he switched to deductive thinking and, in tears, asked, "Will *I* die?" And though I spoke reassuringly of the long and rich life he would lead before that happened, he flapped his hands in despair and wailed, as we all do in one way or another, "But I don't *want* to die!"

That is one kind of inductive thinking. Another, as we said in the last chapter, reaches its conclusion by analogizing from a set of similarities. Still other kinds make rules out of events that occur in some sequence. In general—and this sentence is itself an inductive generalization based on the preceding three—induction refers to those processes by which we group similar objects into categories, or recognize patterns in events that happen in some regular order.

Without these inductive abilities, we could do no thinking more advanced than that of an infant or a laboratory rat. But all of us have such abilities and use them all the time, though usually we are no more conscious of doing so than we are of forming grammatical sentences when we talk. Notice, for instance, how effortlessly and almost automatically you answer this question:

What word does not belong in this group?

    dog    bush    bee    salamander    jellyfish

Probably the answer seemed to "come to" you after a moment's scanning of the words. ("Bush," you saw, doesn't belong because it's a plant, while all the other words refer to members of the animal kingdom.) In getting to the answer, however, you took several inductive steps too fast to be aware of them. But you may be more conscious of them when solving these somewhat harder problems:

What word does not belong in this group?

    book    magazine    note pad    credit card    newspaper

To what classes of figures (1, 2, etc.) do the test items (A, B, etc.) belong? (See Fig. 32.)

In both cases, the search for an answer is more difficult because the nature of the groups or classes is not obvious; indeed, there can be more than one correct answer, depending on the traits you focus on. In the word group, if you take the common trait to be "things that have printed information on them," "note pad" wouldn't belong—but you could also argue that "credit card" doesn't belong since all the others are objects involved in reading or writing (one doesn't normally read a credit card). In the figure group, class 1 is made up of closed, shaded figures, so C belongs to it; 2, of figures containing parallel lines (or four lines), so A goes here; 4, of solid black figures, so E fits it; and 5, of curved figures, so C goes here. But what of class 3? It's made up of figures containing right angles (D would fit)—but you could also say it's made up of closed, unfilled figures (A would fit).

    Clearly, to answer such problems takes a fair amount of mental work. Later we'll look at the steps actually involved; for now I want only to point out that this process—class recognition or categorization—is one of the ways in which the mind makes order out of chaos. The real-life analogs of

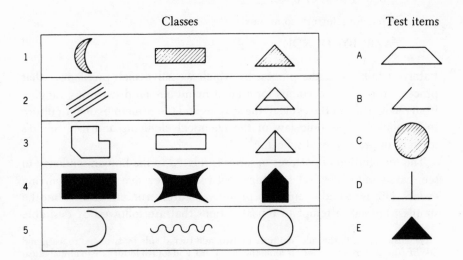

**Fig. 32.**  Figure classification test

these problems are innumerable: they include every act of thought and speech in which we deal with things conceptually (in categories), thus freeing ourselves to think and speak with immense efficiency not just of this oak tree and that oak tree, this squirrel and that squirrel, but of oak trees and squirrels, or of trees and rodents, or of plants and animals.

Another major inductive process is known as pattern recognition. We tend to notice, or actively to seek out, the patterns by which things regularly change, as in these easy examples:

What number comes next?

2 3 5 6 8 9 __

What two letters come next?

AABCCDEEFG __ __

Again, with such simple series problems—these are intelligence test items a ten-year-old can handle—the adult sees the pattern as if by effortless recognition (the answers, of course, are 11 and GH). But with problems at the adult level one becomes aware of some of what goes on in the mind prior to recognition. For instance:

What two numbers come next?

3 6 8 4 8 10 5 10 __ __

What four letters come next?

AZBCBYCDCXDE __ __ __ __

Later I'll talk about the process by which we solve such problems;* that process, in real life, accounts for a great many human discoveries, ranging from recognition of the cycle of the seasons and the principles of agriculture to Mendeleev's periodic law of the chemical elements and each child's mastery of grammatical speech.

The recognition of patterns in series is related to the human tendency to see cause-and-effect relationships between successive or co-occurring events. This is rooted in our most primitive neural structures, for all but the simplest animals attempt to repeat actions that are followed by desirable

---

* The answers: 12, 6 (the rule: multiply by two, add two, divide by two, and repeat); and *DWEF* (the pattern is four letters long: the first, third, and fourth letters are in alphabetical order and this group moves forward by one letter in each four-letter unit, while the second letter moves backward in the alphabet by one letter).

outcomes and to avoid those that are followed by undesirable ones—a basic law of behavior that would never have evolved if there were no regular connections between events and subsequent happenings.

These patterns of behavior are instinctual in simpler creatures, but at the higher levels of evolution they are the essence of learning. Every puppy learns by experience which actions bring a scolding (messing on the floor, biting too hard) and which bring rewards (licking and nuzzling, obeying commands). Even birds learn the art of courtship by making causal connections: in one study, young male parakeets were observed to court females too fast or to approach them in response to the wrong signals, and to get pecked sharply in response; only with time and experience did they become adept at producing more rewarding outcomes.

It is unlikely, of course, that most animals, if any, actually possess the concept of causality; they do clearly perceive, however, that one thing is regularly followed by another, and they behave accordingly. Human beings go much further: they not only acquire the concept of causality as they grow up, but then, as adults—if they are scientists or philosophers—argue about what it really means. While these cognoscenti debate the metaphysics of causality, however, they, like the rest of us, live life on the basis of innumerable expectations about the certainty with which particular events will follow particular others. Flip the switch and the light will go on; hit the ball just so and it will go where you want it to; pay your taxes late and you'll get a bill for interest due, or even a fine; design an airplane according to known principles and engineering specifications and it will fly.

The attribution of causality to an event which is regularly followed by another is so much a part of our everyday thinking that we take it for granted and see nothing extraordinary about it. Nor is there, since the lower animals, too, respond to those regularities; what *is* extraordinary is the human ability to differentiate between events that co-occur and are causally related, and those that co-occur and are not. When we feel ill, we attribute our illness not to any or all of the events of the previous day but only those that are likely to have played a causal part in it. When we feel especially well, we link that feeling not to the date, the positions of the stars and planets—most of us don't, anyway—or other concomitant irrelevancies, but to what we ate, how much sleep we had, the exercise we have taken, and what is going on in our life. Inductive thinking is not simple association but a sophisticated process of hypothesizing, testing, and weighing the evidence; that kind of reasoning is uniquely human.

●

Most people associate inductive reasoning with scientific method, which they assume to be superior to, and somehow different in kind from, everyday thinking. Superior to, it surely is, but different in kind, it is not; indeed, scientific method is only a refinement and elaboration of the natural inductive tendency of the human intellect.

Scientific method does, to be sure, go far beyond natural inductive thinking. Scientists not only look for similarities and patterns, but test whether such regularities are mere coincidences or causally connected by means of such sophisticated techniques as experiments in which only one factor is varied at a time, the analysis of "statistical significance" (the likelihood that the results of any series of observations are not due to mere chance), and so on. But this superstructure is built on the foundation of the mind's natural tendency to sort out the infinite disarray of experience and inductively make sense of it.

The ancient philosophic prejudice in favor of deductive reasoning long kept us from recognizing the central role of induction in comprehending the world around us. Francis Bacon, writing in the early seventeenth century when the sciences were in their sturdy infancy, was the first to recognize the relation of inductive thinking to the scientific understanding of the world, and, in his *Novum Organum,* called induction "the great mother of the sciences." But Bacon did not trust the mind to do sound inductive thinking on its own; he regarded scientific method as a necessary corrective to our natural tendency to distort and misuse the data of our senses.

This note is sounded again and again by later philosophers of science and expositors of scientific method. A tradition running from Bacon to J. S. Mill, and thence to such contemporaries as philosopher Karl R. Popper and psychologists Daniel Kahneman and Amos Tversky, pictures the mind, in its inductive processes, as highly error-prone, and stresses methods of scientific inquiry that overcome this falliblity.

Error-prone the mind is, in some ways—yet most of the time it does rather well in its inductive efforts to make sense of the world. With the advent of cognitive science, we have begun to discover that the mind has built-in methods of self-correction, and that its natural processes are akin to, not at war with, those of scientific inquiry. Scientific method does overcome the mind's natural shortcomings, yet method itself (as Thomas Kuhn points out in his searching analysis of how science develops, *The Structure of Scientific Revolutions*) often holds science fast in outworn theory—until the mind's natural inductive processes lead a few extraordinary scientists to make a breakthrough to a new and better theory.

Natural inductive thinking has led to innumerable wrong conclusions, as witness the history of medicine or of cosmology, but it has eventually produced corrections of most of those errors. The inductive mind, shaping experience into a likeness of the world, fumblingly but regularly arrives at good enough approximations of reality to ensure not only humankind's survival but, for better or worse, its domination of the earth.

## The Concept Maker

Every form of life with a nervous system organizes its experiences to some degree in order to correctly classify unfamiliar objects as harmless or dangerous, friendly or hostile, edible or inedible. But only we human beings assemble our experiences into categories at many levels of abstraction, label the groupings, and then use these conceptual labels as building blocks of thought. Without concept-making ability, we would remain at the mental level of the two-year-old, the grossly retarded adult, or the ape; with it, we become capable of the full range of human intellectual behavior. Concept making is as crucial to human behavior as language and reasoning and is, in fact, so intimately related to both of these that I could well amend my definition of the human difference and make it a cognitive trinity: we are *symbol-using, thinking, concept-making* creatures.

As is true of many other aspects of our mental life, we take concept making for granted; we become aware of what it means to us only under special circumstances, such as when we try to explain the meaning of some high-level category to a child or communicate with a person whose language we do not know.

Imagine that you are the sole survivor of an air crash in Mongolia, a land whose tongue has nothing in common with English. The kindly natives take you to their village, where you have to live until the spring thaw. How are you to communicate with them? You point to things, act out your wants and feelings, and try to learn their words, but you are almost entirely limited to particular objects like "milk," "knife," and "bed," and to specific acts like "drink," "cut," and "sleep." In weeks—or days, if you're verbally gifted— you may be able to talk as well as a two-year-old, but for a long while you will be totally unable to express or to understand any idea much more complicated than "More milk" or "Me sleepy." How would you go about telling them you'd been divorced, are an agnostic, believe deeply in democracy and the presumption of innocence, worry about the world's diminishing supply of fossil fuels, and, being convinced that human beings learn nothing from history, regard yourself as something of a cynic?

Still, it is possible to convey a concept using only specific gestures, provided you and the other person share a certain amount of cultural tradition: in the game of charades, a player can indicate a semiabstract or even abstract concept by making signs for a series of related objects or actions from which his or her teammates inductively arrive at the overall notion. (That technique might or might not work with your Tibetan hosts; in different cultures, the materials of everyday experience can be organized into quite different concepts.)

The same thing is true of American Sign Language (ASL), the signing system used by many deaf persons. ASL, though it is a genuine language with the capacity to convey subtleties of thought and feeling, has few simple signs for concepts, and renders most conceptual terms as a series of signs for three or four related objects or actions plus the sign for "et cetera." For "crime," an ASL user signs "kill-stab-rape-etc."; similarly, "transportation" is "car-plane-train-etc.," "sport" is "football-basketball-track-etc.," and so on. (In their reading and writing, of course, ASL users use the standard conceptual terms available in English.)

As these examples suggest, the major function of concept making is to vastly increase our mental efficiency. Professor Eleanor Rosch of the University of California at Berkeley, a leading investigator of categorization, says that "the task of category systems is to provide maximum information with the least cognitive effort." Professor Marc Bornstein of Princeton speculates that without the economies of categorization our information-processing system would suffer from overload. By way of example, he points out that theoretically there are something like 7,500,000 discriminable colors; if we did not reduce them to a handful of groupings, incoming color information would be an overwhelming visual static in our brains. In an advanced civilization, innumerable areas of knowledge must, like color, be handled in greatly compressed and codified concepts if we are to think and communicate effectively, or at all. (Look back at that last sentence: if I had had to use strings of concrete terms to express such abstractions as "civilization," "knowledge," "color," and "concept," it might have been pages long and all but impossible to follow.)

And there is a second major advantage to categorizing: it enables us to make efficient predictions. Psychologist Jerome Kagan of Harvard exemplifies this by means of a prototypical experiment based on countless actual ones. Take a number of toys, and match each one with a nontoy that resembles it, as in these two lists:

| | |
|---|---|
| cap pistol | revolver |
| building block | brick |
| small rubber ball | orange |
| tricycle | motorcycle |
| drum | barrel |

Now scramble these objects, hide a morsel of food behind each toy but not behind any nontoy, and let an animal—a duck, say, or a rat—loose in front of the display. After it has found food, do the run again, and again. Eventually the animal will learn which of the objects conceal food and which do not—but by rote; it won't generalize, it will not have formed the concept "toy." If you now introduce a new pair of lookalike objects—a basketball, say, and a large cantaloupe—the animal will show no preference for looking behind the basketball. Yet any child of three or four would have formed that concept and known where to look.

But categories are predictive in a more fundamental sense than this. A category is a theory about the nature of the objects in it. If I want to poke up the living-room fire, I use the poker—or similar long metal object—but not a broom handle or anything else that would catch fire. If I want to drive in a nail but have no hammer at hand, I use any heavy, grippable, unbreakable object such as a wrench or even a rock. If I need a doctor, a place to stay for the night, or a new job, I eliminate most of the unsuitable possibilities and concentrate on those that have promise by means of my ability to categorize the candidates.

Thus, the predictive power of categorizing yields efficiency; more than that, it increases well-being and the chances of survival. People often think it sophisticated to speak disparagingly of "pigeonholing," but our tendency to classify new experiences is an essential component of human intellectual behavior and, as much as language and thought, accounts for our huge advantage over all other forms of life in interacting with the environment.

And that's because we pigeonhole our experience in ways that prove functional. We do so, however, not by conscious design and not even because we are taught to, but naturally and inevitably; that is the message of current research in concept formation. Daniel Osherson of MIT, who is currently exploring the nature of the differences between natural categories and artificial ones, put it to me this way: "We can program a computer to deal with any concept, no matter how bizarre or unrealistic—such as, for instance, the class of 'all bachelors and all nonreturnable bottles'—and the computer can handle it, and make valid inferences from it, as easily as any other. But the human mind can't. The computers in our heads simply aren't hard-wired to form or to make use of concepts of that sort but only of natural and realistic ones."

"Hard-wired" is the key word. It's a computer-science term that refers to built-in characteristics—those resulting from fixed circuitry rather than from programming. Applied to human beings, hard wiring refers to innate abilities or, at least, predispositions, as opposed to learned behavior. Osherson was saying, in effect, that the circuitry of the brain develops, under the biochemical guidance of the genes, in such a way as to assemble incoming experience into realistic, useful concepts, and not the converse.

This, the dominant view in cognitive science today, represents a revolutionary break with the behaviorist view of concept formation, which held that the mind has no inherent tendency to compartment its experiences in any particular fashion, and can be trained to do so in many different ways. As proof, behaviorists drew on the data of anthropology, which, in the era of cultural relativism, focused its attention on human differences rather than human uniformities. In English we include in the category "aunts" four biologically distinct kinds of persons (the sisters of each parent, and the sisters-in-law of each parent), but in various other societies these four are grouped in almost every other possible way. Again, we think of colors as falling into physically determined groups, but people in other societies classify them differently from the way we do: for instance, the Shona-speaking people of Zimbabwe divide the spectrum into three color groups, and the Bassa-speaking people of Liberia into only two, whereas we divide it into six.

As for the actual mechanics of how we learn what goes into a category and what doesn't, psychologists conducted hundreds of experiments in concept formation from 1920 on, but, starting from a behaviorist orientation, based them on the assumption that the process is simple and basically associative. In this view, if a child sees a red ball, a red block, and a red toy car, and hears the word "red" in connection with each, the bond between the word "red" and the color will be stronger than the bonds between "red" and any other trait such a size, shape, or texture. Thus, by the strength of association, the child forms or abstracts a concept.

Most of the experiments based on this theoretical model took the form of a kind of game or contest somewhat similar to Twenty Questions. Typically, the experimenter would have a concept in mind, and the subject would figure out, from clues given by the experimenter, what the concept was. Figure 33 shows a set of cards used some years ago in a famous research project of this sort conducted at Harvard by Jerome Bruner and two associates.° The experimenter might decide on a simple concept such as "all shaded figures," a more complicated one such as "crosses with three borders," or a highly complicated one such as "three shaded circles or any constituent thereof—anything with three figures, or shaded figures, or circles, and so forth." The experimenter would then name various cards, one by one, telling the subject whether each one was a positive instance or a negative instance of the concept; the subject was to try to extract the common proper-

° In the actual experiment, the figures were green, red, and black; these colors are represented here as plain, shaded, and black, respectively.

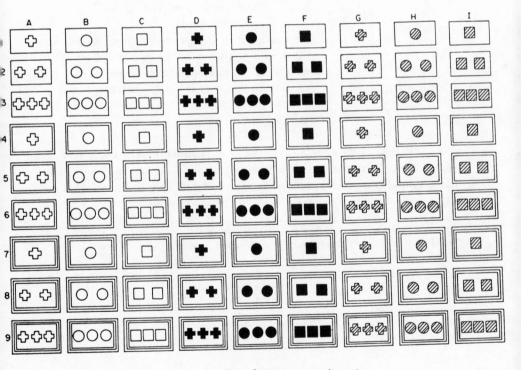

**Fig. 33.**   Raw material for concept-identification experiments

ties and to name the concept whenever he or she had some idea what it might be. A typical protocol might go somewhat as follows:

> EXPERIMENTER: Card F-1 is negative.
> SUBJECT: That might rule out black figures, or squares, or single borders. But I need more information; I can't tell anything yet.
> E.: Card E-1 is positive.
> S.: Well, the only difference between F-1 and E-1 is that E-1 has a black circle, not a black square. Is the concept "one black single-bordered circle"?
> E.: No. . . . Card A-3 is negative.
> S.: That's no help. It doesn't knock out any of my possibilities. Go on.
> E.: Card E-3 is positive.
> S.: Oh, I see—not just *one* black circle. Is the concept "black single-bordered circles"?
> E.: No. . . . Card E-9 is positive.
> S.: So the number of borders has nothing to do with it, and neither does the number of circles. The only thing all three positive examples have in common is black circles. Is the concept "black circles"?
> E.: Yes.*

A good deal of effort was expended in experiments of this sort that revealed a lot about how we identify an artificial concept that someone else has in mind from a series of clues. But this task has little to do with how we

---

* If you'd like to try your own hand at concept identification using these cards, here's a series of identifications to work with. A clue: the concept will include only two characteristics.

> C-6: positive
> E-6: negative
> B-6: positive
> I-4: negative
> B-4: positive
> E-4: negative
> C-1: negative
> C-4: positive
> C-5: positive

The answer: All plain figures with two borders.

usually form natural concepts. The difference isn't just a matter of artificiality versus naturalness; it's a question of *concept identification* versus *concept formation.* In the identification task, there is a right answer, it is quite precise, and the subject tries to identify it by adding and subtracting bits of evidence. But this is nothing like the real-life process by which the child or the adult, experiencing a number of phenomena, sorts them into coherent or useful categories: there is no right answer, the category has no precise boundaries, and the subject creates it by the mental overlapping of percepts that resemble each other in a number of ways.

The new view of categorization emerged from several lines of research, among them studies of how children acquire concept words. When they first begin to talk, they use words for specific objects or actions, but soon begin to form categories—not by subtracting or extracting traits but by generalizing on the traits they see. In fact, *overgeneralizing* on them. The child between one and two will, typically, learn a word like "ball" or "dog" and then call all round things "ball" and all furry, four-legged creatures "dog"; the child is categorizing, and simply needs to have its categories refined.

But it takes time to make these refinements, and even more time to acquire the idea of higher-level categories such as "animals" and "plants" or, higher still, "living things" and "inanimate objects." Eleanor Rosch and several colleagues asked three-year-olds, "Which is different: a Persian cat, a green Chevrolet, or a calico cat?" and the children were able to answer correctly, but when the researchers asked them, "Which is different: a Persian cat, a green Chevrolet, or a cocker spaniel?" the three-year-olds couldn't say; the category "animal" was too abstract for them. Four- and five-year-olds, on the other hand, had no trouble with the question.

Many such experiments have made it clear that concepts are learned, and that high-level, abstract ones are learned later than low-level, basic ones. In either case, however, what is learned is not whatever we choose to teach the child; it is the product of an interaction between incoming experience and the brain's circuitry. We do not possess concepts a priori; rather, the concepts we make out of our experiences are largely predetermined by neural structures. The human brain is concept-prone—but prone to conceptualize experience in certain ways.

This somewhat neo-Kantian view is borne out by recent experiments showing that children do a certain amount of categorizing even before they start to talk. In several different laboratories I watched an ingenious type of experiment designed to test this phenomenon: pictures are projected on a screen placed in front of a baby strapped in an infant seat, while the experimenter, hidden behind the screen, watches the baby's eyes through a peephole, and by seeing what the baby chooses to look at from among the images on the screen, gets indirect evidence as to what is going on in his or her head. One group of researchers showed one-year-old children pictures of furniture, two items at a time; after a long series of such slides, they switched to a slide showing an item of furniture and a face—and almost always the child would look at the face rather than the furniture. But when they showed a series of pairs of faces first, and then a slide of a face and an item of furniture, the children would show a preference for the piece of furniture. Evidently, a one-year-old child is able to categorize the objects he or she sees, and takes more interest in something from a new category than something from an old one.

Even infants only a few months old seem to do simple categorizing. Marc Bornstein and two associates showed four-month-old babies patches of varied blues, greens, yellows, and reds; after seeing a number of examples from one color group, the babies would regularly show a preference for an example from a new color group. Bornstein's conclusion was that hue categorization either is innate, or matures quite soon after birth. In a related observation about four-month-olds, Jerome Kagan says that when they smile at unfamiliar faces, it is because they have already abstracted certain elements of their repeated encounters with people, and classify the unfamiliar face as an instance of a familiar category.

Finally, while cross-cultural studies once seemed to support the behaviorist view of concept formation, recent fieldwork lends credence to the cognitivist view; the variations in how primitive peoples categorize various objects or relationships now seem less noteworthy than the evidence of sweeping similarities. For instance, anthropologist Brent Berlin of the University of California at Berkeley has looked closely at the ways in which people in a dozen different primitive societies categorize plants and animals, and found that they are remarkably similar. For one thing, all people group plants and animals into named classes on the basis of overall perceptual similarity, not on the basis of some dominant trait such as utility or danger. For another, they not only group them in these basic classes, corresponding to genera in scientific biological classification, but have a whole hierarchy of classification, starting with subgroups (similar to our species) within the generalike classes, and moving up to higher-level groupings, the highest of all being comparable to our plant and animal kingdoms. While the various levels of classification by different peoples are not identical with one another or with ours, their systems all are astonishingly similar in this overall hierarchical structure. We often make much of how different from us other peoples are—notably, those we are in conflict with—but cognitively speaking we are all remarkably alike.

It took a revolution in cognitive theory for scientists to see two related facts that seem obvious—now that they have been seen. First, we do not perceive an object as a set or list of distinct attributes (such as having two squares, shaded, and one border), but as wholes (a particular person, chair, house). Second, as a consequence, we do not naturally group objects in categories with sharp boundaries but in clusters that have a dense center and thin out to fuzzy, indeterminate edges, overlapping other categories.

An experiment that illustrates these points was devised a few years ago by linguist William Labov. He showed his subjects the objects in Figure 34 in random order, asking them to imagine each thing in a person's hand, and to name it. If the object was just about as wide as it was deep, everyone called it a cup. The wider it was in relation to its depth, the less it seemed to them to be a cup and the more likely they were to call it a bowl, while the deeper it was, the more likely they were to call it a vase. But these were gradual shifts, not sharp discontinuities in classification. Interestingly, too, these indeterminate boundaries proved to be highly movable: when Labov told his subjects to imagine the objects on a dinner table, filled with mashed potatoes, they tended to call them bowls even if they weren't very wide, and when he told his subjects to imagine them on a shelf, filled with cut flowers, they called them vases even if they weren't very deep. Under all conditions, however, there was a "best" cup—number 5—which everyone called a cup. Thus, Labov's experiment suggests that the center of a natural category is made up of the "best" or most typical instances.

From this study and a number of others has emerged the new view of how we construct categories. We accumulate similar memories in the same region of the memory network, building up a center of greatest density where there is the greatest amount of overlap of similarity. At that center is the prototype—the best cup, the doggiest dog, the average young married man, the typical bird, the ordinary chair; it may be an actual exemplar, or merely a mass of prototypicality. Progressively less prototypical instances are stored increasingly further from the center, until, at some indeterminate distance, there are instances that are no more like that prototype than they are like some other.

A number of kinds of experimental evidence supports the new view of the

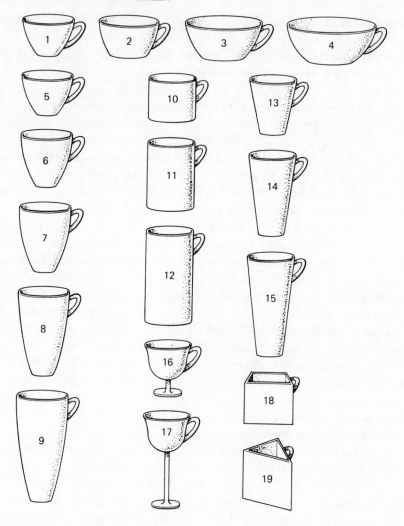

**Fig. 34.** Cup or vase? Materials for a study of the boundaries of concepts

structure of natural categories. We have already seen that when subjects are asked to say "true" or "false" to statements that categorize various objects, they are able to answer fastest for those objects closest to the prototype (they can answer more quickly to "A canary is a bird" than to "An ostrich is a bird"). Experiments with diagrams, stick figures, and dot patterns have yielded similar results: it is easiest to decide what category a typical object fits into, but harder and harder to do so as objects become less and less typical—that is, have less in common with the prototype.

Our method of making categories has a simple and obvious biological rationale: it is the mind's way of representing reality in the most cognitively economical form. In the real world, writes Eleanor Rosch, traits occur in "correlational structures"; observable characteristics tend to go together in bunches. "It is an empirical fact provided by the perceived world," she says, "that wings co-occur with feathers more than with fur," or that things that look like chairs have more sit-on-able traits than things that look like cats. The prototypes and categories that our minds naturally make are isomorphs of clusters of traits in the external world.

This is so simple a notion that you might wonder why it took the revolution of cognitive sscience to discover it. But such was the awesome reputation of Aristotle that his fiats concerning categories—they should be logically defined, clearly bounded, and nonoverlapping—kept us until now from seeing the plain facts about the mind's natural method of sorting out its impressions of the world. And that method, though neither logical nor tidy, is an evolutionary design that maximizes our ability to make sense of our experiences and to interact effectively with the environment.

Nothing about the new view is as sharp a departure from behaviorist doctrines as the notion that the human brain is hard-wired to form certain kinds of concepts even without the benefit of feedback. Where the old view held that children and adults form concepts by being given clues (as in the laboratory experiments) or by being taught ("That's not a dog, that's a cat"), the new view says that we make at least some concepts out of experience wholly by internal neural processes. We may not have innate ideas, as in Platonic and traditional "idealist" psychology, but our minds filter and compile incoming data in such ways that we tend to form some prototypes and categories without help or instruction.

It is, of course, a major advantage of human social life that it greatly speeds up the process of concept formation through the social transmission of both prototypes and boundaries. An example of help with a prototype: I recently heard a father, sitting on a park bench, jokingly say to his little daughter as a Yorkshire terrier went by, "Is that a dog or a dust mop?" and a moment later, patting a stray mutt, tell her, "Now *that's* a real dog!" An example of help with boundary definition: when a neighbor's two-and-a-half-year-old son couldn't get his windup car to run, he said, "It's sick," whereupon his mother explained that "sick" applies to living things but that with toys and such we say "broken." The same process occurs at every age: conceivably any one of us might work out for ourselves the concepts of ratio and permutation, but it is infinitely more economical to acquire them from the high-school math teacher and textbook.

The phenomenon of cultural transmission of concepts is hardly surprising; what *is* surprising is that we ourselves, even if experimentally deprived of any instruction or guidance, can still form categories out of our experiences. This is the finding of a very recent experiment by two young psychologists, Lisbeth Fried and Keith J. Holyoak, of the Human Performance Center at the University of Michigan. They had started with the observation—a part of current perception theory—that the infant gets better at seeing simply as a result of experience and practice; perhaps, they speculated, this might also apply to category formation. Perhaps we get better at sorting out examples of any given kinds of experience merely from a growing recognition of their similarities and differences, without being told whether we're right or wrong in how we sort them. If one could show this in the laboratory, it would strongly support the notion that the mind is predisposed to form concepts out of incoming stimuli on its own.

Holyoak, a tall young man whom I met in his cluttered, manuscript-strewn office, seemed laconic and reserved at first, but rapidly became voluble and enthusiastic as we talked about the experiment he and Lisbeth Fried had conducted. "We made up two geometrical patterns," he said, leafing through an unpublished paper and showing me the designs in Figure 35. "Then, on a computer, we generated a number of distortions of each one, ranging from very minor changes to very major ones. This will give you the idea," he said, turning to the diagrams in Figure 36. "We told our subjects that they were going to see slides of a number of designs by two artists, 'Smith' and 'Wilson,' and they were to try to distinguish the work of one artist from that of the other."

"How were they to know whose work was which?" I asked.

"That didn't matter. They had only to sort the diagrams they saw into two groups. We projected the diagrams one by one, and they would make a choice by pushing one button or another.

"We divided our subjects into two groups. One group got feedback—we told them, after they assigned each slide to one category or the other, whether they were right or not. The other group didn't get any such information. With each subject we ran the experiment until he or she made ten right choices in a row or reached two hundred trials in all. Neither group, you understand, saw the prototypes; they just started sorting out diagrams

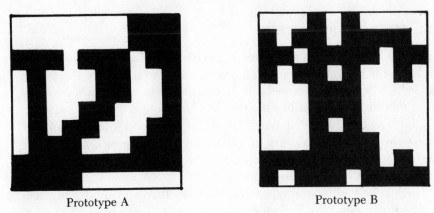

Prototype A                    Prototype B

**Fig. 35.** Designs by "Smith and "Wilson"

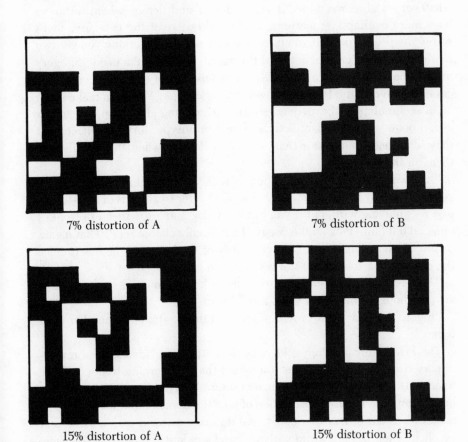

7% distortion of A             7% distortion of B

15% distortion of A            15% distortion of B

**Fig. 36.** Distortions of designs by "Smith" and "Wilson"

on a trial basis and soon got better and better at it. But here's the striking finding—the subjects who got no feedback did as well as the subjects who did get feedback. They formed categories, without being told whether they were right or wrong, just like the people who were told."

"But how could they?" I asked. "How did they know what to look for? Don't children make category mistakes—like calling an acorn a bead or button—until adults set them straight? You're saying that we can make categories correctly without any guidance."

"Right," he said. "Our results show, I believe, that human categorization proceeds naturally. We build up a mental density function of all the features we see in abstract diagrams—or beads, buttons, faces, hats, desks, whatever—and as we do so, it grows denser and denser where instances have more overlapping features. That's the center of the category; that's where the prototype is. If you have two such density functions, you get two clusters—and you can begin to sort things out, putting them in one category or the other. The more an example overlaps the prototype in the center, the easier it is to classify. How do we get that prototype? We often make it out of an accumulation of experiences rather than being given a model. In our experiment, we never identified the actual prototypes for our subjects, but they identified them faster than any other designs when they finally saw them on the screen.

"And we see similar things happening with young children all the time. A very small child may use the word 'doggy' to refer to all sorts of four-footed toys he's playing with, but if you put a toy dog and a toy sheep in front of him and tell him, 'Pick up the doggy,' he'll usually choose right. That means he already has some idea of the centrality of the category; he has to have the category narrowed, but not restructured."

"Apparently, we have a great deal more built-in mental structure than anyone thought only a few years ago," I said.

"Right," he said, "that's my position, and the position of a number of us today."

The Fried-Holyoak study adds a significant bit of evidence for a revolutionary reappraisal of the human intellect that is emerging from cognitive science. It is not a return to the ancient discredited doctrine of innate ideas, but an empirically based description of how the human mind spontaneously makes ideas out of its experiences. We do make a world within—one that excellently mimics the world without—and we do it, to some degree, even if we are not taught to. When we *are* taught, we can recapitulate the evolution of culture within the span of our school years—but we could not do this if we did not have in our heads a highly evolved organ that all but demands that we think in human ways. This interactionist view, neither Platonic nor Lockean—and much more than a simple compromise between them—is surely one of the most important products of cognitive science.

## The Rule Finder

The human mind, as I said earlier, makes order out of its experiences not only by grouping them in categories but by noticing patterns or regularities in the way things happen.

This, too, is a general characteristic of sentient life forms. Every instinctive response of any animal to a stimulus—the sight of food or a foe, for instance, or the sensation of dangerous heat or cold—arose only because the animal's nervous system evolved among regularly patterned events. The tadpole, snapping at a wriggling larva, does so because over the aeons little creatures that wriggled have regularly been edible. But learned behavior in higher animals, too, is possible only because the neural system, as it has evolved, expects there to be regularity in events. The wolf learns to hunt, and the child to speak, on the brain's assumption that what has happened before will happen again when the same circumstances arise.

Indeed, it is not possible to imagine that any form of life, including our own, would ever have arisen if the flow of events obeyed no laws or were unpredictable. Philosophers have labored mightily to prove that the world operates according to reliable causal principles, but they themselves are the proof; modifying Descartes, the philosopher could rightly say, "I exist; therefore the world is orderly."

The assumption that events obey laws is thus built into us at the most basic neural level. In the thinking mind, however, it is transformed from a neural axiom into a purposeful search for rules and patterns. We are, by nature, hungry for rules and take delight in them. One sees this in the year-old baby, endlessly amused by peekaboo, and in the two-year-old, tirelessly piling up blocks and then knocking them down; each is deeply satisfied by the fact that events can be relied upon to follow in the same sequence every time. One sees the same trait, at the other extreme, in the adult motivated by what Einstein called the "passion for comprehension"—the scientist, the explorer, and the philosopher trying to understand how the world runs.

Not only at every age, but at every level of civilization, human beings look for patterns and rules that will enable them to comprehend the world, and so to anticipate outcomes and thereby make their lives more secure and more rewarding. Preliterate natives, drying corn and meat for the winter ahead, are putting to use their recognition of the patterns of seasons, weather, and food metabolism. Civilized human beings, driving to work in their cars, are relying on their culture's accumulated knowledge of the laws governing gases, combustion, electricity, hydrodynamics, torque, and a great deal more.

Pattern finding has very obvious survival value, but it is so deeply rooted in us that we enjoy it even when it has none. We chart quasars and black holes solely for the joy of understanding the mechanics of the cosmos; we find the regularities of rhythm, melody, and structure in music inherently satisfying, though they are not particularly useful; in the games we turn to for recreation, we enjoy trying to perceive the pattern of future events and to mislead our opponent as to what that pattern is. The Thinker, chin on fist, staring into space, is probably not pondering The Meaning of It All but simply trying to figure out how it works.

In investigating how we perceive patterns, cognitive scientists have used a number of simple laboratory tools, the most common of which is the letter or number series like those we saw examples of earlier. Of course, in a simple series like this—

ABMCDMEFM_____

—there are no cause-and-effect relationships, but in our becoming aware of the pattern in such a series we go through somewhat the same mental processes we use to recognize a pattern in a series of events taking place over a period of time.

Herbert Simon is one of the cognitive scientists who have used letter series to explore what people actually do when trying to find a pattern. He and various colleagues analyzed what subjects said while solving such problems, and extracted from their protocols a set of steps that constitute a model of how they did it. He then put this model to the test by writing it out as a computer program; it served very well to spot the patterns in various letter series, thereby lending credence to the model.

According to Simon, the first step we take is to detect the "period"—the length of the repeated sequence. In the case of a rhythmical drumbeat, the rhyming and meter of a poem, or the daily rising of the sun, the period is obvious; we know, without giving the matter conscious consideration, when the next episode will occur. That is how we recognize the period in a very simple, unchanging letter series such as ABCABCABC; visually, we see identical units and know with little effort that the period is three letters long. Even someone unfamiliar with our alphabet would be able to do so, though it might take a little longer. In the case of a slightly more difficult example such as the one given above (ABMCDMEFM_____) the pattern changes; still, it is easy to see that there is a regularly repeated letter, M, by means of which we establish the period as three letters long. It becomes more difficult in the case of a pattern with no regularly repeated letter, such as this one*:

ABRSZBCTUY_____

We hunt around, expecting a regularity. We may notice the two Bs, which suggest a four-letter period, but this doesn't work; finally, we respond to the fact that the first and sixth letters are A and B, while the fifth and tenth are Z and Y; this much orderliness indicates that the period is five letters long.

Next, we turn to the first period and start looking for the rules that generate the symbols within it. According to Simon, we need only a few simple mental abilities to do this, such as the ability to recognize that two letters are the *same* and to recognize that one letter is *next* to (follows) another in a familiar alphabet. (Any two letters in a series might also skip over one, in the alphabet, as in the series ACEGI__; this, however, is *next to next*—a special case of *next*.) At once, we see that in our first period, ABRSZ, the second letter of the sequence is next to the first; that the third skips to a later part of the alphabet but that the fourth is next to the third, and that the fifth skips all the way to the end of the alphabet.

Now we compare the first sequence to the second, to see what rules carry us from one to the other. The first two letters of the first sequence, and the first two of the second sequence, put down side by side, look like this: AB, BC. No problem there; each of these letters in the second sequence is next to the corresponding one in the first sequence. How about the third and fourth letters of each? Here they are: RS, TU; a slightly different rule—next to next—but obvious enough. And the fifth letter of each? Z, Y. That's easy enough, too; next, going backward. The answer, then, to the question is that the series continues as follows: CDVWX.

Such simple processes, Simon maintains, "are sufficient to handle almost any kind of task that can be characterized as pattern identification." That includes everything from clapping hands and singing along to deciphering

---

* Before going further, you might like to try to solve this one and see whether your own way of solving it matches the model I am about to present.

the DNA code, everything from learning how to speak in sentences to predicting the existence of as yet unobserved subatomic particles.

Surely the most important form of pattern recognition is the perception of causality—the recognition that event $X$ is always followed by event $Y$. Everyone knows that the subject of causality is a thorny philosophic problem. (How can we ever know that $X$ causes $Y$ and isn't merely a consistent forerunner of it? What do we mean by "cause" anyway?) But argue about the ultimate meaning of cause as you may, its pragmatic meaning is clear; it is *law*. Ohm's Law, for instance (current equals voltage divided by resistance), says simply that if you apply a current of a given voltage across a conductor of a given resistance, a predictable amount of current will—as a result—flow through it. What, indeed, is any scientific law but a statement of a regularity that implies a necessary connection among the events or conditions named in it?

In cognitive science, the interesting question about causality is whether it is a concept that children slowly acquire over a period of years, as Piagetians believe, or whether it is part of the hard wiring of the human brain. Opinion seems to be swinging toward the latter view; even at a very early age, the preschool child seems not only to notice regularities in the sequence of events but to interpret them causally before possessing words to express this concept.

This has been convincingly demonstrated in a number of "magic experiments" conducted by Rochel Gelman of the University of Pennsylvania and some of her graduate students. Originally, Gelman was looking for something else: she suspected that children have a concept of quantity long before they can count. Even very young children learn to recite a few numbers, but usually they don't know what the numbers mean. They can't add or subtract, and if they count out a number of blocks—say, four—and then are asked to count them again, they may start at the other end and call the first block "four," since that was its name the first time around. Efforts to see whether very young children had a sense of quantity even before they could use numbers correctly had, however, been muddied by the experimenters' use of giveaway words ("more," "same," and "less") in their questions.

Gelman thought of a way around this. It occurred to her that a magician often establishes the audience's expectation as to how many objects he has in his hand or hat, then surreptitiously changes the number and reveals the objects, to the audience's surprise and delight. So Gelman—normally a serious, professorial young woman—began playing tricks on unsuspecting pre-school children.

First, she'd play a game with them. She'd show them two plates, on one of which there were three green toy mice and on the other of which there were two. "This is the winner," she'd say, pointing to the three-mouse plate, "and this one is the loser. Whenever you pick a winner, you get a prize." Then she'd cover the plates with large cans, slide them around, and ask the child to pick the winner. Even three-year-olds quickly learned to choose correctly.

Then came the magic part: Gelman, while distracting the children's attention, would palm or switch a mouse as she covered the plates. When the children picked the one that should have been the winner but wasn't, they were surprised—even if they were only three years old. Their surprise confirmed Gelman's hypothesis that children have a sense of quantity at a very early age; they had not only compared the plates but clearly knew when three became two and two became three.

But there was another and equally important message to be read in their reaction: it indicated that they expected things not to change without cause—yet they had seen no cause. When I visited Gelman, she played for me a videotape recording of one such experiment. On the screen, an impish three-year-old boy with blond bangs was seated at a table on which there were two covered dishes. The voice of a young woman, off-camera, explained about the "winner" and the "loser"; she then lifted the covers and told which plate was which. She explained how they'd play the game; then she covered the dishes, moved them around a little, and asked, "Now, which one is the winner?"

"This one!" he squealed confidently (she had made it very easy for him to follow). She lifted the lids, revealing that he was right, and he laughed with joy.

"Oh, you're *right!*" she said. "You get a prize! You can take any one thing from this box." And she offered him a carton of small trinkets.

After a number of trials, in which he was always right, it was time for the magic phenomenon. As she covered the plates, she distracted the child by saying something about the prizes he had put aside; while he was looking away, she removed one mouse from the plate of three. After sliding the covered plates around again, she asked him which was the winner. He confidently pointed to the one that had had three mice and crowed, *"That* one!" When she uncovered them, he stared in disbelief and looked up at her wonderingly.

**Fig. 37.**  The Snoopy-doll box, phase one

"What happened?" she asked him.

Perplexed, he hunched up his skinny little shoulders toward his ears; then, trying to make sense of the mouse's disappearance, he said, "It got tooken away!"

A very small episode—but in this minuscule grain of behavior one can see a world of mind. As young as the child was, he knew that a toy mouse, or any object, doesn't just disappear; something or someone *makes* it go away. A number of similar magic experiments have repeatedly shown that small children think in terms of causal explanations of changes in the number of mice: "You did it!" they say, or "Something happened," or "It fell off," or "It's underneath the plate." They don't simply take the disappearance to be a natural or causeless happening.

Recently, one of Gelman's graduate students, Merry Bullock, conducted a study for her doctoral dissertation that used another kind of magic trick to explore more deeply the emergence of cause-and-effect thinking in very young children. Bullock showed me a drawing of the apparatus she had designed for her experiment (Fig. 37). "I use two hand puppets," she said, "each one of which drops a ball into one of these runways. The child can see the balls run down and then disappear. A second after the ball on the left side disappears, a Snoopy-doll jack-in-the-box pops up in the opening in the middle. (Actually, we—Dr. Gelman and I—make it pop up by means of a solenoid.) The ball on the right side, however, rolls down just *after* the Snoopy has popped up. We wanted to test a belief of Piaget's that young children are as likely to think a cause comes after the effect as before it. But after the children had seen the demonstration, if we asked them how to make Snoopy pop up they always told us that the left-hand puppet should drop its ball in the slot. It was plain that they thought that the ball that rolled down the runway beforehand was the one that caused the doll to pop up. They had the temporal relationship of causality correct.

**Fig. 38.**   The Snoopy-doll box, phase two

"Then we went further—we tried to find out if they had any concept of physical mediation. Did Y merely follow X, or was there some physical connection between them? So the box, which was made in three parts (but didn't look it), was now pulled apart, on the tabletop [Fig. 38].

"This time, when the ball rolled down the left-hand runway in the separated part and disappeared, and the doll then popped up, you could just *see* how surprised they were. They laughed, they giggled, they wriggled. When we asked them how the ball did it, our four-year-olds and five-year-olds invented ways; they'd say things like, 'When I wasn't looking, the ball slided over,' or 'The ball turned invisible,' or 'It's a trick, right?' Three-year-olds couldn't do that (or maybe we just haven't been able to get them to), but their reactions made it clear that they, too, think in terms of causal relationships, and are surprised by a bizarre event—a seemingly uncaused event."

"If they think in such terms even before they can voice them," I said, "doesn't that imply that the child is prepared in advance to see the world in causal terms even before it is taught the meaning of causation by adults?"

"I think we *are* somehow built to connect events causally," she said. "On the basis of the evidence, it's hard to see how one could argue otherwise. An adult, observing a given sequence of events, can easily say 'This is the cause and that is the effect, and this is why.' Show the same sequence to very young children, and even though they can't offer good explanations, they will exhibit very reasonable responses. The neural mechanism expects a connection between events, and you can see this in children even younger than three-year-olds. The other day I watched a two-year-old girl with a jack-in-the-box, and she would crank it until the jack popped up, and then put it back in, and crank again, and repeat this over and over. I would argue that she's trying to find out how one thing is related to another."

And that aptly describes in the simplest of terms one of the distinguishing features of the human intellect.

•

Yet our grasp of causal patterns is limited. It was only yesterday, in evolutionary terms, that we began to talk and to think, and most of us are not yet very good at handling complicated symbolic patterns. A small minority of human beings—perhaps they are the most highly evolved—can grasp concepts and recognize patterns that the rest of us find too hard or elusive. But they are not the norm, we are; it is normal to find certain concepts hard to grasp, and even when grasped, hard to remember and use.

Most of the concepts and patterns that are difficult for the average person to grasp or use are "nonintuitive"—that is, they cannot be, or are not easily, derived from everyday experience, and therefore are not part of the normal mind's repertoire. Probability is one such; most people can intuitively see the answer to only the simplest problems involving probability. An example: in a group of forty people, picked at random, what are the odds that two of them will have the same birthday? Most people feel that the odds must be quite small; in fact, they're quite large. For though there are only forty people, there are 780 ways those people can be paired up, and the odds, according to probability calculations, are *eight to one* that one such combination does exist.

The concept of correlation, which is related to that of probability, is likewise nonintuitive and not part of most people's thinking, according to research studies by psychologists, mathematicians, and educators. Correlation is the tendency of two phenomena to vary together. If you measure children's height and how much milk they drink, you will find that, on the average, taller children are also bigger milk drinkers. That's a correlation; it *suggests* that milk drinking causes growth, but does not *prove* it absolutely, for it deals only in averages. Some children who drink a lot of milk are short, some who drink little are tall; the correlation shows only that milk drinking is *likely* to be connected to tallness, and to be a cause of it. It takes further research to find out if there is or is not such a causal relationship. Milk drinking might tend to increase height, but it is also possible that children who are naturally taller drink more milk because they have a greater capacity; we need more evidence, based on other kinds of studies, to know for sure.

Moreover, many correlations exist that are not due to any causal connection in either direction between the two phenomena; both may be the side-by-side results of some other cause. There is a correlation between divorce (or desertion) and delinquency in the male children of the broken families, but divorce doesn't produce the delinquency: both of these phenomena are higher in low-income families than in middle- or high-income families, and both, apparently, are effects of poverty rather than being related to each other as cause and effect.

Perhaps the hardest notion to grasp about correlation is that while it always suggests a cause-and-effect connection to us, it may involve nothing more than an accidentally lopsided sample—yet the bigger the sample and the more random it is, the more we can believe that there really is some causal relationship. If I ask the first three redheaded people I meet whether they like oysters, and none of them does, I had better not leap to any conclusions; the fact that all redheads in this sample dislike oysters might easily be happenstance. If I ask a hundred redheaded people, and almost all of them dislike oysters, the chance is much smaller that my finding is accidental. Even so, it isn't a correlation unless I compare it to data on how blonds and brunettes feel about the matter. If just as many of them are antioyster, redheadedness has nothing to do with it; only if there is a marked difference among the groups can I suspect some connection between hair color and oyster dislike.

This concept is very difficult for most people to comprehend, as experiments have often shown. In one of them a Swedish researcher gave a group of nurses 100 cards supposedly representing data extracted from the files of 100 patients. Each card said only whether the patient did or did not have a certain hypothetical disease and did or did not have a particular hypothetical symptom. When the nurses totaled the data, they came up with the following figures:

|  | *Patients with disease* | *Patients without disease* |
|---|---|---|
| *Patients with symptom* | Disease and symptom: 37 cases | No disease, but symptom: 33 cases |
| *Patients without symptom* | Disease but no symptom: 17 cases | Neither disease nor symptom: 13 cases |

The question was: Is there a relationship between the symptom and the diesase? Eighty-five percent of the nurses concluded that there was, pointing out that there were more cases with both disease and symptom (37) than in any other category, or that more than twice as many sick people had the symptom (37) as didn't (17).

But the nurses were wrong. For even among people *without* the disease, the same majority had the symptom (33 had it, 13 didn't). If the proportion is the same in both cases, there's no variance of one factor when the other factor varies; that is, there's no correlation. Look at the data the other way: more people *with* the symptom were sick than were well (37 as compared with 33); but similarly, more people *without* the symptom were sick than were well (17 as compared with 13)—so there's no covariance, no correlation.

Even when two things do vary together, they may not be causally related unless there are no other variables; this is why experiments involve control, in order to vary only one thing at a time. But in everyday thinking, we frequently draw conclusions from a covariance without noticing that other covariances exist. A person who often feels poor the morning after a big party may attribute his or her condition to the overuse of alcohol—but research in alcohol use has shown that even those who drink relatively little often feel poor the morning after, due to party fatigue. The accident rate for small planes is far higher than that for large planes; the intuitive assumption might be that small planes are less safe than large ones, but there is another and more significant variable—small planes are often piloted by amateurs flying for pleasure, while large ones almost never are.

Another reason we often draw faulty conclusions about cause-and-effect relationships is that most of us fail to grasp, or at least to apply, the concept of "regression to the mean." This means that on the whole, an average sort of result is the most likely to occur at any time; thus, after an unusual event, things tend to return to the average. The child of a genius is rarely a genius; after an unusually successful first novel, a writer's second one is often somewhat less successful; the underdog in a tennis tournament who scores an upset victory over a better player is likely to play somewhat less brilliantly in the next match.

This may seem obvious, yet we regularly fail to use the concept in our thinking and, instead, attribute the regression to some coincidental factor rather than to normal distribution. Kahneman and Tversky, when they were at Hebrew University in Israel, were struck by the curious belief of Israeli flight instructors that punishment was more effective than reward in pilot training. Upon investigation, they found that certain instructors had noticed that if a student performed some maneuver unusually well and was praised for it, he was likely not to do as well the next time, while if a student performed the maneuver very poorly and was harshly criticized, he was likely to do better the next time. But according to the principle of regression to the mean, very good and very poor performances are usually followed by more average ones; the praise and criticism had little or nothing to do with it.

Such mislabeling can have grave consequences. Social psychologists Richard E. Nisbett and Lee Ross, in their book *Human Inference*, point out that measures taken to stem a crisis like a sudden increase in crime or disease, or a sudden decrease in sales or rainfall, will, on the average, appear to have had more impact than is the case. The result: "Illusions of personal or social control are likely to result." And not just illusions, but their consequences: wrong theories and inappropriate actions. Many harmful governmental practices, foreign policies, magical beliefs, and superstitions owe their existence to the human tendency to infer that certain actions produced a desired result, when the result was due simply to the normal tendency of events to regress from the unusual to the usual.

How common are such errors? Common enough: one could compile a treasury of human miscalculations resulting from our limited ability to deal with nonintuitive concepts. Reading the Nisbett and Ross book, indeed, one might wonder how any of us manage to survive. But against such a compilation of our miscalculations one must weigh our successes. Most of us do survive, and the evidence of many experimental studies of inference show that in real-life situations, we tend to correctly identify the real cause even when there are a number of coincidental and possible causes. Nisbett and Ross themselves, summing up these studies, conclude that in general, most of us manage to use causally significant data in such a way as to make good predictions a fair amount of the time, and to get through our days without making any serious inferential errors, or at least none with serious consequences.

Still, our ability to do causal analysis well enough to get us through daily life does not explain how we human beings have managed to comprehend and to manipulate the world. It cannot account for our mastery of fire, metalworking, agriculture, our ability to build houses and cities out of whatever material is at hand, our invention of wagons, ships, and airplanes, our creation of tools and technology that have changed the face of the planet, our accumulation of an immense body of scientific knowledge, our fashioning of hundreds of different functional social systems.

How do we do all this if our ability to perform causal analysis is both limited and imperfect? We do it, Donald Norman of the University of California at San Diego suggests, by being "excellent inducers. We leap to correct answers before there are sufficient data, we intuit, we grasp, we jump to conclusions despite the lack of convincing evidence." The faults in our thinking about causation are what enable us to guess how things work, on the basis of inadequate knowledge. "That we are right more often than wrong," Norman says, "is the miracle of human intellect."

## The Hypothesist

But if we can leap from inadequate data to good answers, how do we know which data to notice in the first place? Out of the profusion of objects and events we might pay attention to, how do we choose which to attend to before having any reason to think they form a category or obey a law? Where do we get our notions of what to look for? This may well be the most interesting question about inductive thinking, and the most fiercely debated.

In a few cases, it is obvious how we know: the infant whose attention is commanded by various smiling faces can hardly help grouping them in its mind. But in most situations, infant and adult alike are bombarded by such a wealth of sense impressions that there must be various mechanisms in their minds through which they single out those things that can be classed together or that obey a law. If I say to you, "Look at this paragraph for fifteen seconds and tell me what you see," you will see everything—and nothing; but if I say, "Look at this paragraph for fifteen seconds and notice how many words in it have six or fewer letters," the short words will seem to stand out and you will have a good idea what proportion of all words they make up. In a comparable way, we somehow direct our own attention toward particular or significant sets of sense impressions; we look not at everything in the world around us, but at those things we have in some way decided to look at. We begin with hypotheses, rather than develop them from our experiences.

The philosopher Sir Karl Popper, who lectures at the London School of Economics, sometimes invites his students to take part in a little experiment which, he says, "consists in asking you to *observe*, here and now." The students look a little unsure of what to do. "I hope," says Sir Karl, "you are all cooperating and observing"; there is a rustle of discomfort. "However," he adds in a more jocular tone, "I fear that at least some of you, instead of observing, will feel a strong urge to ask: *What* do you want me to observe?" Laughter and relief wash over the room.

Sir Karl's point is that the mind does not passively take in everything around it and get organizing concepts or principles through induction; answers, he says, do not emerge unbidden from a mass of data, but in response to questions. Accordingly, he regards the belief that scientific investigation consists of unprejudiced observation of the facts as pure nonsense. "There is no such thing as an unprejudiced observation," he asserts. "All observation is an activity with an aim (to find, or to check, some regularity which is *at least* vaguely conjectured). . . . There is no such thing as passive experience. . . . Experience is the result of active exploration by the organism, of the search for regularities or invariants."

He has some impressive allies. Darwin wrote that "all observation must be for or against some view, if it is to be of any service," Einstein said that "it is the theory which decides what we can observe," and Nobel Laureate Sir Peter Medawar recently commented that the purpose of experiment is not to find facts but to test a hypothesis.

But this view runs counter to a long tradition of scientific objectivity and to the generally accepted theory of inductive learning. Francis Bacon, the first great expositor of scientific method, warned at great length against letting preconceptions distort what we perceive, and the fictive Sherlock Holmes, whose opinions on investigation are far better known than those of the real Sir Karl Popper, said, "It is a capital mistake to theorize before you have all the evidence. It biases the judgment." Moreover, as we have seen, the neural system is predisposed to notice regularities among its perceptions without apparent effort or active exploration; recall the one-year-old, growing bored with pictures of furniture and preferring a picture of a face, or the four-month-old, smiling at unfamiliar but friendly people.

Actually, cognitive science furnishes evidence on both sides of the dispute; both views, when suitably qualified, appear to be true. The laboratory studies of preschool children and infants show that our neural systems do spontaneously group similar objects and notice regularities in the sequence of events, but studies of more advanced inductive tasks show that we cannot form highly abstract concepts or perceive obscure causal connections unless we have some idea what to look for, some hypothesis to filter and focus our perceptions. One can see this even in the case of a simple number series such as 1 2 4 8 __, where the very question "What number comes next?" embodies a hypothesis (it implies that there is a rule at work), and where one assumes—without being told—that the numbers are those of our usual decimal system (rather than, say, some alternate such as a base-12 system) and so occur in the same sequence and signify the same quantities that we are accustomed to.

Thus, both sides in the dispute are right; at times we let experience wash over us until a hypothesis emerges, but at other times we start with a hypothesis and use it as a searchlight with which to illuminate certain kinds of evidence. We are all hypothesists in two senses: we are hard-wired to automatically make order out of our experiences, but we also learn to deliberately create hypotheses as a way of seeing more clearly the regularities that exist in the world outside. We all have a little of Francis Bacon in us, and a little of Albert Einstein.

Both Bacon and Einstein, however, despite the difference in their orientations, thought about hypotheses in a way that is alien to most of us. We tend to look for evidence that confirms a hypothesis, while they knew that to prove it one must also look for evidence that would, if it existed, destroy that hypothesis. Here is Bacon on the point, witty despite his cumbersome Elizabethan prose:

> The human understanding when it has once adopted an opinion . . . draws all things else to support and agree with it. And though there be a greater number and weight of instances to be found on the other side, yet these it either neglects and despises, or else by some distinction sets aside and rejects. . . . And therefore it was a good answer that was made by one who when they showed him hanging in a temple a picture of those who had paid their vows as having escaped shipwreck, and would have him say whether he did not now acknowledge the power of the gods,—"Aye," asked he again, "but where are they painted that were drowned after their vows?"

Einstein's general theory of relativity had plenty of confirming evidence, but Einstein himself deliberately sought a test that could disprove it. The theory predicted that light, though it seems to travel in a straight line, would be slightly deflected from its path if it passed through a powerful gravitational field where space was warped. Accordingly, Einstein predicted that during the eclipse of the sun in 1919, light from stars appearing near the edge of the sun—where ordinarily they are invisible—would be bent by the sun's gravity, making them look slightly out of place. If this proved wrong, the theory would be demolished, no matter how many other observations fit in with it. A British expedition headed by Sir Arthur Eddington went to the island of Principe off Africa, measured the position of the stars during the eclipse, and found them out of place as predicted. Einstein's potentially disconfirming test had proved his theory correct.

Most of us, however, do not think in this fashion; we look for and remember those instances that bear out our belief, but not those that do not, a tendency cognitive scientists call "confirmation bias." It is easiest to see this in the case of people with mystical or irrational hypotheses. Believers in astrology tell us endlessly about the various persons they know who are typical Pisces, Virgos, and so on, but say nothing—and perhaps remember nothing—about those who do not fit the patterns. Believers in ESP, according to research studies by psychologists Dan Russell and Warren Jones, have selective memory: they tend to forget whatever casts doubt on their beliefs and to remember what supports them. Russell and Jones gave both believers and skeptics material to read, some of which confirmed and some of which disproved the existence of ESP. Believers remembered confirming materials accurately 100 percent of the time but negative materials only 39 percent of the time; skeptics remembered both kinds accurately about 90 percent of the time. So, too, we often hear of some person who dreamed that his or her father was dying, and, later, discovered that it had indeed happened at about the time of the dream—but how often do we hear about the many dreams of such events that did *not* take place? We hear of people who were cured by the touch of a faith healer, but when do we ever see a report as to how many of those whom the healer touches get better and how many do not?

We strongly tend toward confirmation bias even about nonmystical hypotheses. Most Americans believe, for instance, that almost anything a child does is the result of parental behavior. If the child turns out badly, the parents torment themselves by asking, "What did we do wrong?" If the child turns out well, they are proud of themselves. It never occurs to them that much or most of the end result is due to a number of other forces, both social and genetic, or that parents, while influential, can scarcely be omnipotent if children of the same home turn out as different from each other as they often do—and, indeed, begin to manifest some of those differences in their first hours of life.

So, too, with much social theorizing. Who remembers that his or her political views have been borne out by events only part of the time, and contradicted the rest of the time? Hawks maintain that getting tough is the way to gain our national ends—and although getting tough has failed us at least as often as it has succeeded, they never qualify their views. But doves, too, seem chronically unable to admit that at times—including critical ones—peaceful and nonresistant policies have failed to achieve their goals. The conservative believes none of the charges that this country has supported and connived with corrupt or brutal regimes elsewhere; the radical believes every such charge, even when it comes from the most suspect sources. The advocate of harsh treatment of criminals remembers none of the evidence that it doesn't reduce crime; the advocate of prison reform remembers none of the evidence that even humane prisons rarely rehabilitate their inmates.

A variety of studies suggest that confirmation bias may be a general characteristic of human thinking; only training and deliberate effort enable us to avoid it. Among the simplest of these studies is Wason's little experiment, described in the previous chapter, in which he asked people which of four cards, marked A, D, 4, and 7, they had to turn over to test the rule, "If a card has a vowel on one side, then it has an even number on the other side" (see Fig. 24, p. 127). As you will recall, almost all of Wason's subjects turned over either the A, or the A and the 4, looking for confirmation of the rule, while almost none of them turned over the 7, looking for disconfirmation, or could see why this was absolutely necessary.

In a more complex experiment, a team of researchers at Bowling Green State University had their subjects sit before a video screen on which there appeared assortments of small triangles, squares, and circles that were either solid or crosshatched. By using controls, the subject could "fire" a particle (a moving dot) across the screen at any of them; the particle would either penetrate the figure or be stopped by it. The subjects were asked to test the hypothesis, "Triangles stop the particle," and to choose displays (which had varying assortments of targets on them) to shoot at; almost always they chose those with triangles, but rarely any of those with which they could have tested other alternatives to see if the hypothesis needed to be broadened.

In two disheartening studies of psychotherapists in training, a research team found that once the trainees had made a preliminary diagnosis of a patient's condition on the basis of personality tests, they could then look through a folder full of information contradicting the diagnosis without changing their opinion. They would explain away the negative evidence, or fit it in, emerging with the original diagnosis more firmly entrenched than ever. In other words, they had sought only to confirm their hypothesis—to such an extent that they could not see contradictory facts for what they were.

Sociologists and psychologists offer similar evidence from outside the laboratory. Many millennial cults have been studied in which a leader has predicted the arrival of a messiah or the end of the world; when the event does not take place, the cultists almost never lose faith, but accept their leader's explanation of the Almighty's change of plans and believe in the leader all the more strongly. Similarly, people addicted to dangerous practices—free flight, mountain climbing, drug taking—explain away the mishaps that occur to others ("They couldn't handle it" or "That was bad luck") and focus instead on the positive data ("There are people who've been doing it for half a lifetime and never had any trouble").

How can a flaw of such seriousness be characteristic of human thinking? If we consistently pay attention only to evidence favoring our hypotheses, and ignore or rationalize evidence contradicting them, why have we been so successful a species of life? An answer existed even before cognitive science asked the question: history is a record of mistaken ideas—eventually recognized as such and corrected. Stubborn or willful or biased as we are, we are not incorrigible. The human mind becomes aware of most of its own errors soon enough to forestall disaster; we may not learn to think in terms of seeking disproof of our beliefs, but eventually we generally notice such disproof and take it into account.

Some recent experimental evidence does, in fact, show that while we may not normally look for evidence contradicting our hypothesis, if we do stumble across it we tend to use it to correct our belief. In the Bowling Green experiment, subjects were sometimes presented with a target array that did not include a triangle; when they shot the particle anyway, it was stopped by one of the figures—and with this clear evidence against the hypothesis that triangles alone were impervious to the particle, subjects changed their minds.

Wason and Johnson-Laird conducted an experiment in which subjects had to figure out the rule behind a set of three digits; subjects guessed (usually wrong, at first), then got additional sets of numbers and made further guesses until they got it right. Many of them seemed intent on verifying their first hypothesis rather than trying others—yet after enough negative evidence, they would stumble their way to the right answer. They did not go about the search in an ideal way, but they did eventually see their mistakes and solve the problem.

Of course! How could we human beings solve any problems or figure out how anything works if our confirmation bias kept us from ever abandoning or correcting a wrong hypothesis? Each time you do a crossword puzzle, decipher a cryptogram, or solve a maze, you are living proof that, time and again, you do recognize a wrong hypothesis as being wrong, and try another. The trouble with the laboratory studies aimed at showing how biased we are toward confirmation is that the experimenters themselves have a bias toward confirming their hypothesis; they look at results of experiments set up to show us at our mental worst, seeking only proof of our beliefs. But in real life, disproof is forced upon us, and we do recognize it as such, sooner or later, and adapt. When we fail to adapt, it's likely to be in cases where clinging to the wrong hypothesis makes no practical difference.

What is true of each of us is true of scientists and science. In *The Structure of Scientific Revolutions,* Thomas Kuhn shows that science advances slowly and with difficulty against the stubborn resistance of all who have a stake in currently received theory. The Copernican view of the cosmos, he says, made few converts for almost a century after Copernicus' death; Priestley, though he was the first to isolate oxygen, never accepted the oxygen theory, clinging, instead, to his belief in the nonexistent substance "phlogiston"; and Lord Kelvin just as stubbornly refused to believe electromagnetic theory. Max Planck once said that a new scientific truth does not triumph by convincing its opponents but by outliving them and being accepted by a new generation.

How, then, does a new theory ever arise? As Kuhn pictures the process, scientists use an accepted theory to work out various problems, and, from time to time, are puzzled by certain anomalies—failures of data or events to fit the theory. They either ignore them or make minor adjustments in theory or procedures to account for them. But some anomalies cannot be assimilated, and as their number grows, the scientific community begins to argue about what they mean and to focus research on them, though without changing its theory. But at last, one or a few imaginative individuals weave a new fabric of hypotheses and concepts that incorporates all of what had been previously known plus the existing anomalies; Kuhn calls this process of reconceptualization "scientific revolution." Even though the new theory may not be immediately accepted, it eventually wins out because it is a better fit; it accounts for the anomalous evidence that had long bothered even those who refused to doubt the old theory.

That is what happens within each of us in a matter of seconds when we are solving a crossword puzzle; over a span of months or years when we are acquiring new views in college; and over a matter of decades when we modify our political philosophy or religious beliefs. For average people, like scientists, are prey to confirmation bias—and, like scientists, eventually recognize their erroneous hypotheses for what they are, and cast about for better ones.

If we are far from ideal as inductive thinkers, it is not that we are stupid or even that we are badly engineered; if the parts of our intellect work relatively well but not ideally, it may be because that is best for the intellect as a whole. For as Herbert Simon has shown on the basis of game theory and programming theory, if the parts of a complex system are designed to seek the best possible solutions to their problems, they may not lead to satisfactory solutions for the system as an entirety.

We have already seen that our short-term memory could be far better, but only at the expense of our ability to pay attention to what is urgent, and that our deductive reasoning could be more logical, but only at the expense of realistic good sense. So it is with inductive reasoning. If, as might seem ideal, we abandoned every hypothesis at the first sign of error, we would discard many correct hypotheses because of faulty observations; if we sought only to disprove every hypothesis, we would never accumulate the confirming data that represent the real value of a good theory—its ability to predict what *will* happen rather than what won't.

A splendid paradox, indeed: evolution has produced in us an intellect that is imperfect throughout and finds only tolerable solutions to its problems—and is, therefore, more successful than a perfect design would have been.

# THE ORIGINS OF THE MIND

## Ancient Argument, Modern Compromise

A cognitive scientist who studies the adult mind is in somewhat the same position as an archaeologist who studies the Easter Island statues or the Stonehenge megalith: the archaeologist can measure and describe the objects in detail, but can only conjecture how prehistoric peoples, with their simple hand tools, could have moved, shaped, and erected such mighty stones—or toward what end.

But it is possible to watch the monument of mind being constructed: if one observes the mental processes of infants and children, one sees the adult mind being assembled out of the raw materials of brain and experience. The study of mental development is an area of cognitive science that requires great patience, considerable ingenuity, a genuine fondness for children, and a willingness to engage in various activities that may, on the surface, seem undignified, trivial, or even silly but that have serious and even profoundly important goals. A few examples:

—The eminent Swiss child psychologist Jean Piaget—this scene goes back some years—squats on the floor with a five-year-old boy who is playing with marbles. Piaget, seeking to explore how and when children begin to think in terms of rules and procedures, says to the boy, "I used to play a lot but now I've quite forgotten how. I'd like to play again. Let's play together. You teach me the rules and I'll play with you."

—In a small child-study laboratory at Harvard—a playroom, really—a young woman is talking to a two-year-old girl in a high chair. The young woman puts in front of the child a toy car, a toy animal, and an oddly shaped piece of wood; then, offhandedly, she says, "Give me the zoob." The child, after a moment, picks up the piece of wood and hands it to her. The experimenter is studying the ways in which a child learns new words; her hypothesis is that one way is by reasonable inference—which the child has just demonstrated, since she already knew what the two toys were and so took "zoob" to be the name of the only unfamiliar object before her.

—A one-year-old boy is seated before a miniature stage; from behind it a hand pushes a toy dog into view, and just as the baby is about to reach for it, the curtains close, hiding the toy. The researcher is no petty sadist, of course; he is seeking to find out at what point an infant realizes that a hidden object still exists.

—A three-day-old infant sucks on a pacifier wired to an apparatus that records the intensity of sucking, while a psychologist plays a recording by a string ensemble, and then follows it with one of a woman talking. The recording machine clearly shows a more favorable reaction, in the form of stronger sucking, to the sound of the human voice than to music; the response to human speech may, therefore, be innate—a fact that carries cognitive science yet one more step away from behaviorism.

—In a fourth-grade classroom, a visiting physicist hands a group of ten-year-olds sheets of paper on each of which there is a drawing of a stick figure that he calls "Mr. Short." The children are to measure his height with paper clips. The physicist says that he himself measured Mr. Short with buttons rather than paper clips, and found him to be four buttons high. In his office there is another figure, "Mr. Tall," who is six buttons in height. "Now," says the physicist, "I'd like you to tell me how tall Mr. Tall is, if you could measure him with your paper clips—only you can't, because he's back in my office." This little puzzle is the physicist's way of finding out at what age children are able to grasp the concept of ratio; he discovers that many children do not understand it at an age when, according to Piaget's studies, they should.

—An English baby girl, her diaper sagging around her knees, toddles down a garden path followed by her aunt and uncle, two American psycholinguists, each with pad and pencil in hand. The child looks around and says, "Windy"; the adults capture the comment on their pads. A heavy truck goes by on the highway. "Noisy lorry," says the child, ". . . naughty lorry!" and the adults scribble away. So it goes for half an hour. The aunt and uncle are not unnaturally fond; they are dedicated researchers, gathering data on what kinds of words a child uses prior to speaking in sentences and exactly what kinds of stimuli call them forth.

In thus observing the construction of the intellect, these observers never actually see what is taking place inside; they see only the results. The problem is to figure out, from whatever clues they can spot, what part of the unseen development represents the influence of information genetically encoded in the brain, what part the influence of accumulating experience, and how these two forces interact, in ever-changing ways, to bring about the growth of the intellect.

Which category of influences, or what combination of the two, for instance, can explain the first appearance of thinking in the very young child? Newborn infants do not think, in the customary meaning of the word, and there is no way the people around them can explain to them or demonstrate how to do so, as they can with physical acts; nevertheless, rudimentary thought processes appear in infants within a few months, well before they understand speech, and within three or four years they do fairly complex kinds of thinking, long before they can comprehend explanations of what they are doing.

What could possibly account for this? Could it be that thinking develops spontaneously, as the brain itself matures during the childhood years? The newborn's brain is only a quarter as large as it will eventually grow to be, and its neurons are still in the process of linking up with each other, a process directed by subtle chemical forces that determine the neurons' ultimate, stupendously intricate, wiring pattern. Perhaps, then, the gradual appearance of thought is due to postnatal maturation of the brain itself; it may be that the processes of thinking are, at birth, like our teeth, predetermined in form and function but undeveloped and invisible; this seems to be the opinion of certain cognitive scientists who hold that the emergence of thought and the self-selection of nerve connections in the maturing brain cannot be mere coincidence.

Yet this modern version of an ancient theory seems to be refuted by common sense and abundant evidence. We all know that children's thinking varies greatly according to what adults teach them. Most of us have heard, too, that children in understaffed and ill-run institutions remain mentally retarded, and that children whom psychopathic parents have kept locked away from birth develop neither speech nor, apparently, thought but remain mentally like untamed animals. For that matter, there is even some evidence that without a rich inflow of experience, the brain does not grow properly; laboratory rats that live in enforced idleness have smaller brains, with fewer synaptic junctions among their neurons, than rats that have companions and a changing assortment of playthings. Recent psychobiological studies in Oslo and elsewhere also show that through experience the developing neurons strengthen some of their synaptic connections and allow others to wither away, thus establishing particularly effective pathways; such "synaptic pruning" eliminates potentially inappropriate or conflicting circuits. So on a physiological level, there is evidence favoring a neo-Lockean, environmentalist view: experience wires the brain, and we think only as we have learned to think.

No matter where one looks, there is evidence on both sides of the question. Environmentalists believe that formal education is a major source of the thought patterns of the adult mind—and indeed, as we have seen, the thinking of nonliterate peoples is different in many respects from that of literate ones. On the other hand, schooling cannot produce abstract or logical thinking in the mind of the child until he or she is ready; the mind has its own timetable and will not be hurried. Moreover, even in societies where there is no schooling, as children grow up their thinking undergoes a slow metamorphosis into adult thinking. So the evidence shows that education does—and does not—account for adult thought processes.

Obviously, we are still embroiled in the classic Nature-Nurture problem, the great debate about whether heredity or environment, biology or experience, is the chief determinant of human behavior. As we have already seen, this used to be the key issue in psychology, and it remains a major theoretical issue pervading cognitive science, even though the practitioners of the new discipline are scornful of those lay persons who discuss it in simple either-or terms, or even in terms of how much is due to Nature and how much to Nurture. The consensus among cognitive scientists is that thinking develops gradually, as a result of a continuous and ever-changing interaction between various biological propensities of the brain and the shaping and stimulating effects of experience. But this broad compromise is only a framework; it tells us nothing of the specific processes by which the child comes to organize his or her experiences, to form concepts, to understand speech, to talk, to reason, and so on. What cognitive scientists want to know is exactly what forces interact, and when and how they do so, at each step in the development of each mental ability.

But the influences of neural propensities and of experience are hopelessly intermingled (or, as cognitive scientists say, *confounded*), since they coexist and interact from the moment of birth onward. There is no conceivable way to isolate either component by eliminating the other. Even the Fried-Holyoak experiment in the classification of abstract diagrams, in which the subjects weren't told whether their choices were right or wrong, only minimized the input of experience but did not exclude it, for they experienced similarity among the diagrams and so got progressively better at sorting them; learning played a part in the end result. Moreover, there is no way to know whether those who sorted the diagrams best had some special genetic visual gift, or had simply had more previous experience in dealing with abstract designs.

In such a predicament, the scientist can look for natural experiments—situations in which one component, though not eliminated, varies while the other remains constant. A study of the ways people in different cultures think is a case in point: Nurture varies while Nature is presumably the same. But such studies, though suggestive, are of limited value because there is no way to know whether the hereditary material of different peoples is truly identical. Studies of the schooled and the unschooled within a single society are closer to the mark, but even there, the unschooled are often older, or come from different regions, than the schooled; the experiment lacks rigor. Conversely, many studies have measured mental differences among races in a single society—a situation in which heredity is varied while environment, presumably, remains constant. But it does not: persons of different races have very different life experiences, even if they live in the same neighborhood and go to the same school.

There is, however, another way to investigate the sources of thinking: one can watch the mind grow, from infancy onward, looking for patterns and regularities in the way various mental processes appear and develop. Through intimate, microscopically fine observation of what children say and do, compared and correlated with what they have had the chance to learn, one can make reasonable guesses as to what part biology is playing, and what part experience, in each change that appears in their mental behavior.

This is what the various investigators of mental development are doing in their several ways. They come from two disciplines within cognitive science—child development psychology and psycholinguistics—which are intertwined, although distinct and specialized. Both sides think of themselves as interactionists and claim to have resolved the ancient argument; since, however, child development psychologists focus largely on the outside influences on thinking processes, while psycholinguists are much concerned with maturational and innate influences on language acquisition, the two specialties still carry on the old Nature-Nurture debate to some degree, albeit in modern terms. But this is largely a matter of their special areas of attention. If one watches only the female dancer or only the male dancer in a pas de deux, it becomes hard to see the pas de deux itself; yet just as it does not exist except as an interaction between the two dancers, so human mental development takes place only as a continuous interaction between the predisposed brain and disposing experience.

## Watching the Mind Grow

Aristotle, believing as he did in the natural inferiority of women, said that they had fewer teeth than men; apparently, he never bothered to look. In much the same spirit, empiricists and nativists (innatists) long held opposite views about how the mind is formed, but never bothered to look at it actually taking form.

Not until sixty years ago, that is. Then Jean Piaget began looking, and never stopped until his death in 1980. Piaget set down what he observed, and what he believed it all means, in a prodigious outpouring of publications—sixty books and hundreds of articles. He and his co-workers created a subdiscipline within psychology, the study of cognitive development. In Europe, the United States, and most Western nations, Piaget's theory of intellectual development is the standard; all recent theoretical writing in this field begins by saying how it sides with, is related to, or differs from, his. These days Piaget's ideas are increasingly contested by the new breed of cognitive scientists, but those who disagree with his theory do so on the basis of experiments patterned on his, while even those who find fault with both his theory and his experiments concede that he asked—and made everyone else ask—the right questions: "What do children know at birth? When do they begin to think, and in what terms? When and how do they acquire concepts of time, space, causality, and the conservation of matter? In what sequence does all this take place, and why?" Even if Piaget's grand theory is seriously flawed and his experimental techniques prone to subjective errors, he did look; he counted the teeth.

It began in 1920 when Piaget, then a young psychologist working at the Binet Laboratory in Paris, was developing tests of reasoning. In trying them out on children of various ages, he found his subjects' wrong answers to be more interesting than their right ones. Children of about the same age, he noticed, often gave the same wrong answers, and at different ages children gave different kinds of wrong answers. He concluded that older children are not "brighter" than younger ones, but that their thinking is qualitatively different; younger children simply do not yet comprehend the world in the way they will later on.

This, plus some clinical experience with abnormal children, led Piaget to begin his lifelong quest, in his own distinctive way. For a few years he conducted his studies at home, with his own children; thereafter, for the most part, he continued his research at the University of Geneva. Piaget's method was the very antithesis of controlled, impersonal laboratory experimentation: over a span of six decades, he spent something like a hundred thousand hours watching children play, playing with them, asking them endless questions, offering them problems and puzzles to solve, and discussing with them why they were going about it as they were. With great ingenuity he thought up literally hundreds of questions, games, and tasks to use in this *méthode clinique,* as he called it. For instance:

—When his own children were infants, Piaget performed innumerable little experiments such as showing them a toy and then putting his beret over it, to see if they realized it was still there, underneath. Until the age of about a year, he found, they seemed to forget about the toy the instant it disappeared.

—Piaget would lay down in front of a child a row of half a dozen buttons, spaced out, and another row of half a dozen, close together; then he would ask whether there were as many in one row as the other. Though it may be hard for an adult to see how a child could make the mistake, Piaget found that until the age of six or seven, children would generally say there were more in the longer row.

—He would show a child a bunch of flowers, most of which were yellow, and ask, "Are there more yellow flowers or more flowers?" Preschool children would usually answer this incorrectly, not realizing that "flowers" includes "yellow flowers."

—He would set out ten sticks of different lengths, and ask a child to arrange them from smallest to largest. Generally, four-year-olds were unable to do it at all, or had errors in the final arrangement; six-year-olds did it by trial and error, making and correcting many mistakes along the way; and seven- or eight-year-olds did it easily and in a systematic fashion.

—He would ask children of various ages innumerable questions such as: "When you go walking, why does the sun move with you?" "When you dream, where is the dream, and how do you see it?" and "What is it that makes it all dark at night?" Until five, children might say that we make the sun move with us when we walk; until six, that the dream takes place in their room and that they see it with their eyes; and until seven, that it gets dark at night because we go to sleep. Beyond those ages, however, children cease seeing the world "egocentrically" (as Piaget put it), and become more realistic.

—With schoolchildren up to and beyond adolescence, he would pose problems in physics and chemistry like those we heard about earlier (What makes a pendulum swing faster or slower? Which of the four liquids must you mix to get the yellow color?), or problems in mathematics (Here is a bag with twenty red and twenty blue marbles in it; if you reach in and take two at a time, without looking, how many pairs will be made up of two reds, how many of two blues, and how many of one of each?). Children under eleven or twelve seem unable to tackle such problems in an orderly way or to use hypothetical reasoning; at or after adolescence, however, they can.

What patience the man had, what energy, what persistence! And what originality!—for it is obvious to all of us now that at different points in their development children think about the world in different ways, but until Piaget looked, and told us what he saw, we did not realize this. We did not know that thinking does not just grow but undergoes a series of metamorphoses, arriving only after some fifteen years at the kind that we say is characteristically human.

Piaget said that this development comes about because of the operation of two universal biological principles, *organization* and *adaptation;* the former is the tendency of every organism to arrange its parts and processes in a coherent system, the latter is the tendency of the organism to assimilate nourishment from the environment and to make changes in itself that enable it to deal better with that environment.

Piaget's theory of mental development is analogous to the development of the embryo into a fetus and eventually into a full-term newborn. The fertilized egg divides again and again, absorbing nutrients and transforming them into an ever-multiplying mass of cells; these form specialized clusters, and turn into rudimentary, and then developed, organs, tissues, structures, and systems, efficient at their various functions. The movement throughout is toward complexity, organization, and effectiveness. Each stage of development is the outgrowth of what went before, and the entire process follows an inexorable, genetically determined course.

The intellect, in Piaget's view, has a similar history, though it is determined not by biology but by the logic of experience. The mind of the newborn infant has certain tendencies of a very general sort—to assimilate experiences as if they were nutrients (indeed, he calls experience *aliment*), and to build increasingly specialized structures of thought out of this mental food by way of adaptation to the world. At first, these mental structures—not tissues, but conceptual systems—are simple and crude, but as they grow, they become increasingly complex, highly organized, and effective representations of the outside world.

All this takes place in an invariable sequence of steps, the same adult mental structures being built, in every mind, upon the foundation of the childhood structures. This is due to a kind of inner logic: just as algebra starts with definitions and axioms that determine systems that can be built upon them, so the infant mind starts with perceptions and motions (its simplest experiences) and out of these builds the first simple structures of thought—which, in turn, determine how other experiences will be assimilated and turned into more complex structures of thought, and so on.

If you find this rather murky, be reassured; were it crystal-clear, it would misrepresent Piaget's thinking. But perhaps the theory is less important than the facts. Piaget's greatest contribution may, in the end, prove to have been his choice of material. Even if much of Piaget's theoretical system is eventually superseded, he will remain the one who first systematically observed the mind of the child developing, and so showed all who came afterward where to look if they want to see how the human intellect is assembled.

The best-known aspect of Piaget's work is his stage theory—his characterization of the four major levels of mental development and of the kind of thinking done in each. From birth to about eighteen to twenty-four months infants are in the *sensorimotor* stage, during which they are aware of sensations and can make increasingly purposeful movements but know nothing of the world except their own perceptions; for a time, they have no mental symbols or images of things outside themselves, and even seem unaware that an object they cease to see or feel still exists. They may stare at a toy, or grasp it or suck on it, but if the toy falls out of sight or is hidden under a pillow or blanket, infants do not look for it and instantly become unaware of it, as if the object had ceased to exist. Infants, in other words, cannot think about anything but the here and now.

But by about a year to a year and a half—sooner for some, later for others—children increasingly act as if they know that things still exist even when they neither see nor are touching them; Piagetians call this the attainment of the "object concept," or "object permanence." Out of repeated encounters and developing memory, children begin to have mental images or concepts that they can use in place of sensations. Hide a toy under a pillow or roll a ball under a sofa while a child is watching, and he or she will look for it there; the child has in his or her mind the rudiments of a world that corresponds to external reality.

This is the threshold of the next stage, which runs roughly from two to seven, and which Piaget called the period of *preoperational thought*. During this time, the child rapidly acquires images, concepts, and words that represent external objects and processes, and is increasingly able to remember things and talk about them. But his or her internal representation of the world is still primitive, lacking, at first, such organizing concepts as space, time, causality, and quantity. The child cannot perform mental operations using these ideas, which is why Piaget called this stage preoperational. Tell a three-year-old that his parents, vacationing in Europe, will be back in two weeks; no matter how you explain it, he cannot grasp it, for time, in his mind, is only "now," "before now," or "not yet." Ask a four-year-old, across the room, how objects line up from where you are looking at them; she will describe them as they look from where she is, for her thinking is still close to the infantile egocentric view of the world. Nor has the child in this period any grasp of the principle Piaget called "conservation": the child is unable to recognize that the amount of liquid remains the same when it is poured from a short wide container into a narrow tall one, or that a ball of clay, rolled out into long thin sausages, hasn't changed in weight.

By seven or so, children enter the period of *concrete operations:* now they are able to perform mental operations, that is, manipulate the symbols they have in their minds as if they were manipulating real things. But only concrete ones—mental equivalents of physical objects and actions, not abstract ideas or logical processes. During these years children acquire the notion of conservation, as if, mentally, they could pour the liquid back and forth and see that it does not change in volume. They are able to arrange sticks or other objects by size, recognizing, without having to test it physically, that if $A$ is shorter than $B$, and $B$ shorter than $C$, there is no need to try $A$ against $C$. They can classify better, now; in this period they realize that the class of flowers includes, and is larger than, the class of yellow flowers. Increasingly they are able to see that events outside themselves have causes outside themselves: the sun doesn't really follow them; it gets dark at night for reasons other than that we go to sleep. And they become aware that their own thoughts are separate from external reality: they know that dreams occur within, and that we see them mentally, not with the eyes.

Finally, between about eleven and fifteen children move into the final stage, that of *formal operations*. As we saw in Chapter 4, this is the level at which, according to Piaget, young people become able to think not only about concrete objects and actions but about abstract relationships like ratio, probability, justice, and virtue. They become aware of the form of arguments rather than their content, and can tell whether a piece of reasoning is valid or not, quite apart from their personal knowledge or feelings about the subject. They become able to hypothesize, to classify according to logical principles, and to investigate problems in a systematic fashion. They can become excited by abstract ideas, such as those of religion, philosophy, and science; they can take an arbitrary position in debate for the sheer fun of it; they can imagine the past, the future, and worlds other than this one. Adolescents begin to think as adults; they have reached the inevitable final stage of mental development.

Along with his other accomplishments, Jean Piaget created a minor academic industry—the manufacture of pro-, anti-, neo-, and post-Piagetian studies. Wherever I went in the course of my inquiry, I met or heard of psychologists, educators, experts in artificial intelligence, and others whose lives are devoted to the researching, writing, delivering, and publishing of papers that either add to, modify, or contradict Piaget's findings and his theory. A single Piagetian idea—conservation—has produced something like five hundred published studies to date.

Many Piagetian studies today are, like Talmudic scholarship, glosses upon glosses, but others are more original, and add a wealth of new details to the overall description of the building of the human mind. Here are two examples of the kind of information that fills in the Piagetian design without materially altering its outlines:

—A four-month-old boy is seated in front of a screen on which two pictures of human faces, side by side, are projected. The baby had seen one of the pictures two weeks earlier; today, his eye movements are recorded by the experimenter, to whom it is quickly apparent that the baby is more interested in the new picture than the one he had seen before—persuasive evidence that even at this early stage he has considerable power of recognition, since he clearly discriminates between something not seen before and something seen so long ago. (But recall comes only much later; even at three, as I had heard from Marion Perlmutter, a child is hard put to name more than two toys out of a set of ten or twenty that he or she has just seen. Recognition is probably an innate ability; recall is acquired, and waits upon the mind's developing a symbol system by which to represent the outside world and a set of skills for locating those symbols in memory.)

—A seven-month-old girl is handed a toy cat by an experimenter. She plays with it for a moment; then the experimenter takes it from her and covers it with a cloth; the baby promptly pulls the cloth off and retrieves the toy. Obviously, she has attained an early form of object permanence (which, as many people have found, arrives much earlier than Piaget originally thought it did). The experimenter goes through the same routine again but this time uses two cloths, one hiding the toy, one hiding nothing. The baby pulls off the right cover. The experimenter repeats the procedure but this time slides a screen between the baby and the cloths for three seconds and then removes it. Sometimes the baby pulls away the right cloth, sometimes the wrong one; apparently her memory, at this juncture, doesn't last even for three seconds. But a month later it does; a month after that it lasts for seven seconds; and so on. Such research is dudgery, yet it yields a marvelous time-lapse movie of human memory taking form, a second's worth at a time. It also adds a valuable footnote to Piagetian doctrine—object permanence does not appear of itself, but is a product of the growing ability to remember.

Multiply those examples a thousandfold or so, and you get some idea of the mass of details being added to the Piagetian structure.

Now, a couple of examples of research findings that add to the grand design but that do modify or alter it in some way:

—A psychologist sets on a table, before a five-year-old girl, a simple apparatus, similar to one that Piaget used in experiments with children; it is a straight beam balanced on a central fulcrum, with four equally spaced upright pegs on either side. The psychologist asks the child a series of questions about whether the beam will balance if he puts various combinations of weights at different positions on either side; he also asks her why she thinks it will or won't. He does this with other girls of the same age, and with still others aged nine, thirteen, and seventeen. The five-year-olds and nine-year-olds, he finds, can answer simple problems correctly, but not those involving different weights at different distances from the fulcrum; surprisingly, however, in their explanations they use more reasoning of a primitive scientific sort than Piaget said children are capable of at that age. (The thirteen-year-olds and seventeen-year-olds, of course, do considerably more sophisticated reasoning.) Even more surprisingly, the young children, if they are given some instruction in how to reason about the more difficult problems, get better at solving them, although according to Piagetian theory their reasoning should not be capable of such improvement until their minds reach the stage of formal operations.

—A professor of science education gives a diagnostic test of formal reasoning to a group of first-year engineering students. This is a typical question:

> Write an equation using the variables $C$ and $S$ to represent the following statement: "At Mindy's restaurant, for every four people who ordered cheesecake, there were five who ordered strudel."
>
> Let $C$ represent the number of cheesecakes ordered and let $S$ represent the number of strudels ordered.

Three quarters of the students get it wrong; most of them write $5S = 4C$; the correct answer, however, is $4S = 5C$.* They make the mistake not because they don't know algebra, but because they are deficient in formal reasoning ability. Evidence like this, gathered by science educators at several institutions, shows that most young people, even by the time they complete high school or are in the first years of college, have not reached the stage of formal reasoning (and possibly never will), although in the Piagetian scheme this should be the inevitable outcome of mental development.

Again, multiply such findings manyfold, and you will get some idea of the bewildering complexity of the mass of corrections that have been, and are being, made to the Piagetian edifice, and that modify it to a limited extent.

Now, however, a few specimens of research that radically alter or reconstruct the Piagetian design.

—A two-year-old boy, holding a picture of a house, is asked by an adult to show it to her. He turns it so the front side—the picture side—is toward her. But in Piagetian theory, a child of his age should still be thoroughly egocentric in his thinking and unable to realize that others see things from a different perspective than himself; if so, he should hold up the picture so that he himself sees it. . . . A four-year-old girl's words are recorded as she talks to various people—a playmate her own age, her mother, and her two-year-old sister. Analyzed, her speech turns out to vary greatly, according to the person she is talking to: her conversation with her mother, for instance,

---

* The ratio of $C$ to $S$ is 4 to 5; that is, $\dfrac{C}{S} = \dfrac{4}{5}$. Hence, it takes $5C$ to equal $4S$.

includes comments about her own thoughts, requests for information, and the like, but when she talks to her two-year-old sister, she adjusts her speech to the younger child's level, speaking in short, simple sentences and mostly directing the younger child's attention to things ("Look at the doggy") or issuing orders ("No, don't do that!"). Something, it seems, is very wrong with part of the Piagetian doctrine: three- and four-year-olds are supposed to be quite egocentric, but adapting one's speech to the abilities of the listener is the opposite of egocentrism.

—A three-year-old girl is asked to count the five butterflies under a sheet of plexiglass in front of her. Touching them one by one, she counts slowly, "Two, sixteen, five, four, ten." She looks up and triumphantly announces, "Ten!" You and I might have been merely charmed, but the researcher was impressed: though the girl can't count yet, she already knows several important principles of counting—she tagged each butterfly only once, she assigned each one a different number, and she took the final number to be the answer to how many there were. Like many other children her age, she possesses concepts of quantity and counting that she ought not yet have, according to the Piagetian account of mental development.

—An experimenter, a young woman, puts a heap of wooden blocks of various shapes and colors on the table. She says to her subject, a seven-year-old boy, "Make a building in which all the yellow blocks are square." He misinterprets, just as Piaget said he would, and makes one using only square yellow blocks. "Now make a building in which all the square blocks are yellow," she says; he makes the same mistake again. Finally, he asks a very sensible question: "Why do you keep telling me to make these stupid little buildings?" That, however, has nothing to do with the matter being researched, which is the child's ability to comprehend "inclusion"—the relation of objects to a class that may include other objects as well. So far, all is according to Piaget.

But now the experimenter puts a syllogism to the boy.

> All zorru birds are yellow.
> The animal I am thinking of is a zorru bird.
> Is it yellow?

He gets that one right. She tries again:

> All zorru birds are yellow.
> The animal I am thinking of is not yellow.
> Is it a zorru bird?

He gets that one right, too. Even though he fails on certain other, more difficult syllogisms, he (and others of his age) do virtually as well with syllogisms of these two types as older children and adults. But they're not supposed to, according to Piagetian theory about class inclusion and formal reasoning.

—As we have already seen, three-year-olds show a primitive notion of causality in the form of surprise when the Snoopy doll inexplicably pops up, and one-year-olds show concept formation in the form of boredom with pictures of a familiar category (faces, or furniture) and interest in pictures of a new category. But in Piagetian theory, neither of these abilities should exist—not even in primitive form—until later stages of development.

Multiply such recent findings a hundredfold, or perhaps several times that, and you will get a sense of the serious challenge, now emerging from many cognitive-science laboratories, to the rigorous Piagetian scheme of mental development.

Is there, then, something basically wrong with Piagetian theory? Many educators and cognitive scientists say no, but an increasing minority of the latter now say yes. They agree that Piaget pinpointed the significant phenomena of mental development, but believe that his all-encompassing explanation has two major flaws and that these cannot be fixed by tinkering and reworking.

First, Piaget conceived of adult thinking in terms of formal logic: mental development is aimed at the achievement of formal reasoning, or, to put it less teleologically, the inevitable adaptation of the mind to reality is logical thinking. But we have already seen much recent evidence that contradicts this; the logic model of thinking is apparently wrong. Logical reasoning is a specialized mental activity that has particular value in special circumstances, but it is not the mind's natural way of operating.

Stage theory, moreover, is a product of Piaget's belief in the logic model: in his view, cognitive abilities develop side by side, stage by stage, in accordance with the degree to which the mind has moved from its original sensorimotor simplicity toward the goal of abstract, rigorous logical reasoning. But this is contradicted by the new evidence: some abilities seem to be present very early in a rudimentary fashion when, according to stage theory, they shouldn't exist at all, and some often fail to appear when they should. Stage theory is increasingly contradicted by the evidence of current child development studies, and is becoming more a hindrance than a help in the understanding of cognitive development. Currently, some of the best workers in the field are finding it more fruitful to follow the development of cognitive abilities separately, from their earliest appearance to their fullest flowering, without being concerned as to whether logically they should or shouldn't exist at any given age or stage.

The second major flaw in Piagetian theory is that while it purports to be interactionist, in fact it is almost entirely experiential; it allows for none of the recent evidence of specific propensities—the hard-wired tendencies we have heard so much of. Piaget spoke of the organism's part of interaction as its tendency to assimilate and to accommodate, but that is almost all he said about it. He portrayed all the more complicated mental abilities as arising out of prior, simpler thought structures as they absorb experience; new ideas develop out of the interaction between experience and the ideas the mind has thus far acquired.

Piaget said nothing about the influence of neural propensities or preprogrammed ways of dealing with experience; he explicitly rejected all preprogramming. This was the prevailing attitude in psychology when he began his work, but that was long ago; now, it is increasingly evident that the brain, though it has no innate ideas, comes furnished with tendencies to interpret or to assemble experience in particular ways that yield the concepts of time, space, number, and causality very early in life. Our brains are genetically designed to respond to our experiences of gravity, of three-dimensionality, of time, of quantity, and of causality, forming at first a very shallow and blurred picture of the world but progressively adjusting and correcting that picture.

A number of these neural predispositions to react in specific ways to experience develop only over a period of weeks to years after birth. Thus, many kinds of experience cannot build upon previous experiences until the neural networks are fully assembled and the myelin sheathing—the fatty insulation of the neurons—is completed. What looks like the development of mind due largely to assimilation and accommodation is in fact a continuing interaction between emergent neural potentialities and the increasingly complex ways they enable the mind to respond to experiences.

What, then, remains of the greatness of Piaget's achievement? Plenty. He recognized and identified the phenomena that have proven so rich a source of basic information about cognitive development, and he named and described the major cognitive structures that arise between birth and adulthood. As Rochel Gelman said to me, "He picked the right problems to work on. So he's going to live forever. We who are called anti-Piagetian today are really neo-Piagetian. We're only trying to articulate better, and with more

attention to internal cognitive machinery, the way the mind develops."
Isaac Newton once said, with seeming modesty, that if he had seen farther
than others, it was by standing on the shoulders of giants; today's cognitive
scientists stand on the shoulders of many giants, among whom Jean Piaget is
one of the tallest.*

## The Spoor of Thought

The raw materials from which biologists and geologists construct their
theories are the specimens they gather and the phenomena they observe.
The raw materials of a theory of thinking are thoughts—but how are cognitive scientists to collect or observe them? An action may indicate or result
from a thought but is not a reliable picture of it (a kiss may signify love—
but also betrayal); a brain-wave recording shows the composite effect of innumerable neural events but does not portray specific thoughts; and even
the recording of a single neuron's firing portrays an electrochemical event,
not a meaning. In short, thoughts become observable only when they are
expressed, and while a limited number can be expressed through gestures or
grimaces, nonverbal symbols such as those of mathematics or art, and demonstration (playing an instrument, for instance), most thoughts have no per-
ceptible form except that of spoken or written language.

Many child development psychologists therefore regard language as "the
window to the mind" and peer through words to see the thought processes
inside. But practitioners of another discipline, psycholinguistics, regard
language not just as the means of transmitting thought but as a form of behavior that itself is evidence of how thinking develops in the child and proceeds in the adult. In terms of the metaphor of specimen collecting, language is the *spoor* of thought. By studying not only what is said but how it is
said, psycholinguists seek to deduce what mental processes produced the
verbal trail. For example:

Many a child of two or three, having learned the words *his, hers, its, ours,*
and *yours,* will say *mines* ("Dat yours, dis mines"). Similarly, children will
treat irregular verbs and nouns as regular ones ("He bited me with his
tooths"). Why do they make such mistakes? Not because they have learned
them, but evidently because they have noticed certain regularities in adult
speech and taken them to be simple invariant rules, when, in fact, they have

---

* Newton wasn't all that modest; he reworded an old proverb, which, in its original form,
said that a *dwarf,* if he stands on the shoulders of a giant, is the one who sees farther.

specific exceptions. Thus, the child's speech error is a clear trace of a thought process.

Again, three- or four-year-olds will often use an intransitive verb as if it were transitive ("I'm gonna go my truck 'cross the floor," or "Can you stay the door open for me?"). But the children never heard sentences in which "go" and "stay" were used like this; the mistake shows that children, even in their early speech, are not simply imitating what they have heard but are creatively assembling into a sentence words stored in their memory, according to rules of syntax that they have already somehow arrived at. And though one of the rules, in each of these examples, is imperfect, the overall performance is impressive. No one teaches such rules to little children; how, then, do they come by them? An intriguing question—especially since children surely could not say what they are.

In adult language, likewise, psycholinguists see clues to thought processes. At Stanford University, Herbert Clark and a colleague showed subjects cards like those in Figure 39. The subjects were asked to say as quickly as they could whether the statement on each card was true or false; it took them two-tenths of a second longer to reply to false ones than to true ones. The explanation offered by Clark and his colleague is that when we seek to verify a statement, we normally assume it is true and try to match it against the facts. If they match, we need do no further mental work; if they don't, we have to take the extra step of revising our assumption, thus answering a trifle more slowly. Similarly, as Clark and various others have shown, it takes half a second or more longer to verify denials than affirmations; we

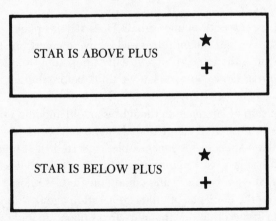

**Fig. 39.**   True or false? It takes longer to identify the false statement than the true one.

seem programmed to think more readily about what is rather than what is not, and have to transform negative sentences into affirmative ones to deal with them. Statements in the passive voice take longer to process than those in the active voice; apparently we more easily notice "agents" (do-ers) than "objects" (done-tos)—perhaps a linguistic outgrowth of our elementary perceptions of cause (first) and effect (afterward).

Psycholinguists thus are interested less in the properties of language itself, as linguists are, than in what it reveals about how the mind develops and operates. We have already seen some of the fruits of psycholinguistic research about the adult mind: how words (and the images and concepts they stand for) are grouped in memory, how listeners supply details from their own store of knowledge in order to understand someone else's speech, how schooling increases the ability to think logically, and how we modify our own speech according to an instantaneous computation of the listener's state of knowledge.

Psycholinguistics also casts a special light on the subject of this chapter's inquiry: the way in which biology and experience assemble the intellect between birth and adulthood. In doing so, psycholinguistics produces valuable information bearing upon two of the most interesting questions in cognitive science:

—To what extent is language built into us by specialized neural mechanisms and to what extent is it acquired through such mechanisms of learning as association and imitation? For if language is innate to any extent, there is an innate substrate to our verbal thinking. But that brings up the second question:

—To what extent is thinking verbal? Does it take place exclusively in words, or in some other medium from which we convert our thoughts into words—or in more than one? Can we really think about matters for which we have no words? Do we know what we think before finding words for our thoughts?

The relationship of language to thought is an old and hotly debated issue. At one pole are those who assert that thought and words are coextensive. "Thought without speech is inconceivable," asserted the philosopher Hannah Arendt in her last work, *Thinking.* "Our mental activities . . . are conceived in speech even before being communicated." Others take a similar view but rely on the evidence offered a generation ago by Benjamin Whorf, a linguist, who argued that our thoughts are confined to and molded by the syntax and the vocabulary of our native language. The concepts of time and space embodied in the verbs and nouns of the Hopi language, for instance, are different from those in the verbs and nouns of English, according to Whorf; therefore, he held, a Hopi and an English-speaking person would see the world very differently. The same thing is true of a large number of other concepts and thoughts; accordingly, our thinking is shaped and bounded by our language. (An English-speaking person, to give a familiar example, cannot express—and, Whorf would have argued, cannot think about—the nuances of meaning implied in the French-speaking person's shift from the polite pronoun *vous* to the familiar *tu*.)

At the opposite pole are those who argue that we think without words, and that words are simply the labels we attach to our thoughts. One piece of evidence offered in support of this view concerns the words for colors in various languages. Anthropological studies have shown that in many other cultures, people do not have the same boundaries for color categories that English-speaking people do; some have fewer basic color terms than we, and one people, the Dani of New Guinea, have only two color terms—*mili* ("dark") and *mola* ("light"). One wonders how the Dani could think about colors in any but the simplest way, yet Eleanor Rosch found that they remember "focal" (basic) colors better than nonfocal ones, just as English-speaking people do, and judge the similarity of color samples in much the same way as we. So at least as far as color is concerned, it is possible to think without words.

But what about more abstract concepts such as those involved in mathematics and the physical sciences? Faraday, Galton, Einstein, and certain other noted scientists have reported that they solved scientific problems in visual images and only afterwards translated their thoughts into words. In a famous instance of this, Einstein, unable to reconcile his special theory of relativity with Newtonian physics, pictured a box falling freely down a very long shaft; inside it, an occupant took coins and keys out of his pocket and let them go. The objects, Einstein saw, remained in midair, alongside him, because they were falling at the same rate as he—a situation temporarily identical with being in space, beyond any gravitational field. From this visual construct, Einstein was able to sense some of those seemingly contradictory relationships about movement and rest, acceleration and gravity, that he later put into mathematical and verbal form in his general theory of relativity.

Psychologist Roger N. Shepard of Stanford University demonstrates the existence of nonlinguistic thinking by means of Figure 40. In which of the

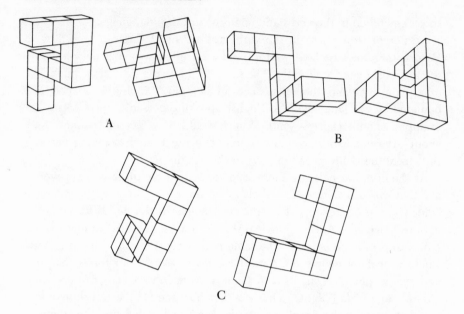

**Fig. 40.**   Are the objects in pair A identical? In pair B? In pair C? To answer, one has to rotate the objects in the mind.

pairs are the two objects identical? The answer is, of course, pairs *A* and *B*, in each of which an 80-degree rotation of one figure will show it to be identical with the other; pair *C*, however, cannot be matched by rotation. But in solving this problem and many like it, one neither needs nor uses words; one mentally rotates the image.

Does such evidence mean we don't think in words? Shepard doesn't make so sweeping a claim; he does say, though, that we think nonverbally most of the time and argues that thinking in spatial analogs or images preceded verbal thinking in human history—and thus is the foundation upon which verbal thinking is erected.

This, however, is speculation; there is no record of prehistoric thought. But more nearly definite evidence may come from the study of the child's acquisition of language; there, one can see and say whether thought comes first and language second, or whether language makes thought possible—or whether both things are true.

A child can talk long before it can tie its own shoelaces, although talking is infinitely the more complex of the two activities. No wonder so many people have found children's acquisition of language marvelous and mystifying. The behaviorists, however, explained language acquisition quite simply in terms of three principles derived from rat psychology—association (of the sight of the object and the sound of the word), imitation (of pronunciation and of sentence structure), and reinforcement (through approval, or success in communicating, when saying something properly). Language was thus nothing but a complicated set of habits established by conditioning.

This seemed to Noam Chomsky, then a young linguist at MIT, mere "play-acting at science," a wholly inadequate explanation dressed up in scientific-sounding terms. In 1959 Chomsky, at thirty-one a leading figure in linguistics, wrote a scathing review of B. F. Skinner's book *Verbal Behavior* that not only demolished the behaviorist view of language but produced an upheaval in psychology, the outcome of which was the emergence of the new discipline, psycholinguistics.

The behaviorist theory of language, Chomsky said, cannot possibly account for some of the most important phenomena of language learning and use. For one thing, children produce all sorts of sentences they have never heard; imitation is thus grossly insufficient as an explanation of sentence formation, even though it undoubtedly plays a part in it. For another thing, children's efforts to make sentences are not random; their sentences, though mostly original, are generally grammatical, the errors in them being superficial and not serious enough to make the speech unintelligible. (No English-speaking child ever produces a sentence in reverse order, such as, "Milk more some want I.") The same is true of adult speech: none of us remember all the sentences we have ever heard but instead generate sentences on our own—and, nearly always, intelligible grammatical ones.

Yet the rules of English grammar—or any grammar—are so intricate and hard to figure out, from merely listening to speech, that one cannot imagine how the child ever manages to do so. Most people suppose that the child learns to speak by being taught and corrected by the parents, but several studies have shown that parents are more concerned with the content of the child's utterances than the grammar. For instance:

CHILD:   Nobody don't like me.
MOTHER:  Oh, yes they do, darling.

Even when, on occasion, parents do try to correct the child's grammar, the child rarely pays attention, but clings to the error (correcting it in his or her own good time), as illustrated by this interchange reported by a psycholinguist:

> CHILD:    Nobody don't like me.
> MOTHER:    No, say, "Nobody likes me."
> CHILD:    Nobody don't like me.
> (eight repetitions of this interchange)
> MOTHER:    No, now listen carefully; say, "Nobody likes me."
> CHILD:    Oh! Nobody don't *likes* me.

And that's a simple problem; how does the child figure out the innumerable harder ones? Earlier, we saw how complicated it is to learn how to turn a sentence in the active voice into one in the passive voice. And it's just about as complicated to turn even simple statements into simple questions. As Chomsky points out, it would be easy and natural for the child, hearing simple declaratives turned into questions, to indirectly extract a rule. From a number of instances likes this—

> The man is tall.
> Is the man tall?

—the child should arrive at the following rule: Start at the beginning; move along to the first appearance of "is" or some other verb; shift that word to the front. But what of a slightly more complex declarative like this one?

> The man who is tall is in the room.

Applying the rule, the child should say:

> Is the man who tall is in the room?

Yet one never hears children make such a mistake; they make plenty of trivial ones, but not substantive ones like that.

There are a multitude of similar problems. Why is the proper answer to some questions a simple "yes" or "no" ("Can you ride a bike?"), but not to other similarly constructed questions ("Can you tell me the time?"—to which a simple "yes" is inappropriate and a simple "no" is hostile). If "John told Mary to water the garden" implies that Mary is going to water it, why does "John promised Mary to water the garden" imply that John is going to water it? Why does "The girl the boy saw threw the ball" mean something completely different from "The girl threw the ball the boy saw"? The list is seemingly endless, the problem of language acquisition monumental; yet children find it easy. How is this possible?

Chomsky's answer was that there must be a specialized neural structure in the brain—a genetically determined formation that he called the Language Acquisition Device, or L.A.D.—that has "preexistent knowledge" enabling it to recognize the ways in which the things and actions represented by noun phrases and verb phrases are related to each other as agent, action, and object. The L.A.D. (or "language faculty" as he also calls it), a highly specialized product of evolution, thus perceives the "deep structure" or underlying connections among the components of spoken sentences. Chomsky calls those relationships—which correspond, in a way, to the connections between things and actions in the world—"universal grammar." It's not a knowledge of English (or any other particular) grammar—that's what accounts for the "surface structure" of sentences—but it underlies every such grammar. To put it another way, no human language anywhere could develop that does not, in its own way, conform to the universal grammar.

Because children are equipped with this organ, they fairly soon sense the connections between the forms of their native tongue and the relationships embodied in the deep-structural grammar already in their head. Those connections—the rules of "transformational grammar"—make it natural for children to speak sentences that conform to proper usage in their own language. Children never make a mistake like "Is the man who tall is in the room" because, based on their innate universal grammar, they *feel* that the phrase "who is tall" belongs to "the man" and shouldn't be broken up when turning the sentence into a question. Nor do children utter sentences backward or string words together in random order; in another tongue, they might learn to use a different word order—but the relationship of the component parts of the sentence—their "mental position," as Chomsky puts it—would remain the same.

All this is a little easier to see in the form of an example Chomsky himself has given. Here are two sentences with the same surface structure:

John is easy to please.
John is eager to please.

In both, in terms of English grammar, "John" is the subject. But if you try to paraphrase each in the same way, one makes sense, the other doesn't:

It is easy to please John.
It is eager to please John.

That's because there's a difference at the level of deep structure: "John," in the first sentence, is the *deep object* of "please" (thus, the paraphrase works), but in the second sentence "John" is the *deep subject* of "please," so that any alternate version has to take the form:

John is eager to please (someone).

Thus, the relationships that exist in the deep structure determine what rewordings can be made in surface structure—something one can't know from surface structure alone. In paraphrasing a statement, we do not apply rules of thumb that we have learned but those rules that are in harmony with, or are generated by, the deep structure of the sentence.

None of this amounts to the claim, often wrongly ascribed to Chomsky, that language is innate; he has never suggested that a child raised without contact with language would spontaneously produce words or sentences. The Language Acquisition Device has no words, no meanings, no ideas, stored in it; it merely has a set of preexisting expectations of the ways in which the components of any natural language go together. If a child were exposed only to language generated by a computer, in an ever-changing code, he or she would surely never crack that code, but the code of every human language can be cracked by the universal grammar that exists within all of them.

That is Chomsky's basic position.

He has modified it somewhat in recent years, however; in the original version, he stressed syntax to the exclusion of meaning, but more recently he has taken a weaker stand and included meaning as part of the mechanism by which the child decodes the structure of language. Yet even in the modified Chomskyan view, there must be an L.A.D. to account for our transformations of sentences—and there seems to be some physiological evidence that something like it does exist: studies of aphasic and brain-injured patients indicate that syntax is governed by Broca's Area but meaning by Wernicke's Area. A lesion of Wernicke's Area results in fluent but meaningless speech; one of Broca's Area results in slow, syntactically flawed speech but unimpaired meaning.

The Chomskyan position is interactionist; it pictures the child as acquiring only the particular language he or she hears, as that incoming speech triggers off the innate responses of the language faculty. But in contrast to Piagetian psychology, Chomskyan theory is strongly innatist—or so it has seemed to all those people reared in the liberal tradition that the human being is totally free of instincts or preexisting mental tendencies. Thus Chomsky, well-known as a left-liberal political activist, espouses a theory of mind that seemingly aligns him with social conservatives who believe in innate ideas and the unchangeability of human nature. But of course Chomsky's theory doesn't posit the existence of innate ideas, attitudes, or ways of behaving toward other human beings; it deals only with the decoding of language and the encoding of thoughts we would like to turn into language.

Although Chomsky's theory liberated the study of language behavior from behaviorist bonds, much of it has been modified or rejected in recent years by other psycholinguists. Some offer alternate explanations of how deep structure works; some doubt that deep structure is innate; and some find evidence, in the child's acquisition of language, that conflicts with Chomskyan theory on many points. But one fact is unarguable: Noam Chomsky, like Jean Piaget, asked questions that cognitive science has been obsessed with ever since—questions whose answers, however incomplete they may be today, suggest how highly specialized an organ the human brain is, and how very far the human mind is from being the passive recipient of experience, a blank slate on which life writes its messages.

Psycholinguistics is so new a field that as yet it offers no unified picture of the mind's development but, rather, a host of tantalizing and suggestive bits and pieces. It is like an anthropological dig that has turned up a tooth, a fragment of brow, and a thumb bone from which one cannot clearly describe the whole creature but only guess at its overall nature. Though psycholinguists differ about exactly what those bits and pieces mean, in general they seem to take a genuinely interactionist view of the mind's origins—a view somewhere between that of Piaget and that of Chomsky. In the minutest details of children's speech, month by month and year by year, they find evidence of the ever-changing interplay of developing neural mechanisms and of developing thought structures.

And minute details are what they have plenty of. Although I likened the findings of psycholinguistics to fragments of prehistoric tooth and bone, they differ from such fossils in being immensely abundant. To gather data, psycholinguists have only to listen to their own children at home, or to other children in other homes, schools, or playgrounds, using no apparatus but a pad and pencil or a tape recorder. (They also, however, do experimental laboratory work of kinds we have already seen, such as reaction-time studies and comprehension studies.) They thus easily accumulate vast masses of childish talk, some of which is illuminating—and, sometimes, charming—but much of which is extraordinarily boring. Undeterred by the latter quality, they often reproduce even the most tedious stuff in their writings in order to make a particular point. Here, for instance, is a specimen from *Language Acquisition*, an excellent textbook by Jill G. and Peter A. de Villiers, both of Harvard, showing how a needed morpheme—a speech sound—is at first haphazardly added by the child (note how the "s" in "Dat's" comes and goes):

> PETER: Which one is that?
> ALEX (30 months; referring to an orange car): Dat's greem.
> PETER: O.K.
> ALEX: Dat greem.
> MOTHER: No, that's orange.
> ALEX: Dat's greem.
> PETER: Is it?
> ALEX: Dat greem.
> (and so on for another 10 lines)

The patience of such researchers is as great as Piaget's. But it is rewarded, for out of endless hours of such childish prattle they winnow and sift enough valuable information to fill book after book. Here are just a few examples of the sort of findings that are completing the picture of how the human mind develops:

—Most children begin to speak in single words—"More!" "Open!" "Doggy," " 'Bye"—at about a year. Why not sooner? Piagetians say that the ability to speak waits upon the development of certain cognitive structures acquired through sensorimotor experience, especially the idea of object permanence (what good is it to know a word if you have no permanent mental object to pin it on?). But object permanence arrives months before words; if it is a prerequisite to speech, it is not the only one. Another prerequisite —this one a contribution from the innate side—is the maturation of the speech centers of the brain. Like those baby birds who play with leaves and straw as a necessary step in getting ready to build nests later on, human babies begin to babble at three or four months as a kind of preparation for speech, and the babbling increases until they begin to form understandable words, after which it declines. The intriguing point about babbling is that it is a spontaneous, self-generated activity and not an attempt to imitate adult speech, the proof being that deaf children, too, babble. It must be a preprogrammed activity that begins when the neural centers that direct it have reached a certain stage of maturation; it is a form of automatic and pleasing play. Yet it does respond to input: in normal children, babbling changes over the months and increasingly comes to include the sounds and intonations of the spoken language; in deaf children, it dwindles away from lack of feedback. Thus it is a hereditary activity, altered by experience, that is a step in the acquisition of speech.

—At the one-word stage of speech, children often seem to be trying to communicate much more than the single word. "Wawa" can signify "I want some water," or "Put some more water in the tub," or "Look at the water over there," and so on; the child's actions and the context often make this clear, especially to the parents or a customary caretaker. But does the child actually have a sentence in mind? Expert opinions differ; there is no doubt, however, that he or she has a *thought* in mind that he or she cannot express. Thus thoughts do exist without words—at least, visual and simple thoughts that are comparable to perceptions and motions.

—At the one-word stage children seem ready for speech, yet they remain stuck at that stage and simply accumulate words for most of the second year; then, rather abruptly, they begin two-word speech. Why the delay? What happens during that year? There is no generally accepted explanation, but one well-regarded theory is that it takes the whole year for children's minds to be able to combine social communication such as requests ("more") with object labels ("milk") into two-word protosentences ("More milk"). But that's only labeling what happens, not explaining it. Perhaps, again, the assembling of social communication and object labels waits upon the growth of the network of neural connections; the fact that in the same home one child will speak in two-word sentences much earlier than another seems to point to a maturation effect.

—The child's two-word utterances are "telegraphic." Like telegrams (SEND CASH), they don't contain articles, prepositions, or auxiliary verbs but consist chiefly of nouns (at the sound of the car in driveway, a little girl cries, "Daddy car!") or nouns and verbs (ready for an outing, she demands, "Go car!"). Significantly, however, the child uses the correct word order; if she were merely uttering labels for objects and actions, she would be as likely to say "Car Daddy" or "Car go." But she doesn't; she uses word order as an expressive device. (In languages that depend not on word order but on inflections, the child begins to use those, instead, in its early speech.) Obviously, the child already has a few rudiments of English grammar, perhaps derived from the hypothetical L.A.D. Another bit of evidence: a child who can manage only two words will sometimes say something like this—"Daddy pat—Pat dog—Daddy dog"—the final utterance being a surface representation of a deep structure that the child cannot yet utter; score a point for the innate language faculty.

—In a recent study of some deaf children in Philadelphia who had not been taught any form of sign language, a team of researchers discovered that the children had made up gestures of their own and, by age three or four, would produce "sentences" (strings of these signs) that had such characteristics of normal early-childhood speech as distinctions between agent, action, and object, word order that parallels the sequence of events, and so on. Since this was all self-generated, the researchers concluded that it strongly suggests the existence of inherent, unlearned "language organizing principles." Score another point for innateness.

—On the other hand—and psycholinguistics is full of on the other hands—it takes children four to six years to understand passive constructions. A preschool child will often take a sentence like "The dog was chased by the cat" to mean "The dog chased the cat." The hypothetical L.A.D. doesn't seem to be operating; the child is dealing on the surface level, not the deep level. Score a point against innate universal grammar.

—A two-year-old knows how to say "No!" as any parent can testify, but learning how to turn affirmative sentences into correct negative sentences is a long and difficult process that goes through several stages and takes many years. Even well into grade school, children still make such errors as "I'm not scared of nothing" and "I don't got no brothers and sisters." Score another point against innate universal grammar.

—The two-word stage lasts a long while; then, beginning at about two and a half or three, children start making longer and longer sentences. For some years, these are relatively simple in construction—without, for instance, interruptions, like this one—but by age eight or ten they have acquired mastery of complex constructions. Some psycholinguists now say that most of these stylistic skills are acquired by means of a variety of learning processes, but not by means of transformational grammar. Yet until adolescence, language learning is easier and faster than it will ever be again, possibly indicating an innate component—a "critical period" during which the neural networks within Broca's Area and Wernicke's Area are still being completed and are easily modified by new information. Further evidence: All during these years the child is effortlessly acquiring words at an astounding rate—four to eight new words a day—and by age six has a vocabulary of somewhere between 8000 and 14,000 words. And that's before schooling. By adolescence children know several times as many; learning new words will never again be as easy. Accent, too, seems all but fixed by adolescence; many people who came here from Europe in their early teens, during the Hitler era, still speak English with a definite foreign accent after forty-odd years.

—The awareness children have of such regularities as the adding of *-s* or *-es* to form a plural or *-ed* to form a past tense is only one of a number of "operating principles," as some psycholinguists term them, that children spontaneously apply in language learning. Attention to word order is another; avoidance of interruption of linguistic units is a third. In a survey of forty different languages, one researcher found that six such principles are used by children learning each of those languages—reasonably good evidence that the mind is innately well-prepared to notice certain kinds of regularities in any natural language.

—And yet what of all the exceptions to those rules? What about the irregular verbs and nouns, the innumerable idioms, the fragments of speech that stand for whole sentences ("Yeah?"—"Yeah!" "Oh, yeah?"—"*Yeah!*"), the shades of meaning of synonyms, the comprehension of metaphoric usages, and so on and on? None of this is universal, and apparently none innate; children learn it, bit by bit, as they learn any other large body of information. Yet they do so more easily than they learn such other subjects as mathematics or chemistry, perhaps because the brain is naturally receptive to language and not to those other bodies of knowledge.

—Mothers talk to infants and small children in special ways, almost without being aware of doing so: they speak in a high-pitched voice, strongly emphasize key words, use simple sentences, and spontaneously reply to the child's primitive utterances with slight expansions that show the child how to say it better (Child: "Mommy soup." Mother: "That's right, Mommy's eating her soup"). In these and many other ways, mothers' speech to children is rather special, and has earned the name among psycholinguists of "Motherese." With considerable unwitting skill, mothers alter their Motherese as the child becomes more linguistically competent; mothers seem to know just about how much more difficult or involved to make their speech to the child in order to keep teaching it language. (There is, though, a dissenting view: some who have analyzed Motherese claim that it isn't grammatically as simple as it sounds, that its real purposes aren't so much to teach the child language as to get its attention and to ensure its obedience, and that its value as a teaching technique isn't at all clear.)

—It's easy to understand how a child may learn from a correction that it is ready for; what isn't so easy to understand is the phenomenon of self-correction. Children apparently acquire many elements of grammar and vocabulary that they don't use until, at unpredictable moments, they consciously improve their own speech, as shown in this bit of dialogue recorded by one researcher:

> JAMIE (age 6 years, 10 months):   I figured something you might like out.
> MOTHER:   What did you say?
> JAMIE:   I figured out something you might like.

What mechanism was at work? Did Jamie match the sounds generated by his speech center against a memory of similar sounds filed elsewhere in that same center? Clearly, learning is involved—but the inherent wiring plan is what seems to allow the learning to take the form of self-correction.

These findings, and hundreds of times as many more, add up to a highly complex interactionist portrayal of the growth of the mind—an ever-changing interplay of maturing neural structures, developing knowledge structures, and the increasingly advanced speech and behavior directed at the child by those around it.

On nearly every point, however, there are disputes; a theory may be in the making, but at present no grand synthesis has appeared. Still, there is a core of agreement that can be summed up in two points:

—One: We human beings bring to the process of language acquisition much more innate information, in the form of neural predispositions and operating principles, than we had any notion of until recent years.

—Two: The experiential aspects of language acquisition are very much more intricate than behaviorists suspected. At every phase of development, the child's linguistic interaction with parents and others—and with his or her own verbal productions—obeys a variety of special principles, many of them peculiar to that moment and that particular linguistic phenomenon.

So we have an answer, of sorts, to the first of the two questions we asked of psycholinguistics—the Nature-Nurture problem—and it is anything but a simple one. But how could it have been simple? The workings of the digestive system require a highly complex explanation; so does even the growth or loss of the hair on the head; and so, all the more, do the processes of the mind.

Now to the second question: What is the relation of language to thought?

Here, too, there are innumerable viewpoints and debates, but a core of agreement.

There is plenty of evidence that thinking of a kind does take place in the infant's and the child's mind before he or she has the capacity to find words or produce sentences to express those thoughts. But for the most part, thought does not develop much ahead of language that can express it. Children deprived of language experience by being kept isolated, or deaf children who are not taught another method of communication, seem to think in only the simplest terms, like two-year-olds or apes.

Language is not well suited to encoding certain kinds of information (in particular, visual and spatial relations); some scientists and certain other people say that they think in images. But while this may be true, it is also true that they have had a lifetime of learning concepts through language. As we know, infants form some concepts before they have words for them but only low-level ones—faces, furniture, colors—and not sophisticated or abstract ideas like probability or romanticism, let alone such unobservable and nonvisualizable realities as the curvature of space or fate. It seems most unlikely that any scientist could think in images about space, or any artist about romanticism, without having learned, through language, what they are.

Thinking in imagery may well have come before thinking in words, as Roger Shepard says, but what kind of images were they and what kind of thinking was it? Probably extremely simple and, like the thinking of a preverbal child, limited to the physical here and now. Advanced thinking depends on the mental manipulation of symbols, and while nonlinguistic symbol systems such as those of mathematics and art are sophisticated, they are extremely narrow. Language, in contrast, is a virtually unbounded symbol system, capable of expressing every kind of thought. It is the prerequisite to culture, which cannot exist without it or by means of any other symbol system. It is the way we human beings communicate most of our thoughts to each other and receive from each other the food for thought. In sum, we do not always think in words, but we would do little thinking without them.

## A Very Special Animal

The ancient argument is settled—more or less.

It is clear from what we have seen that nothing resembling the human mind would develop in an infant who was deprived of all human contact. To fashion that mind takes something like 100,000 hours of child care, socialization, play, schooling, and work experience, and the exchange of hundreds of millions of words. Without that immense infusion of experience, scarcely a trace of intellect would appear. Genie, a girl who had been locked away by her parents all her life, was discovered at age thirteen by Los Angeles authorities, some years ago; she was mute and incontinent, crawled on all fours, and understood nothing that was said to her, a primitive creature without any evidence of mind. But it was not because of gross brain defectiveness; within four years, in foster care, she had developed some language ability, many social skills, and the mental capacity of an eight-year-old.

And yet the human brain is filled with special mechanisms that are essential to the making of mind; without them, experience can never produce it. The most intelligent cat, dog, or ape, even if exposed to a constant stream of cultural experiences, never develops a mind like that of a human being. For it lacks what we have: preprogramming of our neural equipment that enables us to form concepts out of what we see, language out of what we hear, and thoughts out of our experiences.

In being so preprogrammed, we are akin to all the other animals; but of course we are a very special animal, for our preprogramming is both far less specific than theirs and yet, in a sense, far more specialized. The worm, the protozoan, and the spider are born equipped with responses so specific that it takes only the right stimulus to produce a detailed and almost unchangeable pattern of response; they do not need to learn what to do. But the higher in the scale of development we look, the less well specified the response is, and the more the creature must construct its behaviors by means of experiences. Even the cat is not born a mouser, but little by little assembles its mousing pattern out of bits of built-in behavior—eye tracking movements, chasing, catching, biting. Monkeys reared alone, and having no chance to experience a variety of kinds of body contact with other monkeys in play, are all but unable to mate as adults.

In the spectrum of innate-versus-learned behavior, we human beings are at the far end—we have fewer specifically preprogrammed responses, and are in need of far more learning experiences than any other animal. But it was a major mistake of the empiricists and of the environmentalists of recent years to claim that we were totally different from all the other animals and had no hard-wiring whatever—a belief as anthropocentric as that of the Victorians who so angrily rejected Darwinism.

We are very special animals—but animals, still. The human difference is the human mind, but the mind is the product of the same kind of interaction between the environment and built-in information systems that results in the cat's mousing and the monkey's mating. Unlike other animals, we are not constrained by our preprogramming to eat only particular foods, build species-specific kinds of shelters, or go through invariant forms of sexual courtship; but we are constrained to make certain kinds of order out of our perceptions, to count, to recognize cause and effect, to record speech sounds and meanings in our brains, and to recreate the world in our minds by means of our symbol systems. Constraints, of course, are not only limitations, but capabilities; and those that are built into the human brain are our greatest asset, for they force us to construct the human intellect.

Recently, however, we have been hearing a great deal about how much we are like certain other animals and, conversely, how much they are like us. In particular, there has been a flood of enthusiastic reports about the mental and linguistic accomplishments of a handful of culturally overprivileged apes. A decade ago, Allen and Beatrice Gardner of the University of Nevada succeeded in teaching Washoe, a female chimpanzee, well over a hundred words in American Sign Language. Then David Premack, in California, used plastic pieces of varied colors and shapes to symbolize words that he taught to Sarah, his chimpanzee, who learned to put them together to form phrases. Duane M. Rumbaugh, in Georgia, devised a keyboard by which his chimp, Lana, tapped out patterns that represented words. At Stanford, Francine ("Penny") Patterson taught ASL to Koko, a female gorilla who, after eight years, has a working vocabulary of nearly four hundred signs and, Patterson claims, can not only converse in sentences but make jokes and puns.

All of this is very impressive. For a while, some psychologists—and many lay persons—believed that a major discovery had been made, namely, that apes, while they cannot produce spoken words, have semantic and syntactic abilities similar to, though smaller than, those of human beings. Granted that their utterances were brief, simple, and extremely limited in content—"Washoe sorry," "Machine give Lana drink," and the like—was it not a dazzling revelation that they had a modicum of what we human beings had always considered our exclusive and most valuable ability?

Yes, it was dazzling—and, it now seems, a great exaggeration. Among psychologists working with apes, and others who have studied the evidence, serious doubts have cropped up in the last year or so. Herbert S. Terrace, a psychologist at Columbia University, trained his own ape, Nim Chimpsky (named in honor of Noam Chomsky), to converse in ASL, but later, after methodically reviewing videotapes of Nim's performance, Terrace ruefully concluded that Nim's utterances were the result of "pure drill" and of cues unconsciously given by his trainers. Terrace and a growing number of other psychologists now believe that the trained apes do not create new grammatical sentences of their own but only repeat fortuitous combinations of symbols they have used that resulted in reward of one sort of another. A recent review of the professional literature by anthropologists Thomas A. Sebeok (a specialist in animal communication) and Donna Jean Umiker-Sebeok, both of Indiana University, comes to the same conclusions.

Too bad. It was amusing that Koko, angry at Penny Patterson, signed, "You dirty bad toilet." It was impressive that chimps could master a couple hundred signs or symbols and string together two, three, or even sometimes four of them in coherent utterances. It was astonishing that apes could sound like typical two-year-olds, as in this bit of dialogue reported by Penny Patterson:

> PATTERSON:   What did you do to Penny?
> KOKO:   Bite.
> PATTERSON:   You admit it?
> KOKO:   Sorry bite scratch.
> (Patterson shows Koko the mark, which does look like a scratch.)
> KOKO:   Wrong bite.
> PATTERSON:   Why bite?
> KOKO:   Because mad.
> PATTERSON:   Why mad?
> KOKO:   Don't know.

So it is disappointing to hear that, in all likelihood, the apes have not really been creating sentences but merely assembling some of their symbols—pertinent ones, to be sure—and stumbling upon syntactically proper combinations that then are rewarded and reinforced. Nonetheless, it is interesting and important to learn that the ape brain has the capacity to store symbols created by human beings, and to use them to express the kinds of elementary wants and moods that one-year-old or two-year-old human beings exhibit, and even grasp a few concepts such as "same" and "different." But the apes and we branched off from common evolutionary predecessors—and it was almost surely *after* branching off that we developed the remarkable specialization of throat and brain that gave us the gifts of speech and of human thought. Washoe, Sarah, Lana, and Koko may ask for juice, fruit, or a tickle, but there is no reason to believe that they will ever say anything much more advanced than that. Bertrand Russell's sardonic comment about dogs is probably applicable to the apes: "No matter how eloquent a dog is," he once said, "he cannot tell me that his father was poor but honest."

Finally, one trait that gradually appears during the child's mental development may be the most distinctive feature of the human intellect. It is metaknowledge (or metacognition)—the awareness of our own thinking processes. Psychologist John H. Flavell of Stanford University, a specialist in child development, says that children gradually acquire metacognitive capacities such as the awareness that it is having more trouble learning one thing than another, the thought that a fact should be checked out before being taken as true, and the feeling that it would be well to make note of something that they might forget. Metacognition is thus the monitoring and guiding of one's own thought processes; it is mind observing itself and correcting itself. Even as I write this sentence, I am observing the thoughts and words that come next, am dissatisfied with them, change them, observe and judge the product, and finally declare myself content. (In doing so, just now, it seemed to me that I experienced yet a higher level of mind, for I watched my metamind watching my mind—a dizzying experience.)

I wonder, indeed, if this is not the reason we all sense our own freedom of will, even though, aside from those who believe in it on religious grounds, we consider free will an impossibility—an effect without a cause, an event that owes nothing to the past. But if it is an impossibility, why do we all experience it every day in countless ways? We want to make a phone call and change our minds; we think about how to broach some sensitive matter to a friend and then rethink it; we weigh spending money for a pair of new shoes, and freely decide either to do so or not to do so.

Is this pervasive feeling of freedom only a delusion? Perhaps not; perhaps it is a function of examining our own thoughts and modifying them. When we regard our own thinking and either approve of it or decide to alter it, we experience freedom, for we are not bound by the past to think only one set of thoughts and to go no further. We are aware of our own thoughts, and that awareness, in itself, is a force capable of altering those thoughts. We are neither passive nor static; we act upon ourselves, we change. And though from the perspective of the outside observer our thoughts may well appear to be the product of all the past and present forces acting upon us, within our minds we experience freedom: the freedom of the metamind to observe and direct the mind. In terms of the flow of events in the outer world, we are not free agents, but in the inner world of our minds we feel free, and, therefore, in a very real sense, we are.

# THE PROBLEM SOLVER

### A Species-Specific Trait

*Question: What is the subject being studied in all three of the following cases?*

—An instructor asks a freshman engineering class to do the following exercises in their workbooks:

> In a foreign tongue *lev klula buj* means "buy green peppers," *ajm buj gyst* means "big green cars," and *lkuka lev ajm* means "quickly buy cars." How would you say "big peppers" in this tongue?
>
> (a) *buj klula*
> (b) *klula buj*
> (c) *klula gyst*
> (d) *lev gyst*
> (e) *lkuka ajm*

—In a psychology course for upperclassmen in the humanities, the instructor presents the students with this query and the accompanying diagram:

> You are working with a power saw and wish to cut a wooden cube, 3 inches on a side, into 27 1-inch cubes. You can do this by making six cuts through the cube, keeping the pieces to-

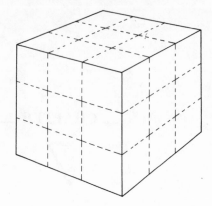

**Fig. 41.** Cube-sawing problem. Can it be done with fewer than six cuts? If not, why not?

gether in the cube shape. [See Fig. 41.] Can you reduce the number of necessary cuts by rearranging the pieces after each cut?

—In a class for students who intend to major in sciences, the professor asks this question:

> A bear, starting from point *P*, walked one mile south. Then he changed direction and walked one mile due east. Then he turned again to the left and walked one mile due north, and arrived exactly at the point *P* he started from. What was the color of the bear?

Now, while I didn't ask you to answer these three questions (I asked you only what subject was being studied in all three cases), you may have done so; first, therefore, here are the answers:

—The only word the first two phrases have in common in the foreign tongue is *buj*, and in English is "green," so *buj* must mean "green." Similarly, one can equate *lev* with "buy" and *ajm* with "cars." If you now substitute English for these known foreign words, you can easily identify the remaining ones, even though the word order is variable. The answer: (c) *klula gyst*.

—Most people try unsuccessfully to visualize a shorter way of cutting the cubes but remain unsure that there isn't one. It is possible, however, to prove by reasoning backwards that none can exist. Some of the cubes-to-be (the ones at the corners of the big cube) already have three exposed sides and thus need only three more—therefore, three cuts; some have two and need four more; some one and need five more; and one cube-to-be—the one in the dead center—has no existing sides and needs six. Therefore six cuts with the saw are the minimum; there is no shorter way.

—Did you say the bear is white because point *P* is the North Pole? Good—but is that the only answer? The North Pole is the only point on the globe to which the bear can return via a different meridian than the one it started out on; but could it, perhaps, return via the *same* meridian? Suppose *P* were a little over a mile north of the South Pole; the bear could then walk south, turn left, and walk around a latitude circle close to the pole one or more times, and, if *P* had been in any one of a number of precise places, it would arrive back at the same meridian after exactly one mile of circling; then it would turn left again, walk a mile due north, and arrive back at *P*. (What color is the bear? Who can say, since there are no bears at the South Pole?)

*Answer: The subject being studied is not language learning, topology, spherical trigonometry (and certainly not bears) but, in all three cases, problem solving.*

In an effort to help students think more effectively, many universities and colleges now offer courses that present practical applications of research in this subject—the subspecialty that many cognitive scientists regard as the most important area within their discipline. And surely problem solving *is* the most valuable of higher mental activities, for it creates a special and consequential interaction between the individual and the environment. It is the source of our ability to adapt ourselves, consciously and deliberately, to situations we have not faced before and for which we have no ready-made built-in response—as extraordinary an evolutionary development as any on record.

We marvel, and rightly so, at the sight of a spider constructing her web; yet for all her skill she is only carrying out a predetermined series of automatic responses to specific stimuli. Any two-year-old child figuring out how to build a simple house of blocks is far more marvelous, because he or she is using intelligence to devise a solution not inherent in the genes.

Or consider how animals deal with their need to create a shelter, and how we do. A robin, at nest-building time, will build her nest in a tree or on a ledge, using grass, twigs, and similar available materials. But if you could move her to a treeless, ledgeless, grassless environment such as a sandspit or barren islet and keep her alive there, she would not be able to nest, even though terns were contentedly doing so in the sand dunes. The robin is programmed by a set of innate responses to build only one kind of nest; she is not a problem solver. A human being, in contrast, is adaptable; explorers and castaways have made all sorts of shelters for themselves—mud huts, log cabins, stone walls with thatched roofs, tepees of animal hide, igloos, whatever could be made from whatever was at hand.

It is true, of course, that the more highly developed the animal's nervous system, the less it is guided by instinctual responses to stimuli and the more it becomes capable of simple problem solving. A hungry chicken in a U-shaped enclosure, seeing food on the other side, will agitatedly rush to and fro along the fence; a dog, in the same situation, will recognize quickly that it has to head away from the food in order to get around the U to the other side. But then comes a quantum leap: the human being is a different kind of animal, vastly more capable of adapting to new situations or, what is the same thing, solving problems. The immense accumulation of tools, skills, knowledge, and folkways that constitutes each human culture is the product of human problem solving. (A few animals have also solved problems new to them and passed these discoveries on to their fellows—the chimps who use slender twigs to fish termites out of their nests are an example—but such instances are extremely rare.) We recognize and prize this special aspect of our nature: we are endlessly entranced by myths such as the cleansing of the Augean stables or stories of the *Robinson Crusoe* genre—or their space-age, sci-fi equivalents—because it is the very essence of humanity to encounter problems for which we are unprepared by either biology or acquired knowledge and to solve them.

I am following Allen Newell and Herbert Simon, the leading expositors of modern problem-solving theory, in using "problem" and "problem solving" in this way. To quote them: "A person is confronted with a problem when he wants something and does not know immediately what series of actions he can perform to get it." If you need to find the square root of 1764 and remember the procedure, you need only carry it out; the problem is a trivial one. But if you have forgotten how to extract square roots, it is a nontrivial problem; you have to figure out how to reach the goal in some other way, such as squaring various small numbers and working your way to the goal by a series of ever-closer approximations.

Some cognitive scientists prefer a much broader definition of problem solving than this; they maintain that all thinking is an effort to arrive at some desired goal. In this view, even trying to remember something is a problem: you choose a strategy (What letter does it start with?), execute it, and, if it doesn't work, choose another (What does it sound like? Where was

I when I heard it? and so on). Similarly, understanding any brief or elliptical utterance can be thought of as solving a problem: you need to add contextual meaning, or choose among possible meanings, to make sense out of it.

But there is little real problem solving in mental acts such as these; the individual has so much information and so many acquired skills that finding the solution involves only routine procedures. As with the extracting of square roots—or double-entry bookkeeping, or flying an airplane—when you are confronted with any task at which you are adept, you don't solve a problem but merely perform a learned and practiced skill. Many problem-solving courses drill the students in working out certain kinds of problems (such as the one above involving the substitution of words to figure out how to say "big peppers" in a foreign tongue), and the students definitely get better at them, but cognitive scientists suspect that some or even many of these students become better at dealing with only those kinds of problems and not others.

Robin Jeffries, of the University of Colorado, recently conducted an experiment that bears on this point. She trained a group of people in solving missionary-cannibal problems like the one on pages 25–26. After her subjects were adept at this kind of problem, she gave them specimens of another standard task known as the water-jar problem. (Suppose, for instance, you have a 9-quart jar and a 4-quart jar, and need to measure out 6 quarts. You can draw as much water, and throw away as much, as you like. How would you get exactly 6 quarts?*) If Jeffries' subjects had acquired general problem-solving skill from their missionaries-and-cannibals training, they should have done better at water-jar problems than a control group without such training, but Dr. Jeffries found that they didn't.

In a sense, the human being trained to extract square roots, do double-entry bookkeeping, or fly a plane is somewhat like the spider building her web or the robin her nest. The difference is that the animal has been equipped for the task largely by instinct, the human being by training, or, as cognitive scientists prefer to say, one has the information coded into its genes, the other has acquired it by learning. In either case, the organism possesses what it needs to solve the problem; hence only trivial problem solving is involved.

But when you do not have all the information you need, you engage in

* The solution: work backwards. How could you pour off 3 quarts from a full 9-quart jar? By having 1 quart in the 4-quart jar. How can you measure 1 quart? Fill the 9-quart jar, pour off enough to fill the 4-quart jar and dump it; repeat. That leaves 1 in the 9-quart jar; transfer it to the empty 4-quart jar; fill the big one; pour off enough to finish filling the little one. That leaves 6 in the 9-quart jar.

serious problem solving. Imagine that you are flying in the right front seat of a two-place plane with a friend who is a pilot. He falls unconscious and you grab the controls. If you happen to be a pilot, you have a task to perform; if you have never flown a plane, you have a problem to solve.

The distinction between solving problems one knows how to solve ("knowledge-based performance") and those one doesn't know how to solve ("real" or nontrivial problem solving) is arbitrary; a great many situations involve some knowledge but some area of uncertainty. Even so routine a process as starting your car may involve a bit of real problem solving if, say, it is cranky one morning, and you have to figure out what has gone wrong. Conversely, even so challenging a problem as figuring out how to safely land a manned spaceship on the moon involves an immense backlog of knowledge of physics, engineering, and human physiology, without which space engineers could not have begun to solve it.

Yet if most problems are neither wholly trivial nor wholly without some knowledge base, they call upon us to perform two distinctly different kinds of mental activity, and it is the latter of these that is so characteristic of humans. The difference between the two kinds of mental activity has been recognized for a long time, as evidenced by the existence of two words, *algorithm* and *heuristic*, each of which has been used for centuries more or less as it is today. An algorithm is a learned, memorized, working plan or procedure. Suppose you are faced with this simple algebraic task:

$$\text{Solve for } x: \frac{2x}{5} + 7 = 13$$

If you remember high-school algebra, you apply the following three-step algorithm: (1) get rid of the denominator of $x$ (to do so here, you multiply each expression by 5):

$$2x + 35 = 65$$

(2) get rid of multiplicands of $x$ (here, you divide everything by 2):

$$x + \frac{35}{2} = \frac{65}{2}$$

(3) and move everything but $x$ to the right side of the equation (changing the sign, as needed):

$$x = \frac{65}{2} - \frac{35}{2} = \frac{30}{2} = 15$$

Assuming you knew the algorithm and applied it to solve for $x$, you solved the problem—but didn't do any real problem solving.

When, however, you possess some but not all of the requisite knowledge to reach a goal, you must use more general strategies for getting there, such as trying to see the problem from various perspectives, testing what seems to be a likely approach up to a point where it seems unprofitable, backing up and trying another route, and so on. These broad principles of exploration and evaluation are known as heuristics. In the water-jar problem above, a heuristic approach might have gone something like this: "Is there an easy answer? If I fill one and pour off into the other, can I get 6? . . . No. . . . What if I fill and pour twice? . . . No, no good. But if I could fill the 9 and pour off 3, I'd have it. How can I do that? I could, if I had only 1 quart in the 4-quart jar," and so forth.

No doubt every algorithm is the end product of what was once a problem requiring heuristic solution. But it is heuristic thinking, not algorithmic performance, that is interesting, for it is the kind of exploratory, unprogrammed mental process that is species-specific to humankind, or nearly so enough to warrant the term.

We are fascinated by instances of intelligent problem solving in individual animals: Wolfgang Köhler's celebrated chimpanzee, slowly realizing that it could fit two jointed bamboo poles together to fish in an out-of-reach banana; Tolman's rats, figuring out which avenues to the food box were blocked, without having to try them all (see pp. 64–65); or any suburbanite's local raccoon, managing to get the lid off the garbage can despite various preventive devices. But after decades of animal watching, ethologists have only a handful of such examples, compared with the infinite panorama of human problem solving.

We seem to have an almost limitless ability to solve problems—and we need to have, since so many of our solutions create new problems we could not have anticipated. Modern medicine and public health practices, for instance, are solving old problems of disease and untimely death but vastly increasing those of overpopulation, malnutrition, and poverty. But it is human of us to create such new problems by solving old ones, and then to seek to solve the new ones in turn. The misanthrope might say that we would do better to simply ignore the old ones, but that is not the way of the human species, and it is to our credit that it is not.

Why is problem solving such a rarity in animals and such a commonplace in human beings?

Some of the reasons are obvious. For one, our nervous systems come equipped with very little instinctual programming, and we therefore need to figure out answers to our problems. For another, we have a vastly greater capacity than even our closest relatives among the animals to store and retrieve information, to think in conceptual and symbolic terms, and to test solutions in our minds by means of these symbol systems.

The most important reason, however, is not so obvious: we *perceive* situations as problems, and therefore undertake to solve them. An ape, coming to a broad river, would see it merely as the end to further travel in that direction; a human being might see it as a body of water to be crossed, and thereupon invent a raft. Innate neural responses and early learning provide each species of animal with the specific procedures it needs to obtain food, avoid enemies, mate, care for its young, and so on; human beings, too, acquire procedures for dealing with these basic problems, but they also solve countless others that did not exist until their own minds saw them as problems. Art and arithmetic, music and money, detergents and democracy, are all solutions to problems created not by Nature but by the human mind.

Problem solving is virtually species-specific, but what is absolutely species-specific and ultimately human is *problem generating*. The problem is in the eye of the beholder, and we are beholders.


### Try This One: Puzzles as a Research Tool

I doubt that there is any reader of this book who has not, at some time in the past, come across the six-stick problem. It goes like this:

> Given: Six matchsticks or toothpicks of equal length. Problem: Arrange them to make four equilateral triangles, the sides of which are one stick long.

If you have forgotten the solution and try to find it by pushing the sticks around on a tabletop, you will soon conclude that there must be a trick to it, for you can make only two equilateral triangles out of the six sticks. (You can also form a square with crisscrossed diagonals, thus making four triangles, but they're neither equilateral nor are their sides one stick long.) Finally, at some point you see the so-called trick: instead of laying the matches out flat on the tabletop, you make a tetrahedron—a four-sided pyramid—like the one in Figure 42.

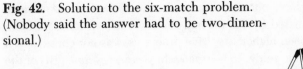

**Fig. 42.**   Solution to the six-match problem.
(Nobody said the answer had to be two-dimensional.)

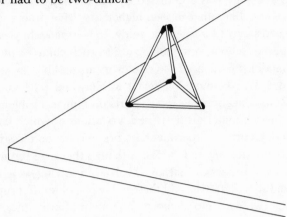

The six-stick problem looks like a mere "brain-teaser"—the kind of puzzle one finds in Sunday papers or airline magazines, meant to while away idle moments. But to psychologists investigating problem solving before the era of cognitive science, it was much more than that; it was a task of a kind ideally suited to the laboratory study of problem solving—that is, simple enough to permit the observer to see, in isolation, a single principle at work.

In this case, the principle behind the solution is known as *reorganization.* The mind, as we have seen, does not passively receive incoming sense data but actively organizes them; if, however, the structure that it imposes on them fails to make sense, it will eventually reorganize the data in some other way. Most people, coming upon the six-stick problem, organize the data two-dimensionally: they visualize the sticks lying on a flat surface. When they can find no solution within this frame of reference, they rearrange the data in a three-dimensional frame. Usually, of course, they do not do so deliberately but in a spontaneous flash of insight. However, reorganization can be, and often is, consciously applied by good problem solvers: they deliberately try to "take a different look" or "turn things around" when they get stuck. Great inventions often come about in this way: efforts to design a sewing machine got nowhere as long as the needle, with a point at one end and the eye at the other, had to pass completely through the fabric and be returned, but in 1846 Elias Howe reorganized the data—he put the eye of the needle in its point—and solved the problem.

The use of puzzles and games as a research tool began not in our own amusement-loving country but in Germany. In the 1920s, when American psychology was dominated by the rat and the nonsense syllable, problem solving, like other unseen higher cognitive processes, was not considered a good subject for scientific study. In Germany, however, psychologists of the Gestalt school were looking at just such complex mental phenomena, and a handful of them whose names mean nothing to most Americans today— Max Wertheimer, Wolfgang Köhler, and Karl Duncker, among others— were concentrating their efforts on human problem-solving behavior. The research materials they used, variations of which continue to be employed today both in experimental work and in the classroom, consisted in large part of puzzles and games. Although these are fun to work on, they require mental processes that are involved in solving weightier kinds of problems, and the Gestaltists and their followers, observing subjects solving such puzzles, were able to enunciate a number of principles, such as reorganization, that are basic to all problem solving.

Duncker would bring a subject into a room in which there were a standing screen, some chairs, and, on a table, three small cardboard boxes containing matches, candles, and thumbtacks. "You are to mount a candle vertically on the screen so it can serve as a light," Duncker would say. Most of his subjects would look around, perplexed, seeing no materials that lent themselves to the task; a majority never did succeed in solving the problem within the time allowed. But with other subjects, Duncker would have emptied the boxes beforehand and put the matches, candles, and thumbtacks alongside them. Most of these people solved the problem easily: they thumbtacked a box top to the screen, and mounted a candle on top of it with melted wax, as in Figure 43. What kept the first group from solving the problem was a learning phenomenon that Duncker called *functional fixedness*. Those who saw the boxes being used to hold various objects perceived them as having that function and were unable to see them as having any other; those who saw them empty had no such limitation.

Many other experiments, performed then and later, have confirmed the validity of Duncker's observation. In one of the more ingenious of them, subjects would enter a room in which a rusty pipe was bolted upright to the floor, with a Ping-Pong ball down inside it; the problem was to retrieve the ball with anything at hand. In the room were a hammer, pliers, rulers, soda straws, bent pins, and an old bucket of dirty wash water. After fishing around in vain with the various tools and objects, most students saw the solution: they poured the dirty water into the pipe and floated the ball to the top. Another group of subjects were confronted by the same problem, but

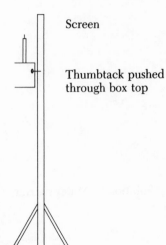

Screen

Thumbtack pushed
through box top

**Fig. 43.** Solution to Duncker's candle-mounting problem lies in seeing that a box can be used as something other than a container.

with one difference: instead of the bucket, there was a crystal pitcher of ice water, surrounded by goblets, on a table covered by a fresh white cloth. Not one of these subjects solved the problem; none of them could dissociate the ice water from its indicated function.

Another aspect of problem solving that interested Gestaltists in Germany and elsewhere was the effect of past experience. At Yeshiva University, Abraham S. Luchins, who had studied under Wertheimer, concocted the classic water-jar problem. He presented his subjects with a list of tasks of which this is part:

| Given containers of these sizes | | | | measure out this much water |
|---|---|---|---|---|
| | A | B | C | |
| Problem 2 | 21 | 127 | 3 | 100 |
| Problem 3 | 14 | 163 | 25 | 99 |
| Problem 4 | 18 | 43 | 10 | 5 |
| Problem 5 | 9 | 42 | 6 | 21 |
| Problem 6 | 20 | 59 | 4 | 31 |
| Problem 7 | 23 | 49 | 3 | 20 |

Most of Luchins' subjects figured out after a while that an easy solution to problem 2 is to fill jar B, pour off enough to fill jar A, and pour off enough more to fill jar C twice; that is, $127 - 21 - 3 - 3 = 100$. They generally solved problem 3 a bit more quickly, and the others even more so; the same

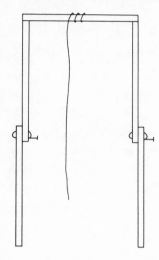

**Fig. 44.**   Solution to Maier's string problem

procedure works in each case. But four fifths of Luchins' subjects failed to notice that problem 7, though it can be solved in the same four steps (49 − 23 − 3 − 3 = 20), can also be solved in only two steps (23 − 3 = 20). What kept them from seeing the shorter solution was the phenomenon Luchins called *problem set*—a mental preparedness to solve the problem in the same way one successfully solved similar problems in the past. (Subjects to whom he gave problem 7 first almost always solved it the quicker way.) Even quite easy problems, Luchins concluded, may be solved inefficiently or not at all if one has a strong set based on past experience.

Yet we know that experience does often help us in problem solving. The question then is: When does it help, and when does it produce problem set? A psychologist named Norman R. F. Maier investigated this by asking subjects to hang a string from the ceiling without defacing it, given only five wooden poles, some clamps, and string. The solution was to tie the string around one pole and brace it against the ceiling with two long supports made by clamping pairs of wooden poles together, as in Figure 44. Then he gave them a second task: with some poles and clamps, make a hat rack. The solution is to clamp two poles together, reaching from floor to ceiling, with the handle of the clamp serving as the hat rack. Of those subjects who hadn't done the string problem beforehand, only one in four solved the hat-rack problem in the allotted time, but of those who had done the string problem, twice as many solved the hat-rack problem—and if the string problem apparatus had been left standing in the room, three times as many did so. This illustrates *positive transfer*: past experience helps when the new problem is closely related to the previous one.

When, then, does experience lead to problem set? Maier didn't say; the difference between his experiment and the Luchins water-jar experiment, however, is easy to see. In the former, there are only two problems, related but somewhat different; in the latter, there is a whole series, all looking very much alike. Evidently, experience both helps and hinders, depending on how much of it you've had and how rigidly patterned it is. That's why academic and commercial think tanks are so productive of good problem solving: specialists think in terms of their specialties, but are broadened in their thinking by contact with people from other fields, who don't have the same problem set.

Another and broader avenue of inquiry by the Gestaltists and others was the search for the general structure of the problem-solving process from beginning to end. One early investigator, the American Graham Wallas, asked problem solvers to say what they had done, and grouped their experiences into a four-stage process: *preparation* (data gathering, and so on), *incubation* (letting it stew), *illumination* (the flash of insight), and *verification* (checking it out).

This four-stage description became the basis of various early books on how to solve problems by means of heuristics appropriate to each stage, such as the classic *How to Solve It*, by George Polya, the Stanford mathematics professor. But while it is useful to be aware of these stages, to know about them is not necessarily to be able to make the right things happen in each. For one thing, much of what happens is not conscious and not under our control. For another, one can use Polya's broad heuristics only to the extent that one has the right information and experience to carry them out.

Take, for instance, the anagram, a much-used genre of research problem, of which Polya offers this tough example:

## DRY OXTAIL IN REAR

Problem: Find one word made up of all these letters. His advice consists of heuristic maxims like "What are the data?" "Decompose and recombine," "Restate the problem," "Can you imagine some other related problem?" But *how*? I might decompose and recombine according to my own experience—and it might not work; you might do so in some way I would not have thought of and move on toward the answer.

Polya's own way is to start by sorting out the vowels and consonants to see whether there will be many syllables:

AAEIIOY DLNRRRTX

Yes, it has many syllables—but I didn't find that that gave me any ideas of how to proceed.

Next, Polya says, try to solve part of the problem, if you can—the ending, perhaps, which might be -ATION or -ELY. That seems reasonable; on the other hand, one can easily get stuck with such a partial solution (neither of which happens to be correct) and fail to move on.

Actually, what really does the job of anagram problem solving, at least for me, is a busy ferment in the mind, much of it unconscious, a shuffling and testing of possible letter combinations until one of them strikes a chord in memory and leads on to a solution. I myself got no place with this anagram until I hit on the notion—not derived from any heuristic in Polya's list—that since X is uncommon, I would look first at ways to use it. In the prefix OXY-? That led nowhere. In the far more common prefix EX-? In a moment, this became EXTRA-, and then, all at once, I saw the answer: EXTRAORDINARILY. What happened between the formation of EXTRA- and the solution I cannot say; it certainly was not an orderly, conscious, or voluntary process.

But at least the early steps of this solution are well described by another model of the problem-solving process, worked out by Duncker in the 1940s. He saw that the route taken by the mind in its groping toward a solution could be described as a "decision tree" or a "solution tree." The problem solver starts out with only a general idea of which way to go, but sees a number of major avenues of thought branching out ahead; each, in turn, branches out into more specific avenues, and those into still more specific ones. Solving the problem consists of making the right choice at each fork, or, if the branch chosen leads in the wrong direction or to a dead end, backing up and trying another, until one has worked one's way to the solution terminus. Here is a difficult problem Duncker posed to his subjects:

> Given a human being with an inoperable stomach tumor, and rays which destroy organic tissue at sufficient intensity, by what procedure can one free him of the tumor by these rays and at the same time avoid destroying the healthy tissue which surrounds it?

In a 1945 account of this experiment, Duncker reported that his subjects tended to think first of a general alternative, then proceed down this branch of thought and its subbranches until each proved unworkable, then back up enough to try another, and so on. One subject came up with the general solution, "Avoid contact between rays and healthy tissue"; followed this to the more specific idea, "Use free path to stomach"; and then proceeded to the still more specific solution, "Use esophagus" (unworkable and imprecise). Backing up, the subject tried other general alternatives, among them, "Lower the intensity of the rays on their way through healthy tissue"; this led to the more specific idea, "Give weak intensity in periphery and concentrate in place of tumor"; and this to an actual solution: "Send a broad and weak bundle of rays through a lens in such a way that the tumor lies at the focal point and thus receives intense radiation." (Duncker adds, as a footnote, "This solution is closely related to the best solution: crossing of several weak bundles of rays at the tumor." Today we have yet another: rotate the patient so that the rays always pass through the tumor but are continually moving through the rest of the body.)

The process of this subject's problem solving, as diagrammed by Duncker (see Fig. 45), does indeed take the form of a sort of tree; the successful route in this diagram is at the far right, all others having led to dead ends.

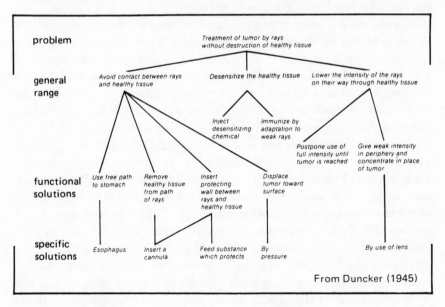

**Fig. 45.** Solution tree to Duncker's tumor problem

**Fig. 46.**   Three-disc Tower of Hanoi problem. Goal: Reassemble discs on peg 2, in same order, in smallest number of moves.

In reality, Duncker's subjects shuttled back and forth in their thinking and did nothing as orderly and logical as the decision tree suggests. That may be because the problem is so complex and does not lend itself to a tidy, logical procedure. Accordingly, most other early investigators of the overall structure of problem solving chose to stick to more controlled and easily analyzed problems, of the puzzle or game kind. In many a problem, for instance, subjects have a goal they cannot immediately reach, and therefore proceed by means of subgoals that they can reach; the forks in Duncker's decision tree are subgoals, but the decision process is far easier to observe in the case of a puzzle like the Tower of Hanoi.

This old puzzle, in an extremely simple version (fit for a small child), is shown in Figure 46. The goal is to assemble the discs on the center peg; the rules are that you may move only one at a time, and that no disc may ever rest on one smaller than itself. The best solution takes seven moves: to reach the goal, one must move disc L to the center peg; to do that, however, the others must be removed from L, which means that disc M has to be moved (subgoal); but to do that, disc S has to be moved (sub-subgoal); and so on. The sequence is as follows: S to 2, M to 3, S to 3, L to 2, S to 1, M to 2, S to 2. The decision tree—the actual track of your thinking—might be diagrammed as in Figure 47. Of course you wouldn't have tried all these dead-end routes, or the many others not shown here; you would have looked ahead or sensed the outcome of those branches that led to dead ends. That's because this is a simple version of the game. But you're likely to proceed down wrong routes in a more sophisticated version of the game such as six-, seven-, or eight-disc Tower of Hanoi. (You can try this, if you have some foreign coins on hand, by making a pile of eight of different sizes. Or you can try six-disc Tower of Hanoi with the six common American coins, or, if you

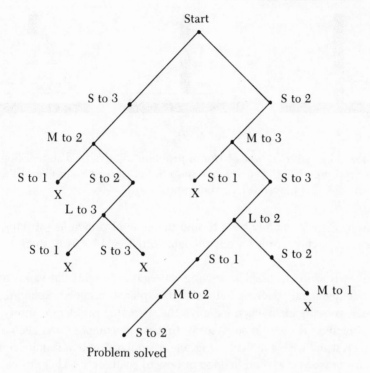

**Fig. 47.**   Decision tree for three-disc Tower of Hanoi problem

have no silver dollar, five-disc Tower of Hanoi.) In these more advanced games, the subgoals used in the three-disc version work at first, but all too soon it becomes clear that you need a whole series of deeper subgoals. For instance, given the situation in Figure 48, how do you get disc 7 onto disc 8? By getting 6 off 7 (but not on 8). But how do you move 6? By getting 5 off it. And so on. If you play eight-disc Tower of Hanoi perfectly, it takes 255 moves; without a perfect goal-structure, it may take you twice that many, or more.* If you try it, talk to yourself—say out loud (or in words, even though unuttered) what you're doing and why; in one study, subjects who verbalized their moves did very much better at Tower of Hanoi problems

* A perfect five-disc game takes 31 moves; a perfect six-disc game, 63 moves; seven-disc, 127 moves. A sixty-four-disc game played perfectly at the rate of one move per second would take a trillion years.

**Fig. 48.**   Eight-disc Tower of Hanoi problem in advanced state. Subgoal: get everything off 7 so it can move onto 8. Sub-subgoal: get everything off 6 so it can be moved off 7. And so on.

than subjects who merely tried to find the general principle—striking evidence that having words for our thoughts often enables us to think better.

The early work on problem solving was rich in insights but vague about details and generally lacking in theory; its explanations need explaining. To say that we reorganize when we solve the six-match problem is surely correct—but how do we do so? To say that we decompose and recombine when wrestling with a difficult anagram or similar problem is quite right— but how do we know when to do so or how to go about it? These things can hardly come about in a random hit-or-miss fashion, since so many of us solve problems in similar ways; there must be specific mental processes that account for such phenomena.

Similarly, to view the overall structure of problem solving as a decision tree through which we work our way corresponds to observed facts and makes sense out of them. But by what means do we avoid having to follow every branch to its dead end? No chess master could ever make his first move if he had to envision and mentally test the hundreds of thousands of possibilities within the first few moves, let alone the $10^{120}$ moves in all possible games (one plus the word "trillion" ten times). Modern computers, programmed to play chess, can test millions of possibilities in a matter of minutes, something the human mind is utterly incapable of—and yet the mind does not need that capability; it "prunes the tree" efficiently, takes only a tiny percentage of wrong forks, and follows most of them only partway. How does it do that? What is the working plan that makes our problem-solving minds operate according to wisdom rather than rely on computerlike mindless searching? The answers to such questions, curiously, emerged only when cognitive scientists borrowed theory from computer science and created a new model of what goes on, unseen and unseeable, in the human intellect.

## Travels in Inner Space

When cognitive scientists began to view thinking as the processing of information, it became possible for them to take a much more detailed look at human problem solving. They could now describe such broad, vague phenomena as problem set and understanding in terms of far more specific steps like the perception, recognition, classification, storage, retrieval, and transformation of data by the human information processor.

Every such description embodies a theory. At the moment, there are many somewhat discrepant versions of problem-solving theory, but one of them is so widely accepted that its major concepts are used even by those that compete with it. It is the theory set forth by Allen Newell and Herbert Simon of Carnegie-Mellon University in their monumental *Human Problem Solving*—the product of seventeen years of work—and in a number of more recent papers written with other colleagues.

Here, first, is a capsule version of the Newell and Simon view of the interaction between the environment and the human problem-solving organism (or, as I shall more simply say, you):

—First, you perceive the raw data and process these perceptions far enough to recognize the *task environment*—the components of the problem or the terms in which it is presented. They may consist of words or other symbols and their meanings, or these plus some objects (six matches; a Tower of Hanoi set; poles, clamps, and string); or perhaps just an object (a stuck door, an unfamiliar TV set in a hotel room, a balky lawn mower).

—Next, you transform this information into what Newell and Simon call your *problem space*—your mental representation of the task environment. This is your interpretation of where the goal is, where you are in relation to it, and what kinds of acts you must perform to get to it—logical or arithmetical procedures, a shaking and jiggling of the parts, trial-and-error juxtapositions, and so on. In the six-stick problem, an important aspect of the problem space is whether you think of the solution as taking place in two dimensions or in three. In dealing with a stuck door, your problem space might picture the goal as getting the door to open—or, alternatively, getting to the other side, a quite different matter with quite different possible solutions.

—Depending on the way you have conceived of the problem space, you use various kinds of information drawn from memory, or given with the problem, to process the data so as to move toward the goal. The total set of mental operations you use in the effort to move from given to goal is what Newell and Simon call your *production system,* a computer-science term that can be roughly translated as your *program.* In the six-stick problem, the program is bound to be very simple; it might consist of orders that cause you to recall what an equilateral triangle looks like, duplicate that pattern with three matches and again with the other three, check your results (two triangles, no solution), slide the matches about in search of a more efficient design (adjoining, crisscrossing), and so on.

—In the course of carrying out the program, you notice whether any step or series of steps decreases the distance to the goal; if so, you continue with it, but if not, you move on to the next step or steps in the program. If the entire program fails to carry you to the goal, you either quit, modify the program, or change the problem space. In the six-stick problem, the latter possibility means conceiving of the problem space as three-dimensional; within this framework, the program leads to the answer almost at once.

Marvin Minsky of MIT even argues—differing somewhat with Newell and Simon—that problem solving is not so much a search for a successful program as for the best problem space. The following problem, though not his example, exemplifes the point:

> Two train stations are fifty miles apart. At 2 P.M. one Saturday afternoon two trains start towards each other, one from each station. Just as the trains pull out of the stations, a bird springs into the air in front of the first train and flies ahead to the front of the second train. When the bird reaches the second train it turns back and flies towards the first train. The bird continues to do this until the trains meet. If both trains travel at the rate of twenty-five miles per hour and the bird flies at one hundred miles per hour, how many miles will the bird have flown before the trains meet?

If your problem space concerns the bird's flight path, you will have a long and difficult mental trip ahead of you. But if it concerns how long the bird will fly—and hence how far it will go—your trip in inner space will be short and simple, to wit: the trains will take one hour to reach each other; hence the bird will be flying for one hour; therefore it will cover one hundred miles.

Newell and Simon derived the basic elements of their theory by first using themselves as experimental subjects: while playing chess and Tower of Hanoi, solving cryptarithmetic problems, and proving theorems in formal logic, they looked closely at their own thought processes and sought to express them in information-processing terms. Then they offered similar problems to a number of other subjects—most of whom were undergraduates at Carnegie-Mellon—asking them to say everything they were thinking as they worked on the problems. Every word was taken down; the protocol of one run-of-the-mill chess player, considering a single middle-game move, contained 241 units of thought (these ranged from single words to complex sentences), while the protocol of our old acquaintance, S3, working on the DONALD + GERALD = ROBERT cryptarithmetic problem (see p. 79), was made up of 311 such utterances. These were, of course, only the subject's conscious thoughts, but what goes on in the unconscious can be inferred from them. As one of Newell and Simon's colleagues puts it, protocol material is like the surfacings of a porpoise: most of the time the creature is hidden from view, but one can pretty well surmise where it has been between sightings.

Here, for instance, are a few lines from the beginning of S3's protocol and what Newell and Simon made of them:

$$\begin{array}{r}\text{DONALD} \\ +\ \text{GERALD} \\ \hline \text{ROBERT}\end{array} \qquad \text{Given: D = 5}$$

S3: . . . Looking at the two D's . . .

Each D is 5;
therefore, T is zero.
So I think I'll start by writing that problem here.

In Newell and Simon's analysis, the thoughts in these lines were generated by two steps of information processing, which they express in this piece of arcane computer notation:

P1:  $D \leftarrow 5 \rightarrow FC(D) \ (\Rightarrow \text{col.1})$;
    $PC[\text{col.1}] \ (\Rightarrow T = 0 \text{ new})$

P11:  $T = 0 \rightarrow TD(T,0) \ (\Rightarrow +)$

This, in English, means roughly: "Find the vertical column that contains the variable $D$; assign the number 5 to instances of $D$ in that column; process the column (add it); assign digit 0 to variable $T$; test digit to see if it results in a contradiction; since it doesn't, add it to the store of knowledge."

It takes only fourteen such processes in all, used again and again in different parts of the problem, to account for nearly all S3's steps in his rambling, error-prone trip through his problem space. (A few steps remain unexplained because of limitations of the theory.) Rambling and error-prone it was, indeed: one can tell that from the words themselves ("I'm not sure" . . . "Now, wait a second" . . . "Just trying to sort of bluff my way through this" . . . "I'm in sort of a dilemma"), but a pictorial representation will make it clear what kind of route S3 traveled. Newell and Simon's graph of the protocol, in which each dot represents a "node"—a definite step in thought— looks like Figure 49. The path that finally led S3 to the solution is the one running down the left side of the graph and across the bottom; all the rest—the earlier parts of the protocol—represents efforts which came to dead ends of contradiction or points beyond which no further movement was possible.

Was S3 particularly inept at solving this problem? Not really; he was merely average. Does this suggest that most human problem solving is grossly inefficient? After all, the ideal solution, as you may remember, can be stated in a few sentences (see pp. 367–68). But that's the solution one can put down after the fact; S3, like all human problem solvers, had to find that path by choosing among many possible avenues of thought, pursuing those that seemed likeliest to him, deciding which way to go at every fork, and, at every dead end, backing up to try another route.

In many of his choices he was wrong—and yet his performance, like most human problem solving, was highly efficient. For there were hundreds of thousands of wrong avenues of thought that he did *not* pursue. The nine unassigned digits could have been assigned to the nine unidentified letters of the problem in 362,880 different ways, 362,879 of which are wrong and won't work. A computer can easily generate and test all of those ways one after another by "brute force," or, as it is more properly called, "serial searching"; according to Simon, a computer so programmed in 1969 might have taken ten hours to solve the problem, while today's far faster computers might need one hour. But S3, whose mental processes were far slower than comparable processes of the most antiquated computer, needed only half an hour to solve the problem, and some of Newell and Simon's more apt subjects did so in ten minutes. How did S3 do it? By *not* performing a serial search; by avoiding the great bulk of the possibilities for various good reasons, and testing only the likely few.

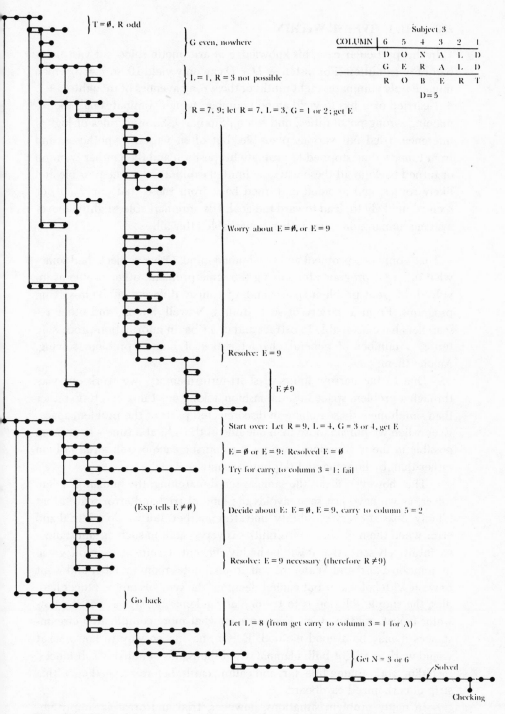

**Fig. 49.** Mental journey of one person through a cryptarithmetic problem

In this particular case, his knowledge of arithmetic ruled out vast numbers of possibilities. (For instance, $D + D$ can only yield 10, so $T = 0$, which immediately eliminates eight ninths of the wrong avenues of thought; $L + L + 1$-carried-over has to yield an odd number, which eliminates half the remaining wrong possibilities; and so on.) Similarly, S3 used rules of logical inference, tried out various plausible (but often wrong) hypotheses, and from time to time stopped to evaluate his position and then either went on or turned back; in all these ways, he limited exploration to the possible and likely routes, and avoided or turned back from those that could not, or seemed unlikely to, lead toward the goal. His unremarkable, slightly above-average human mind was rather remarkable after all.

That's only one protocol and one human mind. Other subjects had somewhat different programs for solving the same problem; other problems involved different problem spaces and, of course, different problem-solving programs. From a variety of such studies, Newell, Simon, and other researchers have been able to extract and describe, in information-processing terms, a number of general characteristics of human problem solving. Among them:

—Due to the narrow limits of short-term memory, we work our way through a problem space in serial fashion, taking one thing at a time rather than simultaneously searching in disconnected parts of the problem space. Even when we pursue more than one line of thought at a time—as appears possible in the unconscious—we seem to pursue each one in serial fashion rather than by hopping and skipping around.

—This, however, is not the same as serial searching; the human problem solver, as we have just seen, avoids the kind of trial-and-error search that blindly looks at every possibility, one after another. But we do use trial and error when the number of possibilities is very small; in such circumstances we intuitively sense that it will be highly efficient. To cite an example given by Johnson-Laird and Wason: if you are in a hotel room in Tibet and want to wash with hot water but cannot decipher the symbols on the faucet handles, the simple solution is to try one at random, and, if it is not the hot-water faucet, try the other. Even in somewhat more complicated circumstances it may be a good method: Edison, having no way to know what would work as a light-bulb filament, tried thousands of unlikely substances, including cork, fishing line, tar, and calling cards, before succeeding with a strip of carbonized cardboard.

—In many problem situations, however, trial and error is simply unworkable. Even the most elementary steps of mental processing take anywhere from forty to a hundred milliseconds each; that sounds fast, but it isn't fast enough when the number of possibilities is large. As simple a problem as an eight-letter anagram—BISETUAL, for instance—could take up to fifty-six working hours, if you solved it by writing out all 40,320 permutations of the letters at the rate of one every five seconds. Most people, however, can solve this anagram in a few minutes at most, making only a dozen or so rearrangements before reaching the answer (which you can find below*). As Herbert Simon observes, "It is a major characteristic of the human problem solver to do a selective search, not an exhaustive search." We wouldn't, for instance, waste time looking for the anagram of BISETUAL among possibilities that begin with BT or SB; we know better. In the same way, a bridge player deciding what to lead doesn't have to consider all thirteen cards in his or her hand and all the consequences that each might entail, but chooses among the few that follow powerful, time-tested strategies, such as leading a card of the suit one's partner bid (which is, presumably, the partner's strongest suit). By means of such bridge heuristics, the player who leads can massively prune the tree of decision, leaving few branches to be considered.

—Another widely applicable heuristic that makes for selective search is to comb through our experience for an analogy—some object or process related to the present problem—and use it as a guide. Confronted by a problem that is new to us—anything from an unfamiliar machine or mysterious leak to an inexplicable piece of behavior by a friend—we may find a solution by thinking of some analogous object or situation from which to draw a reasonable inference. A neighbor of mine unearthed a boulder in his vegetable garden last spring and found it too heavy to carry or even roll, but there was no room to bring in a garden cart. He thought about how houses are moved and tankers are launched, and realized that they're slid. That was his answer: he eased the boulder onto the blade of a shovel and towed it out of the garden. (He merely reinvented the sledge—a conveyance predating the wheel, and regularly used for clearing stones from fields by New England farmers of Colonial days.)

—Of still more general usefulness in pruning the decision tree is a pair of simple heuristics that apply to a great many problems. The first is what Newell and Simon call "best-first search": at any fork in the tree, you first try the next available node that appears closest to the goal. It is highly effi-

* SUITABLE.

cient to seek to move toward the goal with every step (even though sometimes one must move away from it to bypass some obstacle). The second heuristic is "means-end analysis": having observed that some node lies closer to the goal than your present state, you choose an allowable operation (a means) that will get you there. You thus make that node a subgoal, and often even plan ahead through a series of subgoals, as in advanced Tower of Hanoi games. The same heuristic is often used in daily life; the authors of one current textbook of cognitive science say, by way of example, that the problem of serving up a Chinese dinner could be solved by the following train of means-end analysis:

> What's the difference between what I have now (my initial state) and dinner (the goal state)? A cooked meal. What is needed to cook a meal? Food, an oven [the authors should have said "stove"]. I have an oven. I also have some food, but not Chinese food. What do I do to get Chinese food? Go to the grocery store. The grocery store is down the street, but I haven't any money. What can I do to get some money? Go to the bank, etc.

—Finally, we are adaptive creatures: we learn from experience. When a series of steps leads us toward the goal but then comes to a dead end, we do not go back to the beginning but only as far as we must, so as not to discard any valid part of what we have learned. Moreover, in the course of solving a complex problem we may see the shortcomings of our first strategy and alter it to a more effective one. Yuichiro Anzai and Herbert Simon recently analyzed one woman's experience with five-disc Tower of Hanoi: in the course of four attempts to solve the puzzle, she altered her strategy bit by bit as she saw its defects, eventually arriving at a highly effective scheme in which she worked backward through a series of subgoals. She had not only solved the puzzle but learned how to solve other and more difficult Tower of Hanoi puzzles.

The information-processing model of the mind was taken from computer science, and it is by means of computer science that new hypotheses concerning how the mind solves problems are tested. A researcher who works out a detailed explanation of how any person or group of people solves a particular kind of problem can write that explanation in the form of a computer program and run it on a machine. The results of the run show whether the program follows the same general course as the human being, that is, yields a "trace"—a printout—that is comparable to the human protocols; if it does, the assumptions behind the theory are taken to be supported. Such "computer simulation" of human cognitive processes has become the most powerful tool available for the testing of theories about how the mind works.

Accordingly, Newell and Simon have written and run computer simulations, based on protocols, of human problem solving in the areas of cryptarithmetic, the proving of logical theorems, and various games and puzzles. Hans Berliner at Carnegie-Mellon has written a chess program that is not nearly as powerful as some that exist but that plays chess the way a person does. Walter Reitman at the University of Michigan is developing a Go-playing program that uses knowledge, memory, and judgment in much the same way as a good Go player. Scores of other researchers elsewhere are working on computer programs that simulate the human mind's solving of problems in algebra, physics, medical diagnosis, chemical engineering, backgammon, music composition, graphic design, and poetry, among others.

By now, indeed, many cognitive scientists consider a theory about any aspect of problem solving—or any other area of mental functioning—less than respectable until it has been spelled out with the precision of computer simulation and has provided a trace that is comparable to human protocols. Not that a program will make all the mistakes a human being makes—or do as well as the human being in making intuitive leaps. But if the simulation yields a reasonably good likeness, it is taken to confirm the theory that it embodies.

One might argue that this doesn't really prove what goes on in the mind; it is possible that the mind and the machine follow similar paths but for different reasons. Since we can't see inside the mind, we cannot be certain what produces the visible results of the protocols. But elsewhere in contemporary science we regard indirect evidence as good enough. Much of our knowledge of nuclear physics, for instance, consists of inferences about the nature of invisible atomic particles, based on the tracks of condensed water droplets they leave behind them in a cloud chamber. Quarks, the ultimate constituents of many of those particles, do not even leave such tracks, but high-speed electrons are deflected by protons in a way that implies a substructure of quarks within them. Black dwarf stars and black holes are invisible, but their presence can be inferred from the way visible stars are affected by them.

So it is with the human mind. Merely because its workings are invisible, they are not unknowable; the traces of thought tell us what the imperfect but magnificent machinery that produced them is like.


## Novices and Experts

A theory based on how people solve puzzles and play games may explain in part—but not fully—how they solve the problems of real life. For most puzzles and games are "knowledge-poor"; they involve almost no content. To solve a cryptarithmetic problem, we need know nothing but the rules of simple arithmetic, and a little deductive logic. All the rest of the enormous wealth of knowledge each of us has acquired in life has no bearing on how well or poorly we solve problems in this artificial and narrow domain.

But common sense and everyday observation tell us that it is quite otherwise with the problems of real life. It is obvious that the well-trained and the wise solve such problems better than the ill-trained and the foolish. It is apparent, too, that a person may be a poor poker player but an excellent doctor—or, conversely, an excellent poker player but a poor doctor. Some cognitive scientists, accordingly, have little regard for problem-solving research that uses puzzles and games; as one young psychologist said to me, "It's a case of the drunk looking for his keys under the streetlight—it's where the light is but not where the problem is." Many others, though not sharing his scorn, feel that it is time for them to look at problem-solving behavior as ethologists do at animal behavior—that is, in a naturalistic setting rather than an artificial one.

In recent years, therefore, cognitive scientists have begun to study problem solving in certain knowledge-rich areas, among them thermodynamics, cost accounting, engineering, physics, medical diagnosis, commodity trading, the assessing of trial evidence, and even the composing of fugues and the writing of essays.

In a knowledge-rich domain, the question of how people possessing knowledge solve problems compared with those lacking it is trivial. Obviously, a person lacking special knowledge cannot solve a problem requiring it; there isn't any point asking someone who knows nothing of chemistry how to find and identify a suspected toxic agent in the drinking water. Nor on the other hand is there anything to be learned about problem solving by watching a specialist perform a task he or she is thoroughly familiar with: a chemist routinely checking the quality of a chemical plant's product is not solving a problem.

The nontrivial question, however, is why some people who have special knowledge use it efficiently while others who have it, and are equally intelligent, use it inefficiently. It is the difference between experts and novices; though they may have roughly the same body of information, experts who face a problem they have not encountered before solve it in a fraction of the time needed by novices—an everyday observation that has, until very recently, been unexplained.

The inquiry into how experts solve problems in a knowledge-rich domain has focused more on physics than any other subject, partly because it is orderly and rule-bound, and partly because the nation's need for competent physical scientists and engineers has increased greatly in recent years. Indeed, a number of investigators of expert problem solving are physicists or physics teachers by training and cognitive scientists by adoption.

One of them, Frederick Reif, is a professor of physics at Berkeley, and chairman of its Group in Science and Mathematics Education. Reif had had no background in psychology until his efforts to develop better methods of teaching physics drew him, some years ago, to the study of problem solving; today, though he still calls himself a physicist, he is accepted among cognitive scientists as one of them.

Reif, a small pudgy man with thick glasses and rumpled gray hair, spoke with enthusiasm about his work, pacing back and forth in his office and frequently scribbling on the blackboard to make his points clear. "Experts," he said, "faced with certain problems, can solve them easily, but students, even when you've taught them the necessary skills, can't. Why not? I wanted to find out. So one of my graduate students—Jill Larkin—and I gave some relatively simple problems, such as first-year physics students get, to both experts and novices, and did protocol analyses of their thought processes."

"This, for instance, was a typical problem we used." He slashed at the blackboard with such abandon that chalk fragments showered down on his clothing, but he ignored them as he produced the diagram shown in Figure 50. "$A$ is a ten-pound block," he explained, "$B$ is a five-pound weight, and $mu$ is the coefficient of friction, given here as 0.20. Problem: How much more weight must you add—that is, how heavy must block $C$ be—to keep $A$ from sliding? Now, a typical novice would begin writing equations for all sorts of specific phenomena involved in this situation—including those that play no part in the solution, such as acceleration or the tension in the string. As he worked, he would gradually exclude these irrelevant factors and eventually find the right equation and the answer. But a typical expert would, first of all, identify this as being in the general class of 'normal force'

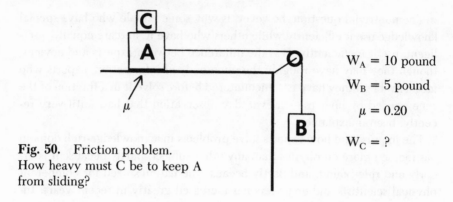

$W_A$ = 10 pound

$W_B$ = 5 pound

$\mu$ = 0.20

$W_C$ = ?

**Fig. 50.** Friction problem.
How heavy must C be to keep A
from sliding?

phenomena, then narrow it down to a question of a subsidiary principle involving friction and motion, and quickly arrive at the right equation and solve the problem."

Experts are able to function in this way, Reif and Larkin concluded after conducting a number of such experiments, because their knowledge is hierarchically organized. In their minds, the specific details and phenomena of physics are logically grouped into chunks, these chunks are grouped into more general topics, and these topics are grouped into still more general ones. Reif drew on the board the diagram in Figure 51 to illustrate the form of such organization. I recognized this as a concept-classification tree such as I had heard about earlier but asked what the dotted lines were that violated its symmetry. They were "pointers," Reif said—particular associations, created by experience, that lead directly from one specific to another, interconnecting the smaller branches of the tree and providing a series of shortcuts. Experts have many such interconnections in their minds—but, he repeated, in general they approach problems from the top down; that's the key to expertise.

How does one achieve hierarchical organization of the knowledge in his or her field? "Chiefly through experience," Reif said. "It takes a *lot* of experience to gradually arrange and structure your information." I said that when talking to other cognitive scientists about memory, I'd heard much the same thing—namely, that there seems to be no substitute for twenty-five years of experience. "Yes," said Reif, "but maybe the process could be shortened somewhat if the material were presented and learned in hierarchical form in the first place. In fact, some of the people in our group are beginning to develop such materials. Bat-Sheva Eylon, an Israeli doctoral candidate, has recently worked up textbook presentations of topics in freshman physics, in two different versions. She wrote a brief chapter about the measurement of buoyancy, for instance—Archimedes' principle—in standard textbook fashion, and also in a format that presented the material in a hierarchical structure and stressed the place of the topic in a broad overview of physics. And what happened? The students who studied the hierarchically organized version"—Reif paused for emphasis—"had *forty* percent higher recall of the material and scored *twenty-five* percent higher in actual problem solving than those who got the standard version! Now *that*," he said, beaming, "is what I call 'human cognitive engineering.'"

For all his enthusiasm, Reif does not suggest that the right kind of teaching could make students into instant experts; perfecting the knowledge structure in the mind will always require a great deal of time and experience.

Time and experience, however, also add all those little crossovers and pointers to the structure, producing much swifter, less logical processes of problem solving than those Reif was describing. Many experts can almost instantly pinpoint the right means of attacking a problem in fields far less amenable to logical organization than physics—medicine, for instance, or business, or law. In such domains, experts develop not just superior organization but innumerable shortcuts and special associations by means of which they solve many problems with extraordinary speed.

That is one of the main findings of recent research by Paul E. Johnson of the University of Minnesota (whom I mentioned earlier, when discussing logical versus "plausible-inferential" thinking). Johnson, a lean, blond youthful man, was as enthusiastic and voluble as Reif had been, but in a dif-

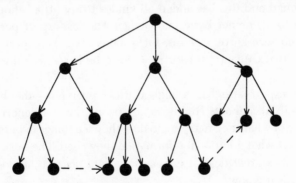

**Fig. 51.** How knowledge is organized in the mind of an expert

ferent way; his style was not chalk-talk professorial but more like that of a skilled showman who uses dramatic shifts of voice and acted-out anecdotes. "My colleagues and I," he said, "have studied experts in four fields so far—cardiology, commodity trading, chemical engineering, and law. The most striking feature of expertise in these less-than-orderly fields is that experts, though they're faster and better at problem solving than novices, have trouble explaining how they do it. 'What did you do?' we'd say. '*I* don't know,' they'd say, 'why don't you watch me and see?' Or they'll say, 'It just comes to me.' A lot of what they do—medical diagnosis, especially—appears to be based on a kind of intuition. Well, fine, but what's that mean? What *is* intuition, and how does it work, and why? We wanted to get behind that appearance and find out what accounts for it.

"My group and I will, typically, give a printed statement about a case to a group of expert diagnosticians, and also to medical students, and we'll do protocol analysis to see how both groups think about the problem. The printed statement might say something like this: 'You're the admitting resident in the Emergency Room, and a six-week-old boy has just been flown in from Frozen Falls, Montana, and there's a scribbled note from the doctors in his hometown that he hasn't been feeling well, his respiration has been this, his other physical data are this and this, and what would you do?' As they think it through out loud, we record everything they say, and then analyze it to see how they perceive the problem, what additional data they feel they need, and what kinds of decisions they make.

"We find that the expert differs from the novice in three ways. One is in domain knowledge. In medicine and certain other areas, the expert and the novice have the same basic information, but the expert has a large experiential background and this has added all kinds of tiny little refinements and distinctions to his or her basic knowledge. The less-expert person is prepared to recognize aortic stenosis, for instance, but the expert can recognize, within that category, subaortic stenosis; he has a finer discrimination net.

"But the expert also has a high-altitude overview—the hierarchical structure Reif talks about. Highly expert people have an enormously efficient picture of what they're trying to do—they see things in perspective, so they know just what additional information they need. The less expert individual collects a great deal of unnecessary data because he doesn't know what he needs to know.

"The third thing, and maybe this is the crucial one, is that the expert has a whole bunch of specifically tailored tricks to make the problem manageable—quick little associations, based on a lot of experience, linking one or two scraps of information with the heart of the problem—pointers, cross-links in the knowledge network. We'll say to an expert, 'There's a six-month-old child coming in from North Dakota, and he's a little bit under-weight and slightly cyanotic—' and he says, 'The problem is this and this'—and we say, '*How* did you *know?* With only three pieces of data, how could you *possibly* know?' And it turns out he doesn't really *know*, but he has a good *hypothesis* based on experience, and he'll immediately set about collecting certain very specific other data to confirm or disconfirm it. But the medical student has no such associations and hypotheses and has to col-lect a lot of data before he can get any good ideas."

I said that this sounded like a process quite different from the linear, goal-and-subgoal problem solving involved in games and puzzles, or even in physics.

"Exactly right!" cried Johnson. "In a domain like medicine, all kinds of other things happen in the expert mind. Of *course* there's planning, of *course* there's hierarchical thinking and means-end analysis—but there's also a great deal of thinking, based on knowledge special to this domain, that consists of shortcuts and tricks and isn't part of any general theory of problem solving. And the paradox of expertise is that the expert can't tell you how he does what he does. As he was growing proficient, he had to think about what he was doing, then he went through a phase where he was practicing those hookups, and finally he got to the stage of automaticity, where all that stuff is filed away, out of sight. So when I ask, 'How did you know? What did you do?' he says, 'You can't reduce diagnosis to rules. It's an *art*—I just *do* it.'

"What he can't tell us—but what we're finding out—is that he's doing top-down and bottom-up thinking at the same time. He's seeing things in a general way but also in a highly specific way, using his tremendous network of experiential associations, and relying on his overlearned, intuitive judg-ments. In our solving of problems in medicine and the other domains I've been studying, we're not logical machines, we're *psychological* machines. Experts are capable of step-by-step reasoning, but most of expert problem solving consists of using shortcuts within the knowledge structure. That's why I and some other people are coming to think that a theory of expert problem solving in any one domain may not have a great deal of carry-over to any other."

That sounded, I said, like something James G. Greeno had said some months earlier, at a Carnegie-Mellon conference on problem solving: in the future, he predicted, cognitive scientists would be teaching more about problem solving in specific domains than about problem solving in general. They'd be teaching students more and more about less and less.

"Exactly right!" said Johnson.

## The Problem of Teaching Problem Solving

If we could teach people to be even moderately better at problem solving, we might realize Omar Khayyám's wish to remold this sorry scheme of things nearer to the heart's desire. If only a few of us could use our minds more effectively, we might find better solutions than now exist to all of humankind's problems—everything from toilet training to terrorism, from neurosis to the nuclear arms race, from perspiration odor to the poisoning of the environment. Could a poet ask for more?

But can problem solving be taught? Some say yes, some strongly doubt it, and the majority opinion, among cognitive scientists, was voiced at the Carnegie-Mellon conference by Jill Larkin, who said somewhat plaintively, "It just seems to be very hard to teach people to solve problems."[*]

The difficulty, as we have just seen, lies in the fact that general problem-solving heuristics that are useful in knowledge-poor domains such as puzzles have little to do with problem solving in knowledge-rich domains. If you were to suffer from intermittent spells of faintness and palpitations of the heart, your disorder would be best diagnosed and treated not by someone who has studied means-end analysis and subgoal planning but by someone who is wholly familiar with the various wave forms of an electrocardiogram, who is able to recognize and distinguish among various kinds of heart murmurs, and who knows the positions you must assume if he or she is to hear the characteristic sound of blood sloshing back through a faulty mitral valve. Such a person, even if following the general principles of problem solving, isn't thinking in those terms but in terms of domain-specific expertise, without which the general principles would be quite useless.

Indeed, the key question about the teaching of problem solving is whether the general principles, which can be taught to all comers, have any significant amount of transfer or carry-over into daily life or into one's area

[*] At least one nation, however, officially believes that it can be taught: since 1979 Venezuela has had a minister of state for the development of human intelligence, whose Learn to Think projects are concerned with improved problem solving.

of specialization. Do future doctors, physicists, and writers get any tangible benefit from a general problem-solving course, or do they need courses in the specific problem-solving techniques of their individual professions? At this point in the development of cognitive science, there is no consensus on the matter.

Not surprisingly, the problem-solving courses now being taught at a score or more of major universities and possibly a hundred junior colleges reflect a variety of views.

Professor Moshe Rubinstein, who has been teaching problem solving at UCLA for ten years, stoutly asserts that his students are able to apply the basic principles he teaches to their own fields of study. The great bulk of the material in the course, as in his book *Patterns of Problem Solving*, explicates general heuristics, chiefly applied to mathematical problems, such as, "Avoid getting lost in detail. . . . Do not commit yourself too early to a course of action. . . . Change representation. . . . Ask the right question. . . . Work backwards," and so on. These are fleshed out with discussions of Gestalt psychology, information-processing theory, and other materials, plus a multitude of intriguing and amusing puzzles. The course must be fun to take, and must make students think about how to think.

I wonder, though, how well they can actually transfer these general principles to specific real-life situations. Here is a typical exercise from the book:

> How can you divide an area bounded by a circle into ten parts with only three lines?

You can doodle for many minutes without finding an answer to that one unless you remember that Dr. Rubinstein has told you to "avoid unnecessary constraints." In this problem you probably have been using straight lines— but who said you had to? If you lay aside that unnecessary constraint—if, that is, you reorganize your problem space—you can solve it easily. Figure 52 shows one solution, using three parabolas. But I don't know how you can apply that principle to knowledge-rich domains unless you know, in advance, which constraints are unnecessary and why. In the case of a geometrical puzzle, the possibilities are limited and clear-cut, but if you are a head of state, considering your options in dealing with a hostile foreign power, what are the unnecessary constraints?

Or consider the often-useful heuristic "Work backwards," which is es-

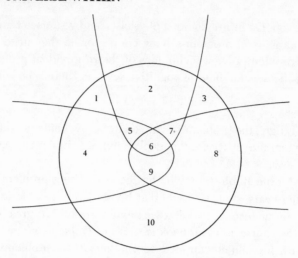

**Fig. 52.**   How to divide the area within a circle into ten parts with three lines. (Nobody said they had to be straight.)

sential to the solution of numerous exercises in Rubinstein's book and which we have seen to be valuable in Tower of Hanoi problems, water-jar problems, and other transformational and mathematical puzzles. All very well—but how does one know, in a knowledge-rich domain, whether working backward will be helpful, or even what it means? In writing a novel would it be best to start with an ending, and work back from it? With a fixed length in mind and fill the pages with words? With a detailed plot, and write scenes that flesh it out? Or would it be best to work forward, letting the interplay of the characters and the writer's own imagination unfold the story from within? It all depends: sometimes a novelist will do one of these things, sometimes another, sometimes none, and sometimes all of them. But no general heuristic can tell the novelist—or any creative artist—which to do or when.

A somewhat different approach is taken at Carnegie-Mellon, where no fewer than six different courses in problem solving are taught, one of them concerned with general principles and the rest with problem solving in specific fields such as engineering and history.

In the general course, now required of all students in humanities and the social sciences, Dick Hayes teaches a mixture of fundamental heuristics, mnemonic techniques for rapid learning and good recall, and some of the elements of decision-making techniques. In the more specific courses, students are given highly specific kinds of problem-solving techniques: for instance, history majors learn how to generate their own hypotheses about such matters as whether French nobles, before the Revolution, sided with their class or with the people of their region; how to construct a plan for testing such hypotheses; and how to gather the data by using computer-stored materials.

Hayes says that the general course does seem to result in some transfer, while the specific courses definitely yield domain-specific skills. He and most of his colleagues at Carnegie-Mellon believe that it is necessary to teach both kinds of problem solving.

At the University of Massachusetts, Amherst, a course in problem solving given from time to time ostensibly deals with physics and calculus problems but, in fact, smuggles in general problem-solving principles. Jack Lochhead, who directs the Cognitive Development Project and is responsible for the content of the course, says, "I have concluded that a low-level course in general problem solving should be disguised within a specific discipline and that it must deal with issues other than general problem-solving heuristics." Lochhead's doctorate is in science education; he is keenly aware of the need to motivate students, as well as of the value of domain-specific material.

An interesting feature of this course is that students work in pairs: in any given problem, one is the problem solver, the other the listener. Problem solvers are required to talk out loud, saying everything that comes to their minds; listeners, who are expressly forbidden to solve the problem, act as feedback mechanisms, pointing out any gaps or jumps in thought, asking for any unuttered details, demanding clarification, and making the problem solvers aware of their own thought processes. This sounds like a tough assignment for the listeners, but a workbook written by Lochhead and psychologist Arthur Whimbey (now at Clark College in Atlanta) guides them in their role. "Thinking out loud," Lochhead says, "isn't the only way to solve problems, and sometimes not the best way, but at least in learning general problem solving and physics problem solving it seems to make students aware of their own thought processes and to give them some command over those processes. We think it works."

What proof is there that these methods do work?

Very little, thus far; all hands agree on that. There are scattered reports of improved grades in other courses, rises in scores on IQ tests, and the like;

for the most part, however, belief in the value of problem-solving courses is subjective and anecdotal: the teachers see the benefit, the students feel it, but it remains largely unmeasured.

Even assuming, however, that general problem-solving skills can be transferred to specific fields, most researchers now think that such transfer isn't automatic but has to be induced. But it isn't clear how to do that, or how to integrate with those basic skills the detailed realities of problem solving in a knowledge-rich domain. Jill Larkin likens it to teaching someone to ride a bike: it helps if you tell and show the learner what to do, but most of what has to take place involves the learner's trying again and again until a multitude of experiences coalesce to form the specific skills that are needed.

There also is no convincing evidence that courses in problem solving can increase one's ability to make the imaginative leaps that are often crucial in problem solving. Teaching students about the reorganization of problem space does not enable them to do it at will. For behind most leaps of imagination there is some ineffable process resulting from an individual's particular knowledge, the way that knowledge is organized in his or her mind, and the freedom he or she unconsciously feels to rearrange that material.

Consider this problem, which comes from that great pioneer Karl Duncker:

> One morning, at sunrise, a Buddhist monk began to climb a mountain, on a narrow path that wound around it. He climbed at varying rates of speed, and stopped from time to time to rest or eat.
>
> At sunset, he reached the top, where there was a temple, and remained there to meditate for several days. Then, at sunrise, he started down, on the same path, again walking at varying rates of speed, though his average speed of descent was somewhat greater than his average speed of ascent.
>
> Show that there is a spot along the path that he will occupy on both trips at exactly the same time of day.

People who try to solve this problem logically or algebraically make little headway with it; a consideration of average speeds and average distances gets them nowhere, and they often conclude that it would be very unlikely that the monk would ever be at the same spot at the same time on both

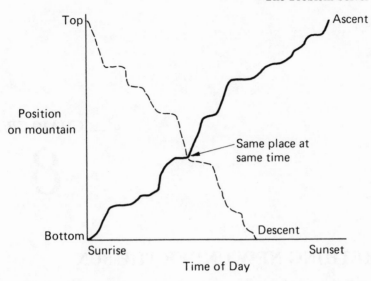

**Fig. 53.** Visual solution to the monk-on-the-mountain problem

days. But Arthur Koestler, in *The Act of Creation*, tells how one young woman solved it by a sudden leap to a different frame of reference:

> I tried this and that, until I got fed up with the whole thing, but the image of the monk ... walking up the hill kept persisting in my mind. Then a moment came when, superimposed on this image, I saw another, more transparent one, of the monk walking *down* the hill, and I realized in a flash that the two figures *must* meet at some point in time—regardless of what speed they walk and how often each of them stops.

Her vision can be turned into a simple graph that charts the monk's position on the mountain against the time of day for each trip; it is obvious that the two lines have to cross somewhere (Fig. 53).

But note the title of Koestler's book; he is talking about creativity. And that is a special, and particularly important, kind of problem solving, which deserves a chapter of its own.

# SOMETHING NEW UNDER THE SUN

### The Junk Shot and *Guernica*

The last time I played tennis with my plump, unathletic friend Dan, he kept winning points with a disgraceful shot that some tennis players call a "pooper" and others call a "junk shot"—a wobbly little pop-up with a bit of cut on it that trickled over the net and died before I could get to it. "Dan," I said at last, to hide my chagrin, "that's *some* shot! How do you do it?" "Don't ask me," said Dan, "I just do it. If I stopped to think about it, I wouldn't be able to do it at all."

Some days later I went to the Picasso retrospective at the Museum of Modern Art in New York, and there marveled once again at *Guernica*, that nightmarish vision of the bombing of a Basque town by German planes during the Spanish Civil War. In the same room with the painting were a number of studies for some of its details, and one might suppose, seeing them, that Picasso had consciously experimented with and modified those details until he had achieved the end he had in mind. But that's not how he worked, according to his own testimony: "I . . . put on canvas the sudden apparitions which force themselves on me. I don't know in advance what I am going to put on the canvas, any more than I decide in advance what colors to use. . . . The picture is not thought out and determined beforehand; rather, while it is being made it follows the mobility of thought."

Thus, the junk shot and *Guernica*—the one so ordinary and the other so extraordinary—have one essential thing in common: both are products of

272

unconscious mental processes. We identify ourselves with the conscious mind, whose thoughts we are aware of and can more or less control, but it is the unconscious, the unruly, mystifying, and often alien other self within us, that is responsible both for our everyday habitual acts and for our rare creative solutions to problems. The most common and the least common of our mental products come from the part of ourselves that we scarcely know.

For at the one extreme, it is the unconscious mind that governs our accustomed and automatic behavior, thereby sparing the conscious mind the burden of continual effort but also permitting us to carry on numerous skilled activities simultaneously, a feat quite beyond the ability of conscious attention. Washing, dressing, eating, driving, typing—these and many comparable trains of acts, though initiated by the conscious mind, are executed in detail by the unconscious one. While you are setting the breakfast table, you can step over the sleeping dog, add hot water now and then to the coffee maker, and stir the oatmeal without paying attention to any of these acts or interrupting a conversation you are carrying on—in which, moreover, though you express conscious thoughts, you rarely need make any conscious effort to find the right words or frame them in a suitable sentence.

All these actions, which once you had to think about consciously, you have long since been able to delegate to unconscious control, thus freeing yourself to turn your attention elsewhere; cognitive scientists call this "overlearning" or "automation." Usually you are unaware of the other self at work, but once in a while you do notice it and are surprised or disconcerted. In the middle of a particularly busy day you may pick up the phone to call home about something, only to find that you have dialed the number of the house you moved from a year ago. Or, deep in thought while driving or walking home by your customary route, you may suddenly notice where you are and be unable to recall having seen the familiar corners and buildings you have passed. One scholar is reported to have taken a bath while considering some difficult theoretical problem and, still engrossed in his thoughts, proceeded to take a second one, as he later realized to his mortification.

These errors are trifling, but daily life is made up of innumerable trifles we handle without erring; it would be ruinously effortful and time-consuming if we had to deal with them consciously. Here is one man's testimony as to how it would feel:

> I'm not sure of my own movements any more. It's very hard to describe this but at times I'm not sure about even simple actions like sitting down. . . . If I'm going to sit down,

for example, I've got to think of myself and almost see myself sitting down before I do it. It's the same with other things like washing, eating, and even dressing. . . . I have to do everything step by step now, nothing is automatic.

His problem: schizophrenia.

At the opposite extreme, numerous writers, artists, scientists, and other creative people have attested that their major innovative ideas and discoveries have not been deliberate constructs of the conscious mind but have come to them mysteriously, and as if of themselves, out of the unconscious mind. This is not to say that creative ideas or solutions to problems arrive gratis, without the cost of hard work; on the contrary, it is most often after intense but unsuccessful efforts to generate a fresh artistic idea or to find a new solution to a problem that one unexpectedly appears in a moment of exhaustion and relaxation, when the mind is floating free.

A famous instance of this is Kekulé's discovery of the structure of the benzene molecule. Friedrich August Kekulé von Stradonitz, a nineteenth-century German chemist, had been doggedly trying to deduce the molecular architecture of benzene, but without success. Then one evening, as he described it:

> I turned myself toward the fire and sank in a reverie. Atoms danced before my eyes. Long chains were firmly joined, all winding and turning with snakelike motion. Suddenly, one of the serpents caught its own tail and the ring thus formed whirled before my eyes. I woke immediately and worked on the consequences the rest of the night.

He had understood instantly the symbolism of the vision: the benzene molecule was a loop or ring of carbon atoms, which are capable of holding onto each other as well as to other atoms (Fig. 54). Experiments proved Kekulé's vision correct; after this breakthrough insight, the field of organic chemistry developed with great speed.

Occasionally, though, new ideas—and even whole works—seem to spring into being from the unconscious without their creator's having made any previous effort to generate them. Probably the most celebrated such case is that of Coleridge's poem "Kubla Khan." In the summer of 1797, the poet was living in a lonely farmhouse in Somerset when one day, feeling ill, he took a dose of laudanum (an opiate); he then sat down to read about the Khan in an old volume entitled *Purchas his Pilgrimage,* and fell asleep. In his sleep, Coleridge composed a poem some two hundred to three hundred lines long—"if," he later wrote, "that indeed can be called composition in which all the images rose up . . . without any sensation or consciousness of effort." Upon awakening, he immediately began to write down the poem, but at line 54 was interrupted by "a person on business from Porlock" (most likely a tradesman from that nearby village, demanding payment of a bill). It took an hour to get rid of the fellow, and when Coleridge returned to his desk, he was dismayed to find that the rest of the poem had vanished from memory. He long intended, he said, "to finish for himself what had been originally, as it were, given to him," but never carried out that intention; the fragment that he captured, however, is generally accounted one of the finest pieces in all of English Romantic poetry.

Most research on thinking has dealt with conscious mental processes— not surprisingly, since they are the ones researchers have direct access to. But cognitive scientists are beginning to take a keen interest in unconscious cognitive processes, which, many of them now believe, underlie and pro- duce most of our complex behavior—and most of our conscious thoughts. One middle-aged psychotherapist said to me, with considerable satisfaction, that cognitive scientists are belatedly realizing what every Freudian has long known about the importance of the unconscious, but this development is less of a vindication than he takes it to be; younger cognitive scientists, when they speak of the unconscious, mean both less and more than Freud did.

Freud's chief interest in the unconscious was in its function as the reposi- tory of thoughts that are threatening to the normal ego or conscious self— impermissible or conflict-producing ideas such as the infantile wish to be totally taken care of, or the childish desire to have sex with one's father or

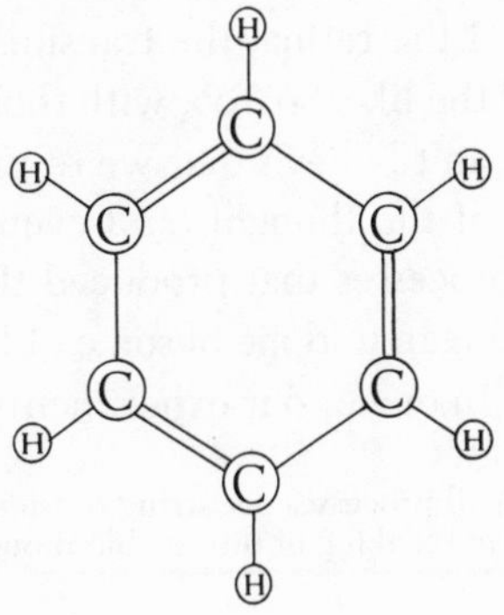

**Fig. 54.** The benzene ring

mother. Such troublemaking thoughts are repressed (forcibly forgotten) and locked away in the unconscious. Freud also described another area of the unconscious mind which contains thoughts that are less severely repressed, or merely forgotten or set aside, but that can rather easily be retrieved or brought into the light of consciousness; this area he called the "preconscious." It was of relatively little interest to him, however; his real concern lay with the repressed and unavailable thoughts, since he believed that flaws in the process of repression were responsible for the neuroses he sought to treat.

Cognitive scientists don't pay much attention to the distinction between preconscious and unconscious or to the sources of neurotic behavior. They are concerned, rather, with the way information is processed outside the conscious mind and the way the products of that processing emerge into consciousness. This is a much larger subject than that which concerns Freudian therapists, since it includes all those complex mental processes—largely preconscious—that have become automatic, as well as those original and creative acts that come from more deeply buried areas outside our conscious control.*

Indeed, some prominent cognitive scientists—George A. Miller of Princeton, Ulric Neisser of Cornell, and others—argue that all conscious thinking is the result of unconscious thinking, that the real reasons we think as we do about any matter are unknown to us, and that we are never aware of what is going on in our minds even when we are keenly conscious of our own thoughts. According to this view, we cannot be conscious of our own thought processes, for the thought is not a mental *process* but its *product.* It's akin to what happens in the act of seeing: when you look at the room around you, you are aware that you see a chair, books, a window, and so on, but you are not and cannot be aware of the processes that produce the perceptual experience—the passage of light through the lens and vitreous humor, the excitation of the optic nerves of the retina, the transmission of impulses to the optic area of the brain, and the like. So, too, with thought: if at this very moment you are thinking, "I can't believe that we're unaware of our thought processes," you are aware of the thought, and even of the thoughts that led up to it, but not of the processes that produced them.

Richard Nisbett of the University of Michigan told me of some of his own research that strongly supports this view. "In one of our experiments," Nis-

---

* From here on I will use "unconscious" to refer to all processes occurring outside of consciousness; it will be clear from context whether I am speaking of retrievable thoughts and memories or those that are not normally so.

bett said, "we asked people to pick out the nylon panty hose of the best quality from a set of four pairs that were arranged in front of them from left to right. Actually, the panty hose were identical, but our subjects picked the right-most pair four times as often as the left-most pair. When we asked them why they picked that pair, they gave reasons of one sort or another but never mentioned position. And when we asked if its position could have influenced them, they denied it and sounded annoyed, or, in some cases, seemed to think that they were dealing with madmen. The evidence of a number of related experiments suggests that most of the time we don't know why we think as we do, even when we feel certain that we do."

Donald Norman, director of the Program in Cognitive Science at the University of California at San Diego, takes a less troubling and more widely accepted stand. He believes that we *are* aware of some of what lies behind our conscious thoughts, but that it is greatly to our advantage to have the unconscious take charge much of the time. "Conscious thought processes," he says, "are very powerful but very slow. Skilled performance, which we need constantly, is fast, but it depends on *not* doing conscious thinking. The airline pilot, the musician, the juggler, and the typist all rely on automatic skills, because if they had to consciously think about what they're doing, they couldn't do it. A pianist may often have to play twenty-five or even more notes a second; he can think about those notes when he's learning the piece, but not when playing it at performance speed. A chess master will look at the board for a minute and then make his move, but it takes him half an hour to tell you why he made his choice.

"It's the same with all of us. Behind a great many of our everyday routine acts, unconscious automatic mental processes are at work. At the conscious level we select the act—we *will* it—and then let the subconscious* complete the details. Or to put it in more formal terms, our conscious intentions activate complex sensorimotor schemas in the subconscious—overlearned detailed routines that produce the actual actions. Including, even, the flow of words in a conversation such as this one."

Thus the unconscious processes that account for routine behavior and skilled performance do not, after all, seem particularly mystifying or hard to explain. What does remain both mystifying and unexplained is that other and far more intriguing function of unconscious thinking: the creation of new ideas and the making of discoveries. How does the unconscious mind do this? What does it do that the conscious mind does not do, and why? And

---

* Norman prefers this word to "preconscious," but the distinction between them need not concern us.

how is the kind of unconscious thinking responsible for automatic perform-ance related to that of the creative kind—what, after all, does the junk shot have to do with *Guernica?*

Not much, and yet more than you might think: both are forms of problem solving, but they're at opposite ends of the spectrum of experience. The au-tomatic action is a problem-solving response in which we know and have repeatedly used the precise algorithms by which the goal can be reached. The new idea or the discovery, in contrast, is a problem-solving response in which we use heuristic search methods to find a trail we have never fol-lowed that leads to a goal we may not clearly see.

This is what sets creative behavior apart from all other forms of problem solving. With routine problems like dressing or driving, we know the exact steps by which to achieve the known goal, and need no new ideas; even with more demanding problems ranging from solving a cryptarithmetic problem to designing a conventional office building, we use a combination of well-learned skills and heuristics, but need not generate innovative solu-tions. I once knew a man who designed suspension bridges and who, with unconcealed vanity, described himself as extremely creative in solving the engineering problems they involved. He was not; he was merely highly skilled at using the recondite technical knowledge he possessed to work out designs suitable to each location, but the truly creative act was that of the unknown genius who, thousands of years ago in India, thought for the first time of suspending a roadway from cables rather than supporting it from below or building a rigid structure. In the arts, similarly, creativity is radi-cally different from the skilled reuse of existing artistic forms and devices. A creator of the stature of Mozart, Verdi, Degas, or Braque is bound to be emulated and imitated, but we rarely admire even the very creditable emulations to the same extent—or even in the same way—as we do the works that were original.

The interesting question about all this—one of the most interesting ques-tions confronting cognitive science—is: How is it possible for the mind to create a concept it has never known, a new idea, simile, shape, melody, image, structure, or device? The behaviorists, with their scorn for all theories involving mental processes, explained creativity as nothing more than the random shuffling of known bits and pieces until, by accident, they fall into a new configuration. As the behaviorist John Watson put it:

> *How the "new" comes into being:* One natural question
> often raised is: How do we ever get new verbal creations such

as a poem or brilliant essay? *The answer is that we get them by manipulating words, shifting them about until a new pattern is hit upon.*

But what series of manipulations of the parts of the old romances and histories that Shakespeare drew upon could ever have yielded one of his plays? What recombination of the sparkling and relatively simple melodies and harmonies of Beethoven's youthful work could ever have yielded the torrential discords and sonorities of his Ninth Symphony? What reshuffling of familiar objects or ideas, in the minds of our ancestors, could have yielded the first wheel, writing, the screw thread, or romantic love?

If behaviorism had failed in no other way, this shortcoming alone would have been enough to ensure its displacement by cognitive science. For the human mind is not a mere kaleidoscope, making the new by randomly scrambling shards of the old. Rather, by some means the human mind *transforms* the old. The screw is merely an inclined plane—but wrapping that plane around a straight rod is an act of transformation. The words of any great literary work (such writings as those of James Joyce aside) are words we know, assembled in sentence structures we are familiar with, but transformed by the mind that had a new thought, and used the old words and sentence structure in a new way to express it. *To be, or not to be: that is the question*—such ordinary words, such commonplace syntax, and yet how transformed. *How do I love thee? Let me count the ways*—such unremarkable parts, but how unforgettable the whole. And by a delightful irony, how original—and hence how self-rebutting—the words of Ecclesiastes:

> The thing that hath been, it is that which shall be; and that which is done is that which shall be done: and there is no new thing under the sun.

## The Creative Work

Ever since human beings began to think about thinking, they have been fascinated by creativity but hard put to explain it. Cognitive science hasn't yet done much to change that. It has produced a mass of tantalizing scraps of information and intriguing conjectures, but although hundreds of articles on creativity appear in the professional journals each year, there is still no generally accepted theory of creativity, no agreed-upon definition of it, and no consensus as to how best to investigate it scientifically.

The oldest—and a still popular—approach is to study works or ideas generally considered to be creative, seeking to identify what makes us think them so. The difficulty, however, begins with the selection of the evidence: how are we to decide what is creative and what is not, when the experts so often disagree? One respected critic tells us that a particular play or novel is imaginative and original; another, equally respected, says that it is pedestrian and derivative. A scientific research proposal is rated frivolous by a conservative member of a grant-making board, but brilliant by a more liberal one.

Even when there is wide agreement that certain works are creative, the verdict may be reversed by a later generation. In the eighteenth century, Shakespeare was thought a rough, unpolished writer, and the nineteenth-century Romantics found Bach's music arid and mathematical. William James and Herbert Spencer were accounted highly original thinkers in their time, denigrated by later generations, and still later reappraised and restored to the intellectual hall of fame.

And yet these are only variations around a baseline of consensus. Although we may argue with each other about the merits of particular works, and although the tides of taste and of veneration ebb and flow, in general most reasonably well-educated people in most eras agree that certain great artistic works and intellectual ideas are creative: there is no argument about the works of Michelangelo, Rubens, and Degas, the discoveries of Galileo, Newton, and Einstein, the ideas of Descartes, Kant, and Marx. By the same token, most well-informed people will agree that greeting-card verse, the kitsch sold in resort gift shops, the majority of prime-time television shows, and the bulk of the so-called improvements in each year's new cars are definitely not works of creativity.

But it is easier to identify examples of clear-cut creativity, or of its absence, than to say what makes them so. We offer all sorts of explanations—works of art are either "fresh" or "hackneyed," "full of ideas" or "repetitious," "honest" or "sentimental," and so on, but these are aesthetic judgments rather than concrete explanations of what the creative person does or how the creative work produces its effects on us. They are not "operational" concepts; they cannot be objectively defined and measured.

Psychologists studying creativity have therefore tried to find operational criteria—simple measurable substitutes for the aesthetic terms—by which to judge how creative any human response to a task is; moreover, they have designed a number of tasks small enough and easy enough to lend themselves to laboratory research.

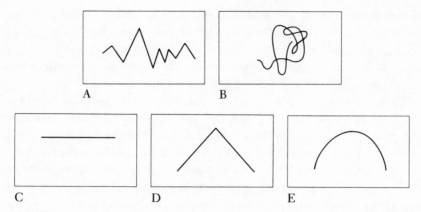

**Fig. 55.** A test of creativity. What do these lines suggest to you?

One such is shown in Figure 55, which is part of a creativity test designed by psychologists Michael Wallach and Nathan Kogan and used with fifth-grade children (its purpose is to measure creativity in the children—but it does so by appraising the creativity of their responses, that is, the *product*). In such a test, the criteria by which the answers are judged are twofold: answers are reckoned creative if, first, they are "unusual" (or "novel" or "original"), and, second, if they are "appropriate" (that is, suitable or valid answers to the problem). In the above test, answers that are obvious and are commonly given, such as (A) mountains, (B) string, (C) a stick, (D) an arrowhead, and (E) the rising sun, are deemed uncreative, even though appropriate. Creative responses, in contrast, are those which are neither obvious nor common, yet are clearly appropriate: for instance, (A) a crumpled piece of paper, (B) paint squeezed out of a tube, (C) a stream of ants, (D) an alligator's open mouth, and (E) a fishing rod bending under the weight of a fish. The creative response thus has two effects on us: in psychologist Jerome S. Bruner's words, it not only produces "effective surprise" but a "shock of recognition" (or sense of satisfaction) that the answer, while unexpected, is a good one. If, however, a child were to say that drawing (E) was a tree or a spaceship, the answer would be novel and a little surprising but not satisfying; it isn't a *good* answer.

Unlike aesthetic judgments, these criteria lend themselves to objective and precise evaluations. For one thing, the novelty of any answer can be reckoned quite accurately: by testing a large number of subjects, tallying the answers to each question, and seeing how often or rarely any answer occurs, it is possible to give each answer a numerical novelty rating. Appropriateness is a bit trickier: the researcher scores answers for that quality on the basis of his or her subjective judgment. But if several judges rate the answers and there is good agreement among their ratings, one assumes that their standards are not bizarre or highly personal.

There is a weakness in this method, however: the judges have no objective criteria by which to appraise the answers, and in difficult cases their consensus, or lack of it, may be meaningless. Consider the well-known Brick Uses test, in which the subject is asked to list all the uses he or she can think of for ordinary bricks. Some responses are unquestionably appropriate (to build a house, a wall, a path, a barbecue, a chimney) but, being common and conventional, are rated uncreative. Others, though uncommon, are clearly appropriate (to drown a cat, to make red powder, to make a tombstone for a bird), and hence are rated creative. The answer "to play catch with," while definitely unusual, is plainly inappropriate, but what if the subject suggested tying a thick towel around the brick and then playing catch with it? One researcher might consider that appropriate and hence creative; another might not. What about gouging out a hollow in the brick and using it for an ashtray? Or breaking it into fragments, putting them in the freezer, and using them as nonmelting ice cubes? Who is to say whether such answers are creative or merely odd?

The distinguished cognitive psychologist J. P. Guilford, discussing creativity in his magnum opus, *The Nature of Human Intelligence,* tells a story which illustrates how hard it may be to judge the appropriateness of unusual answers. In a college physics course, a student was given the problem: "Show how it is possible to determine the height of a tall building with the aid of a barometer." The right answer, presumably, is to take the barometer to the top, note the difference in air pressure between there and the ground, and convert the difference into an altitude reading. But the student, an original fellow if nothing else, said he would take the barometer to the top, lower it to the street, pull it back up, and measure the length of rope needed to reach the ground. Wrong, said the instructor; try again. This time the student proposed to drop the barometer from the top, time the fall to the impact below, and calculate the distance by using a free-fall formula. (Wrong; try again.) The third answer: measure the length of the barometer's shadow, and of the building's shadow; then, knowing the barometer's height, work out the building height by a simple ratio. (Wrong!) Okay: offer the barometer to the building's superintendent in return for telling its height. . . . The answers earn points for originality, but whether any of them seems appropriate may depend on the researcher's sense of humor.

Yet there is no doubt that most of the time, knowledgeable people respond in generally similar ways to creative products. In one study, researchers asked a series of architects and editors of architectural journals to name and to list in order of merit the most creative architects in the country. There was good agreement among the groups of persons making these choices, but what the judges were agreeing on, though ostensibly the names of the architects, was in fact their products, for the judges knew only their work and not their psychological abilities or mental processes.

In her recent doctoral dissertation, Teresa M. Amabile, a cognitive social psychologist at Brandeis University, showed that a "radically subjective" rating of artistic products as creative or uncreative—without the use of any criteria—is a sound way to identify them. Amabile had several groups of high-school and college students make collages from pieces of colored paper that came in a variety of sizes and shapes. The subjects were told to make a "design" that was "silly," this being a way of suggesting the goal of creativity without overtly using that label. Three groups of judges—one composed of psychologists, one of art teachers, and one of artists—evaluated the creativity of the collages without training runs and without being given any definition of creativity or any criteria by which to measure it. (Amabile told them to simply use their own personal definitions of it.) Nonetheless, there was substantial similarity in the judgments made within each group, and fairly good agreement among the groups despite the wide differences in their levels of expertise.

Amabile's conclusion is that in judging the creativity of a work, it isn't necessary to think in terms of novelty, appropriateness, the sense of satisfaction it yields, or any other supposedly objective criteria, or even to define creativity in any particular way. "A product is creative," she says, "to the extent that people tell us it is creative, as long as those people have some familiarity with the type of product being observed, and as long as they agree with one another."

Once more, the findings of cognitive science suggest that our minds are more to be trusted than we had thought. Within the bounds of any particular culture, the human mind recognizes creativity most of the time, despite the vagaries of taste, and despite the lack of objective rules or criteria by which to judge. The creative answer to a problem, it would seem, strikes home and makes us feel good; we recognize and like it. And that is yet another distinctive feature of the human intellect.

## The Creative Nature

Fully as intriguing as the creative product—and as difficult to demystify—is the creative nature. For many centuries, thoughtful people have wondered how those who are creative differ from the rest of us, and what it is about them that enables them to do what they do. Many of us believe in certain traditional stereotypes of the creative personality: we are likely to think of such a person as a loner, sensitive and gentle, emotionally disturbed or neurotic, and unconventional or even distinctly Bohemian. Research studies, however, refute these notions as often as they confirm them. Morris Stein, a psychologist at New York University, recently reviewed the research literature and listed nineteen personality characteristics that have been reported to be associated with creativity, but the list is full of curious contradictions. Some researchers, Stein says, find creative persons to be self-assertive, dominant, and aggressive, but others find them lacking in aggressiveness and, whether male or female, possessed of certain traits traditionally thought to be feminine. Some report that creative persons are introverted and uninterested in interpersonal relationships, others that they are socially sensitive, intuitive, and empathetic. Some say that creative people are emotionally unstable, others that they are actually mentally healthier than less creative people in their same professions. And some find them Bohemian, while others, repudiating literary and operatic tradition, report that they are generally conventional and respectable.

The likeliest explanation of these discrepancies is that there are many kinds of creativity, with certain traits of character being amenable to some kinds and not to others; one would hardly expect the Broadway director and the cellular biochemist to be much alike. Moreover, creativity takes so many different forms even within any one profession that it is not surprising to find sharply dissimilar kinds of personalities in the same field. Wagner was monstrously bold, conceited, and domineering; Tchaikovsky was timid, self-doubting, and passive. Byron was hypersexual and chronically promiscuous; Tennyson was the very model of a faithful and uxorious homebody. Newton was intolerant and contentious; Einstein was unassuming and mild-mannered.

Still, the research studies do agree on some important issues, namely that creative people are hardworking and persevering, that they are relatively independent and nonconformist in their ideas (if not their life-styles), and that they are generally more flexible in their thinking—that is, readier to shift their frame of reference—than noncreative persons. In short, a handful of personality traits are linked to creativity, but in many or most respects creative persons are as diverse in personality as the rest of the population.

Certain other factors that have generally been thought to be linked with creativity have likewise proven, upon study, to have little connection with it. Intelligence is one: highly creative people are more than normally intelligent, but not extraordinarily so; conversely, many highly intelligent people are not particularly creative. One can only conclude that, simplistic though it may sound, there is a good deal more to creativity than intelligence.

The evidence for a connection between sex and creativity is even weaker. Historically, of course, the great bulk of creative work in the arts and sciences was performed by men, and until recently, many authorities held that women were either innately lacking in creative powers or used up their creative urge in childbearing and childrearing. But for more than a generation, women in increasing numbers have been entering and succeeding in the arts and the sciences. The evidence strongly suggests that women's failure to be creative in the past was largely or wholly the result of their lack of education and opportunity, plus an acquired mental block—a part of the traditional female identity—against seeing themselves in the role of creative artist or scientist.

The belief that creative powers are at their peak in early adulthood is another cliché that has not been scientifically examined and now seems questionable. According to tradition and to one well-known but very limited study, great works and great discoveries have chiefly been the work of people in their twenties and thirties. But this correlation may have more to do with quantity than quality of output. Moreover, there is countervailing evidence showing that many creative people grow in their powers throughout adult life, and that some have done their finest work when they were middle-aged or old. Michelangelo, Shakespeare, El Greco, Verdi, Freud, Renoir, and Picasso are cases in point, and a study of Nobel Prize winners in science shows that most of them were near or in middle age when they did the work for which they were later honored. No doubt, some people who do notable scientific or artistic work early in life fail to sustain their output, thus pulling down the average age of peak creativity. But age alone cannot be the crucial factor in the decline of creativity in these people, since so many others do remain creative into later years. Other forces must be to blame—too-early success, with its attendant distractions and temptations; the inhibiting pressure of the world's expectations of them; the ailments that often accumulate with time; and others.

From a purely statistical viewpoint, it is apparently true that older scientists, as a group, produce less creative work than young ones. But an important recent study of the data by sociologist Stephen Cole of the State University of New York at Stony Brook suggests that the "reward system" of the scientific establishment is largely responsible. Scientists who do the best-received work are encouraged to do more of it by various sorts of rewards, while those whose work is unfavorably received are discouraged by the lack of them. As a result, the unrewarded cease to produce. Accordingly, older scientists are less productive, en masse, than younger ones, but it is the lack of success, rather than the aging process, that has diluted the creative output of the older group.

Another avenue of inquiry has linked creativity to various "cognitive styles." Cognitive style is the characteristic manner in which an individual perceives, thinks about, and reacts to the environment. There's an old saw about the difference between the optimist and the pessimist: the former says the glass of water is half full, the latter says it's half empty. That exemplifies one dimension of cognitive style.

Psychologists, using a variety of simple laboratory tests and problems, have identified a number of dimensions of cognitive style along which people differ, and some of the differences seem to have a bearing on creativity. One categorization of cognitive style, for instance, distinguishes between "reflectives" (cautious persons, who need a lot of information before they can solve a problem) and "impulsives" (persons who attempt to solve the problem on the basis of relatively little information). Here's an example of the kind of test that shows the difference: suppose you're shown the following number series, with most of the items hidden but available to you one at a time at your request, and are asked to fill in the number at the question mark:

4:2  ☐  16:?

Not enough? All right; you are given the next clue:

4:2  9:3  ☐  16:?

Some people are willing, at this point, to name the answer, but others ask for yet another clue and still others—the real reflectives—need the whole series:

$$4:2 \qquad 9:3 \qquad 25:5 \qquad 100:10 \qquad 64:8 \qquad 16:?$$

The answer, of course, is 4. Those impulsives who get it right are intuitive and more likely to be creative than the cautious reflectives. (Those impulsives who get it wrong are either bad guessers or not very bright.)

Other researchers have studied the difference between the cognitive styles known as "field dependence" and "field independence." In one famous experiment, the subject sees a luminous rod inside a luminous frame in a dark room, and is asked to adjust the rod until it is truly vertical. But when the researcher secretly tilts the frame, some subjects are unable to ignore it and to correctly adjust the rod: they're dependent on surrounding clues (the tilted frame); that is, they're field-dependent. Others, however, can separate the rod from the frame in their minds and make it vertical despite any tilt of the frame; they're field-independent. Another kind of experiment measuring the same dimension of cognitive style uses an "embedded-figures" test in which one has to pick out a geometrical shape buried in a complicated pattern, somewhat like those children's puzzles with cats (or mice or birds) hidden in a busy picture. Field-dependent people have more trouble with such problems than do field-independent people. Not surprisingly, therefore, field independence appears to be associated with creativity; as we've seen, creative people tend to be independent thinkers, and because they find it easier than other people do to ignore extraneous information, they are better and more creative problem solvers.

One other dimension of cognitive style is said to be related to creativity: it has to do with how narrowly or how broadly people categorize what they perceive. For instance: given a set of cards bearing all kinds of variations on a standard diamond shape and asked to sort out the diamond-shaped figures, some people will reject all but those that are very close to the standard diamond, while others will include variations that are fairly remote from the prototype. The same trait can be measured using colors, sizes, word meanings, and so on. Broad categorizing isn't a matter of lumping all sorts of things into catchall groupings, but of recognizing fundamental similarities in seemingly different things—an ability particularly favorable to the kinds of cognitive leaps involved in creative thinking. Aristotle did such categorizing when he recognized that whales were mammals rather than fish; the sixteenth-century philosopher Giordano Bruno made such a cognitive leap when he suggested that the stars are suns; and it was this kind of thinking that enabled the seventeenth-century mathematician Christian Huygens to suggest that light travels in waves, Einstein to see that gravity and acceleration are identical, and Picasso to perceive a baboon's face in a toy car (Fig. 56).

That brings us closer to understanding the creative person—but only a little; the terms are still vague and general, and while creative people are more likely to have certain cognitive styles than not, a person who has those cognitive styles isn't necessarily creative.

A rather different line of research spells out much more precisely some of the particular mental traits thought to be associated with creativity. Guilford designed a series of tests some years ago (many variants of which were later created by others) to measure a number of mental abilities conducive to *divergent production*—the making of a large number and wide variety of possible responses when faced with a task. This, of course, is what is measured by the Brick Uses test that I referred to a short while ago. Such tests, as we saw, can be used to explore the characteristics of the creative product—the kinds of responses made by creative people—but, conversely, they can be used to measure the differences between the mental abilities of the creative person and the noncreative one.

One noteworthy trait of the creative nature, as judged by these tests, is *fluency*. This trait—or more accurately group of traits—is measured in many ways. A simple test of it is the task of writing out in a limited span of time as many words as possible that end in *-tion;* specifically, this measures *word fluency*. Another task, known as Consequences, asks the subject to list all the things that would happen if some unusual condition prevailed, such as people's no longer needing to sleep; the longer the list, the higher the subject's score in *ideational fluency*, and the greater the variety and unusualness of the answers, the higher the subject's score in *flexibility* and *originality*. The same traits, on a visual level, can be measured by means of tests such as Sketches, in which the subject is presented with a simple familiar form like a circle and asked to make it into real objects by adding a minimum of lines; with a few strokes, one can turn it into a face, a baseball, a wheel, a tunnel, and so on.

The results of such tests indicate that creative people are above average in fluency, flexibility and originality, and a number of other, less notable abilities. Disappointingly, however, the test results do not always correlate well with real-life creativity. Some genuinely creative people don't score particularly high on creativity tests, and many high scorers aren't particularly creative in real life.

**Fig. 56.** Pablo Picasso, *Baboon and Young*, 1951. Bronze (cast 1955), after found objects, 21″ high, base 13 ¼ x 6 ⅞″. Collection, The Museum of Modern Art, New York. Mrs. Simon Guggenheim Fund.

.ne explanation is twofold. First, real-life creative acts are complex and culturally rich; it's not at all certain which abilities are needed for any creative act, or that these are the only abilities needed. Second, the tests are based on psychologists' a priori judgments as to what abilities they expected to find in creative people. It would have been better to start by testing creative people for their abilities—but what ones would you look for? Perhaps, for all their ingenuity, psychologists have overlooked some of the very traits that are most important in creativity.

Even harder to appraise objectively, and yet central to the investigation of the creative nature, is the creative person's ability to see a relationship that other people fail to see spontaneously. That is what underlies the broad categorizing and the cognitive leaps of the mind that we looked at a moment ago. It is what accounts for the power of analogical reasoning—the use of one thing as a model by which to solve the problems involved in another and seemingly different thing. And it is what explains the appeal and value of metaphorical speech or thinking—indeed, a metaphor is a form of analogy—for through metaphors we connect disparate clusters of information to form a new and illuminating concept.

Metaphor is thus not merely an ornament of writing, a beautifying cosmetic laid on the surface of thought; rather, it is a process by which we see more, and more deeply. Listen, for instance, to the fallen Wolsey, in Shakespeare's *King Henry VIII:*

> Farewell! a long farewell, to all my greatness!
> This is the state of man: today he puts forth
> The tender leaves of hope; tomorrow blossoms,
> And bears his blushing honors thick upon him;
> The third day comes a frost, a killing frost;
> And, when he thinks, good easy man, full surely
> His greatness is a-ripening, nips his root,
> And then he falls, as I do.

The literal nonmetaphorical meaning is that when a man has hopes and ambitions, he undertakes actions that lead to success, but also to vulnerability; ill fortune may easily destroy him. But how flat, how thin, how impoverished is the paraphrase—not because it lacks beautification, but because it conveys so much less information, so much less understanding, than the metaphorical writing.

In finding resemblances between remote objects or ideas, metaphorical-analogical thinking opens new pathways of thought and thus of creative problem solving. If the unlike things are really alike in some ways, perhaps they are so in others; that is the meaning of analogy. We pursue the thought, and find new meanings, new understanding, and, often, new solutions to old problems.

The ability to do metaphorical-analogical thinking is thus an essential part of the creative nature. In daydreams like Kekulé's—of the benzene molecule as a snake biting its own tail—the creative mind uses metaphor involuntarily, but many creative people use it deliberately and consciously as a way of generating insights and discoveries. Einstein's *Gedanken* (thought) experiments, to which I referred in an earlier chapter, are a case in point. In one of the most celebrated of these, Einstein visualized himself as a passenger riding on a ray of light and holding a mirror in front of him. He realized that he would see no image of himself, since he and the mirror were already moving at the speed of light and his own image could therefore never reach the mirror. Yet a stationary observer, also holding a mirror and seeing Einstein whiz by, would be able to catch Einstein's image in his own mirror. From this fanciful analogy of physical events, Einstein gained the insight that led him to deduce his special theory of relativity.

It is easy to see how such an analogy can be valuable in solving a problem, but by what mechanism does verbal metaphor produce the deeper understanding I have spoken of? Why does the linking of two remote ideas yield enlightenment or deeper comprehension? George Lakoff, a linguist at Berkeley, and Mark Johnson, a philosopher at Southern Illinois University, recently offered a persuasive explanation: all the propositions connected to one half of the metaphor—all its "entailments," to use their term (its total schema, to use a cognitive-science label)—become transferred to the other half of the metaphor, adding a great deal of conceptual content to it. In a recent paper, Lakoff and Johnson use, as an example, the metaphor "Love is a collaborative work of art"; hearing or reading this, they say, anyone with a reasonable knowledge of what is entailed by the term "collaborative work of art" immediately attaches all those propositions to the concept "love." Here are half a dozen of the twenty entailments Lakoff and Johnson name:

> Love is work.
> Love requires compromise.
> Love is an aesthetic experience.
> Love requires discipline.
> Love is creative.
> Love cannot be achieved by formula.

Each of these may, in turn, have other entailments, all of which, subsumed by the metaphor, provide new meaning to the concept of love. "What we experience with such a metaphor," they say, "is a kind of reverberation down through the network of entailments that awakens and connects our memories of our past love experiences and serves as a possible guide for future ones." Even that statement, you will note, is metaphorical—the terms "reverberation" and "network" are the very means by which Lakoff and Johnson seek to marshal the experiences of their readers to make the concept of metaphor richly meaningful.

But it is not only the creative mind that uses metaphor in this way. All of us have some capacity to use metaphor; indeed, Lakoff and Johnson say that it pervades and structures our everyday thinking. When we are feeling good, we say we're "up," and when we're disheartened, we're "down"; when any project is developing as planned, we say it's "advancing," but if not, it's "stalled" or even "has been set back"; and so on.

The more keenly we feel, the more we are likely to use common metaphors—clichés but, even so, far more vivid and meaningful than nonmetaphorical talk. We say that someone who castigated us "lashed out" at us or "cut us up," and that we, as a result, felt "crushed," "burned up," or "sore." We describe little wavelets in a bay as "dancing," and call a storm-driven sea "angry" or "raging." The ability of the average person to make metaphorical-analogical connections between very unlike areas of experience was entertainingly demonstrated many years ago by Köhler, the Gestalt psychologist: he asked subjects to match two nonsense words, "maluma" and "tuckatee," to the abstract figures shown in Figure 57. Without fail, Köhler's subjects connected maluma to *A* and tuckatee to *B*.

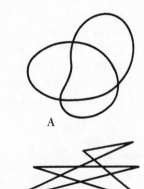

A

B

**Fig. 57.** Which shape looks like "maluma" and which like "tuckatee"?

•

The creative person's ability to connect remote entities, however, is of a different order of magnitude than the average person's. To the noncreative mind, the creative one often seems to make bizarre, disconcerting, and irrational leaps of thought. This may be one source of the old and enduring belief that the creative person is usually somewhat crazy; as Dryden put it, "Great wits are sure to madness near allied."

But there is no evidence that madness is more common among creative people than among noncreative people; it may be that we are simply more aware of it in those who are famous. What the mad and the creative have in common is unconventional thinking, but the similarity is purely superficial. The mad person makes leaps of thought that are definitely original or unusual, but that neither enrich nor illuminate; the creative person makes leaps of thought that dramatically deepen and clarify our thinking.

The easiest way to understand the difference between a psychotic "flight of ideas" and a creative train of ideas is to look at an example of each. Some years ago, while doing research at Pilgrim State Hospital on New York's Long Island, I spoke to a long-term patient, a courtly, silver-haired man who was planting flowers in a garden on the hospital grounds. At first, he talked quite coherently about what he was doing, but when I asked him why there was a small wooden cross in his garden, he opened an envelope hanging from the cross, pulled out a scrap of paper, and produced the following gush of disjointed thoughts:

> Just listen to this Sunogram that I wrote today. "Who are thou, O vipers and earthlings, to question God's terrible power? God forgives you *not* of your debts and sins. Read the Bible, II Peter." I had one of the finest fathers and mothers a man could have had. We are of the clan of Reuben—it's mentioned clear from Genesis to Revelation—people that believe in God, and in tilling the soil. Yet I climbed the ladder and became a professor of economics at Harvard, lecturing before the sons of the wealthy. I'm not trying to glorify myself, I'm nobody but God's judge of the quick and the dead. Your living beings who were on the moon, where did they go? How long ago did the moon stop revolving? What caused it? The same things that the devils are doing on earth right now. They're going to sever the magnetic pulsations, the earth's going to tremble and cease revolving, and what will it profit the wicked then to hold the world?

That involves a number of leaps of thought from one topic to another, but they were produced by short circuits or malfunctions of the mind rather than by creative thought processes.

And now, by way of contrast, here is a passage from the opening pages of E. L. Doctorow's recent novel, *Ragtime*, that impressionistically and somewhat satirically recreates the scene of the early 1900s in this country:

> There seemed to be no entertainment that did not involve great swarms of people. Trains and steamers and trolleys moved them from one place to another. That was the style, that was the way people lived. Women were stouter then. They visited the fleet carrying white parasols. Everyone wore white in summer. Tennis racquets were hefty and the racquet faces elliptical. There was a lot of sexual fainting. There were no Negroes. There were no immigrants. On Sunday afternoon, after dinner, Father and Mother went upstairs and closed the bedroom door. . . . This was the time in our history when Winslow Homer was doing his painting. A certain light was still available along the Eastern seaboard. It gave the sea a heavy dull menace and shone coldly on the rocks and shoals of the New England coast. There were unexplained shipwrecks and brave towline rescues. Odd things went on in lighthouses and in shacks nestled in the wild beach plum. Across America sex and death were barely distinguishable. Runaway women died in the rigors of ecstasy. Stories were hushed up and reporters paid off by rich families.

Here, too, we find a pell-mell succession of ideas and images, an abrupt leaping from one thing to another—but with what a difference! There is a startling logic, a dazzling illumination, in this wild sequence of details; we come away with a vision of America in 1902 that is part real, part caricature, and sharper and more vivid than real life.

The creative person thus is not mad, but presents us with a vision we sometimes find too dazzling for our eyes and prefer to call mad. But how does he or she make those connections? What is the secret? The only way to find out is to observe the creative process itself, if we can.

## The Creative Process

The creative process has been the subject of a great deal of intriguing speculation but very little research, and for good reason: part of the process—

very likely the most important part—takes place outside consciousness and can neither be described by the persons in whose minds it happens nor observed by others. The product of the unconscious cerebration emerges into the light of consciousness, but what takes place in the dark before that emergence remains unknown; cognitive scientists, thus far, can only speculate and make a few inferences about those unseen events.

It was not until late in the last century that there was even any recognition that the unconscious was involved in creative problem solving. One of the first to say something about it was Hermann Helmholtz, a German physiologist and physicist, who described his own scientific investigations as proceeding through three stages. (Graham Wallas, whom I mentioned in the last chapter, did not announce his own four-stage theory of problem solving until some thirty years later.) The first stage, according to Helmholtz, was *saturation;* it consisted of the initial investigation, carried on until he could make no further progress with the problem. Next was *incubation*—a period of rest and recovery during which, without conscious awareness of it, the materials in his mind were moved about and reorganized. Third was *illumination*—the appearance of a sudden and unexpected solution.

In 1908, the French mathematician Henri Poincaré described the creative process in much the same way, but added a fourth step, *verification.* His interest in the creative process grew out of his own experiences, some of which he described and one of which is a classic illustration of the four stages. Poincaré had been attempting to develop a theory of Fuchsian functions (it isn't necessary to know what they are to appreciate the story), and had been working on the problem almost continually for fifteen days, without success. One night, sleepless, it seemed to him that "ideas rose in crowds; I felt them collide until pairs interlocked, so to speak, making a stable combination." The implications of the combination, however, remained unclear, but a day or so later, when he was on his way to a geological expedition and had his mind on the trip, illumination burst upon him as he was boarding a bus:

> At the moment when I put my foot on the step the idea
> came to me, without anything in my thoughts seeming to
> have paved the way for it, that the transformations I had used
> to define the Fuchsian functions were identical with those of
> non-Euclidean geometry. I did not verify the idea; I should
> not have had time, as, upon taking my seat in the omnibus, I
> went on with a conversation already commenced, but I felt a

perfect certainty. On my return to Caen, for conscience's
sake I verified the result at my leisure.

Wallas introduced much the same four-stage description of creative
problem solving into American psychology in 1926, since which time most
investigators of creativity have followed this scheme or some modification
of it of their own devising. Their accounts, and a wealth of testimony by
creative people, essentially agree that:

—The creative act begins with a period of study, fact gathering, and
conscious efforts at creation or problem solving.

—After a while, fatigue, frustration, or the need to attend to other matters causes the attention to be turned away from the problem for anywhere
from a few seconds to months or even years, during which time the materials of the problem are worked over in the unconscious. Some cognitive scientists now say, however, that while incubation may be useful, it is not essential to all kinds of creativity. A musician composing a new work may
need time to incubate, but a musician creatively improvising has no time to
do so, and does not need to.

—At some point after a period of incubation, the result breaks through
into consciousness: it may come as anything from a slow-growing awareness
of a new way to tackle the problem to a sudden, complete, and dazzling
perception of the answer. A. E. Housman sometimes had a whole poem
come into his mind in finished form in the course of an afternoon walk, but
Johannes Kepler, the seventeenth-century German astronomer, experienced his discovery of the first two of the three laws expressing the movements of the planets as a slowly growing illumination. In his own words:

> Eighteen months ago, the first dawn rose for me; three
> months ago, the bright day; and a few days ago, the full sun of
> a most wonderful vision; now nothing can keep me back. I let
> myself go in divine exaltation.

—Finally, there is a stage of testing, developing, and checking out the
details; this may consist of anything from a few minutes' verification of a
mathematical proof to several years' worth of developing and turning an
inspired germ of an idea into a play or novel.

Despite forty-odd years of general agreement as to these stages of the
creative process, only its beginning and end are well understood; the critical steps of incubation and illumination remain almost as unfathomable to
us as they were to the early Greeks, who supposed that they took place out-

side the mind and were of supernatural origin. For so hidden from the conscious mind are the events taking place during incubation that the ancients interpreted new ideas or creative solutions to problems as a gift of the gods—"inspiration" breathed in from outside. Pythagoras, when he discovered and proved his most famous theorem (the square of the hypotenuse of a right triangle is equal to the sum of the squares of the other two sides), sacrificed a hecatomb—a hundred oxen—to the gods who had sent him the idea.

During the nineteenth century the recognition that there was an unconscious part of the mind first began to emerge. (Freud, contrary to common opinion, did not discover the unconscious; rather, he investigated it and established its psychodynamic importance.) Perhaps this is why Helmholtz, later in the century, was able to see that his own creative ideas were the products of incubation, and why Poincaré and others who followed him knew that new ideas come from within us, even though we do not know how we formed them.

This last is an endlessly perplexing but amply documented truth. Once the idea of the creative unconscious had diffused throughout educated society, a number of distinguished creative persons and scientific discoverers testified to the fact that they rarely or never knew what prompted their own creative ideas or solutions to problems. As the poet Amy Lowell wrote in 1930, "In answering the question, How are poems made? my instinctive answer is a flat 'I don't know'. . . . A common phrase among poets is, 'It came to me.' So hackneyed has this become that one learns to suppress the expression with care, but really it is the best description I know of the conscious arrival of a poem." The experience of the famous and the creative has been borne out by hundreds of nameless subjects of laboratory experiments. Norman Maier, giving his volunteers various problems such as we saw in the last chapter, time and again heard them say, after they had figured out a solution, "It just dawned on me," "I just realized—" and the like. A powerful experience, that—epitomized by the familiar story of Archimedes, who, overwhelmed by his sudden illumination concerning specific gravity and the king's gold crown, leaped out of a public bath, forgetting his clothing, and ran home through the streets, crying "Eureka!" ("I have found it!").

The unconscious, though one cannot force it, will not produce new ideas unless it has been painstakingly stuffed full of facts, impressions, concepts, and an endless series of conscious ruminations and attempted solutions. On this, too, we have the testimony of many creative people. Poincaré, as we have heard, had been working intensely at his Fuchsian functions for over two weeks (and at mathematics in general for years) before the solution popped into his conscious mind. James D. Watson's various visions and realizations about the structure of the DNA molecule came only after years of hard work, endless discussions, much model making, and a vast amount of speculation and theorizing.

Sometimes, though, a creative person will be unaware of the immense amount of learning, preparation, and conscious thought that go to make up the prepared unconscious. Amy Lowell spoke of dropping a subject for a poem into her unconscious "much as one drops a letter into the mailbox" and, six months later, finding the words of the poem coming into her head. But of course her mind was richly furnished with images, sounds, words, meters, rhymes, and all the rest; she failed to recognize that the effort of acquiring all these was part of her work.

The same explanation lies behind the seemingly effortless writing of "Kubla Khan." In a famous study, made two generations ago, the scholar John Livingston Lowes showed, from a close study of Coleridge's notebook (compiled from his reading over a three-year period), that virtually every scrap of imagery in "Kubla Khan" and in other poems of Coleridge's prime could be traced back to something the poet had read and written down in his notebook. "In those bizarre pages," wrote Lowes, "we catch glimpses of the strange and fantastic shapes which haunted the hinterland of Coleridge's brain . . . that heaving and phosphorescent sea below the verge of consciousness from which [his poems] have emerged."

That view has become a leading motif in present-day thinking about creativity. Dick Hayes of Carnegie-Mellon University told me that "the current trend, growing out of cognitive-science research, is to stress the relationship between knowledge and creativity. Take that famous figure, worked up by Herb Simon, that the chess master has learned and stored in memory fifty thousand patterns of positions on the board. What that says to me, and what I say to my students, is that to generate creative answers to problems, you need many years of experience and hard work and a lot of information. The old romantic view of the poet lolling around waiting for inspiration to strike is mistaken. In most fields, one has to make a major investment of time and effort before turning out any really creative ideas. We've been studying composers' lives recently, and I claim that the magic number is ten—that is, ten years between the time a composer starts intensive study and the time the first notable compositions appear. It was true of

Mozart, Mendelssohn, Schubert, and others—I now have a sample of seventy-six.

"But, of course, that amount of time and effort is only a necessary condition, not a sufficient one. There are innumerable poor slobs who can spend the same amount of time and effort, and still not produce a creative work of any magnitude. There's plenty more going on, in creative work, than merely stuffing the unconscious with material."

What does go on? Why can the unconscious find answers or at least new approaches to a problem that the conscious mind cannot find? To put it another way: why are interruptions in conscious work or periods of incubation so often helpful in producing those answers or new approaches?

In some cases, the answer is simple: the fatigued mind, after a brief rest, comes back to the problem refreshed. One research team gave their subjects typical divergent-production tests like naming as many consequences of a strange situation as they could think of. (What if, for instance, people could no longer read?) Some subjects worked on the task continuously, but others were interrupted by being given a distracting task for either ten or twenty minutes and were then allowed to finish the test. Those with the ten-minute break did a little better than the ones with no break, and those with the twenty-minute break did a lot better. These results, the researchers claimed, could be attributed largely to recovery from fatigue.

But this accounts only for an increased quantity of ideas; it does not explain why incubation so often yields startlingly *new* ideas and answers. Furthermore, the subjects in the experiment could very well have been unconsciously incubating even while performing the distracting task, and so could have come back to the test with ready-made new material.

Another possibility is that the effect of incubation is chiefly due to selective forgetting. Herbert Simon suggests that the initial plan for solving a problem is held only in short-term memory, but that in working on the problem, we acquire and store in long-term memory all sorts of new information that could lead to a better plan if our attention were not preempted by the first one. During incubation, the fruitless plan is easily forgotten, due to the nature of short-term memory, but the newly stored materials in long-term memory are not, and they lead us—with a feeling of illumination—to try the better route.

This may indeed describe what takes place in some creative experiences, especially those involving slow-dawning discoveries such as Watson's or Kepler's. But it hardly fits the facts of many other cases, such as Poincaré's,

Housman's, or Archimedes', in which the illumination was not an intimation or suggestion of a new approach but an *answer*. And even when incubation yields a new approach rather than an answer, creative people are usually unaware of the process by which that plan is formed; it seems simply to "occur" to them or "come to" them, often when they are thinking of something else altogether. There is more, it would seem, to incubation than the mere forgetting of a poor plan and the noticing of a better one; there is the unconscious *making* of the better one.

What is even more remarkable, incubation may result not only in a new plan but in a new *goal*. This does not happen in most kinds of problem solving, but it does often happen in solving the sort which calls forth creative thinking because, typically, such a problem has an "ill-defined" goal—one that is vague or unclear—allowing or even forcing the problem solver to redefine or change it in order to find a solution.

Such a task is exemplified by Figure 58; the goal is ill-defined, and to solve the problem you have to redefine it. Many people, considering this problem, first construe the question asked to mean, *Find the one odd element in a set of regular ones*, and so name 3 as the answer. But if they then recheck their solution (as most people do), they are likely to notice that 2 is the only shaded element, and so might be the answer, that 1 is the only figure with a·small circle inside it, and that 4 is the only one with a double border. All of which is confusing, but usually leads to a creative leap—a new and sharper definition, namely, *Find the one regular item among a set of odd ones*. The only one that fits—and therefore is the odd one, the one that doesn't fit—is 5.

This problem is an analog of what happens in real-life situations that require creativity. Unlike algebra or chemistry, in which both the goals and the means of reaching them usually are clearly defined, most problems in the arts, and many in the behavioral sciences and in equipment design, have unclear goals and relatively unconstrained means of getting to them.

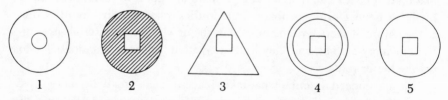

**Fig. 58.** Which of these figures doesn't fit with the others?

When a writer begins to create a novel or an anthropologist sets out to study an alien people, it may be quite unclear what the "real" goal is—and, therefore, what the best plan of attaining that goal will be. Working on the problem creates an influx of new information, and this, at both conscious and unconscious levels, changes the creative person's conception of the goal and of the best means of arriving at it. That is why writers, artists, and scientists so often say that they "had to go where the material led" them. Typically, Dorothy Canfield Fisher, telling how she came to write a particular short story, says that as she was working out the plot in her mind,

> . . . the story got out of hand. The old woman, silent, indomitable . . . stepped to the front of my stage, and from that moment on, dominated the action. I did not expect this, nor desire it. . . .

It led her to write the story in a certain way and to express a given theme that she had not originally had in mind.

The same thing can happen in the sciences, especially those dealing with behavior. Before World War II, Elton Mayo and several other sociologists sought to find out, on behalf of the management of Western Electric's Hawthorne plant in Chicago, what incentives would increase worker output. Mayo and his colleagues separated a group of women from other workers and systematically varied their lighting, coffee breaks, lunch hours, methods of payment, and so on. No matter what the sociologists did, productivity rose; even when the workers were returned to their original conditions, it rose again. Clearly, something was wrong; whatever had caused the increases in productivity, it was not the changes the researchers had introduced. In terms of its original goal, the experiment was a failure. But the sociologists mulled over the matter and eventually recognized what had happened: the women responded to the special attention they were getting, became a tight-knit cooperative group, and tried to please. The unexpected discovery of the "Hawthorne effect," as this phenomenon has been called ever since, could only be counted a success, and the sociologists had definitely arrived at a goal, albeit not the one they had started out to reach.

Finally, an intriguing suggestion as to why incubation is so often productive of creative ideas was made some years ago by Ulric Neisser: in the unconscious, he speculated, where there are no constraints imposed by attention and short-term memory, perhaps multiple chains of thought go on simultaneously—a far more efficient answer-finding procedure than the one-track thinking of conscious problem solving. If any one of these simultaneous lines of thought yields either a new solution or a new goal, it breaks through into consciousness. Neisser's suggestion is appealing, and is often spoken of by cognitive scientists as if it were known to be a reality, but thus far no one has explained how the mechanism might actually work, much less actually demonstrated that it exists. Maybe the idea doesn't lend itself to experimental proof, or at least not to any that has yet occurred to workers in the field. But perhaps one day, some cognitive scientist, after long pondering the matter to no avail, will give up on it and turn to another problem, only to find a way of demonstrating the multiplicity of unconscious thought popping into his or her mind unbidden.

Although what takes place in the unconscious mind of the creative person remains unknown, the visible interaction of the unconscious with the conscious is somewhat better understood, thanks to firsthand accounts by various creative people and to explorations by psychoanalysts of the creative process in their patients.

Sometimes the interaction seems limited to one significant transfer of information: a moment of illumination may be followed by a long period of conscious, highly skilled problem solving. Kekulé worked all night to spell out the consequences of his daydream. It took Einstein ten years to work out the theoretical implications of his vision of riding a beam of light. Tchaikovsky wrote to his patroness, Nadezhda von Meck,

> Generally, the germ of a future composition comes suddenly and unexpectedly ... from the depths of a composer's soul ... [But] what has been set down in a moment of ardor must now be critically examined, improved, extended, or condensed, as the form requires.... Only after strenuous labor have I at last succeeded in making the form of my compositions correspond, more or less, with their contents.

But it is rarely the case that the unconscious furnishes an idea or plan and then remains quiescent while the conscious mind works out the  details; more often, in any extended creative work there is a continuing interplay between conscious and unconscious. Each line of the poem, each measure of the symphony, each step of the working out of the structure of a molecule, feeds new material into long-term memory and, in turn, leads to the emergence of new illuminations from the busy unconscious. If any creative person ever told all that went on in the process of creating any work, he or she might produce an account a hundred, perhaps a thousand, times longer than the work itself. Henry Miller once said that he thought he could write a good-sized book on just one small paragraph selected at random from his work.

The shortcoming of most existing descriptions of the creative process is that they are general, and lacking in details of the mechanisms at work. In other areas of cognitive science, researchers have turned to information-processing theory and protocol analyses to discover such details, but this approach has hardly been used in investigating creativity. And for good reason: because many a creative task has no clear goal or specified set of constraints, the researcher cannot judge the subject's progress toward the solution. Even if one could get a novelist to dictate a protocol while writing part of a novel, against what baseline or toward what known goal would one chart the steps of thought revealed by it? Alternatively, the researcher could think up a task so clearly defined and constrained as to yield analyzable protocols—but no such task would allow much room for creativity.

Dick Hayes and a colleague, Linda Flower, at Carnegie-Mellon, are the only people I heard of who are currently doing protocol analysis of creative tasks (the task, in their case, being writing). It's hard and tedious work reading what people say when they're trying to write, and harder yet trying to perceive the steps of information processing in it. Here, for instance, is a bit of the protocol of one student as she begins the task of writing a short essay on what motivates students in the writing of papers and reports at Carnegie-Mellon University:

> Okay, um, the issue is motivation and the problem of writing papers. For me, motivation here at Carnegie-Mellon is the academic pressure and grades that are involved, so I'd better put that down ... and grades ... Um, they kind of compel me, that's really what motivation is, um, kind of to impel or start or a, momentum. (Pause.) Okay, I suppose from the academic pressure of the grades, I'm not sure whether, I think personal satisfaction is important. ...

Hayes and Flower have painstakingly plodded through hundreds of pages of such stuff, seeking to sort out the steps by which their subjects produced ideas, turned them into words, and modified and polished the result. From their analyses of a number of protocols, they have come up with a diagrammatic model of the writing process that consists of a score of labeled boxes connected by arrows. It indicates that the writer engages in three processes of creative problem solving: planning, translating, and reviewing. Each of these, in turn, consists of several subprocesses (such as retrieving information from long-term memory and feeding it into the plan, or checking the sentence just written to see that it matches what one had in mind). All the processes and subprocesses are watched over and directed by the "monitor," the judgmental, executive part of the conscious mind. A few sentences from a recent paper by Hayes and Flower, talking about one of the three processes, will convey the flavor of their analysis:

> The planning process consists of retrieval, inferencing, and organizing subprocesses. Its function is to take information from the task environment and from long term memory and to generate internal (mental) representations of topic knowledge, the audience, and writing plans. Writing plans may be drawn from long term memory or may be generated by the organizing subprocesses.

This and their other statements about the process of writing are far more down-to-earth and specific than any number of poetic effusions I have read about the art of prose composition. What I miss in it—and I don't find fault with them for this, since it hasn't been one of their goals—is any explanation of how the mind actually originates the plan, the new ideas it feeds into that plan, or the particular sentences by which it translates those ideas into prose. Each of these steps would seem to involve unexplained happenings in the unconscious, but surely explanations of those happenings are crucial to the understanding of the process of writing. It is true that once an image, idea, or sentence is out in the open, we can follow its progress through the flow of the Hayes and Flower diagram, but how did we create it in the first place? Sometimes by various kinds of conscious thinking—but more often by having an image, idea, or expression simply appear while we were thinking. The diagram doesn't show that, and wasn't intended to; and yet, I think, it is an essential part of the process.

To illustrate what I mean, I will turn to a bit of another writing protocol analyzed by Hayes and Flower that I can speak of with special understanding, for it is my own. Before one of my visits to Carnegie-Mellon, I had written ahead to make an appointment with Dick Hayes; his secretary, in confirming it, asked me on his behalf whether I would be willing to act as a subject and provide him with a writing protocol for a new study he and Linda Flower were working on.

So one morning I made my way to his offices on the third floor of Baker Hall, where Sandra Bond, his research assistant, greeted me and installed me in a small room at a table that had on it a tape recorder, pad, and some pencils. She handed me a brown envelope marked #6. "This will tell you what your topic is," she said, and gave me the usual instructions about saying out loud everything I was thinking. I opened the envelope; in it, a handwritten note told me that I was to write an essay on the topic "Abortion, Pro and Con" for the ten-to-twelve-year-old readers of *Children's Digest*.

Because I have been a writer for a long while, I was able to marshal my thoughts and make an outline with far less fumbling and stumbling than the student quoted above; that was to be expected. Although a trifle self-conscious about talking out loud to myself, I felt at home with the task, and said, "Well, the first thing that occurs to me is, uh, I will offer the children some general background—I have to give them an idea what abortion is, and why there's a controversy about it." I wrote that down as the first step in my outline. Then I said that I'd start with the arguments against abortion, since I would find that a harder and weaker argument to make than the other; the piece would therefore build as I moved to the stronger and, to me, more congenial case for abortion.

In this manner I consciously reasoned out an outline with five main topics and a number of subtopics; if there was anything creative about this part of my work, I didn't sense it then, and nothing in the transcript that Hayes later sent me suggests that in this phase there was anything but normal problem solving.

But when it came to writing a lead, I had one of those tiny experiences that make up the creative component of the writing process. (Please understand: I don't claim that what I am about to exhibit is any piece of high-level creativity; it's very small and very low-level—but it isn't explained by any of the boxes and arrows in the diagram.) "I need a lead that seizes my audience," I said when I was ready to write, "and I have to think about how to start this at a level that will be right for ten-to-twelve-year-olds." I speculated about a lead that would directly and flatly state the subject; then, feeling that that would not catch the reader's attention, I considered a more vivid and anecdotal start such as, "Jenny X has a baby in her belly, and one day you see her with a big belly and the next day or two days later you see her and it's flat—" I stopped—not because it had occurred to me that there's no big belly early in pregnancy, when abortion is still feasible, but because I found myself wondering whether to make Jenny X an unwed teenager or a young married woman; I decided on the latter, so as not to load the case unfairly in favor of the abortion. Here is how my protocol reads at this point:

> So I'm going to write now. "One day you see Mrs. Toland, a young lady who lives down the street, and you notice that she has a slightly bulging tummy"—well, I'm in trouble now because most abortions occur before there's really any change in shape, so I'm going to have to kill that one. I'm going to write something that occurred to me [just now] too fast for me to say the protocol aloud. "One day you hear Mrs. Toland, a young woman who lives down the block, has had an abortion"—no—"One day you overhear two women in the A & P"—I'm supposed to talk about the protocol, but these ideas are coming up as I'm writing and I don't even know what's coming next. [And on I went, then, talking and writing as follows:]
>
> "One day you overhear two women in the A & P talking about young Mrs. Toland. One of the women says that Mrs. Toland must be a horrible person to have had an abortion; the other woman angrily replies, 'She had every right to do it—and there's nothing wrong with it.' For the next minute, the two women shout at each other furiously, and at last, after glaring at each other in pure hatred, turn and stomp away."

Some time later, Dick Hayes sent me that protocol and told me about the results of the study. He and Linda Flower had found that professional writers were much more likely than inexpert writers to have a clear image of their audience in mind and to use that image while writing; they had also found that expert writers produced longer sentences than the novices, which indicates that they knew more clearly than the novices what they wanted to say before starting to say it. I found this moderately interesting, since some of it had to do with me and my protocol, but what interested me far more was what the protocol showed about my little flickers of illumination. For having said what I needed to achieve in the lead, and having fumbled around, consciously trying to write one, suddenly—"too fast for me to say the protocol aloud"—I thought of a lead that seemed right, and wrote it down, aware only that "these ideas are coming up as I'm writing and I don't even know what's coming next."

That isn't true of most of what follows in the protocol; a lot of it is a mere restating and expansion of points I had made in my outline. But time and again the protocol indicates that examples, details, and words with which to express them simply popped into my mind, and only after they appeared did I consciously think about how well they did or did not meet the need of the moment.

Two things seem quite clear to me: one, my essay, were it to be published, would win no literary prizes; and two, though I am an experienced writer with a repertoire of skills, I did not know then and do not know now by what means I produced the more imaginative bits and pieces of that little essay when I needed them. Nor do I find anything yet in cognitive-science research that can tell me how I did it. And not until cognitive science can adequately explain a mere amoeba of creativity such as this will it be able to start tackling the vastly higher and more complex forms that human creativity can take.

## Creating Creativity

Despite having only a very imperfect understanding of creativity, human beings have long intuitively recognized the creativity-enhancing value of certain physical and mental conditions that they are able to establish at will. Various primitive peoples and the ancients of our own civilization, for instance, knew that fatigue, sleeplessness, solitary vigils with prolonged meditation (preferably on a mountaintop), and the stimulus of certain drugs would tend to produce visions and, sometimes, what seemed to be answers to problems.

Beside these general and, unfortunately, unreliable methods, a number of creative persons have stumbled upon a variety of specific ways to enhance their own powers. Most of these, however, are purely idiosyncratic, and of no help to the rest of us. Schiller wrote best when smelling rotting apples; Zola was stimulated by the ambience of artificial light, even at midday; the naturalist, Comte de Buffon, felt inspired only when dressed as if for a social event; Ben Jonson responded to the influences of tea, the purring of a cat, and the odor of orange peel; and André Grétry composed with his feet in ice water. Einstein and Freud both worked particularly well during bouts of abdominal discomfort (though neither deliberately induced such distress as an aid to creativity). But these nostrums will do most of us no good; if they were broadly helpful, how could it be that almost no one else has reported finding them so?

Happily, in recent years the intense interest of psychologists, engineers, and lately of cognitive scientists has led to a number of suggestions based either on sound theory or on the results of experience and experiment. These methods are easier and more reliable than mountaintop vigils, and more likely to work for the average person than smelling rotting apples or immersing one's feet in ice water. Herewith a sampling of them; those who want more information can consult the sources listed in the Notes.

Some of the suggestions are obvious implications of the research findings about the creative process. For instance, in books and college courses on creativity, most teachers say that the primary prerequisite is the acquisition of a large "knowledge base"; one must learn a lot of relevant information. Knowledge alone cannot ensure a creative answer to a problem, but the creative mind without the necessary knowledge cannot generate one.

Another obvious implication of existing knowledge, pointed out by psychiatrist Silvano Arieti among others, is that for most people creativity flourishes in isolation. Aloneness, he says, produces something close to sensory deprivation, a condition in which it becomes easier than usual to "listen to the inner self." This, he believes, explains why creative ideas are particularly likely to emerge from incubation during a period of inactivity, somnolence, or daydreaming, when the barriers to unconscious processes are down. It explains, too, the appearance of creative ideas in dreams, though there they are often so heavily disguised by symbolism as to remain inscrutable. Also, dreams fade away so fast when we awaken—even those containing valuable ideas—that often they are gone before we have transferred them to consciousness. Otto Loewi, the German pharmacologist, was investigating the nature of the transmission of nerve impulses in frog muscles many years ago, but at a crucial point in his work he got stuck. One night he awoke from a dream in which both the theory and an experiment by which to test it had appeared to him; he scrawled a few words on a piece of paper and happily went back to sleep. But in the morning the scrawl proved illegible and the dream unrecoverable; he struggled in vain all day to recall it. That night, however, the same dream came to him again. This time he took no chances: he leaped out of bed and got dressed, rushed to his laboratory, and by daybreak had discovered the chemical transmission of nerve impulses—the keystone of the work for which he won the 1936 Nobel Prize in physiology and medicine.

Beyond such general conditions, in recent years a number of specific heuristics to aid and stimulate creativity have been developed by various psychologists, teachers, design engineers and inventors, and others. Some of their recommendations have been backed up by research; others have not but are said to have proven to work well for people in business and in technological development.

One such heuristic is to tackle a problem at a high level of abstraction (the expert method of thinking about a problem that Frederick Reif had told me about). By so doing, we avoid getting locked into one specific view of the problem, and are able to consider many remote and unlikely—but possibly highly creative—solutions. A professor of engineering named John Arnold, in the creative engineering course he taught at MIT in the 1950s, used as an example the problem of thinking of an entirely new type of printing device. If one were to view the problem as a challenge to find a new way to assemble type and transfer ink to paper, he would say, one would be confined to a narrow category of possibilities. But suppose, instead, one were to think in broader terms; suppose one began by listing the basic attributes of a printing device. Type, ink, plates, and rollers aren't basic; what is basic is that a printing device (1) conveys information, (2) transfers it from one form or place to another, (3) renders it visual, and (4) makes multiple copies of the rendering. With that as a start, one would be free to think of possibilities very remote from movable type and ink transfer, such as photographic models of type rather than three-dimensional ones, electronic rather than physical assembling of the master copy, and photostatic copying rather than mechanical transfer of ink from plates to paper. And, in fact, between the time Arnold taught his course and today just such revolutionary developments have come about in printing.

A useful aid to thinking in broad categories and in terms of basic attributes is the avoidance of nouns when naming objects (nouns reinforce rigid classifications), and the use, instead, of verbs, which broadly stress functions. This is a favorite notion of William J. J. Gordon, formerly the head of the Invention Section at the Cambridge consulting firm Arthur D. Little, and at present a partner in the consulting firm SES Associates, also in Cambridge. Gordon once was asked by a client to develop a new type of can opener, but in telling his group about it he avoided the words "can opener" so as not to limit them to the category of mechanical devices used on the top of a container; instead he asked them for ideas about "opening." This produced a free flow of thoughts, including one to the effect that in nature there are self-opening devices such as the soft seam of the pea pod. In turn, this led to such specific suggestions as cans or containers with soft or easily broken seams, like today's pop-tops or tape-opening frozen-juice containers, none of which would have come to mind if one had begun with the words "can opener."

The heart of Gordon's creativity-stimulating system, which he calls "synectics," is the conscious use of analogy. Gordon spells out four kinds of analogies that are helpful in imaginative thinking. In using "personal analogy" we imagine ourselves physically entering into a process—as Einstein did when he fantasied himself riding the light beam. In "direct analogy," we look for something that solves the same problem we are working on, but in a different context or setting: Bell looked at the human ear, and saw in it a way of developing a workable telephone transmitter. "Symbolic analogy" is looser and more visual: it might help the writer of a suspense novel to think of the plot as a sealed vessel being heated up, with the pressure inside increasing continually until at the end there is an explosion. Finally, "fantasy analogy" involves "wild" thinking in which anything goes, even if it violates common sense; when trying to think of new means of transportation, for instance, one might think of flying carpets or teleportation. Impossible and ridiculous? Yes, but ridiculous thoughts sometimes produce useful analogies. One creative-engineering group (not Gordon's), while thinking of ways to fasten wires together, agreed that the most ridiculous suggestion offered during the session was "hold them with your teeth." But while this was manifestly silly, the group swiftly realized that "alligator clips" and other commercially available fasteners analogous to the grip of human teeth were feasible answers to the problem.

Indeed, another often-recommended heuristic is to deliberately think of farfetched and improbable solutions. Psychologists and engineers, theoreticians and pragmatists, agree that in trying to generate imaginative and original ideas, it helps to consciously violate our usual habits of thinking and, at least in the beginning, let the more fanciful and illogical products of the mind break through the barriers of censorship and evaluation. Every recent writer on creativity has stressed the importance of the temporary suspension of critical judgment; it is, in fact, the essential mechanism behind "brainstorming," a method of group problem solving worked out some years ago by Alex Osborn, an advertising executive. The interplay of many minds accounts for part of the effectiveness of brainstorming, but its crucial component is a freewheeling atmosphere in which any and all ideas, no matter how zany or farfetched, are acceptable during the idea-generation phase. Only later, in the idea-evaluation phase, are they subjected to rational consideration.

Gordon, similarly, encouraged the people in his groups to do "irrational" thinking, and claimed that in a permissive atmosphere people are stimulated, made daring, and challenged by others' ideas, with the result that a group can churn out in a few hours a mass of ideas that might take an individual months. But this claim seems excessive to some psychologists; their experiments have sometimes shown that for particular kinds of problems, group sessions yield fewer and poorer ideas than individual endeavors. Moreover, many highly creative people seem disinclined or unable to do their best work except by themselves.

Happily, the most valuable aspect of brainstorming—its suspension of critical judgment during the idea-generation phase—can be successfully employed by the individual working alone, according to Dick Hayes and others. Many creative people intuitively recognized the value of this approach long before the era of cognitive science. Schiller, two centuries ago, had this advice for a friend who complained of his lack of creative power:

> The reason for your complaint lies, it seems to me, in the constraint which your intellect imposes upon your imagination. Here I will make an observation, and illustrate it by an allegory. Apparently it is not good—and indeed it hinders the creative work of the mind—if the intellect examines too closely the ideas already pouring in, as it were, at the gates. . . . In the case of a creative mind, it seems to me, the intellect has withdrawn its watchers from the gates, and the ideas rush in pell-mell, and only then does it inspect and review the multitude.

A contemporary cognitive scientist could hardly say it better.

But what if ideas don't rush in pell-mell? Sometimes one can deliberately produce them by following rules of thumb. Some teachers of creative thinking have compiled checklists of questions and suggestions designed to joggle the mind and to remind us of possible avenues of wild thinking that we might otherwise forget. One such list, put together by Osborn, has nine categories of self-query, each of which asks a number of questions. Under the category *Reverse?* are such questions as, "Transpose positive and negative? How about opposites? Turn it backward? Turn it upside down? Reverse roles? Change shoes? Turn tables? Turn the other cheek?" The other categories include such headings as *Adapt? Magnify? Minify? Substitute?* and so forth, each with its own questions. Such a checklist can prod the mind into searching along many avenues that might have been ignored. Its possible disadvantage is that if we focus on these categories and questions, we may fail to generate some of the wild and creative possibilities of which we are capable but which lie outside the list.

In recent years, group creative thinking has become a commonplace in business and engineering companies, think tanks, and other institutional settings. One of the ways in which it stimulates creative problem solving is through the interaction of experts and outsiders. Experts are very good problem solvers, as long as the problem does not require a novel or radical solution. All the expert's knowledge and training tend to make him or her see the problem in a conventional way and search for answers within that limited view; experts, it is sometimes said, have "hardening of the categories." It is for this reason that some creative-engineering groups bring in people from other scientific disciplines or from the humanities to look at the problem with a "fresh eye"—naive, uninformed, but unfettered by practice and tradition. At think tanks, too, it is common experience that table talk among people of dissimilar backgrounds and expertise often helps open up the ideas of each about his or her own projects.

For though knowledge makes us better problem solvers, practice at using that knowledge makes us less creative ones. The more skilled we are at dealing with a particular kind of problem, the more resistant we are to radically different ways of trying to solve it. And this is the irony not just of the expert but of humankind in general: people admire, celebrate, and reward innovators of all kinds, but also ignore, ostracize, or punish them if they are too radically innovative and if their ideas violate custom and received opinion. Vesalius was called a madman in his time because he dared controvert the established anatomical wisdom of Galen. Ignaz Semmelweis, working in a Viennese hospital before the advent of the germ theory of disease, suspected that the failure of doctors to wash their hands prior to delivering babies was somehow responsible for the high rate of deaths from puerperal fever; he instituted washing and the death rate dropped from 12 percent to 1.5 percent, but the other doctors angrily drove him out of the hospital. Various experts castigated Stravinsky's *Rite of Spring* when it was first performed, laughed at Edison's first light bulb, and sneered at Joyce's *Ulysses*. The Armory Show of 1913—America's first wholesale look at cubist art—created furious controversy and outrage; guards even had to protect such paintings as Marcel Duchamp's *Nude Descending a Staircase* from public attack.

The same cultural ambivalence toward creativity is endemic in our schools; we endlessly praise it to children but teach them to avoid being creative. A number of studies of contemporary teaching practices by psychologist E. Paul Torrance and other researchers show that most teachers react negatively to creative and original notions offered by children in their classes; they tend to characterize unconventional and offbeat work by children as "silly," "wild," or "naughty." But the teachers themselves are only reflecting what they, too, have learned in school and in college: in one study, Torrance found that high-school science teachers who scored high on creativity tests were rated lower by their supervisors for their classroom work than more conventional teachers.

All this is known to every creative person with even a dollop of common sense and life experience. But if it is obvious that one cannot count on acceptance and reward for any major creative effort and may encounter instead silence or obloquy, what motivates the creative person to produce new ideas and works? The hope of success, of course—but perhaps something more, something quintessentially human: the sheer joy of the creative act itself. This is not Panglossian optimism; there is intriguing experimental evidence showing that not just the highly creative person, but the average human being, is more likely to do creative work for its own intrinsic rewards than for external ones. In fact, there is even some evidence that reward or critical evaluation of one's work actually decreases creativity.

In one of Torrance's many studies of creativity in schoolchildren, children were given pencils, crayons, and simple collage materials, and told to make a picture that no one else would be likely to come up with. A variety of kinds of comment and appraisal were given to different groups of the children, and some got no evaluation at all. The upshot: those who worked without evaluation turned out pictures that were more creative than those produced by children receiving the most constructive commentary. In a study by another researcher, a group of students were told they would earn a reward for thinking up the largest number of plot titles and stories; their output was less imaginative and original than that of another group who expected no reward. Merely knowing that one's work will be critically appraised by experts after it is finished has a negative influence. Teresa Amabile, in her collage studies, told one group of college women that their efforts would be judged by artists, while another group was told nothing; the latter group did significantly more creative work.

How can this be? Haven't nearly all great writers, artists, and other creative persons labored for money and in the hope of fame? Isn't it well-known that most scientists are fiercely competitive and eager to be recognized for their discoveries? If the need to earn a living by one's work or the hunger for acknowledgment and prestige could undermine creativity, how can we account for the work of professionally creative people?

Amabile offers two possible answers. First, consistently creative people may be so skilled at what they do that they are not diverted from their pathways of thought by the lure of reward or public opinion. Second, outstandingly creative people may have so much intrinsic interest in what they are doing, while they are doing it, that they are able deliberately to shut out the influence of external motives; thoughts of success or failure and other outside incentives and constraints do not affect them, at least for the time being.

If so, highly creative people deserve admiration not only for what they produce but for the spirit in which they produce it. But the research data indicate that even less creative people are at their most creative when playing with ideas or solving problems for the sheer pleasure of manipulating the inner world and the outer world better than they had been doing. Every day each of us does some things for the pure joy of figuring out a puzzle, finding a better way to do some ordinary task, or arriving at a fresh scrap of insight about a friend or about ourselves. We are all more or less creative—the more when we have no need to be; that is another of the paradoxes and splendors of the human intellect.

# MIND AND SUPERMIND

### A Specter Is Haunting the World

*The scene: The computer room of Bolt Beranek and Newman, the Cambridge consulting firm, early on a Saturday morning not many years ago. Enter a vice-president of the firm, who intends to demonstrate a system on the computer to some prospective customers later that day. On the machine's teletype he finds a note that reads, TYPE ALL MESSAGES INTO THIS TELE-TYPE, AND END THEM WITH A PERIOD. Momentarily puzzled, he decides the note was left by Daniel Bobrow, a psychologist who often works with the computer late at night from a teletype terminal in his own home. Supposing Bobrow to be still hooked into the computer, the VP types out a message to him, with the following results:*

| | |
|---|---|
| VP: | Do you think I can use the computer this morning? |
| TELETYPE: | Why do you ask? |
| VP: | I might be able to make some additional tele-com sales. |
| T: | Why aren't you sure? |
| VP: | My prospective customers have never seen a demonstration of the system. |
| T: | Does this mean very much to you? |
| VP: | Of course it does. |
| T: | You seem very positive of that. |
| VP: | This is ridiculous. |

> T:  What do you mean this is ridiculous?
> VP: Is there any reason why I can't use the computer now?
> T:  Tell me more about your prospective customers.

In a fury, the VP called Bobrow on the phone and snapped, "Why are you being so snotty with me?" Bobrow, who had been asleep, asked what he was talking about. The VP read him the teletype exchange, and Bobrow, amid spasms of laughter, explained that the VP hadn't been conversing with him but with the machine itself.

Or, to be more accurate, with a program left on the machine by another employee. It was an adaptation of the famous ELIZA program (later known as DOCTOR), written by Professor Joseph Weizenbaum of MIT, that simulates the responses of a Rogerian psychotherapist talking to a patient. It wasn't half as intelligent as it sounded to the VP—in fact, it wasn't intelligent at all; Weizenbaum had designed DOCTOR to pick up key words or punctuation marks in the patient's typed-in statements and use them to trigger off preprogrammed replies that deceptively appear to be understanding and responsive. For instance, when DOCTOR receives a series of words ending in a question mark, it automatically replies, "Why do you ask?"; when it receives a sentence containing the word "might," it responds, "Why aren't you sure?"; and using key words such as "you" and "me," it replies to a sentence such as, "I think you don't like me" with the question, "What makes you think I don't like you?" It understands nothing; if you spoke nonsense to it, you'd get nonsense back. Were you to tell it, "You gyre and gimble me," it would ask, "What makes you think I gyre and gimble you?"

Weizenbaum was startled and discomfited, however, to find that people who talked to DOCTOR, knowing full well what it was, tended to take its replies seriously; some of them would confide in it, become emotionally involved with it, and insist that it did, in fact, understand them. He was even more disturbed when several psychologists in California, Wisconsin, and England took DOCTOR's success to mean that therapy by computer is feasible and began to develop post-DOCTORATE programs of their own, with an eye toward their widespread use.

One can hardly blame Weizenbaum for being alarmed; he had meant the exercise to be a mere parody, but somehow it had taken on a life of its own or, at least, affected people as if it had. The VP at Bolt Beranek and Newman, all unknowing, was easily misled by the formula responses of the program into thinking that he was having a conversation of a very annoying sort with another human being, but how could one explain the people who knew what it was they were talking to and yet reacted as if it were a living (or at least operating) intelligence?

The explanation is that they *wanted* it to be. It is a phenomenon with a long history: for many centuries, human beings have been entranced by the idea that somehow we might be able to create lifelike mechanisms in our own image—robots, androids, animated dolls, and thinking machines. The archetypal plot of our fantasies has never wearied us nor its conclusion failed to satisfy: the mannequin at first obeys its maker, then grows bold and impudent, then dangerous, and at last, in a breathtaking encounter, is defeated by the wisdom and courage of the human being. From the medieval tale of the golem to the modern one of HAL, the malevolent computer of the movie *2001: A Space Odyssey*, the story has been essentially the same: we have played God, been endangered by our creation, and finally turned it back to dust.*

Until now, these have been nothing but fantasies; now they seem to be something else. Even an electronic bag of tricks, without any intelligence, can come dangerously close to having power over us, but what if computers could be programmed to perform genuinely intelligent processes with the information they possess and receive? What if they could understand, reason, make decisions, and act upon them? How would the story end then?

And in fact since 1966, when DOCTOR was born, computer scientists have developed programs that not only ape the human intellect in many ways but already outstrip it in some. Computers calculate thousands of times faster than we and, as we hear every day, can now perform a number of sophisticated tasks far beyond our capabilities: they prescribe the choice of sails and the headings for America's Cup contenders better than any seasoned skipper, they are far better than any human being at routing air traffic, predicting the weather, and directing the flow of parts and materials in factories, and they are better than poets or scholars at deciding whether or not certain disputed literary works could have been written by particular authors. Some of them can even read and summarize news stories, understand spoken sentences and carry out orders, deduce simple mathematical laws from raw data fed to them, diagnose diseases from given medical information, prove logical theorems, and play games—at which they get bet-

---

* One notable exception: Karel Čapek's 1923 play *R.U.R.*, in which robots successfully revolt against their masters and wipe out the human race—only to begin exhibiting human emotions.

ter as they play. In the view of a number of AI researchers, there is nothing the human mind can do that computers will not soon do just as well and, someday, infinitely better.

From all of which it is only a step to conjectures about the takeover by the Superminds. Such speculations, offered on TV shows or in potboilers that titillate the public, can be viewed as mere entertainment, but they also come from a number of scientists, including some designers of the very programs that, they say, will soon surpass human intelligence and then . . . but let a few of them speak for themselves:

> —Robert Jastrow, director of the Goddard Institute for Space Studies, and professor of astronomy at Columbia University: "In another fifteen years or so—around 1995, according to current trends—we will see the silicon brain as an emergent form of life, competitive with man."
> —Edward Fredkin, professor of electrical engineering and computer science at MIT: "Eventually, no matter what we do there'll be artificial intelligences with independent goals. It's very hard to have a machine that's a million times smarter than you as your slave." Once artificial intelligences start getting smart, he says, their smartness will grow with explosive speed. "If that happens at Stanford, say, the Stanford AI Lab may have immense power all of a sudden. It's not that the United States might take over the world, it's that the Stanford AI Lab might."
> —Marvin Minsky of MIT, the computer scientist and artificial intelligence authority, believes that in the foreseeable future when a machine finally reaches the general intelligence of an average human being, "the machine will begin to educate itself . . . [and] in a few months it will be at genius level . . . A few months after that its power will be incalculable. . . . If we are lucky, they might decide to keep us as pets."

How can this be? If we cannot yet create even the simplest form of life, how can we suppose that we have created (if even at a low level) actual thought, the most complex product of life? How can the inanimate wires and transistors of the computer—infinitely simpler, despite their complexity, than the circuitry of the brain—produce anything comparable to the thinking of a living mind?

To some AI people, this is not an interesting question: what matters is not the hardware (the physical structure) of the computer, they say, but its software (the functions it performs). They maintain that whether one uses gears and wheels, vacuum tubes and magnetic storage, or silicon chips containing microscopic conductors and transistors, one can "build a machine"—AI jargon for writing a program—that processes information in ways comparable to those of the human intellect; mind is mind, no matter what its physical embodiment. Yet the outsider may reject the thought that the inanimate object can acquire the inner essence of the animate; a machine can never be more than a machine unless . . . unless what? What might turn a mere automaton, a device that records data we feed into it and then juggles the data according to our commands, into an apparatus that actually *thinks*?

Although computer science lies beyond the scope of this book, there are a few simple concepts that can clarify this question and permit us to ask the larger one, namely: Can artificial intelligence match and outstrip our own in every respect? And if not, what does artificial intelligence tell us about ourselves? What is it that is unduplicable about us?

First, the building block of the contemporary computer—its neuron, so to speak—is the transistor, a tiny bit of semiconductor crystal. Depending on the applied voltage, a transistor can range from nonconductive to highly conductive; it can therefore be used as a microscopic switch which is either "on" or "off." Two transistors, moreover, can be wired together in such a way that when one is on, the other is off, and they will maintain this state until control signals tell them to switch states—at which point "on" switches off and "off" switches on. This device is known, accordingly, as a "flip-flop." Because it can maintain either one of two states (on-off or off-on), it is an elementary information-storage unit; it's like a pointer one can set to point to either a "yes" or a "no," or, what is the same thing, to a "0" or a "1."

That's not much information—only a single "bit"—but flip-flops can be interconnected with other flip-flops to form a "register" capable of storing any conceivable number by means of the binary (0 or 1) system instead of our familiar decimal system. Here, for instance, is how numbers up to 7 are represented by flip-flops (in the lower line, each digit represents a flip-flop):

| Decimal system | 0 | 1 | 2 | 3 | 4 | 5 | 6 | 7 |
|---|---|---|---|---|---|---|---|---|
| Binary system | 0 | 1 | 10 | 11 | 100 | 101 | 110 | 111 |

Larger numbers merely require more flip-flops; a twenty-bit (twenty-flip-flop) register, for instance, can store the binary equivalent of any number up to 1,048,576.

The rest of computer technology need not concern us here. We need know only these four facts:

—Flip-flops can be interconnected to form registers that can store any number.

—Groups of these registers can be combined to form a "memory array" capable of storing sets of numbers.

—The content of any register in such a memory array can be retrieved and passed along to other elements of the computer system through circuits controlled by other transistors; those circuits can perform various operations on the data such as addition or subtraction.

—Finally, large numbers of flip-flops to record information, plus many others to process it, can be assembled in a tiny "chip." Figure 59 shows one recently designed and made by IBM that contains 64,000 flip-flops and measures less than one quarter inch square. A contemporary research-level

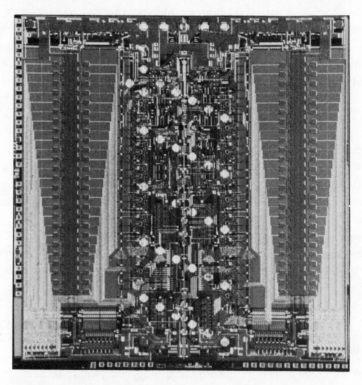

**Fig. 59.** IBM's 64,000-bit memory chip; area of actual chip is only about 1/300th this size.

computer may contain thousands of such chips, totaling many millions of bits of information-processing capacity.

Now, how can even so immense a machine think, if its flip-flops can record only 0s and 1s or combinations of them, and if it can perform only simple arithmetical operations? The answer is that it does something akin to thinking if it guides its own operations. A *calculator* is a reckoning device that you, the operator, have to tell what to do, every step of the way; it carries out those procedures that you tell it to, and only when you do so. But with some additional circuitry, the same kind of machine can hold your entire series of orders in its memory; once you have given it that *program* (as the series of orders is called), you need tell it only what numbers to process, and start it. It will then carry out the operations step by step, even making decisions at various points based on the results thus far, just as you would have done had you been doing it yourself. This is the essence of the *computer:* it is a programmable calculator, capable of carrying out on its own any series of instructions you program it with.

And what if other kinds of mental processes, richer in ideational content than arithmetic, could be translated into numbers? If a machine can deal with numbers—which are one species of symbol—why not with letters? For any letter can be translated into an equivalent number (that's what is meant by "coding"), and that being so, the computer can be programmed to solve algebraic equations: each letter is represented by a string of 0s and 1s, and dealt with according to whatever program you provide.

If algebra, why not symbolic logic? For it, too, uses letters, plus algebra-like symbols that signify "add," "either-or," "not," "if-then," and the like. This was the leap of thought made in the 1950s by Allen Newell and Herbert Simon when they created Logic Theorist, a program that enabled a computer to carry out a series of logical steps by which it turned certain given theorems (using symbols, not words) into other theorems—in effect, "proved" any theorem that could logically be derived from the given ones. Thus, Logic Theorist performed the first acts of artificial intelligence by manipulating symbols in a way only human beings had been able to do until then.

In so doing, it was only one remove from dealing with meaningful thoughts. For if the computer could deal with symbols, why couldn't those symbols stand for words? Indeed, why couldn't the computer handle actual words? The letters of any word can be turned into a string of 0s and 1s, and those strings stored in memory—and *voila!* we have a machine with a human vocabulary, capable of recognizing an incoming word typed onto a terminal, handling it via some programmed set of steps, and replying with a word that it then flashes on the terminal's screen.

That makes it sound simple, and it's anything but that. I've skipped over all the monumental problems of how to locate the words stored in memory, how to connect those words to others so as to have them possess meaning (DOCTOR, you remember, didn't really understand words, it only parroted them), and how to write programs that can manipulate both incoming and stored materials in the same immensely subtle and complex ways the human mind does. But even without going into the technology, it should be apparent that the computer can, in theory, translate any verbal or other symbols into its own kind of symbols, manipulate them according to its programmed instructions, and so process information in ways that are intelligent and can be called thinking.

That being so, the fact that the computer is made of semiconductors and wire, and not living cells, is of no significance, according to most AI people. But many, and perhaps most, cognitive scientists disagree. The differences between computer hardware and the brain's neuron network are so great, they say, that the intelligent functions carried on by the computer are not really clones of human thought; they reach the same ends but by different means. And those means have distinct limitations as well as advantages, so that while artificial intelligence can perform certain intellectual feats far better than any human can, it cannot at all simulate certain more complex and characteristically human mental processes. As Donald Norman puts it, "There may be an information-processing explanation for every mental phenomenon, but the information processing of the digital computer isn't a good model of what takes place in the human mind. Contemporary computers are not a good example of how the mind works."

For despite the complexity of the modern computer, its circuitry is basically linear (each flip-flop is connected to a preceding and a following one), and its ultimate component, the flip-flop, has only two conditions, on-off or off-on. In contrast, every neuron in the brain has thousands of linkages to other neurons, and its condition, far from being limited to on or off, is the infinitely variable resultant of those thousands of inputs. The computer, moreover, deals with information serially, in a single line; the brain does so via millions (perhaps even trillions) of parallel channels, each capable of acting at the same time as the others. Accordingly, the complexity of even a very simple animal cannot be replicated by a computer having an equivalent number of flip-flops and control devices. A few years ago, Claude Shannon, one of the authentic geniuses of computer science, was talking to

Pamela McCorduck, author of *Machines Who Think*, about the differences between artificial and natural circuitry; marveling at the behavior of ants, he said, "They're able to survive and live in this very hostile environment we have, and reproduce and eat and do everything they have to. And they have only a few hundred nerve cells in them. It seems utterly incredible, because if I had to do that with a few hundred relays, I really couldn't—and I'm pretty good at relays."*

If Shannon could not simulate ant behavior with an appropriate number of relays, how can AI experts simulate the full range of human thinking with transistors—even with many millions of them? If circuitry using on-off switches cannot match the complexity of the ant's mind, how can it match ours? What has been simulated thus far is only the tiniest part of what the human mind can do; whether the rest of it can ever be simulated is, in the opinion of many cognitive scientists, extremely unlikely.

History, of course, records innumerable such statements by those who have been unable to envision the future. But simply because people cannot always see what is possible does not mean that every vision of the future comes true. Those who say that artificial intelligence can never match ours may be as wrong as those who said humans could never fly; but it is also possible that those who say it can and will surpass ours are as wrong as those who have been sure that the end of the world was at hand.

What, then, is the chance that artificial intelligence will ever outstrip human intelligence? Is it likely to do so by thinking as we do, but better? Or by thinking in some totally different, nonhuman fashion? Laying aside science-fiction fantasies and our ancient love-hate relationship with homunculi, mannequins, and robots, let us look at the existing evidence, and then make our best guess.

## What the Computer Can Do Better Than the Human Mind

Computers are clearly superior to the human mind in certain respects: they can effortlessly remember immense masses of data and perform prodigious feats of lightning-swift calculation. Most of them, however, can't do anything else, and are only electronic idiot savants.

Yet we regard them with respect and awe because their special powers are so important to technological society. Bankers and brokers rely on computers to maintain up-to-the-minute records of the many millions of daily

* Like a transistor, a relay controls the amount of current flowing through a circuit.

transactions in their customers' accounts; managers of industry and business depend on them for a continuous and current reckoning of the stockpiles and flow of goods throughout the land; government economists count on them for ongoing analyses of the nation's money supply, the cost of living, and the employment status of the labor force. Because these are superhuman tasks, we tend to ascribe superhuman intelligence to such computers, although in truth all they do is count much faster than we can. But speed of reckoning has nothing to do with most of the phenomena of higher intelligence, such as the ability to understand, to organize experiences into new concepts, to reason, to create and test hypotheses about reality, and to solve problems.

It is natural, too, to attribute superior mental powers to any machine that can see through our false statements to the truth behind them. The Internal Revenue Service summons for special audit those taxpayers whose returns look as if they could easily involve unreported income, exaggerated deductions, and other kinds of fudging. In 1968, when human IRS agents were still picking out suspect returns by hand, they were right only a little better than half the time; since then, however, a computer programmed to use some fifty criteria simultaneously has been doing the picking, and it's right three quarters of the time. Apparently the computer knows better than a human agent which returns are likely to conceal taxpayer "errors," as they are euphemistically called. In actual fact, it makes its selection mechanically, on the basis of the rules given it by human beings; it merely has a greater ability than they to weigh the multiple factors at great speed, but it is witless and cannot use judgment to waive those rules. It cannot, for instance, evaluate a notarized document attached to a return, explaining unusual expenses or losses; it can only accuse. It is the ultimate bureaucrat.

In general, while computers have revolutionized our lives, they have done so not because of any intellectual superiority to us but because, like the broom in the tale of the sorcerer's apprentice, they are both tireless and quick to draw and fetch. And broom-stupid. Lawyers looking for precedents in a case can punch their needs into a computer terminal in a law library and, in a twinkling, get back a readout of data, but it will be as good or poor as the form of their request. Scholars and scientists looking for titles of books and articles on a subject they are studying will get helpful or worthless listings, or too many or too few, depending on how they put the question. Sociologists looking for the causes of some change in national eating, voting, or sexual habits can get the computer to uncover any significant connection between those changes and such possible causes as educational level, geographical mobility, or size of the community that respondents grew up in, but the computer will not notice any correlation that it has not been told to compute.

To retrieve and manipulate information in this fashion, these computers apply a fixed set of algorithms to the data provided by their human operators; despite their superhuman output, they perform no heuristic problem solving. Whether they are juggling thousands of flight reservations, working out the airflow characteristics of a new wing or fuselage, integrating weather data from all over the country to make a thirty-day forecast, or predicting the positions of the stars a million years from now, they function at a low intellectual level. They can figure out in minutes or seconds what a human being would need months to calculate, but they do not refine or alter the questions they ask on the basis of what they find, much less think them up in the first place.

Such is the nature of the computers that are in widest use throughout our society today. But in the laboratories of a handful of universities, and of such companies as Xerox, IBM, and Bell Labs, computers have been programmed to do much more advanced kinds of tasks: formal logical reasoning, puzzle solving, game playing, and medical diagnosis, among others. In most of these activities, computers can now match or outperform average human beings. Again, however, their superiority is due more to their speed—the smaller the chip, the faster it works—than to the quality of their thinking. When Newell and Simon created Logic Theorist a generation ago and ran it on JOHNNIAC, a vacuum-tube computer, it could prove various theorems in formal logic in anywhere from under a minute to fifteen or more minutes—roughly as fast as an average college student. On one of today's computers, using miniaturized transistors embedded in chips, the program would do the same job in something like a thousandth of the time.

Logic Theorist, however, was no idiot savant: it used some heuristics, as well as algorithms, in its search for proofs of theorems. It didn't, for instance, make any and every allowable change in the symbols of a theorem, in hopes of stumbling blindly onto a proof, but only those changes that, for one good reason or another, showed some likelihood of leading to a solution. Moreover, it compared any new theorem it was trying to prove to those it had already proved; if they were similar in certain ways, it would first try the method of proof that had worked in the past. In short, it learned from experience.

Newell, Simon, and a colleague named Cliff Shaw then went on to construct a more advanced program they called General Problem Solver. This was more broadly intelligent than Logic Theorist, and was meant to incorporate certain basic problem-solving methods of the human mind, or methods that achieved the same ends by other means. General Problem Solver's program included ways of looking back on its own experience, generating possibilities of its next move but testing them to see if they advanced it toward the goal, looking ahead a certain distance, and so on. Of course, these abstract principles would work only if, in every case, a batch of special rules and information pertaining to the particular subject were also provided. Supplied with the right rules and data concerning logic, it could prove theorems; with those concerning trigonometry, it could work out certain kinds of trigonometry problems; and if properly tutored, it could deal with puzzles like cryptarithmetic, missionaries and cannibals, and the Tower of Hanoi.

Here is an example of a simple problem that General Problem Solver figured out easily, early in its career:

> A heavy father and two young sons have to cross a swift river in a deep wood. They find an abandoned boat, which can be rowed across, but which sinks if overloaded. Each young son is 100 pounds. A double-weight son is just as heavy as the father and more than that is too much for the boat. How do the father and the sons cross the river?

(The problem was not actually offered to General Problem Solver in these words but in algebralike symbols, since the program was unable to understand natural language.) The solution of the problem, though it may seem absurdly simple to you, cannot easily be achieved by mindless trial and error because it requires a seeming retreat in order to advance.* In generating and testing this possibility, General Problem Solver did something akin to human problem solving, and by means of the same heuristic it was able to solve similar but far more difficult problems.

Thereafter, the development of programs that could solve advanced puzzles and play difficult games such as chess went on rapidly in a number of laboratories. It was not that cognitive scientists and AI researchers foresaw today's market for chess-playing machines or thought chess intrinsically valuable, but that the problems involved in constructing a good chess-playing program could be applied to many other kinds of problem solving.

* Both sons get in and row across; one debarks, and the other rows back and debarks on the first shore; the father rows across and lands on the far shore; the son on that side rows back, picks up his brother, and the two of them row across to the far shore.

For many years, AI researchers made their chess-playing programs smarter and smarter, providing them with all kinds of heuristic programs so that they could selectively search rather than try everything. To look ahead only five plies (five half-moves) would involve from twenty million to fifty million calculations—more than computers of the 1950s could handle in normal game-playing time—so for a long while, chess-playing programs were designed to evaluate the first moves and to search in depth (that is, to look ahead at) only those that looked promising.

Based on the early advances in this area, Herbert Simon boldly predicted, in 1957, that in ten years there would exist a chess program that no human being could beat. That didn't come true, and hasn't yet. Simon says that he merely overestimated the time and effort people would be willing to devote to it, but that it's coming. Hans Berliner now believes that such a program will exist by 1990, if not sooner. And in fact several chess programs, most notably Bell Labs' Belle and Northwestern University's Chess 4.7, can beat 99.5 percent of all competition chess players—but they've gotten that good by reverting to stupidity. The intelligent programs kept making mistakes, although slower brute-force programs that simply tried all possible moves did not. As the technology of computer hardware advanced, brute force increasingly became the method of choice; in the past five years chess programs have become dumber, faster, and much harder to beat.

A simple example will strikingly illustrate the difference between brute force and high-level inference—a difference which says a great deal about the relationship of artificial intelligence to human intelligence. Figure 60 is a standard checkerboard whose sixty-four squares you can completely cover with thirty-two dominoes that are two squares long and one square wide. Now cut two squares out of the checkerboard as in Figure 61. Can this board of sixty-two squares be exactly covered by thirty-one dominoes? A computer can test every combination—there are a colossal number of them—and so prove that it cannot be done. A human being can prove the same thing by these four steps of inferential reasoning:

1. Each domino covers one white and one black square.
2. Hence any number of dominoes will always cover equal numbers of black and white squares.
3. But the mutilated board has thirty black and thirty-two white squares.
4. Therefore it is not possible to exactly cover the board with thirty-one dominoes.

**Fig. 60.** Standard checkerboard

**Fig. 61.** Checkerboard minus two squares

As Newell and Simon once commented, "We would award a system that found [this] solution high marks for intelligence." But while it would be very difficult to construct a program that could employ such reasoning, it is easy to construct one that can solve the problem by brute force.

And so the technical improvements in computer hardware have determined the course taken by the development of chess-playing programs in recent years. Ken Thompson and Joe Condon of Bell Labs, the codevelopers of Belle, say that it can now examine 160,000 positions per second. It performs a "full-width search"—it looks at all possible moves—and then pursues each one in depth, examining up to 29 million positions in three minutes, the average amount of time per move in tournament play. Even so, it has to do some tree pruning, since there are far more than 29 million possibilities in even a six-ply total look-ahead; Belle assigns high priority to moves against the opponent's king, it remembers positions it has already considered, and so on. But these procedures merely make its brute-force approach more efficient; Belle's game-playing process remains quite unlike that of the expert human chess player who, as I said earlier, can recognize the few potentially important configurations, and so needs to search in depth only two to four possible moves and some hundreds of ensuing positions. All the same, some time in the near future the world's chess champion will be a machine—a very dumb one, but better at what it's doing than any human being, however intelligent.

One might object that I am guilty of anthropocentric bias: even if computers primarily rely on brute force, is that not as intelligent—as long as it solves the problems—as the human method? But a more meaningful conception of intelligence is that it involves *adaptability* and *change*. An intelligent organism modifies itself in various ways as it interacts with the environment, in order to solve problems better, in new ways, in future interactions. To do that, it must minimize the use of brute force and, instead, deduce general principles, as in the mutilated checkerboard example; the discovery of such principles can beget innovation, but brute force cannot. Nonetheless, it remains true that within a circumscribed problem area such as chess—or even certain real-life areas such as chemistry and medical diagnosis—an artificial intelligence can function with great effectiveness on the basis of a fixed program and sheer power, without any ability to learn, change its own program, or adapt itself to the environment. An example of a program that does extremely competent problem solving in a real-life domain though it functions only a little above the intellectual level of a chess-

playing machine is DENDRAL, the creation of AI researcher Edward Feigenbaum of Stanford University and Nobel Laureate Joshua Lederberg,
now president of Rockefeller University. Chemists working with a new
compound often need to know its molecular structure—the exact way in
which its constituent atoms are linked together. By qualitative and quanti-
tative analysis, they can discover what elements are in the compound, and
in what proportions, but that doesn't reveal the way the atoms are arranged. Suppose, for instance, that such analyses showed that the molecules
of a given compound contained eight carbon atoms, sixteen hydrogen
atoms, and one oxygen atom; chemists could then write its formula,
$C_8H_{16}O$, but they still wouldn't know how those twenty-five atoms were assembled. How can they discover that internal structure?

The technique used in recent years is called "mass spectrography." A
sample of the substance is broken up in a heated chamber, and the particles—single atoms or clumps of atoms—are shot forward by electrical impulses and passed through a magnetic field. That field deflects them from
their course, the deflection being greater if they are light rather than heavy,
and if they carry a considerable electrical charge rather than a small one.
The particles hit a photographic plate, making it darker where they land;
the resulting lines thus show the weight and the charge of the particles, and
their relative number. When the photograph is turned into a chart, $C_8H_{16}O$
comes out looking like Figure 62.

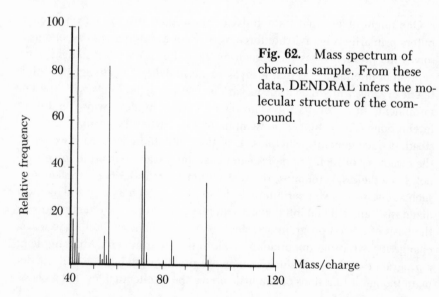

**Fig. 62.**   Mass spectrum of
chemical sample. From these
data, DENDRAL infers the molecular structure of the compound.

But while each of these lines indicates the weight and the charge of the particles that made it, how are they arranged in the compound? The spectrographic data are fed into DENDRAL, which tests it against all imaginable ways in which the twenty-five atoms could be combined, looking for a good fit. If DENDRAL knew nothing about chemistry, it would crank out many thousands of impossible combinations (as well as some possible ones) and compare their theoretical spectrograms to the actual one it is investigating. But it has in its memory a list of combinations of atoms that never occur in stable compounds. Guided by these rules, DENDRAL limits itself to thinking up 698 chemically feasible arrangements of the twenty-five atoms; then it compares each arrangement to the mass spectrogram—rapidly, thanks to its innate speed of computation—and concludes that only 40 of them could have made such traces. This is a small enough number for the chemists to work with; by experiments they can easily eliminate all but a single candidate—

$$CH_3-CH_2-\overset{\displaystyle O}{\overset{\displaystyle \|}{C}}-CH_2-CH_2-CH_2-CH_2-CH_3$$

—a compound called N-propyl ketone-3. DENDRAL has proven so helpful that it is now in use in research centers all over the country.

Likely to be in general use soon are a number of medical diagnosis programs developed at Rutgers, Stanford, the University of Minnesota, and elsewhere. One of them, MYCIN (already in use in hospitals in the San Francisco area), is stocked with certain kinds of medical information and a decision-tree program, and is designed to help the physician who is trying to diagnose and treat a mysterious infection. First, it asks him or her for certain items of information: where the infective organism was found (in the blood, in a tissue, and so on), whether the organism takes a gram-negative or gram-positive stain, whether it is suspected of having entered through the mouth, the skin, or some other route, and the like. As the doctor feeds answers into the terminal, MYCIN uses the data to narrow down the list of possible bacteria that might be causing the infection; at every decision point, it assigns each possibility a "certainty factor" based on all its information, and whenever a hypothesis has become very improbable drops it. Finally MYCIN narrows down the possibilities to a highly probable diagnosis, which may include more than one possibility, and issues a set of recommendations for drug treatment to cover these possibilities.

Another program, MEDINFO, will be able to do a comparable job, acting as specialist to the family doctor in recondite areas such as pediatric cardiology. The family doctor who has a computer terminal in his or her office could, upon finding that a child had high blood pressure, consult MEDINFO, name the problem, answer MEDINFO's questions, and follow it through a line of reasoning ending in diagnosis and recommendations—a procedure which would otherwise have to be carried out by a specialist and laboratory assistants, at considerably greater cost and time.

A somewhat startling development is a computerized interview for mental patients—very different from DOCTOR, though of its lineage—that has been developed at the University of Wisconsin Medical School by John H. Greist, a psychiatrist, and David Gustafson, a professor of preventive medicine. The program, designed to spot potentially suicidal patients, asks a number of simple personal questions, and then abruptly shifts to blunt talk with questions like, "Are you thinking of suicide?" and "By what method do you plan to commit suicide?" Further questions are chosen by the computer according to the patient's answers. On the basis of these replies, the computer assigns a probability that the patient will attempt suicide. Greist and Gustafson believe that clinicians dealing with such patients find it hard to handle such questions, and even harder to objectively evaluate the answers. Although the researchers say that their experimental design was far from perfect, the results are intriguing: in one study involving sixty-three patients, the computer correctly picked out the three who would attempt suicide within the next forty-eight hours while doctors, nurses, and medical students attending the same patients guessed wrong about all three. The computer also was nearly three times as correct in predicting which patients would attempt suicide in the next three months as were the clinicians. Even though the program is not very intelligent, in its thoughtless way it seems to solve this particular problem rather well.

## What the Human Mind Can Do Better Than the Computer

At Stanford University not long ago, AI researchers developed a sophisticated program, hooked to a mechanical arm, that could understand a handful of spoken commands such as "Pick up the small block on the left," and properly carry them out. This impressive show of intelligence was somewhat flawed, however, by the fact that the robot could understand instructions only when uttered by one or the other of its designers, both of whom had foreign accents.

This illustrates a central truth about the difference between artificial intelligence and human intelligence: computers are very much better than we at computing, but we are very much better than they at "matching." The robot could match incoming words against those stored in its memory only if they were exact counterparts; any two-year-old child could do better.

In the early days of AI research, matching was not a problem: computers were concerned with numbers or arbitrary logical symbols that were devoid of content, and that could be easily assigned to storage space in the computer's memory and just as easily retrieved, when needed. But real-world knowledge—perceptions, facts, ideas, relationships, and concepts expressed in natural language—is quite another matter; classifying, storing, and finding it again is an extraordinarily difficult business. If you were plunked down on a street in an unfamiliar city and were looking for a particular building on that street, you'd simply walk until you came to the right number; if, however, you wanted to locate someone you had met at a party whose name you couldn't remember but who was forty-five, divorced, and a specialist in Etruscan art, you'd have to do a much more complex and intelligent form of searching.

In recent years, the major direction of AI research has been to make computers capable of dealing with real-world subjects, but many of the mental processes involved, though easy for a human being, turn out to be extremely hard to simulate on a computer, largely because of matching problems. Suppose a computer has a scanning TV camera and you ask it whether there is a chair in a picture you put before it; would it recognize all of the objects in Figure 63 as being chairs? It would be impractical, of course, to store pictures of every possible chair, seen from every possible angle, in the computer's memory; instead, the word "chair" would be linked in its memory to a series of general characteristics—size, shape, location, function, and so on—and the computer would generate a number of

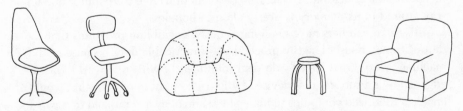

**Fig. 63.** To recognize all of these as being chairs is no simple matter; it takes a lot of "world knowledge."

lists of such facts about chairs and test them, one by one, in a programmed sequence, to see which objects in the picture, matching some but not necessarily all the criteria, might fill the bill.

Every step in the most ordinary act of thinking about real-world matters involves similarly prodigious labors when performed by a computer. For instance, although any word can be turned into a digital number and stored in numerical sequence, that gives it no meaning. To understand what it means in any particular sentence, the computer has to store it in a complex fashion, with links to every possible interpretation, so that the one that makes most sense in context can be chosen. How onerous this can be is illustrated by an example Dick Hayes gives. The sentence "Grasp the red block and put it on the green block" has five content words (*grasp, red, block, put,* and *green*), none of which has fewer than seven distinct meanings and one of which (*block*) has twenty-two, according to an unabridged dictionary; hence, says Hayes, there could be nearly three million interpretations of the sentence, many of them as senseless as this one: "Understand the communist obstruction and blame it on the immature coalition." To deal with the sentence, the computer might have to generate lists of all the meanings of each word, check each meaning against a set of restrictions, and eliminate the impossible ones (for instance, "grasp" in the sense of "comprehend" cannot take a person or other physical entity as its object); this would be only the first of a number of steps necessary to understand the sentence.

The human mind matches incoming perceptions and words to meanings in a very different fashion. Rather than working our way through lists, item by item, we seem to process the incoming perception or word through thousands or even millions of parallel circuits at the same time, arriving at a match far more efficiently than any computer system. Hans Berliner put it this way: "Although human beings have a minuscule computing power, they can store large amounts of knowledge—and get at it. Computers have lots of trouble doing that. In fact, the problem of having a computer find its way around in its memory is pretty close to hopeless."

Still, AI researchers have been ingeniously assembling programs that by dint of tremendously lengthy procedures—practicable only because of the machine's very great speed—do deal intelligently with real-world knowledge. Here is a subprogram devised by Patrick Winston of MIT that would enable a robotized computer to understand and obey a command to shove a table with a lamp on it from where it is to a nearby spot:

PRODUCTION P1:
If STM contains                       (PUT-ON > OBJECT > SUPPORT)
Then             mark         the first item in STM
                   shove       (PUT-AT < OBJECT (SPACE ON < SUPPORT))

PRODUCTION P2:
If STM contains                       (PUT-AT > OBJECT > NEWPLACE)
Then             mark         the first item in STM
                   shove       (TARGET < OBJECT < NEWPLACE)
                   shove       (GRASP < OBJECT)

PRODUCTION P3:
If STM contains                       (MOVE > OBJECT)
                             (> SUPPORT SUPPORTS < OBJECT)
Then             mark         (< SUPPORT SUPPORTS < OBJECT)

PRODUCTION P4:
If STM contains                       (MOVE > OBJECT)
Then             mark         the first item in STM
                   notice      (TARGET < OBJECT > NEWPLACE)
                   send        (MOVE-HAND < NEWPLACE)
                   send        (UNGRASP)

PRODUCTION P5:
If STM contains                       (GRASP > OBJECT)
                             (< OBJECT SUPPORTS NOTHING)
Then             mark         the first item in STM
                   shove       (MOVE < OBJECT)
                   send        (MOVE-HAND (TOP OF < OBJECT))
                   send        (GRASP < OBJECT)

PRODUCTION P6:
If STM contains                       (GRASP > OBJECT)
                             (< OBJECT SUPPORTS > OBSTRUCTION)
Then             shove       (PUT-ON < OBSTRUCTION FLOOR)

PRODUCTION P7:
If STM contains                       (GRASP > OBJECT)
Then             send        (WHAT IS ON < OBJECT)
                   receive
                   notice      (GRASP < OBJECT)

When the specifics are supplied (table, lamp on table, goal XYZ, and the like), the robot proceeds step by step, feeding information from its sensors back into the program. Here is a bit of the resulting trace (the robot's short-term memory is now registering the fact that it has moved the lamp onto the floor and can finally prepare to shove the table to XYZ):

```
>>> (WHAT IS ON TABLE)

(GRASP TABLE)
(TABLE SUPPORTS NOTHING)
(TARGET LAMP (SPACE ON FLOOR))
(MARK (MOVE LAMP))
(MARK (TABLE SUPPORTS LAMP))
(MARK (GRASP LAMP))
(LAMP SUPPORTS NOTHING)
(MARK (PUT-AT LAMP (SPACE ON FLOOR)))
(MARK (PUT-ON LAMP FLOOR))
(TARGET TABLE XYZ)
(MARK (PUT-AT TABLE XYZ))
NIL
NIL
NIL
```

The full trace runs a dozen times as long as this.

Ask any two-year-old to push the table from one place to another and he or she will do so by means of some far easier (and paradoxically far more complex) way of matching the words to the right objects and actions. Of all the uses artificial intelligence has for us, the most important may be telling us what questions we must ask if we are to understand not only why the mind does so poorly what the computer does well, but more important, why the mind does so well what the computer does poorly.

In much AI research, questions, data, and commands are fed into a computer from the keyboard of a terminal. But a truly intelligent machine would be able, like us, to gather information for itself directly from the environment. That entails perception and the ability to interpret what is perceived. If a computer with vision scans a piece of paper looking for numbers and finds them, it then must match them against "templates"—models of numbers—stored in its memory in order to know what it is seeing. But while a bank's computer can easily read stylized numbers on checks and deposit slips such as those in Figure 64, it isn't clever enough to read numbers printed in other styles and sizes, like those in Figure 65. Smarter computers can do better: with an oversized, stylized, sideways number or letter like the one in Figure 66, the computer will look for the long axis, turn the letter straight up, reduce it to template size, and then check it against the tem-

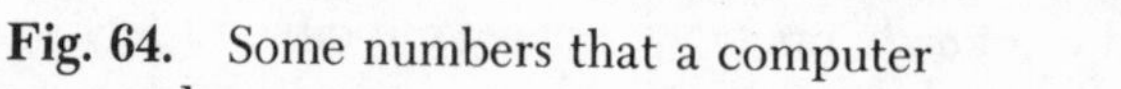

⑈0 2 14 ⑽ 10 30⑈   33 0  1 1080⑊

**Fig. 64.** Some numbers that a computer can read . . .

1234567890          1234567890

1980

1971          1          7

Fig. 65.   . . . and some that it can't.

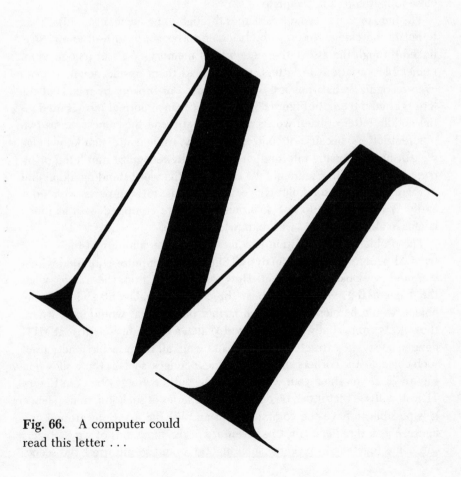

Fig. 66.   A computer could
read this letter . . .

**Fig. 67.** . . . but not these, though any literate person could.

plate, accepting even an approximate fit. But it would be unable to recognize most of the variations in Figure 67, none of which would even come close to matching the template.

The human mind recognizes shapes through some mechanism other than template matching; we do so by bringing to bear a wealth of knowledge, linked through the associative networks of memory. We can recognize innumerable variations in letters; we can read them upside down; we can even recognize what they are, when distorted or broken, by means of the letters around them. In Figure 68, for instance, an abnormal form is used for the middle letter of each word; we effortlessly read the same form as two different letters, because of context. Similarly, using contextual knowledge we can supply missing information and thereby recognize mutilated or incomplete letters. In Figure 69, we can't read the word standing alone, but in Figure 70, with an inkblot concealing the same missing parts, we read it easily. A machine could not do so unless it were equipped with as much language ability and real-world knowledge as we.

The problem of recognition becomes even more complex in the case of what AI people call "scene analysis." Suppose a computer equipped with a scanning eye looks at Figure 71. How can it know, from these lines, what the shapes of the objects would be in three-dimensional reality, which of the objects would be closer and which farther off, or what would exist where the objects are partially hidden? David Waltz, a computer scientist at MIT, devised a way: he extracted from such drawings all the possible junctions of such objects—the corners and the meetings of edges, such as those shown in Figure 72. If you trace your way around the outline of any object in Figure 71, you will see that it can be described as a series of such junctions. Hence it is possible to have the computer spot and list the junctions around any figure, check that list against its inventory of the thousands of ways objects can come together to produce such junctions, and so interpret the scene.

# THE CAT

**Fig. 68.**   One shape, two interpretations

**Fig. 69.**   This unreadable mutilated word . . .

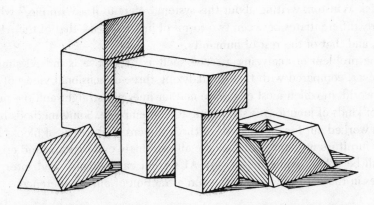

**Fig. 70.**   . . . is easily readable in context.

**Fig. 71.**   To make three-dimensional sense of this simple
scene is a far-from-simple task for a computer.

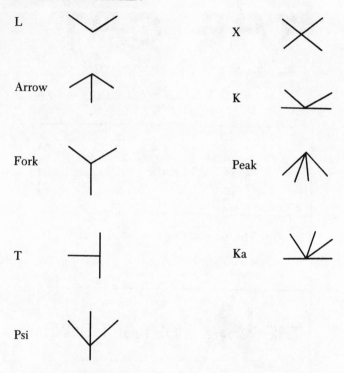

**Fig. 72.** Common junctions, and names given them by David Waltz

Patrick Winston, writing about this system, refers to it as "simple," which clearly differentiates between two forms of intelligence—that of the AI expert, and that of the rest of humanity.

The problem of analyzing a scene such as the above is indeed simple, however, compared with that of analyzing three-dimensional views of the real world, in which most edges are neither lines nor straight and the number of kinds of junctions is staggering to contemplate. Some methods have been worked out for the analysis of three-dimensional scenes of blocks and even furniture in rooms, but they are all extremely cumbersome and crude; it will be a long while before any AI system can perceive and interpret scenes in the natural world with even a fraction of our competence.

The symbol system of natural language has proven particularly difficult for computer programs to cope with. Ten or fifteen years ago, AI researchers, trying to develop machines that could translate from one tongue to another, thought it might be possible to do so without having the machine understand. They hoped that if the computer merely recognized the grammatical relationships among the parts of a sentence, and translated word for word or phrase for phrase, that would serve. A possibly apocryphal story exemplifies the results: a machine translation into Russian of "The spirit is willing, but the flesh is weak" came out meaning something like, "The vodka is fine, but the meat is tasteless."

Reluctantly giving up this approach, researchers turned to systems that used not only syntax but knowledge. The example I gave above—the narrowing down of meanings of the words in the sentence, "Grasp the red block and put it on the green block," by the use of lists of definitions, rules about when each did or did not apply, and other limiting factors—is an instance of a knowledge-based system. Much of the recent progress in the development of machines that understand natural language has come about through the design of programs that use recognition techniques comparable to those that human beings use.

Psycholinguistic research suggests, for instance, that when we read an ordinary sentence, we first recognize the words (or, with unfamiliar words, start by recognizing the letters and sounds). Next we identify the function words, such as prepositions and conjunctions, and begin to anticipate the structure of the sentence. Then we look at the content words (nouns, verbs, and so on) and begin to make possible meaningful connections among them. Holding all this in memory, we read on, winnowing out our hypotheses in the light of the later words. As we complete the sentence and finally understand it—that is, confirm a single hypothesis as to its meaning—we purge short-term memory of the exact words but retain the sense of the sentence. Actually, these steps are probably not applied one after another but more or less simultaneously, or overlapping, in a process using not only syntactical information but the whole wealth of knowledge the reader possesses about the words and ideas involved.

If the sentence is heard rather than read, yet another series of processes is involved. And what a feat of matching they constitute! When tape recordings of human speech are analyzed spectrographically, it turns out that the beginnings and endings of words are not pronounced the same in connected speech as they are when we say the words singly. If you cut up the words of a sentence on a tape recording and play the fragments back, many of them will prove incomprehensible. But as listeners, we correct distortions and supply missing sounds, and hence usually understand what we hear, despite the innumerable additional distortions of accent and individual pronunciation, the variations of pitch and timbre, and the competition of background noise.

No wonder it has been so difficult to develop AI programs that understand natural language. Whether they deal with language delivered via the keyboard or the voice, they have had to be limited, thus far, to very small vocabularies dealing with extremely narrow topics.

Currently, the most advanced AI system for dealing with written language is the one that most closely resembles the human mind; it is the program SAM (and various descendants of SAM), devised by Roger Schank and his associates at Yale. SAM has three subprograms going simultaneously: one analyzes the sentence, breaking it up into parts that correspond to real-life experiences of time, place, objects, and actions; one draws upon a mass of real-world knowledge to see which interpretation of each part of the sentence fits in best with other parts; and one stores the resulting interpretation in a coherent memory. The core of the system is its body of real-world knowledge, assembled in the form of one or more "scripts" that Schank has fed into its memory. A script is a series of cause-and-effect relationships about a subject; on the subject of car accidents, for instance, the script connects the idea of a crash to ideas about ensuing damage, connects the idea of impact to ideas about personal injury, and so on. In consequence, SAM can be given a short news item about a car crash and, after working through it, can correctly answer questions about it. This story, for instance, was fed into SAM:

> A New Jersey man was killed Friday evening when the car in which he was riding swerved off Route 69 and struck a tree. David Hall, 27, was pronounced dead at the scene by Dr. Dana Blanchard, medical examiner. Frank Miller, 16, of 593 Foxon Road, operator of the vehicle, was taken by Flanagan Ambulance to Yale-New Haven Hospital. He was treated and released. The Branford Fire Department extricated the passenger from the vehicle. No charges were made. Patrolman Robert Onofrio is continuing the investigation.

After digesting the story, SAM was able to answer questions about it as follows:

Q1:  Was anyone killed?
A1:  YES, DAVID HALL DIED.

Q2:  Was anyone hurt?
A2:  YES, FRANK MILLER WAS SLIGHTLY INJURED.
Q3:  Why was Frank Miller hurt?
A3:  BECAUSE THE AUTOMOBILE HIT A TREE.
Q4:  Did Frank Miller go to the hospital?
A4:  YES, HE WAS IN YALE-NEW HAVEN.
Q5:  How did Frank Miller get to the hospital?
A5:  AN AMBULANCE TOOK HIM TO YALE-NEW
       HAVEN.

It is a monumental accomplishment, all in all. But consider: it took SAM ten minutes of reflection to understand that brief story, using high-speed computing and a large amount of storage space. To store another script so that SAM could understand another small topic would require another large amount of space and another program of interpretation. The total amount of space and number of programs needed to match the average adult's knowledge of the world and ability to understand language is staggering— or, to be more accurate, incalculable.

Certain programs deal with recognition of the spoken word (rather than the written word), coupled with analysis of sentence structure and meaning. One of them, HEARSAY, developed by Raj Reddy at Carnegie-Mellon, begins by turning a heard sentence into a spectrogram, and then comparing it to an inventory of spectrograms in memory. In an early version, HEAR-SAY was limited to understanding commands to move chess pieces. If it heard "Bishop to Queen Knight Three," it would turn it into a spectrogram as shown in Figure 73. HEARSAY would then guess how much of the wave form was the first word, and test that portion against its memory file (rejecting out of hand any words that could not come first in the sentence). It might conclude that "bishop" looked most like the first word, but the fit might not be perfect and it would hold onto other possibilities, assigning them lower ratings. Word by word it would work its way through the sentence, somewhat like a human being, compiling a number of interpretations on the basis of sound, sentence structure, and sense, and finally choosing the one that had the highest score. The first version of HEARSAY had a total vocabulary of thirty-one words, and identified correctly about 88 percent of those it heard. A later version had a larger vocabulary and a slightly higher level of accuracy.

A rather different system called HARPY, recently constructed at Carnegie-Mellon, performs distinctly better than HEARSAY. In a quiet room, it can recognize careful, electronically filtered speech from a number of dif-

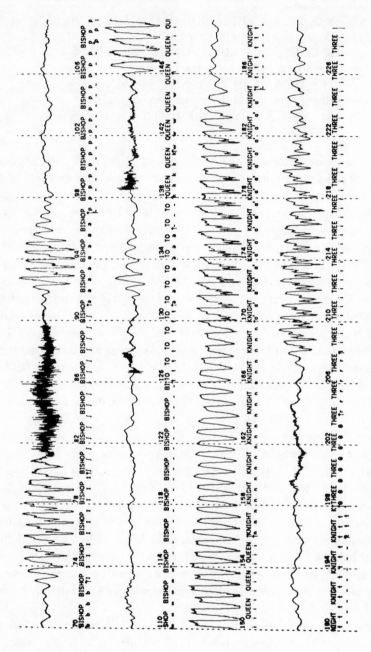

Fig. 73.  Spectrogram of the spoken words, "Bishop to Queen Knight Three"

ferent speakers (HEARSAY was far more finicky about whom it could understand), and it has a vocabulary of about a thousand words. HARPY can correctly understand and respond to 90 percent of the commands or questions it hears, all of which concern the retrieval of certain documents from computer files. (Example: "Have you anything on speech comprehension systems by John Doe?" "No.") But despite the extremely narrow limits of its world, HARPY needs three times as long to figure out what was said to it as it took to say it, and if its world were enlarged, the time lag would increase proportionately. Or perhaps exponentially: an IBM system dealing with a body of material somewhat more complicated than HARPY's world needs three hours to figure out each minute of speech.

HARPY is a significant achievement, and a forerunner of even more significant ones to come, but it will be a long time before the descendants of HARPY can begin to approach the descendants of Adam and Eve in speech understanding. The average adult knows anywhere from fifty to seventy-five times as many words as HARPY, can understand thousands of times as many different speakers (unfiltered, and speaking without particular care, against all kinds of background noise), and is hundreds to thousands of times better than HARPY in the breadth of subject matter and the variations in grammatical structure that he or she can handle. The human mind, in terms of the space it needs, the cost of keeping it running, and the scope of its accomplishments, is still a vastly more efficient knowledge processor than the most advanced computer in existence or on the drawing boards.

As remarkable as today's artificial intelligences are, all of them are dependent infants in the sense that whatever they know about the world has been fed to them by their creators. A more mature intelligence would acquire knowledge of the world directly and construct new concepts or understandings from that knowledge on its own.

Thus far, talk of computers that can acquire information directly from the world is only science-fiction fantasizing; even AI people speak about it with a smile. But in several laboratories researchers have been designing programs that can, at least, spot a regularity in raw data, extract that regularity from the particular instances, and so discover a concept, rule, or law.

One such program was constructed very recently at Carnegie-Mellon by a doctoral candidate named Pat Langley. He calls it BACON because like its namesake, Sir Francis Bacon, it is concerned with the basic process of scientific discovery. When BACON is given data from which a general law can be extracted, it does so by means of a series of built-in steps of heuristic reasoning. Specifically, when fed a series of numbers that express the distances of planets from a sun, and their periods (how long it takes them to circle it), BACON notices at once that the farther away the planet, the longer the period. Then it looks for some relationship between the increase of distance and the increase of the period. It tries one thing after another, and after a while comes up with Kepler's third law of planetary motion: the ratio of the planet's distance from the sun, cubed, to its period, squared, is always the same; that is, $d^3/p^2 = c$.

BACON does this by means of seventy-four "productions" or programmed steps, many of which are hypotheses assembled in an efficient problem-solving sequence. When it looks at a series of numbers representing distance and period for three hypothetical planets, it talks to itself as follows:

> DISTANCE AND PERIOD SEEM TO GO UP TOGETHER
> THE SLOPES AREN'T CONSTANT SO I'LL CONSIDER
>    THE RATIO OF DISTANCE AND PERIOD
> WHAT SHOULD I CALL IT?
>
>    ＊ distance-over-period

This bit of reasoning takes place because BACON has the following heuristic in its program: *If the values of two attributes go up together, consider their ratio* (in this case, distance-over-period). So it does just that, but finds, disappointingly, that the ratio doesn't remain constant—as it would if it expressed a law—but decreases for planets farther from the sun. So BACON says to itself:

> DISTANCE SEEMS TO GO UP AS DISTANCE-OVER-
>    PERIOD GOES DOWN
> THE SLOPES AREN'T CONSTANT SO I'LL CONSIDER
>    THE PRODUCT OF DISTANCE AND DISTANCE-
>    OVER-PERIOD
> WHAT SHOULD I CALL IT?
>
>    ＊ distance-squared-over-period

In this bit of monologue, BACON has just applied a second heuristic from its bag of tricks. This doesn't yield the answer either, but when BACON uses the heuristic twice in a row, it gets distance-cubed-over-period-squared, which does yield the same ratio for every planet. Ergo, a law.

Langley, though proud of his creation, is careful not to overstate its achievement. "You've built a smart machine," I said, "BACON is really intelligent." But Langley stroked his beard thoughtfully and said, "Well, there's a question about that. A question about how much knowledge I put into it. In trying to write a program that will learn from experience, you have to worry about whether you've put knowledge in there that it's drawing on, or whether it's really getting it from out in the world." He explained that perhaps the heuristics he gave it for discovering Kepler's third law incorporate the answer in themselves; BACON starts out with far better ideas as to what to look for than Kepler had. (And yet Kepler, without such ideas, discovered it.)

BACON has other important limitations compared with a human being. It can discover only a few simple concepts. It can extract rules only from perfect data—data which, unlike those of real life, have no irregularities. And finally, it deals with preselected data: the numbers or other materials that Langley feeds it are all pertinent to its task; it doesn't get planetary distances and periods mixed in with observations on, say, the planets' mass, color, reflectivity, number of moons, astrological significance, or other irrelevant matters. Its attention has been focused on the problem—but that, of course, is the larger part of any discovery task; what comes after is easy.

The same thing was true, I found, of an entertaining but essentially serious program designed by Elliot M. Soloway (who is now at Yale) for his doctoral dissertation in computer science at the University of Massachusetts in Amherst. Soloway, tee-shirted and sandal-clad, bounced about his office incessantly as he talked, radiating immense enjoyment of his subject as he explained why he had chosen to write a computer program that would figure out the rules of baseball by observing the events of a typical nine-inning game. "In AI," he said, "people were working on concept formation the same way they used to in the laboratory. Let a machine see this design and this one and this one, have it look for the most common components—the intersection, so to speak—and that's the 'concept.' But people don't usually do it that way. In the real world, there are so many comparisons among things we see that computationally it gets out of hand. So I started to think about how to have a machine extract the right features from a ball game. How would it recognize a single, for instance, when so much else is going on—throwing, catching, players walking around and scratching themselves, and all that?"

Would his machine actually *see* all that happening? I asked. "No, no," he said, chuckling, "that would be too hard, though it's possible. No, I feed in the data in a special form." He flipped open a copy of his dissertation. "It gets strings of numbers and letters like this," he said, showing me a passage that read:

(201 HOLDOBJ A1 PM BALL)
(202 THROW A1 PM)
(203 AT A1 PM)
(204 AT A2 HP)
(205 CATCH A2 HP BALL)

"That represents a pitch. The rest of this"—he pointed to more of the same on the page—"shows that the batter didn't swing. But I had to give my machine a lot of knowledge by means of which to figure it all out. For instance I gave it a rule: *If it's a physical action that takes skill, it gets rewarded, but if it doesn't represent skill, it doesn't get rewarded.* With that kind of rule, the machine extracts a different meaning from a swing and a hit than it does from a swing and a miss.

"In other words, my machine filters out what's happening in terms of what it already knows. That's the only way it can understand the data and draw conclusions from them. I didn't *want* the recognition and interpretation process to be this way. I wanted to build a machine that could simply learn, from zero. But it turned out that to get my machine to do anything, I had to give it a tremendous amount of knowledge. The whole program involves hundreds of packets of knowledge like, *Keep only things that change,* so it can ignore two guys throwing a ball back and forth but pay attention to a guy moving from one base to another.

"Even so, it doesn't understand very much. After a single inning it has figured out the rules about a swing and about a base hit. After a nine-inning game it has figured out what strikes are, and the different kinds of outs and the different kinds of hits. But I didn't give it the ability to count, so it can't figure out the score or who won. That, and a lot of other things, were just too much to try for. The more I worked on it, the more I was amazed that people can understand *anything.* It's really very *hard* to make sense of the world—and yet we do. Even little kids do. It just blows me away!"

One of the complex realities of life that children come to understand on their own is, as I mentioned in an earlier chapter, that we have to adjust our conversation to the needs and abilities of the person we're talking to. All of us do it all the time, and without giving it thought. Imagine, for instance, that you are asked "Where is the New York Public Library?" If a child asks you, your answer will probably be simpler and less precise than if an adult asks you, since you wouldn't expect the child to go there on its own. You would answer a stranger visiting New York in more detail than someone who is familiar with the city. You would answer in one fashion if asked the question by a Greek while you were in Athens, and in another fashion if asked by a Midwesterner on West Forty-fifth Street. In each case, you instantly create in your mind a model of the other person's state of knowledge, and adapt your answer to that model.

Until recently, computers had no such self-modifying capacity; now a few programs do, to a limited degree. At the University of California at San Diego, psychologist Donald R. Gentner has been developing a program called FLOW that teaches a student the rudiments of a computer language by that same name. Unlike the simpleminded teaching machines B. F. Skinner devised many years ago, FLOW is aware of what its student knows at any moment, and adjusts its questions and answers to suit. "As the student goes along," Gentner told me, "FLOW keeps track of what concepts he has read about and what ones he uses successfully. It doesn't really know much—only enough for a half-hour teaching session—but in the course of that half hour it changes the nature of its responses according to the changes it perceives in the student. For instance, early on, if the student makes a certain kind of mistake, FLOW might tell him he needs to make such and such modifications in his program, spelling it out right down to what keys to press. But later, when the student knew all those details, FLOW would just tell him something like, 'You need a loop in your program,' because it would know he knew what that meant."

Thus FLOW, ostensibly a teaching program, is something more important—it is a program that learns and adapts. But, of course, on a very limited scale and within very narrow bounds; as Gentner himself said to me, "Every time I get cocky about some program, I come up against something or other that human beings can do so much better. It just knocks me over the head time and again."

A rather different approach toward building machines that can learn and adapt involves programs that solve problems and then rewrite their own instructions so as to benefit from what they've experienced. One such program, called HACKER, was built a few years ago by Gerald J. Sussman at MIT; it deals with a very small world—a set of blocks, portrayed on a video screen, that are to be piled up in some way, according to the researcher's command—but the concepts embodied in it could be extended to other worlds. HACKER might first be presented with the situation shown in Figure 74, and asked to put *A* on *B*. Using its store of knowledge, it does so. Then it is given the situation in Figure 75 and told to put *B* on *C*. HACKER starts to go about it the same way, but gets an error message from its program: part of its store of information tells it that it can't move a block that has another block on top of it. HACKER solves this minuscule problem by removing *A* and setting it on the table, then moving *B* onto *C*. But having done so, it stores this scrap of learning in its program: now, whenever a block is on top of another that has to be moved, HACKER immediately takes it off without first attempting to move the lower block and getting an error signal. It has gotten smarter. Eventually, it can change the formation of blocks in Figure 76 to that of Figure 77 without fumbling or backing up, thanks to routines it has acquired piecemeal.

This may sound like child's play, but it is not; not for HACKER, at any rate, which, Sussman says, is a "rather complex problem-solving program built from many diverse mechanisms." It could, he thinks, perform and learn in many other domains, although for each one it would need a whole additional set of data structures and procedures. To become a general-purpose learning machine such as every human being is, it would need an encyclopedic library of world knowledge. But simply piling up knowledge would not do; the program would become an unwieldy or unworkable mishmash. Sussman says that sometimes, as he extends a program to do more and more than it formerly did, it becomes a clumsy, incomprehensible patchwork; then he attempts to rethink and radically reorganize it. How? He is vague about that process because, he says, "I don't understand it. But I know that HACKER just doesn't have anything like that ability."

HACKER, General Problem Solver, and other problem-solving programs piece together more efficient problem-solving procedures out of their experiences, but they don't invent or devise new solutions to problems; that is, they don't reconstruct their view of the problem, make leaps of thought, or suddenly perceive new goals. In a word, they aren't creative. But will they become so with further development? Will they ever generate new ideas, inventions, works of art? Will they ever think of things their designers did not already know?

A dozen years ago, in the first flush of excitement about artificial intelligence, people tried to get computers to produce creative works. At the University of Illinois a computer composed music, at the University of Manchester another one wrote love poems, and elsewhere still others generated

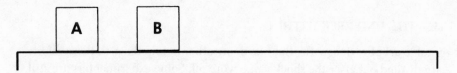

**Fig. 74.** HACKER easily puts *A* on *B* . . .

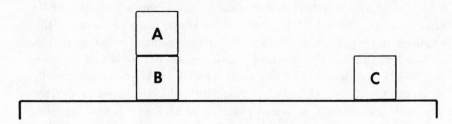

**Fig. 75.** . . . but when told to put *B* on *C*, it makes mistakes—and learns by experience (that is, modifies its own program).

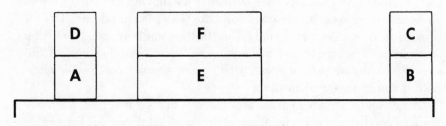

**Fig. 76.** Much later, HACKER has learned enough from experience to be able to turn this . . .

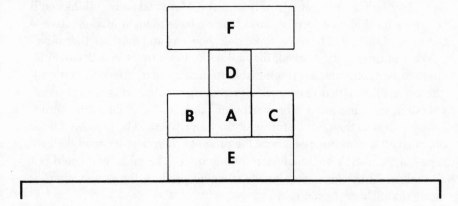

**Fig. 77.** . . . into this, without stumbling.

graphic art of various sorts. But like many other fads in the arts, these efforts largely died out after the shock value wore off. Some experimenters are still tinkering with such programs, but very few of the AI people I met take them seriously.

Still, most AI researchers do not admit to any ultimate limitation of the capabilities of artificial intelligence. As we know, many of them say that whatever the mind can do, the machine will someday be able to do better—and that includes all forms of creative work. But some find the question "Will computers ever be able to do creative work?" naive and simplistic. At the Xerox research facility in Palo Alto, California, when I raised this issue with Ira Goldstein, a former professor at MIT who is now designing highly intelligent teaching programs, the question seemed to pain him somewhat. "In biology," he said patiently, "it once made sense to say that something was 'alive' or 'not alive.' But now that distinction seems too simple, because viruses and DNA are both alive and not alive in the old sense. So we ask more specific questions now, like 'Does it reproduce?' 'Does it respond to its environment?' and so on. In the same way, creativity is an amorphous, ill-defined term, and doesn't lend itself to questions one can answer. But when we tease it apart, we'll be able to ask more specific questions that may have real answers.

"If a machine plays a good game of chess, is that creative? Yes and no— it's not a good question. It's more useful to ask: 'What does it do? Exhaustive search? Or does it use heuristic reasoning and a lot of knowledge?' That's the level at which I'd prefer to ask questions. If a machine produces poetry, is that creative? I'd rather ask: 'How does it do it? By rote procedures? Or by understanding the meanings of the words?' More and more, I think you'll be seeing machines performing tasks that we have thought of as creative— but some of them will be doing those tasks one way and some another way."

What of originality, I asked, the hallmark of creativity in art? Could he envision any computer ever being able to create songs, quartets, and symphonies as filled with original melodies as those of Schubert in his last years? Goldstein gave me an answer worthy of Laplace, the eighteenth-century astronomer who thought the future of the universe could be predicted if we only had all the information about the present. "If you understood the processes of Schubert's life, microstep by microstep," he said, "and could put all that into a machine, presumably it would produce the same wondrous music that Schubert produced."

Outside the ranks of the artificial intelligentsia (as AI people are sometimes called), few cognitive scientists share Goldstein's view. They see basic differences between natural and artificial intelligence that may make true originality inherent in the former but impossible for the latter.

For one thing, as Walter Reitman pointed out to me, artificial intelligences work toward "known end states"—goals defined by their creators. That means that even a machine that learns and improves its own program has no way of setting a new goal for itself. Where would it get such a goal? Out of itself? But *why* would it seek to set itself a new goal?

For another thing, Joseph Weizenbaum believes that computers simulate the logical processes of the left half of the brain, but that there is no way in which a linear, step-by-step artificial intelligence can simulate the intuitive and nonlogical processes of the right half, or of the unconscious (wherever that is). Yet a large part of creative work is nonlogical and unconscious.

Many other experts feel that the extraordinary multiplicity of parallel pathways in the brain yields a kind of thinking impossible to simulate on a computer. Today, computers can be programmed to look as if they're doing parallel processing: the computer pursues one line of thought for a few microseconds (millionths of a second), then switches to another one for the next few microseconds, and so on, giving the overall appearance of pursuing a number of avenues of thought at the same time. But it's only an illusion. When the human mind pursues a number of lines of thought at once, as it does at the unconscious level, much of the time each line is probably continuous, and interactive with the others. The result, sometimes, is a new idea—something that has not yet, to my knowledge, been produced by any machine.

## What the Human Mind Can Do That the Computer Can't

Like creative acts, there are a number of important mental phenomena that have not yet been simulated by any computer program and, many cognitive scientists believe, probably never will be. Surprisingly, most of these are everyday aspects of our mental lives that we take for granted and that seem as natural and uncomplicated to us as eating and sleeping.

The first is that obvious, seemingly simple, but largely ineluctable phenomenon, consciousness. To philosophers through the centuries, and to psychologists of recent decades, this concept has proven as elusive as a drop of mercury under one's finger, but the only question we need ask ourselves here is: Can a machine be conscious? Let's say the current is on, the machine has a program stored in it, you address it from a terminal and, in response, it goes through various steps of solving a problem in very much the way a human being would. Now ask yourself: Was it conscious of its cognitive processes as you were of yours? The question answers itself: There is no reason to suppose so. Nothing built into any existing program that I have heard of is meant to, or does, as far as one can tell, yield a state corresponding to consciousness.

Much of our own thinking, to be sure, takes place outside of consciousness, but the results of these processes become conscious, and each of us *experiences* those conscious thoughts; we know them to be taking place in our own minds. We not only think, but perceive ourselves thinking. Artificial intelligence has no analog to this. As Donald Norman put it—and he was only one of many cognitive scientists who made similar remarks to me— "We don't have any programs today that are self-aware or that even begin to approach consciousness such as human beings have. I see this as a critical difference between human intelligence and artificial intelligence. The human mind is aware of itself as an identity, it can introspect, it can examine its own ideas and react to them—not just with thoughts about them but with emotions. We can't begin to simulate consciousness on a computer, and perhaps never will."

Not everyone would agree that consciousness may forever remain impossible to simulate, but what is clear is that it cannot be simulated at present—and for one very good reason: it remains the least understood and most puzzling of psychological phenomena. I am aware of my own thoughts, to be sure, but what is this "I"? How do I distinguish the "I" from the identity of other people or the rest of the world? Surely it is not a matter of the borders of my physical being, for in the dark, or blindfolded and bound, or even cut off by spinal anesthesia from all feeling, I would know myself: the borders are those of thought, not body. Actually, the question "What is this 'I'?" rarely concerns us, for we experience our own identity as a self-evident reality. But that ineluctable sense of I-ness does not exist in any computer; there is no evidence that any computer program has ever realized that it is itself, running in a particular machine, and not a similar program, running on another machine somewhere else.

Cognitive science does offer at least a rudimentary explanation of consciousness: it is thought to be the product of our internalizing the real world in our minds in symbolic form. We perceive not only the real world but also our own mental representation of it; the experience of the difference between the two results in self-awareness. We recognize that there is not only a real world but a simulacrum of it within us; therefore there must be an *us:*

*cogito ergo sum*, yet again. The thought that we have thoughts is the crucial one that becomes consciousness; it is what Douglas Hofstadter, in *Gödel, Escher, Bach*, calls a "strange loop" of the mind, an interaction between different levels, a self-reinforcing resonance. "The self," he says, "comes into being at the moment it has the power to reflect itself." We contemplate our thoughts, but the awareness of doing so is itself a thought, and the foundation of consciousness.

Perhaps the key factor is that consciousness develops in us as a result of our cognitive history. As we have seen, the infant gradually becomes capable of thinking about external objects by means of mental images and symbols stored in memory. The newborn does not seem to be aware of the boundaries between itself and the rest of the world, but it perceives them more and more distinctly as its internal image of the world builds up. Consciousness emerges as a product of the child's mental development. The computer, in contrast, though it may acquire an ever-larger store of information, has no such sense or experience of its own history. Nor does it recognize that what is in its memory is a representation of something outside. To the computer, what is in its system is what *is;* it does not contemplate its thoughts as thoughts, but as the only reality. How could it, then, be aware of itself as an individual?

Some AI enthusiasts do, however, argue that if a program examines its own problem-solving behavior and modifies it to improve it, as HACKER does, this is the equivalent of consciousness; so says Pamela McCorduck in *Machines Who Think.* John McCarthy of Stanford University, one of America's leading computer scientists, goes even further: he says it is possible to ascribe beliefs, free will, consciousness, and wants to a machine. In his view, even as simple a machine as a thermostat can be said to have beliefs (presumably the thermostat "believes" that the optimum temperature is the one it is set for). But such talk is either metaphorical or, more likely, anthropomorphic; it reads into the machine what the human observer feels, much as primitive people attribute rage to the volcano and prudence to the ant. There is no reason to suppose HACKER or a thermostat experience anything like awareness of the self; they merely respond to certain incoming stimuli with mechanical reactions. HACKER, to be sure, does register corrections in its program for future use, but so does a vine, growing around an obstruction. It seems most unlikely that anywhere within HACKER some small voice says, "I made an error, but I'm correcting it and I'll do better next time."

•

What difference does it make? If a machine can respond to its own errors and correct them, what does it matter that it isn't aware of doing so?

It matters a lot. Awareness of self is the essence of what being alive means to us. If, through some accident, you remained able to talk and reason but could not realize that you were doing so, would you not be as dead, from your own viewpoint, as if your brain had been destroyed?

More than that, with awareness of self we become conscious of the alternatives in our thoughts; we become conscious of our choices, and of our ability to will the things we choose to do. Choice and will are difficult to account for within a scientific psychology, since it views existence as a continuum in which no phenomenon occurs uncaused. If no event is, itself, a first cause, but is the product of antecedent forces, then the experience of choice and of will must be illusory; the acts of choosing and of willing, though they seem to be within our power, must be products of all that has happened to us in the past and is happening at the moment.

And yet when we are conscious of our own alternatives, that self-awareness is another level of causality—a set of influences in addition to those of the past and present. We are not automata, weighing all the pros and cons of any matter and inevitably acting in accord with our calculations. In mathematical decision theory, the totally rational human being does just that and always selects the most advantageous option; so does a well-designed computer program. But in reality we are aware of our own decision making, and that awareness in itself brings other forces to bear upon the decision—emotional responses to the situation, loyalties, moral values, a sense of our own identity—and these resonances, these loops of thought, affect the outcome.

A simple example: you are annoyed by something a friend has said or done, you fume about it, you imagine a conversation in which the two of you argue about it, you prepare your crushing remarks—and suddenly perceive all this as from a distance; in perspective, you see yourself as an outsider might see you, question your own thoughts and feelings, alter them, and, as a result, accept the friend's behavior and dismiss your anger, or, perhaps, call the friend and talk the matter over amicably.

Another example: like every writer I know, when I am writing a first draft I rattle away at the typewriter, setting down words; but once I see them I think, That isn't quite right—that's not exactly what I mean, and tinker and revise and rewrite until the words are right. But it wasn't that the first words didn't say what I meant; rather, in seeing my thoughts, I had thoughts about them; the strange loop yielded something like freedom—the

**Fig. 78.** Young girl or old hag? You can see whichever you will to see.

freedom to make a different choice among my thoughts. If the experiences of choice and will are not what they seem to be, they nonetheless reflect real processes that produce results different from those that would come about without them.

In any case, there is no doubt that we do not experience our thought processes as automatic but as within our control. Figure 78 shows a well-known ambiguous figure, created some years ago by the psychologist Edwin G. Boring; you can see it as a young woman, facing away, or as an ugly old hag (in left profile). The interesting thing is that you can make yourself see it as either one—and can decide *when* you want to see it as either. "I can make it do what I want it to do," David Rumelhart of the University of California at San Diego said to me, speaking of a similar ambiguous figure. "That's a trivial example of willing to do one thing rather than another, but the phenomenon itself is anything but trivial. And it's one of the essential human experiences that I can't see any way to simulate on a machine."

"I can make it do what I want it to do," Rumelhart said. But what does "want" mean? Can a machine want? In a sense: if its program calls for it to assign different weights to various subgoals and goals, it will proceed to choose that option which its program reckons to have the greatest numerical value. All very neat and simple. Human beings are far less neat and far more complicated. We often desire things but lack the motivation to pursue them; conversely, we are sometimes so strongly motivated by beliefs, values, and emotions that we pursue a particular goal with a devotion far beyond what any realistic evaluation would warrant.

Of all the components in human motivation, the one least likely ever to be simulated by a computer is our capacity to find things interesting. It is a mystifying phenomenon. Why do we find any matter interesting? What makes us want to know about, or understand, something—especially something that has no practical value for us, such as the age of the universe or when human beings first appeared on earth? Why do we want to know if there is life elsewhere in the cosmos, if its replies to our messages could not arrive back here for centuries? Why did Pythagoras feel so powerfully impelled to prove his celebrated theorem?

This tendency in us, some cognitive scientists believe, is an intrinsic characteristic of our nervous system. We are driven to think certain thoughts, and to pursue certain goals, by an inherent neurological restlessness, a need to do something with the thoughts in our minds and with the world they represent. The computer, in contrast, is a passive system: its goals and the strength of its drive to reach them are those given it by its designer. Left to itself, it will sit inert, awaiting further orders. We will not; we look for new goals, and, to reach them, are forced to solve problems we did not have before; we do not let well enough alone.

Why don't we? Call it restlessness, call it curiosity, or perhaps, like the historian Huizinga, call it playfulness. Other animals play, but with us playfulness becomes cognitive: we play with our ideas, and afterward with the real-world counterparts of those ideas. How would you simulate that on a machine? Allen Newell and a few other AI researchers say there is no reason why a program could not be designed to be curious and to create new goals for itself, but they are a small minority; most cognitive scientists think otherwise. Yet even if a machine could be programmed to cast about in some way for new goals and new problems, it would do so because it had been programmed to; it wouldn't do so because it wanted to. It wouldn't give a damn.

And that would be bound to affect the kinds of new problems it chose to tackle and the strength of its motivation to solve them. Maybe the biggest difference between artificial and human intelligence is just that simple: we care about the things we choose to do. Solving a new problem, discovering some new fact, visiting a new place, reading a new book, all make us feel good; that's why we do them. But how would one make a computer feel good? Some AI people have built rewards into their programs: if the machine makes right decisions, its program is automatically altered to strengthen that kind of response, and so it learns. Theoretically, a program could be rewarded if it did something new and different, so that its tendency would be not to maintain itself, unchanged, but to keep changing. But would it *want* to do so or *like* doing so? And lacking that, would there be any meaning to its changes? Perhaps computer-written music and poetry have been unimpressive because the computer itself was neither pleased nor displeased by its own product, as every creative artist is. Without that test, it wasn't able to tell whether it had created a work of genius or a piece of trash. And it didn't care.

We, on the other hand, care—and care most of all about those thoughts which express moral values. Each of us is not just an information processor but the product of a particular culture and its belief system. We perceive the world through the special focus of the values we have learned from parents, schools, books, and peers. Those values become a part of our decision-making processes; in making many of our choices, we weight the alternatives in accordance with our moral, religious, and political beliefs.

This aspect of human thinking can be, and has been, simulated on the machine, as we saw earlier, in the form of the simulations of political decision making created by Jaime Carbonell and his colleagues when he was at Yale (he is now at Carnegie-Mellon). POLITICS has simulated the reasoning of either a conservative or a liberal considering what the United States should do if, for instance, Russia were to build nuclear submarines. Both as conservative and as liberal, POLITICS flawlessly came to conclusions consonant with the assumptions it was programmed to draw upon. Carbonell's purpose was to test his theoretical model of the way in which ideology affects the decision-making process; he did not suggest that POLITICS could be developed into a machine that could do our political thinking for us. But his work does have two important implications for this discussion of what the human mind can do that the computer can't do.

First, even though POLITICS can simulate archetypal conservative or liberal political reasoning, it does so in a wholly predictable way; it produces decisions Carbonell could foresee because they are based entirely on the terms and conditions he had put into it. But that is not the way human beings think. Within any party or ideological group, there is a wide range of variations in how individuals interpret the tenets of that ideology. There are always mavericks, dissenters, and innovators, without whom every party, every church, and every culture would atrophy and die.

Second, within any given ideological group, some people have the emotional maturity, the richness of human experience, and the soundness of judgment to use its tenets wisely; others do not, and use them foolishly. This is not to say that wise persons will reach the same conclusions everywhere; I would not want the wisest judge in Russia, India, or Iran to hear a civil liberties case in which I was accused of slandering the state. But if it is true that within any culture, its ethical system has internal validity, some of its people will interpret those beliefs wisely, others foolishly, and the majority somewhere in between. Moral wisdom is not so much the product of a special method of reasoning as of an ability to harmonize moral beliefs with fundamental individual and societal needs. I do not see how artificial intelligence can simulate that.

Will artificial intelligence, then, ever outstrip human intelligence? Yes, astronomically—in certain ways; and clearly it is already doing so. But in other ways it does not now match our powers, much less exceed them, and seems unlikely to do so soon. And in still other ways it seems incapable of simulating human intellectual functioning at all.

For until it acquires perceptual systems as sophisticated as our own, it will not be able to learn directly from the environment. But the development of such systems is bound to prove more difficult, by many orders of magnitude, than the creation of a living cell—a feat not now imaginable—and lacking such perceptual systems, the machine will remain dependent on the human being for its information.

But that is the least of it. Until artificial intelligence can duplicate human mental development from birth onward; until it can absorb the intricacies and subtleties of cultural values; until it can acquire consciousness of self; until it becomes capable of playfulness and curiosity; until it can create new goals for itself, unplanned and uninstigated by any human programmer; until it is motivated not by goals alone but by some restless compulsion to be doing and exploring; until it can care about, and be pleased or annoyed by, its own thoughts; until it can make wise moral judgments—until all these conditions exist, the computer, it seems to me, will not match or even palely imitate the most valuable aspects of human thinking.

There is no doubt that the computer has already transformed our lives, and will continue to do so. But its chief influence will continue to be its utility as a tool. Supercalculators have radically changed, and will continue to change, all human institutions that require reckoning. Artificial intelligence will reconstruct many areas of problem solving—everything from the practice of medicine to literary and historical research and the investigation of the cosmos—and in so doing will change our ways of thinking as profoundly as did the invention of writing. Tools have powerful effects on the thinking of those who use them (the plow radically altered humankind's view of itself and of the world around it), but tools of the mind have the most powerful effects of all. Still, they are our tools, we their users.

But is it not possible that the computer will take over, outthink us, make our decisions for us, become our ruler? Not unless we assign it the power to make our decisions. Joseph Weizenbaum, in *Computer Power and Human Reason*, passionately argues that the computer represents a major danger to humanity not because it can forcibly take over but because we are heedlessly allowing it to make decisions for us in areas where we alone ought to make them. He sees the problem as a moral one rather than a struggle between human and machine: we ought not let the computer function as a psychotherapist, ought not rely on it to tell us whether to bomb civilian enemy targets or only military ones, ought not have it function as a judge in court.

Of course we ought not, but is there any real danger that we will? I hope not; I think not. The computer does not set its own goals; we do, and we human beings are jealous of our own powers. We have often delegated them to some leader—a human being, like ourselves, but one we took to be a greater person than we. Or we have asked some god (who often looks like us, enlarged) to make our decisions for us. But would we ever delegate our intellectual responsibilities to a machine that we ourselves created? I doubt it. Though human beings have often enough been fools, I find it hard to believe that we would ever be foolish enough to think our machines wiser than we; at least, not as long as we are aware of, and proud of, the human difference.

# AN AFTERWORD

In 1748 David Hume expected philosophic inquiry soon to "discover, at least in some degree, the secret springs and principles, by which the mind is actuated in its operations." He was ahead of his time; most of what is known of those secret springs and principles has been discovered only in the past twenty years. Our knowledge is far from complete, but we know more now about how the human intellect works than human beings have ever known since they first stood upright and became aware of their own thoughts.

I asked nearly every cognitive scientist I met whether there yet existed an overarching grand theory that explained all of human mental phenomena. Not one said yes. Nearly all of them considered information-processing theory the most useful model of human thinking but pointed out that it pictures only as much of the operations of the mind as can be simulated on a computer—and, as we have seen, there is far more to human thinking than that.

Moreover, many of them said that the field was not at the stage of development when a unifying theory was feasible. Unifying theories are typical of a very young, speculative science, or of a mature, highly developed one. Cognitive science is halfway. It's developing good detailed explanations of memory, problem solving, and other specific phenomena of cognition; it's concerned with what sociologist Robert K. Merton calls "theories of the middle range"—explanations that do not disagree with each other but that seem to deal with different sets of rules rather than constitute specific applications of general rules.

Some cognitive scientists expect, or at least hope, that a sophisticated synthesis will emerge soon. But others say that the human mind is too complex, and exhibits too many diverse phenomena, to be explained by one set of principles. Perhaps, too, the laws that apply to a simple mental phenomenon are only distantly related to those that apply to a more complex one.

363

As George Mandler said, "The biology of the cell, the biology of the liver, and the biology of the whole person are different enterprises. They're not discrepant, but they're not encompassed by a single overall theory."

But if there is no grand theory unifying all cognitive phenomena, one informing concept does appear in area after area: there is a tremendous evolutionary advantage to each of the various special aspects of the human intellect. Time and again one sees that the special mechanisms of the mind are invaluable adaptations in our interaction with the world. Both individually and collectively they enable us to model the world in our minds, manipulate it, and, having seen what would happen, carry out in reality what we have done successfully in imagination or avoid in reality what we have failed at in imagination. The world is full of evolutionary adaptations that we never tire of admiring—the moth that cannot be seen against the bark of the tree it is resting on, the giraffe, whose neck is long enough to reach the leaves of the trees it feeds on and whose blood pressure is high enough to pump the blood up to that head—but what evolutionary adaptation is as remarkable, and as powerful, as that of the human mind?

The self-esteem in which human beings have traditionally held themselves is no longer anthropocentric and self-flattering. In the past, it may have been based, in part, on errors and misperceptions, but now that we know so much about our minds, we have reason to appreciate and value ourselves after all. And if we truly value ourselves, if we appraise the human difference at its real worth, how can we then, except in self-defense or the defense of others, treat any other person or people as less than precious?

# SOLUTIONS TO PROBLEMS

Here is one of several possible solutions to the missionaries-and-cannibals problem on pages 25–26:

STEP 1: Start with:

MMM
CCC        [river]                [opposite bank]

One M and one C cross (arrowhead stands for boat):

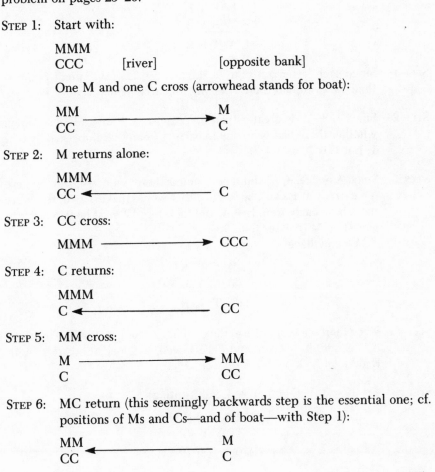

MM ⟶ M
CC       C

STEP 2: M returns alone:

MMM
CC ⟵ ——— C

STEP 3: CC cross:

MMM ⟶ CCC

STEP 4: C returns:

MMM
C ⟵ ——— CC

STEP 5: MM cross:

M ⟶ MM
C       CC

STEP 6: MC return (this seemingly backwards step is the essential one; cf. positions of Ms and Cs—and of boat—with Step 1):

MM ⟵ M
CC       C

STEP 7:   MM cross:

CC   ———————————→    MMM<br>
                                      C

STEP 8:   C returns:

CCC ←———————————  MMM

STEPS 9, 10, and 11: CC cross, C returns, and CC cross.

*

The cryptarithmetic problem on page 26 is solved as follows:

L E T S<br>
+W A V E<br>
———————<br>
LA TER

STEP 1:   Since each letter stands for a single digit, L + W cannot be more than 19, even had there been one to carry; hence L must be 1.

STEP 2:   Since L + W is greater than 9, W must be 8 or 9 (depending on whether there had been one to carry). A can therefore be only 0 or 1; but L is 1; so A = 0.

STEP 3:   Since A = 0, E + A would be E unless there is a carry. Hence there is a carry. But E can't be 9, since that would make T = 0; therefore there is no carry from E + A, and therefore W must be 9 in order to have L + W greater than 9.
We now have:

(1) E  T  S<br>
(9) (0) V  E<br>
———————————<br>
(1) (0) T  E  R

STEP 4:   Since there's a carry of 1 to the column E + 0, E + 1 = T. Therefore if E is odd, T is even, and if E is even, T is odd. Let's start with E/odd. Only 3, 5, and 7 are available.

STEP 5:   Try E = 3. If E = 3, T = 4. Substituting:

(1) (3) (4)  S<br>
(9) (0)  V  (3)<br>
———————————————<br>
(1) (0) (4) (3)  R

But then V could only be 8 or 9; 9 is already assigned; and if V were 8, the second column from the right would require a carry of 1 from S + 3. But then S would have to be 7 (impossible; R can't be 0), or 8 (impossible; we just made V = 8); and 9 is taken. The assumption that E = 3 leads to contradictions; therefore E cannot be 3.

STEP 6:   Try E = 5. If E = 5, T = 6. V can, again, be only 8 or 9, but 9 is taken; so V = 8. Substituting:

$$\begin{array}{cccc} (1) & (5) & (6) & S \\ (9) & (0) & (8) & (5) \\ \hline (1)(0) & (6) & (5) & R \end{array}$$

Since 6 + 8 needs a carry to make 15, S + 5 must be greater than 10. S can't be 5, 6, 8, or 9 because they're all taken; therefore S = 7. Substituting:

$$\begin{array}{r} 1567 \\ 9085 \\ \hline 10652 \end{array}$$

•

Solution to the cryptarithmetic problem on page 79:

It is possible to solve the DONALD + GERALD problem in more than one rigorous way, but here is the briefest and most efficient solution I have seen; it comes from *Human Information Processing* (pp. 559–60) by Peter H. Lindsay and Donald A. Norman. If your own solution is nowhere nearly as brief and neat as this, do not be downcast; Lindsay and Norman have observed many people solving this problem and report that the typical solution is fumbling and tortuous. (In what follows, zero is printed with a slant through it, like this—∅—to avoid confusion with the Os of DONALD and ROBERT.)

$$\begin{array}{ll} \text{(Column} & 654321) \\ & \text{DONALD} \\ + & \text{GERALD} \\ \hline & \text{ROBERT} \end{array}$$

1. D = 5, so T must be ∅ (with a carry to column 2).
2. Look at column 5: O + E = O. This can happen only if ∅ or 1∅ is being added to O. Therefore, E must be 9 (plus a carry) or ∅. But T is already ∅, so E must be 9 (with a carry from column 4).

3. If E is 9, then in column 3, A must be 4 or 9 (with a carry in either case). E is already 9, so A must be 4.
4. In column 2, L + L plus a carry = R plus a carry to column 3. R must be odd. The only odd numbers left are 1, 3, and 7. But from column 6, 5 + G = R, so R must be greater than 5. So R must be 7, which makes L = 8 and G = 1.
5. In column 4, N + 7 = B + carry. Therefore, N is greater than or equal to 3. The only numbers left are 2, 3, and 6, so N is 3 or 6. But if N were 3, B would be Ø, so N must be 6. That makes B = 3.
6. That only leaves the letter O and the number 2: O = 2.

$$
\begin{array}{r}
5\,2\,6\,4\,8\,5 \\
+\ 1\,9\,7\,4\,8\,5 \\
\hline
7\,2\,3\,9\,7\,\cancel{0}
\end{array}
$$

# NOTES

I owe more, to more other people, than I can conveniently spell out here. Accordingly, these notes do not generally name the sources of data or views that can easily be found in textbooks of cognitive science (a few of which are included in the List of Cited Sources), or that are sufficiently identified in the text. I cite chiefly sources of important or controversial data that might be hard for interested readers to locate.

All published sources are given in short form (author's name and year), and can be located in the List of Cited Sources.

Where quotations by cognitive scientists are not otherwise identified, they come from my tape-recorded interviews with those persons.

## CHAPTER ONE (pp. 17-47)

*Page*

18.  50,000 to 75,000: Estimates of typical adult vocabulary size vary somewhat; this often-cited figure refers to educated Englishmen, but Gough and Cosky, 1977, say they see no reason to suppose that educated Americans know fewer words.

22.  50,000 configurations of chess pieces: Chase and Simon, 1974; also, Simon and Gilmartin, 1973.

22.  John Griffith's estimate of the human memory capacity is cited in Rose, 1976, pp. 269–70; the original statement is to be found in Horn and Hinde, 1970.

23.  avoid the word "thinking" . . . others still use it: Variant definitions can be found in almost any textbook; the two quotations come from Radford and Burton, 1974, pp. 30 and 186.

24.  This convergence: The origins and emergence of cognitive science are recounted in Newell and Simon, 1972, pp. 873–89.

26.  "three five-handed extraterrestrial monsters": Hayes and Simon, 1977.

27.  The Kpelle farmer's reaction to the syllogism is related in Scribner, 1977.

28.  programs that think right-wing thoughts: Carbonell, 1977.

28.  BEM, TAQ, MUZ: Ceraso, 1967.

28.  "Bah, gah, gah": Crowder, 1978.

29.  "The yigs wur vumly": Epstein, 1961.

29.  wired that way genetically: See below, chap. 6, third section.

29.  2500 slides: Standing, Conezio, and Haber, 1970. (Standing later went even further and showed a few sturdy volunteers 10,000 pictures.)

30.  "ghost in the machine": The phrase was coined by the philosopher Gilbert Ryle, but has been borrowed by many cognitive scientists.

32. A knowledge of psychobiology: Estes (among many others), in Estes, 1978, pp. 3–4.
33. *epineural:* Newell and Simon, 1972, pp. 875–76.
33. a Danish team: Lassen, Ingvar, and Skinhøj, 1978.
33. computer-generated diagrams: ibid.
36. four hundred words: Terrace, 1979, citing Patterson; see also Patterson, 1978.
36–37. two hundred times that many: See note to p. 18, above.
38. *ten billion:* Hubel, 1979; Stevens, 1979; Nauta and Feirtag, 1979.
38. a *hundred billion:* Stevens, 1979.
38. anywhere from 1000 to 10,000 synapses: Stevens, 1979.
41. The significance of the brain's redundancy is stressed by many writers; see, for example, Roe, 1976, pp. 55, 134, 259.
41. some twenty to thirty . . . "neurotransmitter" substances: Iversen, 1979.
41. The description of neurotransmission is drawn from Hubel, 1979, and from Iversen, 1979.
44. L-tryptophan: Hartmann, 1978.
44. lecithin: Wurtman, 1978.
44–45. Details of the explosive evolution of the brain are from Leakey and Lewin, 1978, and Washburn, 1978. The disagreement is between followers of Leakey and followers of Johanson; see Johanson and Edey, 1981, chap. 14.
45. stood upright three to four million years ago: Johanson and Edey, 1981, pp. 180–81 and elsewhere (see their index).
45–46. On the relation between tool use and brain size, see Washburn, 1978.
46. On animal self-awareness, see any of numerous works on animal psychology, or Ernest Hilgard's review of *The Question of Animal Awareness* by Donald Griffin; the review appeared in *Jour. of Psycholing. Res.* 7 (1978): 243. On self-awareness in apes, see report on the work of Gordon G. Gallup of the State University of New York, Albany, in *The New York Times,* August 7, 1979.

## CHAPTER TWO (pp. 48–83)

49. Watson's famous boast: Watson, 1926.
50. "We're always controlled . . . the world could be improved": Skinner made these statements in the course of a *Nova* (Public Broadcasting System) documentary about his life and work, 1979.
50. Skinner on mentalism as akin to primitive animism: Skinner, 1964, p. 106.
50. "We do not need": Skinner, 1972, pp. 12–13, 22–23.
50. Skinner on the science of behavior: Skinner, 1965, p. 35.
51. Liddell's work is reported in his own publications, but the eyewitness details given here are from my article "Neurosis Factory," *Esquire,* July 1952.
51. Wolpe's work is reported in his own publications, but the statements by him quoted here are from my article "A Neurosis Is 'Just' a Bad Habit," *The New York Times Magazine,* June 4, 1967.
55. The proper goal of psychology: Watson, 1930, p. 18.
56–60. The particular experiments described here are drawn from Bugelski, 1975; Hintzman, 1978; Kagan and Havemann, 1972; and Levine, 1975, in all of which the original sources are cited.
61–62. The case of Albert B.: Watson and Rayner, 1920.
62. Skinner's "air crib": Ekstrand and Bourne, 1974, p. 136, and *Nova* (Public Broadcasting System) documentary on Skinner, 1979.
62. short-term sex therapies: Hogan, 1978; Levay and Kagle, 1977.
62. behavioral marriage therapy: Gurman and Knudson, 1978; Gurman and Kniskern, 1978.
62–63. On the poor results of aversive therapy: Korchin, 1976, pp. 345–46.
63. Watson's statement: Watson, 1924, p. 24.
63. built-in neural circuitry: Hintzman, 1978, 180–81; Moore and Stuttard, 1979.
65. Pick's experiments in spatial mapping: Hazen, Lockman, and Pick, 1978.

67. chemical tags . . . complex and precise plan: Stevens, 1979; Cowan, 1979.
68. The shortcomings of teaching machines: Hintzman, 1978, pp. 194–96.
68. The cue-reversal experiment (red and green lights): Grings, Schell, and Carey, 1973.
69. Psycholinguists maintain: de Villiers and de Villiers, 1978, pp. 199–203; Clark and Clark, 1977, p. 335–38. See also chap. 6, below. The concept is Chomsky's.
70. *deep structure* . . . deep significance: de Villiers and de Villiers, 1978, pp. 54–61.
73. Conditions under which rats and human beings act like behaviorist automata: Hintzman, 1978, pp. 191, 207.
74. On the emergence of information-processing theory: Newell and Simon, 1972, chap. 2; Lachman, Lachman, and Butterfield, 1979, chap. 4; and Estes, in Estes, 1978.
77. The experiment with pairs of letters: Posner and Mitchell, 1967.
77–78. The experiment with paired words: Gough and Cosky, 1977.
80. "guiding metaphor": Bower, 1978*b*.
80. Kuhn's comment: Kuhn, 1970, passim, but see esp. pp. 93, 109 and 140–41.
81. On epiphenomena: The view I espouse can be found in the writings of many cognitive scientists; for other views, see Fodor, 1981; and Popper and Eccles, 1977.

## CHAPTER THREE (pp. 84–120)

84. four fifths of what is learned in classrooms: Paul E. Johnson, University of Minnesota, personal communication.
85. Griffith's estimate of lifetime memory capacity: Rose, 1976, pp. 269–70; the original statement is to be found in Horn and Hinde, 1970.
85. von Neumann's estimate: von Neumann, 1958, pp. 63–64.
86. "the workshop of thought": Charles Perfetti, in Resnick, 1976, p. 288.
87. would need something like four hundred years: Tomkins, 1970, p. 63.
87. less than two seconds: The example is my own, but the figure is based on Collins and Quillian, 1969; see also studies summarized in Glass, Holyoak, and Santa, 1979, pp. 356–57.
87. Typically, one volunteer: Williams, 1978.
89. much of our most important and creative thinking: See, for instance, Shepard, 1978*a* and 1978*b*.
89. The penny study: Nickerson and Adams, 1979.
90. only a minority of slips of the tongue: Clark and Clark, 1977, p. 275.
90. The 1964/1974 comparison study is described in Loftus, 1980, p. 142–44. See also Cohler, 1981.
90–91. The Piaget episode: Piaget, 1962.
93–94. William James described his experiment in *The Principles of Psychology*, 1890; it is retold in Norman, 1976, and in Farb, 1978.
94. thousands of experiments have shown: Glass, Holyoak, and Santa, 1979, pp. 142–43.
95. The thirty-two-word list; Deese and Kaufman, 1957.
96. Hofstadter's explanation: Hofstadter, 1980, p. 98.
97. Both of Elizabeth Loftus' studies are recounted in Loftus and Loftus, 1976, pp. 121–23.
98. Figure 20 is an adaptation of data in Collins and Quillian, 1969, by Lachman, Lachman, and Butterfield, 1979.
98. The use of images alone to solve certain problems: The clock-hand visualization study was by Paivio 1978; the window-recall problem is from Rumelhart, Lindsay, and Norman, 1972.
99–100. On hemispheric specialization and its limits: Geschwind, 1979*b*; Glass, Holyoak, and Santa, 1979, pp. 311–24.

100. Lashley's experiment and the redundant storage of memory: Many sources, but see esp. Lindsay and Norman, 1977, pp. 439–40.
101. Theories of the self: See Shaw and Bransford, 1977, passim.
101n. On demons: Riesbeck, 1974; Goldstein and Papert, 1977; Lindsay and Norman, 1977.
101. The IP metaphor of memory: Many current works use this in one form or another. My diagram (Fig. 21) synthesizes Hintzman, 1978; Estes, in Estes, 1978; Norman, 1976; Lindsay and Norman, 1977; Lachman, Lachman, and Butterfield, 1979; Loftus and Loftus, 1976; and Loftus, 1980.
102–04. The tachistoscope experiment: Sperling, 1960.
104. The aural buffer: Darwin, Turvey, and Crowder, 1972.
104–05. The experiment in the prevention of rehearsal: Peterson and Peterson, 1959; Peterson, 1966.
105–06. The case of H.M.: Milner, 1966; Milner, Corkin, and Teuber, 1968.
106. the greatest part of elaborative processing: My gerbil example is meant to illustrate "depth of processing," a notion first explicated by Craik and Lockhart, 1972.
107. "An ostrich is a bird": Lindsay and Norman, 1977, p. 406–8.
107. Figure 22 is an adaptation of Collins and Loftus, 1975, by, and appearing in, Lachman, Lachman, and Butterfield, 1979.
108. The recall study at Texas A & M: Smith, 1979.
109. Studies of hypnotized subjects on recall of videotape: E. Loftus, personal communication; Loftus, 1980, pp. 54–59.
109–10. Penfield's work: Penfield, 1959; Penfield, 1969; Penfield and Perot, 1963; Loftus, 1980, pp. 50–54.
113. The feat of memory of Steve Faloon: Ericsson, Chase, and Faloon, 1980.
114. The peg-word method: Miller, Galanter, and Pribram, 1960, pp. 125–29, 134–36.
115. twenty-six words arranged hierarchically: Bower, Lesgold, and Tieman, 1969.

## CHAPTER FOUR (pp. 121–156)

122. Some of the beekeepers: Johnson-Laird, 1979.
123. Our ability to be logical when the subject matter is real or familiar: Wason and Johnson-Laird, 1972, p. 245.
126–27. The four-card problem: Johnson-Laird and Wason, in Johnson-Laird and Wason, 1977, pp. 143–57.
128. smokers tend to reject logical inferences about smoking: Aronson, 1973.
129. On the irrational processes in high-level decision making: Axelrod, 1977; Holsti and George, 1975.
131. "All the important inferences": Russell, 1945, p. 199. For a more recent statement of the same position: Calder, 1979.
132. The upper-brow logic textbook is Jeffrey, 1967.
133. Minsky's statement: Minsky, 1974.
134. "All of John's children are asleep": Johnson-Laird and Wason, in Johnson-Laird and Wason, 1977, p. 79.
134. "She inherited a fortune": The example and comment are from Johnson-Laird and Wason, in Johnson-Laird and Wason, 1977, pp. 79–80.
134. Osherson's example and comment: Osherson, in Falmagne, 1975.
135. Osherson's study: ibid.
136. The "scandal": Wason and Johnson-Laird, 1972, p. 244.
136. Minsky's example: Minsky, 1974.
140. "If it's good, then it's expensive": Wason and Johnson-Laird, 1972, p. 43.
142. the most important of our reasoning processes: Shepard, 1978a and 1978b; Sternberg, 1977a.
144–45. The Sternberg example is from Sternberg, 1977b, pp. 138–47; the quote is from Sternberg, 1977a.

145–47.  Collins, 1979, drawing upon Collins, 1978.
147.  The Kahneman and Tversky experiments: Kahneman and Tversky, 1972 and 1973; Lindsay and Norman, 1977, pp. 578–81.
149.  recent studies showed only minor differences: Maccoby and Jacklin, 1978, vol. I., pp. 108–10.
149.  structural difference between the male brain and the female brain: McGlone, 1980; Restak, 1979, pp. 196–204.
150.  Piaget's theory: See chap. 6, below.
150.  The quote by Piaget: Piaget, 1972.
151–52.  Piaget's many studies in formal operations are described briefly in Flavell, 1963, chaps. 6 and 10, and in Ginsburg and Opper, 1969, in chap. 5.
152.  Piagetian studies in England: Lovell, 1961; in Australia: Dale, 1970.
152.  Possible explanations of replication failures of Piaget's experiments: Vinacke, 1974, pp. 140–41; Pitt, 1976, pp. 25–26.
152–53.  The fourth argument against Piaget's formal operations: Gelman, 1978; Pitt, 1976; and personal communications from Gelman, Pitt, and many others.
154.  Luria's findings, and those of Sharp and Cole, are summarized in Scribner, 1977, where the original sources are cited.
154.  The effects of schooling on thinking: Scribner, 1977; Neisser, 1976.

**CHAPTER FIVE (pp. 157–195)**

161.  The basic law of behavior: Lindsay and Norman, 1977, pp. 501–2.
161.  The parakeet study: The work of William Dilger of Cornell; see Hunt, 1973.
164.  Conceptual signing in ASL: Newport and Bellugi, 1978.
164.  The quote by Rosch: Rosch, 1978.
164.  Bornstein, on colors: Bornstein, 1979, p. 71.
164–65.  Kagan's prototypical experiment: Kagan and Havemann, 1972, p. 157.
166.  The behaviorist view of concept formation: Rosch and Lloyd, 1978, p. 2.
166.  Aunts: Brown, 1965, p. 316.
166.  Color groupings: Brown, 1965, pp. 315–16.
167.  Bruner and associates' study: Bruner, Goodnow, and Austin, 1956.
169.  Overgeneralizing by the child: Kogan, 1976, pp. 68–72.
169.  Rosch et al.'s study: Rosch et al., 1976.
170.  The study using slides of furniture and of faces: Unpublished doctoral dissertation by G. Ross, described in Kagan, 1979.
170.  Bornstein and associates' color categorization study: Bornstein, 1979, p. 51.
170.  Kagan, on infants' recognition of faces: Kagan, Kearsley, and Zelazo, 1978.
170.  Berlin's cross-cultural study of biological categorizing: Berlin, 1978.
171.  fuzzy, indeterminate edges: Glass, Holyoak, and Santa, 1979, pp. 342–53.
172.  The ostrich and canary example: Lindsay and Norman, 1977, pp. 406–8.
172.  Experiments with diagrams, stick figures, and dot patterns: Glass, Holyoak, and Santa, 1979, pp. 326–53.
173.  The quote by Rosch: Rosch, 1978, p. 29.
174–76.  Fried and Holyoak's study is reported more formally in Fried and Holyoak, 1978 and 1981.
177.  the brain's assumption: von Glasersfeld, 1978.
177.  Einstein's quote: Einstein, 1950.
177–78.  The survival value and sheer enjoyment of pattern finding: Simon and Sumner, 1968.
178–80.  Simon's analysis of our handling of letter or number series: Simon, 1976. The example given, however (ABRSZBCTUY_____), is mine; I apply his principles to it.
180–81.  Gelman's "magic experiments": Gelman, 1972b and 1977.
184.  Probability and correlation as nonintuitive concepts: Schweder, 1977; however, except for the case of two people having the same birthday, the examples are mine.

184. Divorce and delinquency: Herzog and Sudia, 1971, p. 61.
185. The disease-and-symptom study in Sweden: Smedslund, 1963.
186–87. The case of the Israeli student pilots: Kahneman and Tversky, 1973.
187. Nisbett and Ross, 1980, discuss the harm of mislabeling in their chap. 7.
187. Weighing our miscalculations against our successes: Nisbett and Ross, 1980, chaps. 6, 7, and 11.
188. Popper in the classroom: So quoted by Johnson-Laird and Wason, in Johnson-Laird and Wason, 1977, p. 258.
189. Popper's view of scientific investigation: Popper, 1977; see also Popper, 1972.
189. Darwin: Quoted in Copi, 1972, p. 438. Einstein: Quoted in Heisenberg, 1971, p. 63. Medawar: Quoted from his *Advice to a Young Scientist* (New York: Harper & Row, 1979) in *The New York Times*, in a book review by John Leonard, October 29, 1979.
189. The Holmes quote is from *A Study in Scarlet.*
190. Bacon: *Novum Organum*, First Part, Aphorism xlvi.
191. Influences on child behavior: Skolnick, 1978; Thomas and Chess, 1977.
192. The Bowling Green study: Mynatt, Doherty, and Tweney, 1977.
192. The student psychotherapists: Chapman and Chapman, 1967.
193. The experiment with sets of numbers: Wason and Johnson-Laird, 1972, pp. 207–9.
195. Simon: Simon, 1979, pp. 18–19, and Simon, 1970, pp. 64–65, 75–76.

**CHAPTER SIX (pp. 196–232)**

196. Piaget on the floor: Piaget, 1948, p. 13.
197. "Give me the zoob": Kagan, Kearsley, and Zelazo, 1978, p. 40.
197. The disappearing toy dog: Personal observation at several laboratories.
197. The measurement of sucking response: Butterfield and Siperstein, 1974.
197. "Mr. Short" and "Mr. Tall": Karplus, Karplus, and Wollman, 1974.
197. The English two-year-old's utterances: de Villiers and de Villiers, 1978, p. 1.
198. On the link between the appearance of thought and brain maturation: Trevarthen, 1978; Kagan, 1972; Kagan, Kearsley, and Zelazo, 1978, p. 38.
199. Effect of stimulation on rat brain size: Rosenzweig, Bennett, and Diamond, 1972.
199. Synaptic pruning: Greenough and Juraska, 1979.
202–06. Details of Piaget's principal experiments and theories given here can be found in Flavell, 1963, and in Ginsburg and Opper, 1969, along with references to Piaget's own writing (which are relatively inaccessible, due to his terminology).
204–06. Stage theory: Same sources as preceding note, plus Brown, 1965, pp. 209–33; Lindsay and Norman, 1977, pp. 507–16; and Piaget, 1972.
206–07. Recognition in the four-month-old child: Fagan, 1973.
207. Object permanence in the seven-to-nine-month-old: Kagan, 1979.
207–08. Beam balance experiment: Siegler, "The Origins of Scientific Reasoning," in Siegler, 1978.
208. The cheesecake and strudel problem: Clement, Lochhead, and Monk, 1979.
208. have not reached the stage of formal reasoning: Clement, Lochhead, and Monk, 1979; Siegler, in Siegler, 1978; Karplus, 1977 and 1979; Karplus et al., 1975.
208–09. The evidence that two-to-four-year-olds are not limited to egocentric thinking: Gelman, 1979.
209. Counting by the three-year-old girl: Gelman, personal communication.
209–10. Yellow blocks and zorru birds (inclusion experiments): Bucci, 1978.
210. serious challenge . . . to the rigorous Piagetian scheme: A roundup is in Gelman, 1978.
210. Stage theory as hindrance rather than help: Kagan, Kearsley, and Zelazo, 1978, pp. 22, 26.

211.  he explicitly rejected all preprogramming: Inhelder, 1978.
211.  Emergence of neural predispositions: Kagan, Kearsley, and Zelazo, 1978, pp. 7, 50.
212.  brain-recording wave shows the composite effect: On the computer analysis of brain waves, see Schmeck, 1980.
212–13.  Speech errors by children as traces of thought: de Villiers and de Villiers, 1978, p. 206; Clark and Clark, 1977, pp. 342–43.
213–14.  Clues to thought in adult language: Clark and Clark, 1977, pp. 102, 105–10; H. Clark, 1977c; Lachman, Lachman, and Butterfield, 1979, pp. 386–87.
215.  The color terms of the Dani: Heider [E. Rosch], 1972; Heider and Olivier, 1972.
215.  Use of imagery by Faraday and other scientists: Shepard, 1978a; Arieti, 1976, p. 281; Rothenberg, 1979. Einstein's vision: R. W. Clark, 1973, p. 125.
216.  Mental rotation of objects: Shepard and Metzler, 1971.
216.  Preverbal thinking, in human evolution: Shepard, 1979.
217.  Chomsky's review: Chomsky, 1959.
217.  Chomsky's views are succinctly presented by Lyons, 1978, and by Chomsky himself in brief form in Chomsky, 1975.
217.  Parents' concern with content rather than grammar of child's speech: Clark and Clark, 1977, p. 336.
217–18.  "Nobody don't like me": Clark and Clark, 1977, p. 336.
218.  Problem of passive voice: Chomsky, 1975, pp. 31–32.
219.  L.A.D., universal grammar, transformational grammar: Chomsky, 1975, chap. 3; de Villiers and de Villiers, 1978, chap. 3; Lyons, 1978, chaps. 7 through 9.
219–20.  "John is easy to please": Chomsky, 1957, cited in de Villiers and de Villiers, 1978, pp. 64–65.
220.  The modified Chomskyan view: Lyons, 1978, chap. 7.
220.  Lesions of Broca's Area and Wernicke's Area: Geschwind, 1979b.
221.  The typically interactionist view of psycholinguists: Clark and Clark, 1977, p. 298.
222.  "Dat's greem," etc: de Villiers and de Villiers, 1978, p. 90.
222–23.  Babbling: de Villiers and de Villiers, 1978, pp. 35–38.
223.  The rather sudden development of two-word speech: Nelson, 1979.
223–24.  Child's use of correct word order: de Villiers and de Villiers, 1978, pp. 72–79.
224.  Deaf children and "language organizing principles": Feldman, Goldin-Meadow, and Gleitman, 1978.
224.  Child's difficulty with passive constructions: de Villiers and de Villiers, 1978, p. 200; Clark and Clark, 1977, pp. 501–2.
224.  Difficulty with negative sentences: de Villiers and de Villiers, 1978, pp. 102–5.
224–25.  Details of development beyond the two-word stage are spelled out in de Villiers and de Villiers, 1978, passim, and Clark and Clark, 1977, passim. The rate of acquisition of words: Gelman, 1979.
225.  The survey of forty languages: Slobin, 1973.
225.  The brain's natural receptiveness to language rather than science: Chomsky, 1975, pp. 24–28.
225.  "Motherese": Newport, Gleitman, and Gleitman, 1978; Clark and Clark, 1977, pp. 320–30.
225–26.  Self-correction: Moskowitz, 1978.
227.  Language is not well suited to encoding certain kinds of information: Huttenlocher, 1976.
227.  Language and thought: Farb, 1978, pp. 68–71; Newell and Simon, 1972, p. 66; Huttenlocher, 1976; and many others. Clark and Clark, 1977, and de Villiers and de Villiers, 1978, both offer good summaries of the debate.
228.  The case of Genie: Curtiss et al., 1975.
229–31.  On the complex question of the language abilities of apes, see Terrace, 1979 and

1980; Sebeok and Umiker-Sebeok, 1980; Krauss and Glucksberg, 1977; and M. Gardner, 1980. The subject is also reviewed in both Clark and Clark, 1977, and de Villiers and de Villiers, 1978.

230. The Patterson quote: Patterson, 1978.
231. Metaknowledge: A common concept; discussed in many cognitive-science writings. Flavell's comments: Flavell, 1976.

## CHAPTER SEVEN (pp. 233-271)

233. *lev klula buj:* This problem is quoted from Whimbey and Lochhead, 1979.
233-34. The wooden cube problem: Wickelgren, 1974, p. 32.
234. The bear's route: Polya, 1973, p. 234.
236. Animal problem solving and cultural transmission: Bonner, 1980, passim.
236. The quotation from Newell and Simon: Newell and Simon, 1972, p. 72.
236. Remembering, as a species of problem solving: Lindsay and Norman, 1977, p. 366; Newell and Simon, 1972, pp. 94-95.
238. The gray area between knowledge-based performance and real problem solving: Greeno, 1980.
238-39. The definitions of algorithm and heuristic vary somewhat, according to the specialty of the user; I am enunciating the median position.
240. The six-stick problem: Mayer, 1977, pp. 56-57, and elsewhere.
242. Duncker's experiment and functional fixedness: Duncker, 1945.
242-43. Rusty pipe and Ping-Pong ball experiment: Described by the late John Arnold of MIT in personal communication; see Hunt, 1955.
243-44. Water-jar experiment: Luchins, 1946.
244-45. Maier's experiments: Maier, 1945.
245. Wallas, 1926.
245-46. Polya's difficult anagram is discussed in Polya, 1973, pp. 160-62.
246-47. The decision tree and the tumor problem: Duncker, 1945.
248-49. The decision tree in the three-disc Tower of Hanoi problem is my own simplified version. For a complete version of the tree in a two-disc problem, see Raphael, 1976, p. 81; a complete three-disc tree would be many times larger.
248-50. Tower of Hanoi problems: Simon, 1976; Wickelgren, 1974, pp. 103-4. The trillion-year figure is from Raphael, 1976, p. 80. Talking out loud while solving Tower of Hanoi problems: Gagné and Smith, 1962.
250. Number of moves in all possible chess games: Simon and Newell, 1971.
252. Minsky's dissenting view: Minsky, 1977*b* and 1974.
252. The two-train problem is quoted in Mayer, 1977, pp. 100-1, from M. I. Posner, *Cognition, An Introduction* (Glenview, Ill.: Scott, Foresman, 1973).
254-55. Newell and Simon's graph of the protocol from Newell and Simon, 1972, p. 181, omits the left-most line running more than halfway down; Lindsay and Norman, 1977, from whom Figure 49 is reprinted, have added it.
254. a computer so programmed in 1969 . . . while today's far faster computers: The 1969 figure is from Simon, 1970, p. 27; the figure for today's computers is my own, based on the performance of IBM's model 3033.
256-58. The information-processing description of human problem solving is drawn chiefly from Newell and Simon, 1972, pp. 796-98, and elsewhere in the same work.
256. The hot-water/cold-water example is from Johnson-Laird and Wason, 1977, p. 13.
256. Edison's trial-and-error efforts: Conot, 1979, pp. 157, 161.
257. BISETUAL: The anagram is my own, but the estimate as to how quickly most people would solve it is based on one of similar length discussed in Glass, Holyoak, and Santa, 1979, p. 405-6.
257. Analogy as a heuristic: See Index listings of analogical reasoning and of metaphor.

257. "best-first search": Newell and Simon, 1976.
258. "means-end analysis": Newell and Simon, 1972, passim; Simon, 1978. The Chinese dinner example is from Glass, Holyoak, and Santa, 1979, p. 409.
258. Anzai and Simon, 1978.
259. One might argue that this doesn't really prove: Anderson, 1976, pp. 5–15.
261. The comparative speed with which experts and novices solve problems: Simon and Simon, 1978.
261–62. Larkin and Reif, 1979.
262–63. Hierarchical organization: Reif, 1977 and 1979.
262–63. Eylon's work: Eylon, 1979.
263–66. See List of Cited Sources for papers by P. E. Johnson, and P. E. Johnson and colleagues; also, Swanson, Feltovich, and Johnson, 1977. Greeno's comment: Greeno, 1980.
266. Larkin's comment: Larkin, 1980.
269. scattered reports of improved grades . . . rises in scores on IQ tests: Whimbey, 1977; Whimbey and Lochhead, personal communications.
270. The Buddhist monk problem is presented in Glass, Holyoak, and Santa, 1979, pp. 401–2; I have slightly abridged it here.

**CHAPTER EIGHT (pp. 272–314)**

272. Picasso's statements: The first is in Stein, 1974, p. 30, the second in Ghiselin, 1952, p. 57; in each case, the original sources are cited.
273. Unconscious control of routine behavior: Norman, 1979a.
273–74. The schizophrenic patient: McGhie and Chapman, 1961.
275–76. Freud's views and interest: Freud, "The Unconscious," 1915, in vol. XIV of the standard edition of his *Complete Psychological Works* (Hogarth Press).
276. some prominent cognitive scientists: Nisbett and Wilson, 1977.
276–77. The Nisbett experiment: Personal communication, but also recounted in Nisbett and Wilson, 1977.
278–79. The Watson quote is from Watson, 1930, p. 247.
279. the human mind *transforms* the old: Guilford, 1967, p. 319.
279. The current state of creativity theory: Amabile, 1980b.
280. most reasonably well-educated people: Stein, 1974, p. 40.
282. The lack of objective criteria in judging creativity test answers: Amabile, 1980a.
282–83. The Guilford story: Guilford, 1967, p. 148.
283. The architects: MacKinnon, 1961.
283. Amabile, 1980b.
284. Traits of creative persons: Stein, 1974, pp. 58–60.
285. Intelligence and creativity: Hayes, 1978, pp. 220–21.
285–86. Age and creativity: Lehman, 1953; Kuhn, 1970, p. 90; Arieti, 1976, pp. 382–83.
286. Older scientists and the "reward system": S. Cole, 1979.
286–88. Cognitive styles are discussed in many texts. For the study using the test on pp. 286–87, see Westcott, 1961.
287. Field dependence: See Guilford, 1967, pp. 179–80, for brief discussion and sources.
287–88. Narrow and broad categorizing: Cropley, 1967, pp. 34–43.
288. Divergent production: Guilford, 1967, chap. 6.
288–90. Failure of creativity tests to correlate with real-life creativity: Hayes, 1978a, pp. 225–26.
290–91. Analogy and metaphor: Pollio et al., 1977, passim.
291. Einstein and the ray of light: Einstein, 1970 [1949], p. 53; Dreisdadt, 1968, p. 107.
293. Leaps of thought by psychotics and by creative persons: Arieti, 1976, pp. 7–8, 113.
293. The patient at Pilgrim State Hospital: Hunt, 1962, pp. 43–44.

295.    Helmholtz: Stein, 1974, pp. 13–14.
295–96. The four stages: I have drawn freely from Arieti, 1976, Guilford, 1967, Hayes, 1978a, and Stein, 1974.
297.    Amy Lowell: Ghiselin, 1952, pp. 109–12.
297.    Maier's subjects: Nisbett and Wilson, 1977.
298.    Amy Lowell: See note to p. 297.
299.    The interrupted task: Fulgosi and Guilford, 1968.
299.    Simon's explanation of incubation effect: Simon, 1966.
300.    Ill-defined problem: Reitman, 1964; Simon, 1973.
300.    *Find the one regular item among a set of odd ones:* Hayes, 1978, pp. 211–12.
301.    Canfield Fisher: in Ghiselin, 1952, pp. 168–76.
301.    The Hawthorne experiment: Roethlisberger and Dickson, 1939.
301.    Neisser, 1963.
302–03. The continuing interaction between unconscious and conscious mind: Pine, 1959; Arieti, 1976, passim (see his index heading "tertiary process").
302.    Tchaikovsky's statement is in letters of February 17 (March 1), 1878, and June 25 (July 7), 1878.
303.    Henry Miller's statement is in Ghiselin, 1952, p. 183.
303–04. Hayes and Flower, 1978.
308.    Knowledge as a prerequisite: Hayes, 1978, p. 237; Arieti, 1976, pp. 373–75.
308.    Loewi, 1953.
309.    Arnold's printing problem: Guilford, 1967, p. 325.
309–10. Gordon's work: Stein, 1974, pp. 200–1; Gordon, 1961, passim.
310.    Use of the ridiculous: Cited by Stein, 1974, pp. 221–22.
311.    But this claim seems excessive: Guilford, 1967, p. 332.
311.    Schiller's famous quote: Brill, 1938, p. 193.
311.    Osborn's checklist appears in Whiting, 1958, p. 62.
312.    Group problem solving and group stimulation of creativity are dealt with in Stein, 1975, passim.
313.    Torrance, 1962, pp. 8, 78.
313.    Pressure on teachers to be conventional: Torrance et al., 1964, p. 33.
314.    Amabile's two possible answers are in an early draft of Amabile, 1980b, and do not appear in the shorter final version.

## CHAPTER NINE (pp. 315–361)

315–16. The incident at Bolt Beranek and Newman: Bobrow's account, quoted in McCorduck, 1979, p. 225n.
316.    ELIZA/DOCTOR: Weizenbaum, 1976, pp. 2–10, 189; Alexander, 1978; Hayes, 1978, p. 161.
317.    perform a number of sophisticated tasks: Most of those listed here are discussed later in the chapter; the rest are common news items.
318.    Jastrow: Quoted in Jastrow, 1981.
318.    Fredkin: Quoted in McCorduck, 1979, pp. 349, 351.
318.    Minsky: Quoted in Jastrow, 1981.
318–19. what matters is not the hardware . . . mind is mind: Simon, 1970, p. 18, and many others.
322–23. Shannon: Quoted in McCorduck, 1979, p. 103.
324.    The Internal Revenue Service data were furnished by the IRS Public Affairs Office.
325.    The Logic Theorist work is recounted in Newell, Shaw, and Simon, 1963, and in Newell and Simon, 1972, pp. 105–40.
325.    On one of today's computers: Newell and Simon, 1972, p. 138, say that modern machines are a hundred times faster than JOHNNIAC, but between 1972 and 1981 there has been an increase of roughly tenfold in speed.
325–26. General Problem Solver is described in Newell and Simon, 1972, pp. 455–502, and pp. 853–54 (where the river-crossing problem appears).

327. five plies: Newell and Simon, 1972, use thirty possibilities per move as an average; others (see for instance, "Science and the Citizen," *Scientific American*, April 1981) use the figure thirty-five. Five plies, at thirty possibilities, would give about twenty million positions; at thirty-five, about fifty million.

327. only those that looked promising: Berliner, 1973.

327. Simon's 1957 prediction: McCorduck, 1979, p. 187 (the paper was published in 1958).

327. Simon's present-day explanation: McCorduck, 1979, p. 189.

327. Berliner's prediction: "Follow-Up on the News," *The New York Times*, January 11, 1981.

327. can beat 99.5 percent: Levy, 1978.

327. The reversion to brute force: Ken Thompson, Bell Labs, personal communication.

327-29. The mutilated checkerboard problem: Newell and Simon, 1976.

329. Belle: Ken Thompson, Bell Labs, personal communication; also, "Science and the Citizen," *Scientific American*, April 1981.

330-32. DENDRAL: Buchanan, Sutherland, and Feigenbaum, 1969.

331. MYCIN: Winston, 1977, pp. 241-45.

331-32. MEDINFO: Johnson, Severance, and Feltovich, 1979.

332. The computerized interview for suicide detection: Greist et al. [n.d.; ca. 1979].

332. The accent-dependent program at Stanford: Raphael, 1976, p. 281n.

333. we are very much better than they at "matching": Norman, 1978.

333. the major direction of AI research: McCorduck, 1979, pp 228-29, 237-38; Herbert Simon, personal communication; Goldstein and Papert, 1977.

334. Hayes' examples: Hayes, 1978, pp. 167-68.

334-36. Winston, 1977, pp. 357-63.

338. The human mind recognizes shapes: Lindsay and Norman, 1977, pp. 10-11.

340. Winston, 1977, p. 227.

340. The difficulties of scene analysis in the real world: Shaw and Pittenger, 1978.

341-42. The general description of human language processing is drawn from Clark and Clark, 1977, pp. 49-79; some details come from Shankweiler, Strange, and Verbrugge, 1977.

342-43. SAM: Schank, 1978a; Nelson, 1978.

343. HEARSAY: Reddy and Newell, 1974; Norman, 1978.

343-45. HARPY: Newell, 1978; Norman, 1978.

345. The IBM system: "Science and the Citizen," *Scientific American*, October 1980.

345. Human superiority to HARPY: Norman, 1978.

350. Sussman's comments: Sussman, 1975, pp. 118, 121.

353. Weizenbaum, 1976, p. 214-16.

353. The simulation of parallel processing: Herbert Simon and others, personal communications. Simon believes the mind does "time sharing," like the computer. Many others, especially at the University of California at San Diego, believe in the simultaneity and multiplicity of human thought. See also Neisser, 1963.

353-54. Lack of consciousness in computers: Dreyfus, 1972; Dreyfus, quoted in McCorduck, 1979, chap. 9.

354. rudimentary explanation of consciousness: Mandler, 1975; Newell, Minsky, and Margaret Boden, separately, cited by McCorduck, 1979, pp. 339-343.

355. Hofstadter, 1980, p. 709.

355. McCorduck, 1979, p. 262; McCarthy, 1979.

358. an intrinsic characteristic of our nervous system: Weimer, 1977.

361. Weizenbaum, 1976, passim, but especially chaps. 8-10.

# A LIST OF CITED SOURCES

This is a guide to those sources cited in the Notes or referred to in the text. A proper bibliography would be many times as long as the following list; any reader who wants to pursue the subject further can find such bibliographies in those recent textbooks of cognitive science prefaced by an asterisk (*).

Alexander, G. "Terminal Therapy." *Psychol. Today*, September 1978.

Amabile, T. M. 1980a. "A New Approach to the Assessment of Creativity." Paper. Waltham, Mass.: Brandeis University, 1980.

———. 1980b. "A New Model for Creativity Research." Paper. Waltham, Mass.: Brandeis University [n.d., 1980].

Anderson, J. R. *Language, Memory, and Thought*. Hillsdale, N.J.: Lawrence Erlbaum, 1976.

Anzai, Y., and H. A. Simon. "The Theory of Learning by Doing." Pittsburgh: Carnegie-Mellon University, 1978. *Computer Information Processing Working Paper* No. 386.

Arendt, H. *The Life of the Mind:* Vol. 1: *Thinking*. New York: Harcourt Brace Jovanovich, 1977, 1978.

Arieti, S. *Creativity: The Magic Synthesis*. New York: Basic Books, 1976.

Aronson, E. "The Rationalizing Animal." *Psychol. Today*, May 1973.

Axelrod, R. "Argumentation in Foreign Policy Settings." *J. Conflict Resolution* 21 (1977): 727–55.

Berlin, B. "Ethnobiological Classification." In Rosch and Lloyd, 1978.

Berliner, H. J. "Some Necessary Conditions for a Master Chess Program." In *Third International Joint Conference on Artificial Intelligence*. Stanford, Calif.: Stanford Research Institute, 1973.

Bonner, J. T. *The Evolution of Culture in Animals*. Princeton, N.J.: Princeton University Press, 1980.

Bornstein, M. H. "Perceptual Development: Stability and Change in Feature Perception." In Bornstein and Kessen, 1979.

———, and W. Kessen, eds. *Psychological Development from Infancy*. Hillsdale, N.J.: Lawrence Erlbaum, 1979.

Bower, G. H. 1978a. "Experiments on Story Comprehension and Recall." *Discourse Processes* 1 (1978): 211–31.

————. 1978*b*. "Contacts of Cognitive Psychology with Social Learning Theory." *Cognitive Therapy and Research* 2 (1978): 147–64.

————; A. M. Lesgold; and D. Tieman. "Grouping Operations in Free Recall." *J. Verbal Learning and Verbal Behavior* 8 (1969): 481–93.

Brill, A. A., ed. *The Basic Writings of Sigmund Freud.* New York: Random House, 1938.

Brown, R. *Social Psychology.* New York: Free Press, 1965.

Bruner, J. S. "Learning the Mother Tongue." *Human Nature,* September 1978.

————; J. J. Goodnow; and G. A. Austin. *A Study of Thinking.* New York: Wiley, 1956.

Bucci, W. "The Interpretation of Universal Affirmative Propositions." *Cognition* 6 (1978): 55–77.

Buchanan, B.; G. Sutherland; and E. A. Feigenbaum. "Heuristic DENDRAL: A Program for Generating Hypotheses in Organic Chemistry." In *Machine Intelligence 4,* edited by B. Meltzer and Donald Michie. New York: American Elsevier, 1969.

Bugelski, B. R. *Empirical Studies in the Psychology of Learning.* Indianapolis: Hackett, 1975.

Bullock, M., and R. Gelman. "Preschool Children's Assumptions About Cause and Effect: Temporal Ordering." *Child Development* 50 (1979): 89–96.

————; ————; and E. Meck. "Young Children's Understanding of Object and Action in Simple Event Sequences." Paper presented at Society for Research in Child Development meeting, San Francisco, March 1979.

Burtt, H. E. "An Experimental Study of Early Childhood Memory: Final Report." *Journal of Genetic Psychology* 58 (1941): 435–39.

Butterfield, E. C., and G. N. Siperstein. "Influence of Contingent Auditory Stimulation upon Non-Nutritional Suckle." *Proceedings Third Symposium on Oral Sensation and Perception.* Springfield, Ill.: Charles C. Thomas, 1974.

Calder, A. "Constructive Mathematics." *Scientific American,* October 1979.

Carbonell, J. "Ideological Belief System Simulation." New Haven: Yale University Department of Computer Science, May 1977. Research Report #111.

————. "POLITICS: Automated Ideological Reasoning." *Cog. Science* 2 (1978): 27–51.

Castellan, N. J., Jr.; D. B. Pisoni; and G. R. Potts, eds. *Cognitive Theory,* vol. 2. Hillsdale, N.J.: Lawrence Erlbaum, 1977.

Ceraso, J. "The Interference Theory of Forgetting." *Scientific American,* October 1967.

Chapman, L. J., and J. P. Chapman. "The Genesis of Popular but Erroneous Psychodiagnostic Observations." *Journal of Abnormal Psychology* 72 (1967): 193–204.

Chase, W. G., and H. A. Simon. "Perception in Chess." *Cog. Psychol.* 4 (1974): 55–81.

Chomsky, N. *Syntactic Structures.* The Hague: Mouton, 1957.

————. Review of B. F. Skinner's *Verbal Behavior. Language* 35 (1959): 26–58.

————. *Reflections on Language.* New York: Pantheon, 1975.

Clark, E. "What's in a Word? On the Child's Acquisition of Semantics in His First

Language." In *Cognitive Development and the Acquisition of Language*, edited by T. E. Moore. New York: Academic, 1973.

———, and H. H. Clark. "When Nouns Surface as Verbs." *Language* 55 (1979): 767–811.

Clark, H. 1977*a*. "Inferences in Comprehension." In *Basic Processes in Reading*, edited by D. LaBerge and S. J. Samuels. Hillsdale, N.J.: Lawrence Erlbaum, 1977.

———. 1977*b*. "Linguistic Processes in Reasoning." In Johnson-Laird and Wason, 1977.

———. "Inferring What Is Meant." In *Studies in the Perception of Language*, edited by W. J. M. Levelt and G. B. Flores. London: Wiley, 1978.

———, and W. G. Chase. "On the Process of Comparing Sentences Against Pictures." *Cog. Psychol.* (1972): 472–517.

———, and E. V. Clark. *Psychology and Language*. New York: Harcourt Brace Jovanovich, 1977.

Clark, R. W. *Einstein: The Life and Times*. London: Hodder and Staughton, 1973.

Clement, J.; J. Lochhead; and G. Monk. "Translation Difficulties in Learning Mathematics." Paper. [Amherst, Mass.: University of Massachusetts, Department of Physics], September 1979.

Cohler, B. J. "Adult Developmental Psychology and Reconstruction in Psychoanalysis." In *The Course of Life*, edited by S. Greenspan and G. Pollock. Washington, D.C.: U.S. Government Printing Office, 1981.

Cole, M., and S. Scribner. "Cross-Cultural Studies of Memory and Cognition." In *Perspectives on the Development of Memory and Cognition*, edited by R. V. Kail, Jr., and J. W. Hagen. Hillsdale, N.J.: Lawrence Erlbaum, 1977.

———; D. W. Sharp; and C. Lave. "The Cognitive Consequences of Education: Some Empirical Evidence and Theoretical Misgivings." *Urban Review* 9 (1976): 218–33.

Cole, S. "Age and Scientific Performance." *American Journal of Sociology* 84 (1979): 958–77.

Collins, A. *Studies of Plausible Reasoning: Final Report, October 1976 to February 1978*. Vol. 1: *Human Plausible Reasoning*. [Cambridge, Mass.: Bolt Beranek Newman], BBN Report No. 3810.

———. "Fragments of a Theory of Human Plausible Reasoning." Paper delivered at colloquium, University of Minnesota, Minneapolis, April 1979.

———, and E. Loftus. "A Spreading Activation Theory of Semantic Processing." *Psychol. Rev.* 82 (1975): 407–28.

———, and M. R. Quillian. "Retrieval Time from Semantic Memory." *J. Verbal Learning and Verbal Behavior* 8 (1969): 240–47.

Conot, R. *A Streak of Luck*. New York: Seaview, 1979.

Copi, I. *Introduction to Logic*. New York: Macmillan, 1972.

Cotton, J. W., and R. L. Klatzky, eds. *Semantic Factors in Cognition*. Hillsdale, N.J.: Lawrence Erlbaum, 1978.

Cowan, W. M. "The Development of the Brain." *Scientific American*, September 1979.

Craik, F. I. M., and R. S. Lockhart. "Levels of Processing: A Framework for Memory Research." *J. Verbal Learning and Verbal Behavior* 11 (1972): 671–84.

Crick, F. H. C. "Thinking About the Brain." *Scientific American*, September 1979.

Cropley, A. J. *Creativity.* London: Longmans, Green, 1967.

Crowder, R. G. "Audition and Speech Coding in Short-Term Memory: A Tutorial Review." In *Attention and Performance, VII*, edited by J. Requin. Hillsdale, N.J.: Lawrence Erlbaum, 1978.

Curtiss, S., et al. "An Update on the Linguistic Development of Genie." In *Georgetown University Roundtable in Language and Linguistics*, edited by D. P. Data. Washington, D.C.: Georgetown University Press, 1975.

Dale, L. G. "The Growth of Systematic Thinking: Replication and Analysis of Piaget's First Chemical Experiment." *Australian Journal of Psychology* 22 (1970): 277–86.

Darwin, C. J.; M. T. Turvey; and R. G. Crowder. "An Auditory Analogue of the Sperling Partial-Report Procedure: Evidence for Brief Auditory Storage." *Cog. Psychol.* 3 (1972): 255–67.

Deese, J., and R. A. Kaufman. "Serial Effects on Recall of Unorganized and Sequentially Organized Verbal Material." *J. Experim. Psychol.* 54 (1957): 180–87.

de Villiers, J. G., and P. A. de Villiers. *Language Acquisition.* Cambridge, Mass.: Harvard University Press, 1978.

di Sessa, A. "Intuition as Knowledge: A Clinical Study of the Cognitive Basis of Elementary College Physics." Project proposal submitted to the National Science Foundation. [Cambridge, Mass.: MIT, ca. 1977.]

Doctorow, E. L. *Ragtime.* New York: Random House, 1974, 1975.

Dreisdadt, R. "An Analysis of the Use of Analogies and Metaphors in Science." *Journal of Psychology* 68 (1968): 97–116.

Dreyfus, H. *What Computers Can't Do: A Critique of Artificial Reason.* New York: Harper & Row, 1972.

Duncker, K. "On Problem Solving." *Psychol. Monographs* 58, whole no. 270 (1945).

Einstein, A. "Autobiographical Notes." In *Albert Einstein: Philosopher-Scientist*, edited by P. A. Schilpp. London: Cambridge University Press, 1970.

――――. "On the Generalized Theory of Gravitation." *Scientific American*, April 1950.

Ekstrand, B., and L. E. Bourne, eds. *Principles and Meanings of Psychology: Readings.* Hinsdale, Ill.: Dryden, 1974.

Epstein, W. "The Influence of Syntactical Structure on Learning." *Am. J. Psychol.* 74 (1961): 80–85.

Ericsson, K. A.; W. G. Chase; and S. Faloon. "Acquisition of a Memory Skill." *Science* 208 (June 1980): 1181–82.

Estes, W. K., ed. *Handbook of Learning and Cognitive Processes.* Vol. 5: *Human Information Processing.* Hillsdale, N.J.: Lawrence Erlbaum, 1978.

Eylon, B. "Effects of Knowledge Organization on Task Performance." Ph.D. dissertation, University of California at Berkeley, 1979.

Fagan, J. F. "Infants' Delayed Recognition Memory and Forgetting." *Journal of Experimental Child Psychology* 16 (1973): 424–50.

Falmagne, R. J., ed. *Reasoning: Representation and Process.* Hillsdale N.J.: Lawrence Erlbaum, 1975.

Farb, P. *Humankind.* Boston: Houghton Mifflin, 1978.

Feldman, H.; S. Goldin-Meadow; and L. Gleitman. "Beyond Herodotus: The Creation of Language by Linguistically Deprived Deaf Children." In *Action, Gesture, and Symbol: The Emergence of Language,* edited by A. Lock. New York: Academic, 1978.

Flavell, J. H. *The Developmental Psychology of Jean Piaget.* Princeton, N.J.: D. Van Nostrand, 1963.

———. "Metacognitive Aspects of Problem Solving." In Resnick, 1976.

Fodor, J. "The Mind-Body Problem." *Scientific American,* January 1981.

Fried, L. S., and K. J. Holyoak. "Learning Fuzzy Perceptual Categories: Is Feedback Necessary?" Paper presented at nineteenth meeting of the Psychonomic Society, San Antonio, November 1978.

———, and ———. "Induction of Category Distributions: A Framework for Classification Learning." Chicago/Michigan Cognitive Science Technical Report, 1981.

Fulgosi, A., and J. P. Guilford. "Short-term Incubation in Divergent Production." *Am. J. Psychol.* 7 (1968): 1016–23.

Furst, C. *Origins of the Mind: Mind-Brain Connections.* Englewood Cliffs, N.J.: Prentice-Hall, 1979.

Gagné, R. M., and E. C. Smith. "A Study of the Effects of Verbalization on Problem Solving." *J. Experim. Psychol.* 63 (1962): 12–18.

Gardner, H. "Strange Loops of the Mind." *Psychol. Today,* March 1980.

Gardner, M. "Monkey Business" (review of H. S. Terrace, *Nim,* and T. A. Sebeok and D. J. Umiker-Sebeok, *Speaking of Apes*). *The New York Review,* March 20, 1980.

Gelman, R. 1972*a.* "The Nature and Development of Early Number Concepts." *Advances in Child Development and Behavior* 7 (1972): 115–67.

———. 1972*b.* "Logical Capacity of Very Young Children: Number Invariance Rules." *Child Development* 43 (1972): 75–90.

———. "How Young Children Reason About Small Numbers." In Castellan, Pisoni, and Potts, 1977.

———. "Cognitive Development." *Annual Review of Psychology* 29 (1978): 297–332.

———. "Preschool Thought." *Am. Psychologist* 34 (1979): 900–5.

Gentner, D. 1979*a.* "Coach: A Schema-Based Tutor." Paper. University of California at San Diego, 1979.

———. 1979*b.* "Toward an Intelligent Computer Tutor." In *Procedures for Instructional Systems Development,* edited by Harold F. O'Neil. New York: Academic, 1979.

Geschwind, N. 1979*a.* "Neurological Knowledge and Complex Behaviors." Paper delivered at La Jolla Conference (University of California at San Diego) on Cognitive Science, 1979.

———. 1979*b.* "Specializations of the Human Brain." *Scientific American,* September 1979.

Ghiselin, B., ed. *The Creative Process: A Symposium*. New York: New American Library [n.d., originally published 1952].

Ginsburg, H., and S. Opper. *Piaget's Theory of Intellectual Development: An Introduction*. Englewood Cliffs, N.J.: Prentice-Hall, 1969.

°Glass, A.; K. J. Holyoak; and J. L. Santa. *Cognition*. Reading, Mass.: Addison-Wesley, 1979.

Goldstein, I., and S. Papert. "Artificial Intelligence, Language, and the Study of Knowledge." *Cog. Science* 1 (1977): 84–123.

Gordon, W. J. J. *Synectics*. New York: Harper & Row, 1961.

Gough, P. B., and M. J. Cosky. "One Second of Reading Again." In Castellan, Pisoni, and Potts, 1977.

Greeno, J. G. "Trends in the Theory of Knowledge for Problem Solving." In Tuma and Reif, 1980.

Greenough, W. T., and J. M. Juraska. "Synaptic Pruning." *Psychol. Today*, July 1979.

Greist, J. H., et al. "Suicide Risk Prediction by Computer Interview: A Prospective Study." Document. University of Wisconsin. U.S. Public Health Service Grant MH-21348 (NIMH) [n.d., ca. 1979].

Grings, W. W.; A. M. Schell; and C. A. Carey. "Verbal Control of an Autonomic Response in a Cue Reversal Situation." *J. Experim. Psychol.* 99 (1973): 215–21.

Guilford, J. P. *The Nature of Human Intelligence*. New York: McGraw-Hill, 1967.

Gurman, A. S., and D. P. Kniskern. "Behavioral Marriage Therapy: II. Empirical Perspective." *Family Process* 17 (1978): 139–47 and 165–80.

———, and R. M. Knudson. "Behavioral Marriage Therapy: I. A Psychodynamic-Systems Analysis and Critique." *Family Process* 17 (1978): 121–38.

Hartmann, E. "L-Trypotophan—the Sleeping Pill of the Future?" *Psychol. Today*, December 1978.

°Hayes, J. R. *Cognitive Psychology: Thinking and Creating*. Homewood, Ill.: Dorsey, 1978.

———, and L. S. Flower. "Identifying the Organization of Writing Processes." Paper. Pittsburgh: Carnegie-Mellon University [1977].

———, and ———. "Protocol Analysis of Writing Processes." Paper presented at 1978 meeting of American Educational Research Association, Toronto.

———, and H. A. Simon. "Psychological Differences Among Problem Isomorphs." In Castellan, Pisoni, and Potts, 1977.

Hazen, N. L.; J. J. Lockman; and H. L. Pick, Jr. "The Development of Children's Representations of Large-scale Environments." *Child Development* 49 (1978): 623–36.

Heider, E. R. "Universals in Color Naming and Memory." *J. Experim. Psychol.* 93 (1972): 10–12.

———, and D. Olivier. "The Structure of the Color Space in Naming and Memory for Two Languages." *Cog. Psychol.* 3 (1972): 337–54.

Heisenberg, W. *Physics and Beyond*. New York: Harper & Row, 1971.

Herman, J. B. "Cognitive Processing of Persuasive Communications." *Organizational Behavior and Human Performance* 19 (1977): 126–47.

Herzog, E., and C. E. Sudia. *Boys in Fatherless Families*. U.S. Department of

Health, Education, and Welfare, DHEW Publication No. (OCD) 72-33. Washington, D.C.: U.S. Government Printing Office, 1971.

*Hintzman, D. L. *The Psychology of Learning and Memory.* San Francisco: W. H. Freeman, 1978.

Hofstadter, D. *Gödel, Escher, Bach: an Eternal Golden Braid.* New York: Vintage, 1980.

Hogan, D. R. "The Effectiveness of Sex Therapy. A Review of the Literature." In *Handbook of Sex Therapy,* edited by J. LoPiccolo and L. LoPiccolo. New York: Plenum, 1978.

Holsti, O. R., and A. L. George. "The Effects of Stress on the Performance of Foreign Policy-Makers." *Political Science Annual* 6 (1975): 255–319.

Horn, G., and R. A. Hinde, eds. *Short-Term Changes in Neural Activity and Behaviour.* New York: Cambridge University Press, 1970.

Horn, J. L. "Intelligence—Why It Grows, Why It Declines." *Trans-action,* November 1967.

Hubel, D. H. "The Brain." *Scientific American,* September 1979.

Huizinga, J. *Homo Ludens: A Study of the Play Element in Culture.* Boston: Beacon, 1950.

Hunt, M. "The Course Where Students Lose Their Earthly Shackles." *Life,* May 16, 1955.

———. *Mental Hospital.* New York: Pyramid, 1962.

———. "Man and Beast." In *Man and Aggression,* edited by A. Montagu. New York: Oxford University Press, 1973.

Huttenlocher, J. "Language and Intelligence." In Resnick, 1976.

Inhelder, B. "Language and Thought: Some Remarks on Chomsky and Piaget." *Journal of Psycholinguistic Research* 7 (1978): 263–68.

Iversen, L. L. "The Chemistry of the Brain." *Scientific American,* September 1979.

Jastrow, R. "The Post-Human World." *Science Digest,* January–February 1981.

Jeffrey, R. C. *Formal Logic: Its Scope and Limits.* New York: McGraw-Hill, 1967.

Jeffries, R. "The Acquisition of Expertise on Simple Puzzles." Paper delivered at 1979 meeting of American Educational Research Association, San Francisco.

Johanson, D., and M. Edey. *Lucy: The Beginnings of Humankind.* New York: Simon and Schuster, 1981.

Johnson, P. E. "Expert Problem Solving: Theory and Data from the Diagnosis of Congenital Heart Disease." Paper delivered at 1979 meeting of American Educational Research Association, San Francisco.

———; D. G. Severance; and P. J. Feltovich. "Design of Decision Support Systems in Medicine." In *Proceedings 12th Hawaii International Conference on System Sciences,* edited by B. Shriver et al. 3 (1979): 105–18.

——— et al. "Expertise in Oral Advocacy: An Enquiry into Its Nature and Development." Paper. University of Minnesota, Center for Research in Human Learning, 1978.

Johnson-Laird, P. N. "Mental Models in Cognitive Science." Paper presented at La Jolla Conference (University of California at San Diego) on Cognitive Science, 1979.

## 388   A LIST OF CITED SOURCES

°————, and P. C. Wason, eds. *Thinking: Readings in Cognitive Science.* Cambridge, England: Cambridge University Press, 1977.

Kagan, J. "Do Infants Think?" *Scientific American,* March 1972.

————. "Structure and Process in the Human Infant: The Ontogeny of Mental Representation." In Bornstein and Kessen, 1979.

————, and E. Havemann. *Psychology: An Introduction.* New York: Harcourt Brace Jovanovich, 1972.

————; R. B. Kearsley; and P. R. Zelazo. *Infancy: Its Place in Human Development.* Cambridge, Mass.: Harvard University Press, 1978.

Kahneman, D., and A. Tversky. "Subjective Probability: A Judgment of Representativeness." *Cog. Psychol.* 3 (1972): 430–54.

————, and ————. "On the Psychology of Prediction." *Psychol. Rev.* 80 (1973): 237–51.

Kantowitz, B. H., ed. *Human Information Processing: Tutorials in Performance and Cognition.* Hillsdale, N.J.: Lawrence Erlbaum, 1974.

Karplus, E. F.; R. Karplus; and W. Wollman. "Intellectual Development Beyond Elementary School IV: Ratio, the Influence of Cognitive Style." *School Science and Mathematics* 74 (1974): 476–82.

Karplus, R. "Science Teaching and the Development of Reasoning." *Journal of Research in Science Teaching* 14 (1977): 169–75.

————. "Teaching for the Development of Reasoning." In *The Psychology of Teaching for Thinking and Creativity,* edited by A. E. Lawson. Columbus, Ohio: EIRC-SMEAC, 1979.

————, et al. "Proportional Reasoning and Control of Variables in Seven Countries." Berkeley: University of California, 1975. AESOP Report ID-25.

Keating, D. P. "Toward a Multivariate Developmental Theory of Intelligence." In *Intellectual Development Beyond Childhood,* edited by D. Kuhn. San Francisco: Jossey-Bass, 1979.

Koestler, A. *The Act of Creation.* New York: Dell, 1964.

Kogan, N. *Cognitive Styles in Infancy and Early Childhood.* Hillsdale, N.J.: Lawrence Erlbaum, 1976.

Köhler, W. *Gestalt Psychology.* New York: Liveright, 1929.

Korchin, S. J. *Modern Clinical Psychology.* New York: Basic Books, 1976.

Kosslyn, S. M. "Information Representation in Visual Images." *Cog. Psychol.* 7 (1975): 341–70.

————. "Measuring the Visual Angle of the Mind's Eye." *Cog. Psychol.* 10 (1978): 356–89.

————, and S. N. Alper. "On the Pictorial Properties of Visual Images: Effect of Image Size on Memory for Words." *Canadian Journal of Psychology* 31 (1977): 32–40.

————, and J. R. Pomerantz. "Imagery, Propositions, and the Form of Internal Representations." *Cog. Psychol.* 9 (1977): 52–76.

Krauss, R. M., and S. Glucksberg. "Social and Nonsocial Speech." *Scientific American,* February 1977.

Kuhn, T. S. *The Structure of Scientific Revolutions.* Chicago: University of Chicago Press, 1970.

Labov, W. "The Boundaries of Words and Their Meanings." In *New Ways of An-*

*alyzing Variation in English,* edited by C.-J. N. Bailey and R. W. Shuy. Washington, D.C.: Georgetown University Press, 1973.

°Lachman, R.; J. L. Lachman; and E. C. Butterfield. *Cognitive Psychology and Information Processing: An Introduction.* Hillsdale, N.J.: Lawrence Erlbaum, 1979.

Lakoff, G., and M. Johnson. "Toward an Experientialist Philosophy: The Case from Literal Metaphor." Paper presented at La Jolla Conference (University of California at San Diego) on Cognitive Science, 1979.

Langley, P. "BACON 1: A General Discovery System." Pittsburgh: Carnegie-Mellon University Department of Psychology, 1978. Computer Information Processing Working Paper No. 383.

Larkin, J. "Teaching Problem Solving in Physics: The Psychological Laboratory and the Practical Classroom." In Tuma and Reif, 1980.

―――, and F. Reif. "Understanding and Teaching Problem Solving in Physics." *European Journal of Science Education* 1 (1979): 191–203.

Lassen, N. A.; D. H. Ingvar; and E. Skinhøj. "Brain Function and Blood Flow." *Scientific American,* October 1978.

Leakey, R. E., and R. Lewin. "Origins of the Mind." *Psychol. Today,* July 1978.

Lehman, H. C. *Age and Achievement.* Princeton, N.J.: Princeton University Press, 1953.

Levay, A. N., and A. Kagle. "A Study of Treatment Needs Following Sex Therapy." *American Journal of Psychiatry* 134 (1977): 970–73.

Levine, M. *A Cognitive Theory of Learning: Research on Hypothesis Testing.* Hillsdale, N.J.: Lawrence Erlbaum, 1975.

Levy, D. "Man Beats Machine." *Chess Life & Rev.,* November 1978.

°Lindsay, P. H., and D. A. Norman. *Human Information Processing: An Introduction.* New York: Academic, 1977.

Lochhead, J. "An Introduction to Cognitive-Processing Instruction." Paper presented at University of Massachusetts, Amherst, Conference on Cognitive Process Instruction, 1978.

―――. "An Anarchistic Approach to Teaching Problem Solving Methods." Paper presented at 1979 meeting of American Educational Research Association, San Francisco.

Loewi, O. *From the Workshop of Discoveries.* Lawrence, Kans.: University of Kansas Press, 1953.

Loftus, E. F. "The Incredible Eyewitness." *Psychol. Today,* December 1974.

―――. "Leading Questions and the Eyewitness Report." *Cog. Psychol.* 7 (1975): 560–72.

―――. *Memory.* Reading, Mass.: Addison-Wesley, 1980.

―――; D. G. Miller; and H. J. Burns. "Semantic Integration of Verbal Information into a Visual Memory." *J. Experim. Psychol.* 4 (1978): 19–31.

Loftus, G. R., and E. F. Loftus. *Human Memory: The Processing of Information.* Hillsdale, N.J.: Lawrence Erlbaum, 1976.

Lovell, K. "A Follow-Up Study of Inhelder and Piaget's *The Growth of Logical Thinking.*" *Brit. J. Psychol.* 52 (1961): 143–53.

Lowes, J. L. *The Road to Xanadu.* Boston: Houghton Mifflin, 1927.

Luchins, A. S. "Classroom Experiments on Mental Set." *Am. J. Psychol.* 59 (1946): 295–98.

Luria, A. R. *The Mind of a Mnemonist.* Chicago: Regnery, 1976.

Lyons, J. *Noam Chomsky.* New York: Penguin, 1978.

McCarthy, J. "Ascribing Mental Qualities to Machines." Stanford: Stanford Artificial Intelligence Laboratory, Memo AIM-326, March 1979.

Maccoby, E. E., and C. N. Jacklin. *The Psychology of Sex Differences.* Vol. 1: *Text.* Stanford: Stanford University Press, 1978.

McCorduck, P. *Machines Who Think.* San Francisco: W. H. Freeman, 1979.

McGhie, A., and J. Chapman. "Disorders of Attention and Perception in Early Schizophrenia." *British Journal of Medical Psychology* 34 (1961): 103–16.

McGlone, J. "Sex Differences in Human Brain Asymmetry: A Critical Survey." *Behavioral and Brain Sciences* 3 (1980): 215–63.

McKeachie, W. J., ed. *Learning, Cognition, and College Teaching.* San Francisco: Jossey-Bass, 1980.

MacKinnon, D. "Fostering Creativity in Students of Engineering." *Journal of Engineering Education* 52 (1961): 129–42.

Maier, N. R. F. "Reasoning in Humans III: The Mechanisms of Equivalent Stimuli and of Reasoning." *J. Experim. Psychol.* 35 (1945): 349–60.

Mandler, G. "Consciousness, Respectable, Useful, and Probably Necessary." In Solso, 1975.

———. "Thought Processes." In *Human Stress and Cognition: An Information-Processing Approach,* edited by V. Hamilton and D. M. Warburton. London: Wiley, 1979.

*Mayer, R. E. *Thinking and Problem Solving: An Introduction to Human Cognition and Learning.* Glenview, Ill.: Scott, Foresman, 1977.

Miller, G. A. "The Magical Number Seven, Plus or Minus Two: Some Limits on Our Capacity for Processing Information." *Psychol. Rev.* 63 (1956): 81–97.

———; E. Galanter; and K. Pribram. *Plans and the Structure of Behavior.* New York: Holt, Rinehart and Winston, 1960.

Milner, B. "Amnesia Following Operation on the Temporal Lobes." In *Amnesia,* edited by C. W. M. Whitty and O. L. Zangwill. London: Butterworths, 1966.

———; S. Corkin; and H. L. Teuber. "Further Analysis of the Hippocampal-Amnesic Syndrome: 14 Year Follow-up Study of H.M." *Neuropsychologia* 6 (1968): 215–34.

Minsky, M. "A Framework for Representing Knowledge." Cambridge, Mass.: MIT Artificial Intelligence Laboratory, 1974. Artificial Intelligence Memo No. 306.

———. 1977*a*. "Plain Talk About Neurodevelopmental Epistemology." Cambridge, Mass.: MIT Artificial Intelligence Laboratory, 1977. Artificial Intelligence Memo No. 430.

———. 1977*b*. "Frame-system Theory." In Johnson-Laird and Wason, 1977.

Moore, B. R., and S. Stuttard. "Dr. Guthrie and *Felis domesticus* Or: Tripping over the Cat." *Science* 205 (September 7, 1979): 1031–33.

Moskowitz, B. A. "The Acquisition of Language." *Scientific American,* November 1978.

Mynatt, C. R.; M. E. Doherty; and R. D. Tweney. "Confirmation Bias in a Simulated Research Environment: An Experimental Study of Scientific Inference." *Quarterly Journal of Experimental Psychology* 29 (1977): 85–95.

Nauta, W. J. H., and M. Feirtag. "The Organization of the Brain." *Scientific American,* September 1979.

Neisser, U. "The Multiplicity of Thought." *Brit. J. Psychol.* 54 (1963): 1–14.

———. "General, Academic, and Artificial Intelligence." In Resnick, 1976.

Nelson, K. "The Role of Language in Infant Development." In Bornstein and Kessen, 1979.

Nelson, R. "The First Literate Computers?" *Psychol. Today,* March 1978.

Newell, A. "Harpy, Production Systems and Human Cognition." Paper presented at Fourteenth Annual Symposium on Cognition, 1978. Pittsburgh: Carnegie-Mellon University Department of Computer Science, 1978.

———; J. C. Shaw; and H. A. Simon. "Empirical Explorations with the Logic Theory Machine: A Case Study in Heuristics." In *Computers and Thought,* edited by E. A. Feigenbaum and J. Feldman. New York: McGraw-Hill, 1963.

°———, and H. A. Simon. *Human Problem Solving.* Englewood Cliffs, N.J.: Prentice-Hall, 1972.

———, and ———. "Computer Science as Empirical Inquiry: Symbols and Search." *Communications of the Association for Computing Machinery* 19 (1976): 113–26.

Newport, E. L., and U. Bellugi. "Linguistic Expression of Category Levels in a Visual-Gestural Language: A Flower Is a Flower Is a Flower." In Rosch and Lloyd, 1978.

———; H. Gleitman; and L. R. Gleitman. "Mother, I'd Rather Do It Myself: Some Effects and Non-Effects of Maternal Speech Style." In *Talking to Children,* edited by C. E. Snow and C. A. Ferguson. Cambridge, England: Cambridge University Press, 1978.

Nickerson, R. S., and M. J. Adams. "Long-Term Memory for a Common Object." *Cog. Psychol.* 11 (1979): 287–307.

Nisbett, R. E., and L. Ross. *Human Inference: Strategies and Shortcomings of Social Judgment.* Englewood Cliffs, N.J.: Prentice-Hall, 1980.

———, and T. D. Wilson. "Telling More Than We Can Know: Verbal Reports on Mental Processes." *Psychol. Rev.* 84 (1977): 231–59.

°Norman, D. A. *Memory and Attention: An Introduction to Human Information Processing.* New York: Wiley, 1976.

———. "Copycat Science or Does the Mind Really Work by Table Look-up?" Paper presented at Carnegie-Mellon Symposium on Problem Solving and Education, 1978.

———. 1979a. "Slips of the Mind and an Outline for a Theory of Action." University of California at San Diego, Center for Human Information Processing, November 1979. CHIP Report No. 88.

———. 1979b. "Twelve Issues for Cognitive Science." Paper presented at La Jolla Conference (University of California at San Diego) on Cognitive Science, 1979.

———. 1980a. "Cognitive Engineering and Education." In Tuma and Reif, 1980.

## 392 A LIST OF CITED SOURCES

————. 1980b. "What Goes on in the Mind of the Learner." In McKeachie, 1980.

Osborn, A. F. *Applied Imagination*. New York: Scribner's, 1963.

Osherson, D. "Logic and Models of Logical Thinking." In Falmagne, 1975.

Pachella, R. G. "The Interpretation of Reaction Time in Information-Processing Research." In Kantowitz, 1974.

Paivio, A. "Comparisons of Mental Clocks." *J. Experim. Psychol.: Human Perception and Performance* 4 (1978): 61–71.

Patterson, F. "Conversations with a Gorilla." *National Geographic*, October 1978.

Penfield, W. "The Interpretive Cortex." *Science* 129 (1959): 1719–25.

————. "Consciousness, Memory, and Man's Conditioned Reflexes." In *On the Biology of Learning*, edited by K. Pribram. New York: Harcourt, Brace & World, 1969.

————, and P. Perot. "The Brain's Record of Auditory and Visual Experience." *Brain* 86 (1963): 595–696.

Perlmutter, M. 1978a. "What Is Memory Aging the Aging of?" *Developmental Psychology* 14 (1978): 330–45.

————. 1978b. "Development of Memory in the Preschool Years." In *Childhood Development*, edited by R. Greene and T. D. Yawkey. Lexington, Mass.: Lexington, 1978.

Peterson, L. R. "Short-Term Memory." *Scientific American*, July 1966.

————, and M. J. Peterson. "Short-Term Retention of Individual Verbal Items." *J. Experim. Psychol.* 58 (1959): 193–98.

Piaget, J. *The Moral Judgment of the Child*. New York: Free Press, 1948.

————. *Play, Dreams, and Imitation in Childhood*. New York: Norton, 1962.

————. "Intellectual Evolution from Adolescence to Adulthood." *Human Development* 15 (1972): 1–12.

————. *The Origins of Intelligence in Children*. New York: International Universities, 1974.

————, and B. Inhelder. *The Psychology of the Child*. New York: Basic Books, 1969.

Pick, H. L., Jr. "Mapping Children—Mapping Space." Paper presented at 1972 American Psychological Association meeting, Honolulu.

————, and E. Saltzman, eds. *Modes of Perceiving and Processing Information*. Hillsdale, N.J.: Lawrence Erlbaum, 1978.

————; A. Yonas; and J. Rieser. "Spatial Reference Systems in Perceptual Development." Paper. University of Minnesota. NIH Grant HD 05027 [n.d., ca. 1977].

Pine, F. "Thematic Drive Content and Creativity." *Journal of Personality* 27 (1959): 136–51.

Pitt, R. B. "Toward a Comprehensive Model of Problem-Solving: Application to Solutions of Chemistry Problems by High School and College Students." Ph.D. dissertation in psychology, University of California at San Diego, 1976.

Pollio, H. R., et al. *Psychology and the Poetics of Growth: Figurative Language in Psychology, Psychotherapy, and Education*. Hillsdale, N.J.: Lawrence Erlbaum, 1977.

Polya, G. *How to Solve It: A New Aspect of Mathematical Method*. Princeton, N.J.: Princeton University Press, 1973.

Popper, K. *The Logic of Scientific Discovery.* London, Hutchinson, 1959.
————. *Objective Knowledge.* Oxford: Clarendon, 1972.
————. "On Hypotheses." In Johnson-Laird and Wason, 1977.
————, and J. C. Eccles. *The Self and Its Brain: An Argument for Interactionism.* Berlin: Springer Verlag, 1977.
Posner, M. I., and R. F. Mitchell. "Chronometric Analysis of Classification." *Psychol. Rev.* 74 (1967): 392–409.
*Radford, J., and A. Burton. *Thinking: Its Nature and Development.* London: Wiley, 1974.
Raphael, B. *The Thinking Computer: Mind Inside Matter.* San Francisco: W. H. Freeman, 1976.
Reddy, R., and A. Newell. "Knowledge and Its Representation in a Speech Understanding System." In *Knowledge and Cognition,* edited by L. W. Gregg. Potomac, Md.: Lawrence Erlbaum, 1974.
Reif, F. "Problem-Solving in Physics or Engineering: Human Information Processing and Some Teaching Suggestions." Paper. University of California at Berkeley, 1977.
————. "Cognitive Mechanisms Facilitating Human Problem Solving in a Realistic Domain: The Example of Physics." Paper. University of California at Berkeley, 1979.
————. "Theoretical and Educational Concerns with Problem Solving: Bridging the Gaps with Human Cognitive Engineering." In Tuma and Reif, 1980.
Reitman, W. "Heuristic Decision Procedures, Open Constraints, and the Structure of Ill-Defined Problems." In *Human Judgments and Optimality,* edited by M. W. Shelley and G. L. Bryan. New York: Wiley, 1964.
Resnick, L. B., ed. *The Nature of Intelligence.* Hillsdale, N.J.: Lawrence Erlbaum, 1976.
Restak, R. *The Brain: The Last Frontier.* Garden City, N.Y.: Doubleday, 1979.
Riesbeck, C. K. "Computational Understanding: Analysis of Sentences and Context." Working paper, Fondazione Dalle Molle per gli studi linguistici e di comunicazione internazionale. Castagnola, Switzerland, 1974.
Roethlisberger, F. J., and W. J. Dickson. *Management and the Worker.* Cambridge, Mass.: Harvard University Press, 1939.
Rosch, E. "Principles of Categorization." In Rosch and Lloyd, 1978.
————, and B. B. Lloyd, eds. *Cognition and Categorization.* Hillsdale, N.J.: Lawrence Erlbaum, 1978.
————, et al. "Basic Objects in Natural Categories." *Cog. Psychol.* 8 (1976): 282–339.
Rose, S. *The Conscious Brain.* New York: Vintage, 1976.
Rosenzweig, M. R.; E. L. Bennett; and M. C. Diamond. "Brain Changes in Response to Experience." *Scientific American,* February 1972.
Rothenberg, A. "Creative Contradictions." *Psychol. Today,* June 1979.
Rubinstein, M. *Patterns of Problem Solving.* Englewood Cliffs, N.J.: Prentice-Hall, 1975.
Rumelhart, D. E. "Schemata: The Building Blocks of Cognition." University of California at San Diego, Center for Human Information Processing, 1978. CHIP Report No. 79.

———; P. H. Lindsay; and D. A. Norman. "A Process Model for Long-term Memory." In *Organization of Memory*, edited by E. Tulving and W. Donaldson. New York: Academic, 1972.

Russell, B. *A History of Western Philosophy*. New York: Simon and Schuster, 1945.

Russell, D., and W. Jones. "Reactions to Disconfirmation of Paranormal Beliefs." *Personality and Social Psychology Bulletin* 6 (1980): 83–88.

Ryle, G. *The Concept of Mind*. London: Hutchinson, 1949.

Schank, R. C. 1978*a*. "Computer Understanding of Natural Language." *Behavior Research Methods & Instrumentation* 10 (1978): 132–38.

———. 1978*b*. "Inference in the Conceptual Dependency Paradigm: A Personal History." New Haven, Conn.: Yale University Department of Computer Science Research Report #141, September 1978.

———. "Language and Memory." Paper presented at La Jolla Conference (University of California at San Diego) on Cognitive Science, 1979.

———, and R. Abelson. *Scripts, Plans, Goals, and Understanding*. Hillsdale, N.J.: Lawrence Erlbaum, 1977.

Schmeck, H. M., Jr. "Signals Allow Scientists to Eavesdrop on Mind." *The New York Times*, March 11, 1980.

Schweder, R. A. "Likeness and Likelihood in Everyday Thought: Magical Thinking and Everyday Judgments About Personality." In Johnson-Laird and Wason, 1977.

Scribner, S. "Modes of Thinking and Ways of Speaking: Culture and Logic Reconsidered." In Johnson-Laird and Wason, 1977.

Sebeok, T. A., and D. J. Umiker-Sebeok, eds. *Speaking of Apes: A Critical Anthology of Two-Way Communication with Man*. New York: Plenum, 1980.

Shankweiler, D.; W. Strange; and R. Verbrugge. "Speech and the Problem of Perceptual Constancy." In Shaw and Bransford, 1977.

Shatz, M., and R. Gelman. "The Development of Communication Skills: Modifications in the Speech of Young Children as a Function of Listener." *Monographs of the Society for Research in Child Development* 38, no. 152 (1973).

Shaw, R., and J. Bransford, eds. *Perceiving, Acting, and Knowing*. Hillsdale, N.J.: Lawrence Erlbaum, 1977.

———, and J. Pittenger. "Perceiving Change." In Pick and Saltzman, 1978.

Shepard, R. N. 1978*a*. "Externalization of Mental Images and the Act of Creation." In *Visual Learning, Thinking, and Communication*, edited by B. S. Randhawa and W. E. Coffman. New York: Academic, 1978.

———. 1978*b*. "The Mental Image." *Am. Psychologist* 33 (1978): 125–37.

———. "Psychophysical Complementarity." In *Perceptual Organization*, edited by M. Kubovy and J. R. Pomerantz. Hillsdale, N.J.: Lawrence Erlbaum, 1979.

———, and J. Metzler. "Mental Rotation of Three-Dimensional Objects." *Science* 171 (1971): 701–3.

Siegler, R. S., ed. *Children's Thinking: What Develops?* Hillsdale, N.J.: Lawrence Erlbaum, 1978.

Simon, D., and H. A. Simon. "A Tale of Two Protocols." Paper presented at University of Massachusetts, Amherst, Conference on Cognitive Process Instruction, 1978.

Simon, H. A. "Scientific Discovery and the Psychology of Problem Solving." *Mind and Cosmos: Essays in Contemporary Science and Philosophy.* Pittsburgh: University of Pittsburgh Press, 1966.

————. *The Sciences of the Artificial.* Cambridge, Mass.: MIT Press, 1970.

————. "The Structure of Ill-Structured Problems." *Artificial Intelligence* 4 (1973): 181–201.

————. "Identifying Basic Abilities Underlying Intelligent Performance of Complex Tasks." In Resnick, 1976.

————. "Information-Processing Theory of Human Problem Solving." In Estes, 1978.

————. "Cognitive Science: The Newest Science of the Artificial." Paper presented at La Jolla Conference (University of California at San Diego) on Cognitive Science, 1979.

————, and K. A. Gilmartin. "A Simulation of Memory for Chess Positions." *Cog. Psychol.* 5 (1973): 29–46.

————, and A. Newell. "Human Problem Solving: The State of the Theory in 1970." *Am. Psychologist* 26 (1971): 145–59.

————, and R. K. Sumner. "Pattern in Music." In *Formal Representation of Human Judgment,* edited by B. Kleinmuntz. New York: Wiley, 1968.

Skinner, B. F. "Behaviorism at Fifty." In *Behaviorism and Phenomenology: Contrasting Bases for Modern Psychology,* edited by T. W. Wann. Chicago: University of Chicago Press, 1964.

————. *Science and Human Behavior.* New York: Free Press, 1965.

————. *Beyond Freedom and Dignity.* New York: Bantam/Vintage, 1972.

Skolnick, A. "The Myth of the Vulnerable Child." *Psychol. Today,* February 1978.

Sloan Foundation. Report of the State of the Art Committee. "Cognitive Science, 1978." [New York], October 1, 1978.

Slobin, D. I. "Cognitive Prerequisites for the Acquisition of Grammar." In *Studies of Child Language Development,* edited by C. A. Ferguson and D. I. Slobin. New York: Holt, Rinehart and Winston, 1973.

Smedslund, J. "The Concept of Correlation in Adults." *Scandinavian Journal of Psychology* 4 (1963): 165–73.

Smith, S. M. "Remembering In and Out of Context." *J. Experim. Psychol.: Human Learning and Memory* 5 (1979): 460–71.

Soloway, E. M. *"Learning = Interpretation + Generalization": A Case Study in Knowledge-Directed Learning.* Ph.D. dissertation, University of Massachusetts, Amherst, September 1978. COINS (Computer and Information Science) Tech. Rept. 78-13.

Solso, R. L., ed. *Theories in Cognitive Psychology: The Loyola Symposium.* Hillsdale, N.J.: Lawrence Erlbaum, 1974.

————, ed. *Information Processing and Cognition: The Loyola Symposium.* Hillsdale, N.J.: Lawrence Erlbaum, 1975.

Spear, N. *The Processing of Memories: Forgetting and Retention.* Hillsdale, N.J.: Lawrence Erlbaum, 1978.

Sperling, G. "The Information Available in Brief Visual Presentations." *Psychol. Monographs* 74, whole no. 498 (1960).

Standing, L.; J. Conezio; and R. N. Haber. "Perception and Memory for Pictures: Single-Trial Learning of 2560 Visual Stimuli." *Psychonomic Science* 19 (1970): 73–74.

Stein, M. I. *Stimulating Creativity.* Vol. 1: *Individual Procedures.* New York: Academic, 1974.

——. *Stimulating Creativity.* Vol. 2, *Group Procedures.* New York: Academic, 1975.

Sternberg, R. J. 1977a. "Component Processes in Analogical Reasoning." *Psychol. Rev.* 84 (1977): 353–78.

——. 1977b. *Intelligence, Information Processing, and Analogical Reasoning: The Componential Analysis of Human Abilities.* Hillsdale, N.J.: Lawrence Erlbaum, 1977.

Stevens, C. F. "The Neuron." *Scientific American,* September 1979.

Sussman, G. J. *A Computer Model of Skill Acquisition.* New York: American Elsevier, 1975.

Swanson, D. B.; P. J. Feltovich; and P. E. Johnson. "Psychological Analysis of Physician Expertise: Implications for Design of Support Systems." *Medinfo 77: Proceedings of the Second World Conference on Medical Informatics,* pp. 161–64. Amsterdam: North-Holland Pub., 1977.

Taplin, J. E., and H. Staudenmayer. "Interpretation of Abstract Conditional Sentences in Deductive Reasoning." *J. Verbal Learning and Verbal Behavior* 12 (1973): 530–42.

Terrace, H. S. "How Nim Chimpsky Changed My Mind." *Psychol. Today,* November 1979.

——. *Nim: A Chimpanzee Who Learned Sign Language.* New York: Knopf, 1980.

Thomas, A., and S. Chess. *Temperament and Development.* New York: Brunner/Mazel, 1977.

Tolman, E. C. "The Determiners of Behavior at a Choice Point." *Psychol. Rev.* 45 (1938): 1–41.

——, and C. H. Honzik. " 'Insight' in Rats." *Univ. of California Publications in Psychology* 4 (1930): 215–32.

Tomkins, S. S. "A Theory of Memory." In *Cognition and Affect,* edited by J. S. Antrobus. New York: Little, Brown, 1970.

Torrance, E. P. *Guiding Creative Talent.* Englewood Cliffs, N.J.: Prentice-Hall, 1962.

——, et al. *Role of Education in Creative Thinking.* U.S. Office of Education, Department of Health, Education, and Welfare Cooperative Research Project No. 725. Minneapolis: Bureau of Educational Research, University of Minnesota, 1964.

Trevarthen, C. "Modes of Perceiving and Modes of Acting." In Pick and Saltzman, 1978.

Tuma, D. T., and F. Reif, eds. *Problem Solving and Education: Issues in Teaching and Research.* Hillsdale, N.J.: Lawrence Erlbaum, 1980.

Underwood, B. J. "Forgetting." *Scientific American,* March 1964.

Uttal, W. R. *The Psychobiology of Mind.* Hillsdale, N.J.: Lawrence Erlbaum, 1978.

Vernon, P. E., ed. *Creativity.* Harmondsworth, England: Penguin, 1970.

Vinacke, W. E. *The Psychology of Thinking.* New York: McGraw-Hill, 1974.

von Glasersfeld, E. "Cybernetics, Experience, and the Concept of Self." In *Toward the More Human Use of Human Beings,* edited by M. N. Ozer. Boulder, Colo.: Westview, 1978.

von Neumann, J. *The Computer and the Brain.* New Haven, Conn.: Yale University Press, 1958.

Wallach, M., and M. Kogan. *Modes of Thinking in Young Children.* New York: Holt, Rinehart and Winston, 1965.

Wallas, G. *The Art of Thought.* New York: Harcourt, 1926.

Waltz, D. "Generating Semantic Descriptions from Drawings of Scenes with Shadows." Cambridge, Mass.: MIT AI Laboratory, 1972. AI Memo TR 271.

Washburn, S. L. "The Evolution of Man." *Scientific American,* September 1978.

Wason, P. C., and P. N. Johnson-Laird. *Psychology of Reasoning: Structure and Content.* Cambridge, Mass.: Harvard University Press, 1972.

Watson, J. B. *Behaviorism.* Chicago: University of Chicago Press, 1924. Also: rev. ed.: New York: Norton, 1930.

————. "What the Nursery Has to Say About Instincts." In *Psychologies of 1925,* edited by C. Murchison. Worcester, Mass.: Clark University Press, 1926.

————, and R. Rayner. "Conditioned Emotional Reactions." *J. Experim. Psychol.* 3 (1920): 1–14.

Weimer, W. B. "A Conceptual Framework for Cognitive Psychology: Motor Theories of the Mind." In Shaw and Bransford, 1977.

Weizenbaum, J. *Computer Power and Human Reason: From Judgment to Calculation.* San Francisco: W. H. Freeman, 1976.

Westcott, M. R. "On the Measurement of Intuitive Leaps." *Psychological Reports* 9 (1961): 267–74.

Whimbey, A. "Teaching Sequential Thought: The Cognitive-Skills Approach." *Phi Delta Kappan,* December 1977.

————, and J. Lochhead. *Problem Solving and Comprehension: A Short Course in Analytic Reasoning.* Philadelphia: Franklin Institute Press, 1979.

White, S. H. "Psychology in All Sorts of Places." In *Psychology and Society: In Search of Symbiosis,* edited by R. A. Kasschau and F. S. Kessel. New York: Holt, Rinehart and Winston, 1978.

Whiting, C. S. *Creative Thinking.* New York: Reinhold, 1958.

Whorf, B. L. *Language, Thought, and Reality.* Cambridge, Mass.: MIT Press, 1956.

*Wickelgren, W. A. *How to Solve Problems: Elements of a Theory of Problems and Problem Solving.* San Francisco: W. H. Freeman, 1974.

Williams, M. D. "The Process of Retrieval from Very Long Term Memory." University of California at San Diego, Center for Human Information Processing, September 1978. Technical Report No. 75.

Winston, P. H. *Artificial Intelligence.* Reading, Mass.: Addison-Wesley, 1977.

Wurtman, R. "Brain Muffins." *Psychol. Today,* October 1978.

# ACKNOWLEDGMENTS

Many people helped me with this book—so many that I must compress these thanks (even to omitting the omnipresent "Dr." and, for the most part, university affiliations). I rely on those named here to understand that if I could, I would make much more of my obligation and my gratitude.

Jack Lochhead, Director of the Cognitive Development Project at the University of Massachusetts, Amherst, was my first guide to the content of cognitive science and to the persons doing important work in the field. Without his freely given help and the benefit of his overview of the field, I would long have floundered around, trying to find my way.

Donald A. Norman, Director of the Program in Cognitive Science at the University of California at San Diego, spent more time with me and did more to shape my thinking about his field than any one other person. He also, with great generosity, agreed to read the book in manuscript, and made a great many valuable corrections and suggestions, plus a few vigorous dissents.

Kenneth A. Klivington, Program Officer of the Alfred P. Sloan Foundation, was wonderfully helpful as to the major places where cognitive science is being done and the persons doing it. He, too, read my book in manuscript and offered many important corrections.

Others who gave me good guidance concerning the various centers of cognitive science and workers in it were Lawrence Erlbaum, the publisher of so many valuable books in this new field (as a glance at the List of Cited Sources will make clear), and Joseph L. Young, Program Director for Memory and Cognitive Processes, National Science Foundation. The National Clearinghouse for Mental Health Information, National Institute of Mental Health, furnished me with a most useful set of printouts of abstracts of recent and current work in cognitive science.

Bernice Hunt, my wife—an accomplished author and editor—gave me the benefit of her scrupulously careful reading of the manuscript. Frederic W. Hills, my editor, provided me with the enthusiastic support I needed to begin and sustain the work, and with his own creative and tasteful editorial guidance. My friends Francis Bello and Bruce Gavril earned my gratitude, the first by sending me a number of useful science news-notes, the second by painstakingly reviewing and correcting the pages dealing with computer science.

My sincere thanks to all the following, who took the time to talk to me about their work and, in many cases, demonstrate their current research:

Harold Abelson, John R. Anderson, René Baillargeon, Hans J. Berliner, Gordon H. Bower, Merry Bullock, Aaron V. Cicourel, Herbert H. Clark, John Clement, Michael Cole, Roy D'Andrade, Andrea di Sessa, Bat-Sheva Eylon, Paul Fox, Norman Fredette, Rochel Gelman, Donald R. Gentner, Lila Gleitman, Ira Goldstein, Robert Gray, John R. Hayes, Geoffrey Hinton, Keith J. Holyoak, Edwin Lee Hutchins, Jr., Paul E. Johnson, John Jonides, Jerome Kagan, Robert Karplus, Stephen M. Kosslyn, Pat Langley, Jill H. Larkin, Jim Levin, Herbert Lin, Elizabeth F. Loftus, David McArthur, George Mandler, Michael Maratsos, Hugh Mehan, Ian Moar, Shirley Moore, Frederick J. Morrison, Allen Newell, Richard E. Nisbett, Gary Olson, Daniel N. Osherson, Robert G. Pachella, Marion Perlmutter, Herbert L. Pick, Jr., Ruth B. Pitt, Frederick Reif, Judith Reitman, Walter Reitman, Christopher Riesbeck, David E. Rumelhart, Mark St. John, Roger N. Shepard, Herbert A. Simon, Elliot M. Soloway, Len Talmy, Arthur Whimbey, Sheldon H. White, J. Frank Yates, and Albert Yonas.

Finally, my thanks to all who answered my questions by letter and who sent me their publications. They include:

Teresa M. Amabile, Arnold Arons, Robert Axelrod, Marion Blank, G. Matthew Bonham, Lyle E. Bourne, Jr., Wilma Bucci, Jaime Carbonell, Norman Chonacky, Eve V. Clark, Allan Collins, Robert G. Crowder, J. A. Easley, Jr., Herbert Ginsburg, John H. Greist, Joseph B. Hellige, Jeanne B. Herman, Douglas L. Hintzman, Ole R. Holsti, John L. Horn, David Klahr, John McCarthy, Lillian McDermott, Marvin Minsky, J. Anthony Paredes, Fred Pine, Mary C. Potter, Roger C. Schank, Alan H. Schoenfeld, Robert J. Sternberg, Endel Tulving, Michael Wessells, and J. Kenneth Whitt.

and Donald A. Norman in *Human Information Processing,* 2nd ed., © 1977, Academic Press, Inc.; courtesy of both publishers.

Figure 50: from "Skilled Problem Solving in Physics: A Hierarchical Planning Model," by Jill H. Larkin, printed at the Department of Physics, University of California at Berkeley, 1977; courtesy of Jill H. Larkin.

Figure 51: from "Cognitive Mechanisms Facilitating Human Problem Solving in a Realistic Domain: The Example of Physics," by F. Reif, printed at the University of California at Berkeley, October 19, 1979; courtesy of F. Reif.

Figure 53: from Arnold Lewis Glass, Keith James Holyoak, and John Lester Santa, *Cognition,* © 1979, Addison-Wesley Publishing Company, Inc., adapted from Chapter 12, Figure 12.4, page 402.

Figure 55: from Michael A. Wallach and Nathan Kogan, *Modes of Thinking in Young Children,* © 1965, Holt, Rinehart and Winston.

Figure 56: courtesy of The Museum of Modern Art.

Figure 57: from Howard Pollio et al., *Psychology and the Poetics of Growth,* © 1977, Lawrence Erlbaum Associates, Inc.; courtesy of the publisher and Howard Pollio.

Figure 59: courtesy of International Business Machines Corporation.

Figure 62: from "Heuristic DENDRAL: A Program for Generating Hypotheses in Organic Chemistry," by B. Buchanan, G. Sutherland, and E. A. Feigenbaum, in Bernard Meltzer and Donald Michie, eds., *Machine Intelligence* 4 (1969), © 1969 by Elsevier North Holland, Inc.

Figures 69 and 70: from Peter H. Lindsay and Donald A. Norman, *Human Information Processing: An Introduction to Psychology,* 2nd ed., © 1977, Academic Press, Inc.

Figure 71: from "Understanding Line Drawings of Scenes with Shadows," by David Waltz, in Patrick H. Winston, ed., *The Psychology of Computer Vision,* © 1975, McGraw-Hill Book Company.

Figure 72: from Patrick Henry Winston, *Artificial Intelligence,* © 1977, Addison-Wesley Publishing Company, Inc., adapted from Chapter 3, Figure 3-3, page 47.

Figure 73: from Donald A. Norman, *Memory and Attention,* 2nd ed., ©1976, John Wiley & Sons, Inc., reprinted from "Knowledge and Its Representation in a Speech Understanding System," by Raj Reddy and Allen Newell, in L. W. Gregg, ed., *Knowledge and Cognition,* © 1974, Lawrence Erlbaum Associates, Inc.; courtesy of both publishers.

Figures 74, 75, 76, and 77: adapted from Gerald Jay Sussman, *A Computer Model of Skill Acquisition,* © 1975, Elsevier North Holland, Inc.

Figure 78: from R. L. Gregory, *The Intelligent Eye,* © 1971, McGraw-Hill Book Company.

Figures 5, 10, 12, 13, 17, 18, 21, 23, 24, 25, 26, 27, 28, 41, 42, 43, 44, 46, 47, 48, 52, 54, 58, 60, 61, 63, 64, 65, 66, 67, and 68 were drawn by Kathleen Costick.

# INDEX

**403**